AF726260

OXFORD STUDIES IN EUROPEAN LAW

Series Editors

PAUL CRAIG

Professor of English Law at St John's College, Oxford

GRÁINNE DE BÚRCA

Professor of Law at New York University School of Law

EU Health Law & Policy

The Expansion of EU Power in Public Health and Health Care

OXFORD STUDIES IN EUROPEAN LAW

Series Editors

Paul Craig, Professor of English Law at St John's College, Oxford and
Gráinne de Búrca, Professor of Law at New York University School of Law

The aim of this series is to publish important and original research on EU law. The focus is on scholarly monographs, with a particular emphasis on those which are interdisciplinary in nature. Edited collections of essays will also be included where they are appropriate. The series is wide in scope and aims to cover studies of particular areas of substantive and of institutional law, historical works, theoretical studies, and analyses of current debates, as well as questions of perennial interest such as the relationship between national and EU law and the novel forms of governance emerging in and beyond Europe. The fact that many of the works are interdisciplinary will make the series of interest to all those concerned with the governance and operation of the EU.

OTHER TITLES IN THIS SERIES

EU Powers Under External Pressure
How the EU's External Actions Alter its Internal Structures
Christina Eckes

Frontex and Human Rights
Responsibility in 'Multi-Actor Situations' under the ECHR and EU Public Liability Law
Melanie Fink

EU Equality Law
The First Fundamental Rights Policy of the EU
Elise Muir

Subnational Authorities in EU Law
Michèle Finck

Accessing Asylum in Europe
Extraterritorial Border Controls and Refugee Rights under EU Law
Violeta Moreno-Lax

National Parliaments after the Lisbon Treaty and the Euro Crisis
Resilience or Resignation?
Davor Jancic

Environmental Integration in Competition and Free-Movement Laws
Julian Nowag

EU Agencies
Legal and Political Limits to the Transformation of the EU Administration
Merijn Chamon

Coherence in EU Competition Law
Wolf Sauter

Foreign Policy Objectives in European Constitutional Law
Joris Larik

Economic Governance in Europe
Comparative Paradoxes and Constitutional Challenges
Federico Fabbrini

EU Health Law & Policy

The Expansion of EU Power in Public Health and Health Care

ANNIEK DE RUIJTER

Associate Professor of European Law, University of Amsterdam

OXFORD
UNIVERSITY PRESS

OXFORD
UNIVERSITY PRESS

Great Clarendon Street, Oxford, OX2 6DP,
United Kingdom

Oxford University Press is a department of the University of Oxford.
It furthers the University's objective of excellence in research, scholarship,
and education by publishing worldwide. Oxford is a registered trade mark of
Oxford University Press in the UK and in certain other countries

© Annick de Ruijter 2019

The moral rights of the author have been asserted

First Edition published in 2019

All rights reserved. No part of this publication may be reproduced, stored in a retrieval system, or transmitted, in any form or by any means, without the prior permission in writing of Oxford University Press, or as expressly permitted by law, by licence or under terms agreed with the appropriate reprographics rights organization. Enquiries concerning reproduction outside the scope of the above should be sent to the Rights Department, Oxford University Press, at the address above

You must not circulate this work in any other form
and you must impose this same condition on any acquirer

Crown copyright material is reproduced under Class Licence
Number C01P0000148 with the permission of OPSI
and the Queen's Printer for Scotland

Published in the United States of America by Oxford University Press
198 Madison Avenue, New York, NY 10016, United States of America

British Library Cataloguing in Publication Data
Data available

Library of Congress Control Number: 2018957187

ISBN 978–0–19–878809–6

Links to third party websites are provided by Oxford in good faith and for information only. Oxford disclaims any responsibility for the materials contained in any third party website referenced in this work.

Series Editors' Preface

Like several of the European Union's supplementary or coordinating competences, EU health law and policy is both uncertain in its scope and boundaries while at the same time constituting a field of major social and political importance for the EU. The EU can intervene in the field of public health in a variety of ways, and not only through its explicit health policy powers, but its role in this field is shaped in part by other EU objectives and in particular by those of the internal market.

In this book, Anniek de Ruijter approaches the field of EU health law and policy from various perspectives, with a view to shedding greater light on this important area, and to appraising its impact. She uses the framework of fundamental rights as a lens through which to assess the impact and significance of EU health policy in various respects. Thus the book considers the range of positive as well as negative rights that underpin and inform aspects of health law and policy, as well as the effect of EU law and policy in this field on rights such as human dignity and personal integrity, and on the ways in which member states regulate and protect health.

The aim of the book is to describe the growth and extent of EU powers in the field, as well as analyzing their impact on fundamental rights and other values in the area of human health. And while it is primarily a book about law rather than policy, it goes beyond a doctrinal approach to describing and appraising the field and integrates information derived from interviews carried out with civil servants working on health policy within the EU as well as material drawn from the legislative archives. The author describes the expansion of EU activity in the field of public health as a stealthy one, or a 'silent revolution', given that it is achieved not just by the use of explicit regulatory powers but by a range of other EU policy actions and initiatives too.

The book includes two detailed and interesting case studies as part of its analysis, one on the EU's response to the outbreak of swine flu and the declaration of a global pandemic, and the other on cross-border health care in the EU and the adoption of a directive on patients' rights in that context. Each of these case studies reflects the broader themes of the book by illustrating the growth and scope of EU powers in the field of health law and policy, the role of various institutional actors at national and EU level in that field, and the implications they have for fundamental rights and other values.

The book raises important questions about the EU's role and interventions in the field of health law and policy, and its impact not just on the rights of individuals and communities but also on the policy powers and competences of the member states. It should be of interest to students and teachers of EU law and policy, as well as all of those interested in health law and policy and fundamental rights in Europe.

Paul Craig Gráinne de Búrca

Acknowledgements

This book is the result of the support of many of my great colleagues at the Amsterdam Centre for European Law and Governance. I am indebted to Professor Christina Eckes, who has encouraged me to write this book. I am grateful to Dr Madalina Busuioc and Professor Deirdre Curtin who have been a great support and given me indispensable advice. I also thank my dear colleagues for shared interests and wonderful conversations. The great people at OUP, Natalie Patey and Elinor Shields, thank you so much for your patience and helpful guidance through the process of getting the book out. Hannah van Kolfschooten, we care about in the same things, which makes it a true inspiration to work together. Thank you for your help with this book. And of course, to Professor Tammy Hervey, Dr Scott Greer, Dr Mark Flear, Professor Johan Legemaate, and many other colleagues who have been an inspiration through their writing and advice over the years, thank you very much. I am also thankful to the students at the Faculty of Law in Amsterdam, for their questions and their shared enthusiasm for EU (health) law and policy. Last, and most importantly, I want to express the utmost gratitude to my friends and family, for their patience and support. And to my parents: Pap, Mam, dank voor alles. Sean, Maya†, Wendel, and Benjamin, together we are strong.

Anniek de Ruijter

Amsterdam
July 2018

Contents

Table of Cases

EU

ECtHR

Table of Legislation

EU TREATIES

EU REGULATIONS

EU REPORTS, COMMUNICATIONS, AND RESOLUTIONS

UNITED NATIONS

OTHER

List of Abbreviations

ARGUS	general European rapid alert system
ASHTI	Alerting System for Chemical Health Threats
AWG	Ageing Working Group
BISCHAT	Rapid Alert System for Biological and Chemical Attacks
BSE	bovine spongiform encephalitis
CAP	Common Agricultural Policy
CASSTM	Administrative Commission on Social Security for Migrant Workers
CBHC	Cross-Border Health Care
CEC	Commission of the European Communities
CECA	Communauté européenne du charbon et de l'acier
CEDAW	Convention on the Elimination of All Forms of Discrimination against Women
CELENEC	European Committee for Electrotechnical Standardization
CEN	European Committee for Standardization
CERD	International Convention on the Elimination of All Forms of Racial Discrimination
CFREU	Charter of Fundamental Rights of the European Union
CHMP	Committee for Medicinal Products for Human Use
CJEU	Court of Justice of the European Union
COCOR	Commission de coordination du Conseil des Ministres
CoE	Council of Europe
COREPER	Committee of Permanent Representatives
CRC	Convention on the Rights of the Child
CRPD	Convention on the Rights of Persons with Disabilities
DG	Directorate General
DNA	Deoxyribonucleic acid
EAHC	Executive Agency for Health and Consumers
ECDC	European Centre for Disease Control
ECFIN	Directorate General Directorate General for Economic and Financial Affairs
ECHR	European Convention on Human Rights
ECOFIN	Economic and Financial Affairs Council
ECPT	European Convention for the Prevention of Torture and Inhuman or Degrading Treatment or Punishment
ECR	European Court Reports
ECSC	Treaty establishing Coal and Steel Community
ECtHR	European Court of Human Rights
EDPS	European Data Protection Supervisor
EEC	European Economic Community
EFSA	European Food and Safety Agency
EFTA	European Free Trade Association
EGKS	Europese Gemeenschap voor Kolen en Staal
EMA	European Medicines Agency
EMCDDA	European Monitoring Centre for Drugs and Drug Addiction
ENVI	Committee on the Environment, Public Health and Consumer Protection
EP	European Parliament
EPC	Economic Policy Committee

EPIET	European Programme for Intervention Epidemiology Training
EPSCO	Employment, Social Policy, Health and Consumer Affairs Council
ESC	European Social Charter
EU	European Union
EUCO	European Council
EUPC	EU Poisons Centres
Euratom	The European Atomic Energy Community
EUROFOUND	European Foundation for the Improvement of Living and Working Conditions
EWRS	Early Warning and Response System (Communicable Disease)
FVO	Food and Veterinary Office
GDP	gross domestic product
GMO	genetically modified organism
HEDIS	The Health Emergency and Disease Information System
HIA	health impact assessment
HLG	High Level Group
HLPR	High Level Process
HLY	Healthy Life Year (Indicator)
HSC	Health Security Committee
ICCPR	International Covenant on Civil and Political Rights
ICESCR	International Covenant on Economic, Social and Cultural Rights
IHR	International Health Regulations
ILO	International Labour Organization
IMCO	Internal Market and Consumer Protection
ISO	International Organization for Standardization
IVF	in-vitro fertilization
MARKT	Directorate-General Internal Market and Services
MEDDEV	Commission Guideline relating to medical devices directives
MEP	Member of the European Parliament
NGO	non-governmental organization
OMC	open method of coordination
OSHA	European Agency for Safety and Health at Work
RAS	Rapid Alert System
SANCO	Directorate General Health and Consumers
SARS	severe acute respiratory syndrome
SCCS	Scientific Committee on Consumer Safety
SCENIHR	Scientific Committee on Emerging and Newly Identified Health Risks
SCHER	Scientific Committee on Health and Environmental Risks
TEU	Treaty on European Union
TFEU	Treaty on the Functioning of the European Union
UDHR	The Universal Declaration of Human Rights
UN	United Nations
US	United States
VWG	Vaccine Working Group
WHO	World Health Organization
WMA	World Medical Association

List of Respondents

Respondent 1, Representative of the Council General-Secretariat (2010)
Respondent 2, Deputy Permanent Representative for Health in the Council (2010)
Respondent 3, MS Representative Working Party on Public Health in the Council (2010)
Respondent 4, MS Representative Working Party on Public Health in the Council (2010)
Respondent 5, MEP (ENVI Committee) (2010)
Respondent 6, Assistant to MEP (2010)
Respondent 7, MEP (2010)
Respondent 8, Representative Secretariat General European Commission (2010)
Respondent 9, Representative Secretariat General European Commission (2010)
Respondent 10, Representative Commission Services DG MARKT (2010)
Respondent 11, Representative DG Research (2010)
Respondent 12, Representative Commission Services DG SANCO (2010)
Respondent 13, High-level representative Commission Services, DG SANCO (2010)
Respondent 14, Representative Commission Services, DG SANCO (2010)
Respondent 15, High-level representative Commission Services SANCO (2010)
Respondent 16, Representative Commission Services, DG SANCO (2010)
Respondent 17, Representative Commission Services, DG EMPL (2010)
Respondent 18, Representative Commission Services, DG EMPL (2010)
Respondent 19, High-level representative European Medicines Agency (2010)
Respondent 20, High-level representative European Medicines Agency (2010)
Respondent 21, Representative European Medicines Agency (2010)
Respondent 22, MS representative for the CHMP in the EMA (2010)
Respondent 23, MS representative for the CHMP in the EMA (2010)
Respondent 24, MS representative for the CHMP in the EMA (2010)
Respondent 25, High-level representative ECDC (2010)
Respondent 26, Representative ECDC (2010)
Respondent 27, Representative ECDC (2010)
Respondent 28, Henriette Roscam-Abbing, Professor of International Health Law, Senior advisor to the Dutch Health Department (2010)

1

The Silent Revolution in EU Health Law and Policy

> With health policy in Europe there has been an intrinsic development going on, a silent revolution. It's like grass, you don't see it grow, but you cut it every week.[1]

Mr Kohll's legal case was, seemingly, an unremarkable one.[2] At the beginning of the 1990s Mr Kohll took his daughter to a doctor for dental treatment.[3] The doctor in Luxembourg recommended braces for the girl and, in order to avoid waiting times, advised going across the border to Trier, Germany. The request by Mr Kohll for reimbursement of the costs was refused by his national insurance body because the treatment was not deemed urgent. Mr Kohll challenged this decision and the national Luxembourg court referred a question to the Court of Justice of the EU (CJEU). The question concerned whether the EU law on free movement of services applied (Article 49 TFEU) and if the denial of reimbursement constituted a breach of EU law.[4]

The CJEU determined that the denial of reimbursement of the costs of health care by the Luxembourgian authorities did indeed violate the principle of free movement of services, which meant that Mr Kohll's health-care costs had to be paid for by the home-state insurance authority. The outcome of this case became highly publicized and politicized. The EU was seen as disrupting slowly and carefully balanced-out national health-care systems. Member States in particular argued that the judgment was not in line with European Treaties, which determine that the redistribution of access to health care—a key policy in deciding national elections and taking up a high part of the national budget—is not in the purview of EU 'market-making' and therefore does not give the EU the power to make decisions about the reimbursement of costs (Art 168 (7) TFEU).[5]

Fourteen years have already passed since the *Kohll* case, but it illustrates one way that—as the statement by the EU civil servant at the opening of this chapter states—the involvement of the EU in human health is expanding, notwithstanding limited legislative competence.[6] The paradoxical growth of EU health policy indicates that

[1] Respondent 2 (Deputy Permanent Representative for Health in the Council, 2010).

[2] T. K. Hervey, 'Re-Judging Social Rights in the EU', *Critical Legal Perspectives on Global Governance* (Oxford: Hart, 2014) 347.

[3] Case C-158/96 *Raymond Kohll v Union des caisses de maladie* [1998] ECR I-1931.

[4] Regulation (EC) No 883/2004, 'Regulation (EC) No 883/2004 of the European Parliament and of the Council on the Coordination of Social Security Systems (OJ L166, 3-4-2004)'.

[5] 'Treaty on the Functioning of the EU (OJ 115/49)' <13488829440080509en00470199.pdf>. A. de Swaan, *In Care of the State: Health Care, Education and Welfare in Europe and the USA in the Modern Era* (Oxford: Oxford University Press, 1988); C. Newdick, 'Disrupting the Community-Saving Public Health Ethics from the EU Internal Market', *Health Care and EU Law* (The Hague: Asser, 2011).

[6] The EU only has limited legislative competence in the area of public health, Article 168 TFEU; E. Randal *The European Union and health policy* (New York: St. Martin's Press, 2000); E. Mossialos et al. (eds) *Health Systems Governance in Europe, the Role of European Union Law and Policy* (New York: Cambridge University Press, 2010); S. Boessen and H. Maarse 'The Impact of the Treaty

EU Health Law & Policy: The Expansion of EU Power in Public Health and Health Care. Anniek de Ruijter © Anniek de Ruijter 2019. Published in 2019 by Oxford University Press.

formal legal rules alone do not explain its development, because much EU health activity is either 'non-legislative'[7] or takes place under a different policy heading, such as agriculture or economic policy.

This book describes the growth of EU power in the fields of *health care* and *public health*, and it analyses the implications of this expansion in these distinct and 'functional' policy fields for EU *health values* and *health rights*. The book is legal in that it uses a framework of EU fundamental rights to ascertain the qualitative impact, in terms of rights and values, of the growth of EU power in the field of human health. At the same time, qualitative semi-structured interviews illustrate the legal and policy developments that are involved in the growth of EU power described in the book. Rather than choosing one theoretical narrative to explain the growth of EU power in the field of human health, several theoretical explanations are mapped and related to the functional divides that define the nature of certain choices that are made in EU human health policy and law—the connecting factor, however, is a *legal analysis* in terms of EU fundamental rights and values.

1. Human Health, Values, Rights, and the European Union

The denial or approval of authorization of a specific controversial medication, or the payment of health-care insurance in a Member State other than the home state—and many of the other questions and issues that are addressed in the EU with regard to human health—illustrate that the involvement of the EU in human health can involve controversial questions, where fundamental rights, bioethical issues, and regulatory problems or redistributive choices may intertwine. This calls into question the power the EU has in this regard, particularly if we take into consideration that human health law and policy are often seen in light of a special reciprocal relationship with fundamental rights.[8] Infringements of fundamental rights can harm human health, for instance in cases of torture or discrimination against people with a particular disease, such as HIV/AIDS or mental disorders. At the same time, health policy can affect fundamental rights, for instance when obligatory vaccination programmes or quarantines are ordered.[9]

The connection between fundamental rights and human health is integrated into both the law of numerous states and the legal framework of a number of international organizations.[10] Moreover, the relationship between health policy and fundamental

Basis on Health Policy Legislation in the European Union: A Case Study on the Tobacco Advertising Directive' (2008) *BMC Health Services Research* 8 (77); T. K. Hervey and J. V. McHale *Health Law and the European Union* (Cambridge: Cambridge University Press, 2004); M. Steffen (ed.) *Health Governance in Europe: Issues, Challenges, and Theories* (New York: Routledge, 2005).

[7] D. M. Curtin *Executive Power of the European Union. Law, Practices and the Living Constitution* (Oxford: Oxford University Press, 2009) 3: 'Non-legislation basically refers to executive action in one form or another from implementation and standard setting to operational decisions by both majoritarian and non-majoritarian actors.'

[8] Jonathan M. Mann and others 'Health and Human Rights' (1994) *Health and Human Rights* 1 6.

[9] S. Gruskin et al. 'Health and Human Rights: History, Principles and Practice of Health and Human Rights' (2007) *The Lancet* 370 449–55; G. J. Annas 'Human Rights and Health: The Universal Declaration of Human Rights at 50' (1998) *New England Journal of Medicine* 339 (24) 1778–81.

[10] B. Toebes 'The Right to Health and Other Health-related Rights' in B. Toebes et al. (eds) *Health and Human Rights in Europe* (Cambridge: Intersentia, 2012); E. D. Kinney and B. A. Clark 'Provisions for Health and Health Care in the Constitutions of the Countries of the World' (2004) *Cornell International Law Journal* 37 285–355.

rights is increasingly put forward by scholars as an 'inextricable connection', and is as an instrument to judge the *legitimacy* of the involvement of public and private authorities in health efforts.[11] In other words, fundamental rights are a benchmark for analysing the legitimacy of health policy. On one hand, a rights-based approach to policymaking makes the values that are affected by authoritative decisions of policymakers explicit.[12] On the other hand, fundamental rights can define who is a rights holder and duty bearer and clarify the nature of a particular obligation. In this regard, fundamental rights create a range of legal mechanisms to assess the legitimacy of the exercise of public power.[13]

In the literature on the involvement of the European Union in human health, the connection with fundamental rights has been highlighted and a great deal of work is done in outlining the importance of EU fundamental rights applicable to Member States' health policies.[14] Yet, only 'limited attention has been devoted to the growth of EU legislation that has implications for the protection of fundamental rights'.[15] At the same time, in scholarship fundamental rights are deemed to be of pivotal importance for the EU in a more abstract sense:

> [F]undamental values [. . .] may be said to underpin all health regimes within the EU although the interpretation of those values may differ considerably in practice. [. . .] One key element of the EU's role may be seen in the protection of such 'European values' inherent in European national health systems in the context of increasing international economic pressures.[16]

Yet although the importance of the connection between fundamental rights and the growing involvement of the EU in health is recognized in the literature,[17] there is no

[11] S. Gruskin et al. 'Rights-based Approaches to Health Policies and Programs: Articulations, Ambiguities, and Assessment' (2010) *Journal of Public Health Policy* 31 (2) 129–45; S. Gruskin and D. Tarantola 'Health and Human Rights' in S. Gruskin et al. (eds) *Perspectives on Health and Human Rights* (New York: Routledge, 2005); World Health Organization Europe *Health Impact Assessment: Main Concepts and Suggested Approach* (Brussels: European Centre for Health Policy, Gothenburg consensus paper, 1999); and for a global overview of some of these efforts, see A. Scott-Samuel and E. O'Keefe 'Health Impact Assessment, Human Rights and Global Public Policy: A Critical Appraisal' (2007) *Bulletin of the World Health Organization* 85 212–17.

[12] L. London, 'What is a Human-Rights Based Approach to Health and Does it Matter?' (2008) *Health and Human Rights* 10 (1) 65–80 at p. 72.

[13] Ibid. at p. 68. In the EU there is the Fundamental Rights Agency (EUFRA), which has the policy objective of 'mainstreaming' fundamental rights in all EU public policies, and there is of course the possibility for litigation and legislative review.

[14] The EUFRA in particular has issued a number of studies on discrimination in health-care settings across the EU: EUFRA, 'Involuntary placement and involuntary treatment of persons with mental health problems' (June 2012); EUFRA, 'Inequalities and multiple discrimination in access to and quality of healthcare' (March 2013); EUFRA, 'Legal capacity of persons with intellectual disabilities and persons with mental health problems' (July 2013). Also see J. V. McHale 'Fundamental Rights and Health Care' in E. Mossialos et al. (eds) *Health Systems Governance in the EU: The Role of EU Law and Governance* (New York: Cambridge University Press, 2012). In this regard, the *European Journal for Health Law* in particular has focused on EU fundamental rights. See e.g. H. Nys 'The Right to Informed Choice and the Patients' Rights Directive' (2012) *European Journal of Health Law* 19 (4) 327–31; H. D. C. Roscam Abbing 'Patients' Right to Quality of Healthcare: How Satisfactory Are the European Union's Regulatory Policies?' (2012) *European Journal of Health Law* 19 (5) 415–22.

[15] E. Muir 'The Fundamental Rights implications of EU Legislation: Some Constitutional Challenges' (2014) *Common Market Law Review* 51 219–46 at p. 220.

[16] Hervey and McHale (2004) supra note 6 at p. 5. And see further T. K. Hervey 'The Right to Health in European Union Law' in T. K. Hervey and J. Kenner (eds) *Economic and Social Rights Under the EU Charter of Fundamental Rights* (Oxford: Hart, 2003); T. K. Hervey 'The "Right to Health" in European Union Law' in ibid.; and see Council Conclusions on Common values and principles in European Union Health Systems(2006/C 146/01) (OJ 146/1).

[17] See ibid. Hervey (2003).

neatly circumscribed concept of EU health policy or law, nor a determination of the *de jure* and *de facto* power of the EU in human health. But as long as the existence of European Union health policy is a 'silent revolution' and remains undefined,[18] its possible implications for fundamental rights and values remain implicit. Health policy in that case does not require legitimation, even though our lives may depend on it.

2. The Expanding Power of the EU in Human Health

The scope of power that can currently be exercised by the EU goes far beyond what was envisioned for the international organization founded in the 1950s for the purpose of creating a common market.[19] The EU has powerful institutional actors: the Court of Justice of the EU (CJEU) and the European Commission (the EU's central executive and administrative body that can initiate legislation). The Member States are represented at ministerial level in the Council of the EU and the Heads of State are represented in the European Council. Besides the Council's central role, together with the European Parliament, in adopting legislation, it also holds significant executive powers.[20] Moreover, operating below the core institutions of the EU are a number of actors that play an important role in the involvement of the EU in health, such as European agencies that work on various health issues and to which Member States and the EU have delegated tasks in this regard.[21] Furthermore, in the initiation and implementation stages of EU legislation and policy, there are numerous working groups, experts, committees, and high-level groups that are involved in health in the EU.[22]

Leaving aside the difficulty of defining the nature of the EU's political system,[23] the European Union can be described as a political union that on the surface has developed through major treaty reforms and 'constitutional sedimentation' by way of authoritative and far-reaching treaty interpretations of the Court of Justice and the settlement of institutional mechanisms.[24] However, below the surface, there are numerous empirical

[18] Or merely captured in its 'contours', see T. K. Hervey 'Mapping the Contours of European Union Health Law and Policy' (2002) *European Public Law* 8 (1) 69–105.

[19] See Curtin (2009) supra note 7.

[20] Ibid.; and see the Treaty on European Union (OJ 115/15).

[21] M. E. Busuioc *European Agencies: Law and Practices of Accountability* (Oxford: Oxford University Press, 2013); and see G. Permanand and E. Vos 'EU Regulatory Agencies and Health Protection' in E. Mossialos et al. (eds) *Health Systems governance in Europe: The Role of EU Law and Governance* (New York: Cambridge University Press, 2010).

[22] E. Vos *Institutional Frameworks of Community Health and Safety Regulation: Committees, Agencies and Private Bodies* (Oxford: Hart, 1999).

[23] See D. M. Curtin 'The Constitutional Structure of the Union: A Europe of Bits and Pieces' (1993) *Common Market Law Review* 30 (1) 17–69. The use of the term 'political system' refers to Easton's classic notion of institutions and processes that are involved in the authoritative allocation of values in a given society. D. Easton 'An Approach to the Analysis of Political Systems' (1957) *World Politics* 9 (3) 383–400 at p. 384. The concept of a 'political system' is helpful as it is able to 'encompass pre-state/non state societies as well as roles and offices that might not be seen to be overtly connected with the state'; see S. E. Finer 'Almond's Concept of the Political System' (1970) *Government and Opposition* 5 (1) 3–21 at p. 5, in P. Mair 'Popular Democracy and the European Union Polity' (2005) *European Governance Papers* C-05-03 p. 16; also see S. Hix *The Political System of the European Union* (London: Palgrave Macmillan, 2005); Curtin (2009) supra note 7 at p. 40 et seq.; in relation to health policy specifically, see G. Walt *Health Policy, an Introduction to Process and Power* 5th edn (London: Zed Books, 2001); and see further Chapter 2.

[24] See Curtin (2009) supra note 7 at p. 11; also see D. M. Curtin 'The Sedimentary European Constitution: The Future of 'Constitutionalisation' without a Constitution' in I. Pernice and E. Tanchev (eds) *Ceci n'est pas une Constitution—Constitutionalisation without a Constitution?* (Baden-Baden: Nomos, 2009).

policy practices that take place, for instance in implementation phases, in the form of coordination between Member States' policies in areas where there is little formal legislative competence, or merely as a matter of institutional dynamics.[25]

2.1 Limited legislative power . . .

The EU has limited legislative power in the field of human health, as a result of Member States' resistance to transferring any major powers to the EU. Article 168 TFEU is not very helpful in this regard, as it simply outlines: 'A high level of human health protection shall be ensured in the definition and implementation of all Union policies and activities.'[26] On the basis of this article it could be inferred either that EU health policy is non-existent as an autonomous policy area, given that it is mainstreamed in all other policies, or that it is basically everything, in that all EU public policy is also health policy. However, at the same time Article 168 TFEU restates, in two places, the limited role of the EU:

> The European Parliament and the Council, acting in accordance with the ordinary legislative procedure and after consulting the Economic and Social Committee and the Committee of the Regions, may also adopt incentive measures designed to protect and improve human health [. . .] excluding any harmonisation of the laws and regulations of the Member States.[27]
>
> Union action shall respect the responsibilities of the Member States for the definition of their health policy and for the organisation and delivery of health services and medical care.[28]

One explanation for the resistance of Member States to EU power is that health services form the centre of nation states' welfare provisions, and in most EU Member States health spending is one of the largest single chunks of the national social welfare budget.[29]Equally significantly, health-care and public health provisions have 'state building' capacity,[30] in that the collectivizing of arrangements and instruments to cope with health-related adversity interacts with a 'civilizing process' in which all citizens have come to expect care as an expression of solidarity, organized by the nation state.[31]

The persisting national welfare provisions as a legitimating factor for the nation state and the absence of popular support and solidarity felt across EU Member States make the growing expansion of the EU's role for human health a politically charged

[25] See Curtin (2009) supra note 7.

[26] Treaty on the Functioning of the EU (OJ 115/49); see further Article 6(a) TFEU which attributes supportive, coordinative, or supplementary competence to the EU with respect to the protection and improvement of human health; also see Article 9 TFEU which contains a mainstreaming provision of the protection of human health in the definition and implementation of all EU policies and activities.

[27] Article 168(5) TFEU. [28] Article 168(7) TFEU.

[29] B. Przywara 'Projecting Future Health Care Expenditure at European Level: Drivers, Methodology And Main Results, Directorate General of Economic and Financial Affairs of the European Commission' (July 2010) *Economic Papers* 417.

[30] Public health policy addresses the health of a population at large. See L. O. Gostin *Public Health Law: Power, Duty, Restraint* (Berkeley, CA: University of California Press, 2000). Healthcare policy relates to public activity aimed at creating access and providing healthcare services to individuals, rather than for the population at large. Steffen (ed.) (2005) supra note 6; also see K. Lenaerts and J. A. Gutierrez-Fons 'The Constitutional Allocation of Powers and General Principles of Law' (2010) *Common Market Law Review* 47 1629–69 at p. 244.

[31] A. de Swaan *In Care of the State: Health Care, Education and Welfare in Europe and the USA in the Modern Era* (New York: Oxford University Press, 1988) at pp. 246–57; also see G. Majone 'The European Community between Social Policy and Social Regulation' (1993) *Journal of Common Market Studies* 31 153–70, at p. 159.

issue.[32] In this respect it is not likely that Member States will transfer major powers in the field of health to the EU any time in the near future, nor is there any indication that a collectivizing process is repeating itself at the European level. However, there are numerous accounts testifying that the role of the EU in health keeps expanding, slowly chipping away at the Member States' autonomy to arrange their public health and health-care policies.[33] The EU's involvement in health, then, may not be as clear-cut as the Treaty or Member States' resistance would suggest.

2.2 … but ever-growing policymaking authority

Although the precise nature of the EU political system may remain unclear, the 'bits and pieces' of the EU's institutional and political structure do present a 'living whole' that wields significant political and executive power over its citizens, including with respect to human health.[34] EU involvement in health is often conceptualized as only amounting to an array of health *policies*.[35] This 'patchwork picture' of EU health policy makes it difficult to comprehensively analyse EU activity in the field. This picture is explained by the fact that, in general, much of EU policy activity in health has evolved as a by-product of other policies; for instance food safety in the EU was for a long time regarded as part of the Common Agricultural Policy (CAP). Generally—although from its inception the EU was not supposed to have a central role in human health issues—its involvement grew due to different pressures and constraints and as a result of continuous reconciliations of market aspirations with health concerns.[36]

A particularly important explanation of the EU's increasing role in health—even a justification for some—was that the EU represented a shift in the functions of the state, whereby its main instrument for social change was formed by the regulation of health and safety rather than redistributing welfare entitlements with regard to health, which remained within the autonomy of the Member States.[37] The 'welfare aspect' of

[32] See Majone (1993) supra note 31, at p. 161 (on the unlikelihood of the harmonization of health policies due to the vast differences in health policy arrangements across the EU Member States).

[33] See de Swaan (1988) supra note 31 at p. 257; S. L. Greer 'Uninvited Europeanization: Neo-functionalism and the EU in Health Policy' (2006) *Journal of European Public Policy* 13 (1) 134–52; S. L. Greer et al. 'Mobilizing Bias in Europe: Lobbies, Democracy and EU Health Policy-Making' (2008) *European Union Politics* 9 (3) 403–33; Mossialos et al. (eds) (2010) supra note 6; R. Hamalainen *The Europeanisation of Occupational Health Services: A Study of the Impact of EU Policies* (Tampere: Juvenes, 2008); A. de Ruijter and T. K. Hervey 'Healthcare and the Lisbon Agenda' in P. Copeland and D. Papadimitriou (eds) *The EU's Lisbon Strategy, Evaluating Success, Understanding Failure* (New York: Palgrave Macmillan, 2012); P. Minogiannis *European Integration and Health Policy: The Artful Dance of Economics and History* (New Brunswick, NJ: Transaction Publishers, 2003); A. P. van der Mei *Free Movement of Persons within the European Community: Cross-Border Access to Public Benefits* (Oxford: Hart, 2003); D. S. Martinsen 'The Europeanization of HealthCare: Processes and Factors' in T. Exadaktylos and C. M. Radaelli (eds) *Research Design in European Studies, Establishing Causality in Europeanization* (Basingstoke: Palgrave Macmillan, 2012); R. Baeten et al. (eds) *The Europeanisation of National Health Care Systems: Creative Adaptation in the Shadow of Patient Mobility Case Law* (Brussels: European Social Observatory paper series, 2010); M. McKee et al. (eds) *Health Policy and European Enlargement* (New York: World Health Organization, European Observatory on Health Systems and Policies, 2004).

[34] Curtin (1993) supra note 23; Curtin (2009) supra note 7.

[35] Majone (1993) supra note 31 at p. 154. [36] See Chapter 3.

[37] The concept of the EU as a 'regulatory state' as developed by Majone refers to the phenomenon in which the regulation of health and safety aspects are delegated to largely expert and non-majoritarian authorities that have derived their legitimation from their relative independence and scientific output. Regulation usually refers to specialized and more long-term control (credible commitment) over activities that are socially valued, such as the safety of consumer products generally. G. Majone 'The Regulatory State and Its Legitimacy Problems' (1999) *West European Politics* 22 (1) 1–24 at p. 2; also see Majone (1993) supra note 31; and see E. Vos 'The Rise of the Committees' (1997)

health policy could be separated from the 'regulatory aspect' and so the influence of the EU could grow relatively free from political influence, which in the end eroded the 'Member States' ability to make authoritative political decisions' as a result of policymaking that was not explicitly recognized as health policy, but rather as an issue of market regulation.[38] At the same time, the CJEU addresses the 'welfare aspects' of health policy, in the context of market integration rather than as a particular aspect of social welfare that may escape the influence of EU internal market law.[39] Moreover, on other welfare aspects of health issues Member States *did* coordinate health policies through a range of 'non-legislative' mechanisms and policy practices, which in some cases became formalized to a greater or lesser extent.[40]

As a result of the role of the CJEU, and the EU's various ways for addressing human health, the latter's involvement in health is usually captured as a sum of its parts rather than as a whole: 'EU health policymaking is currently made up of the various extensions of bureaucratic models developed in other fields and for other fields.'[41] Even in relation to public health,[42] where there is a stronger legislative EU competence, the baseline is that:

> it is not possible to discern a distinctive all encompassing 'supranational' public health model that would apply to the EU. Rather what emerges is a series of partially connected EU laws and policies that have various effects on public health.[43]

> [W]e can expect an interaction, or set of interactions, between legislative and governance processes [...]. However, this set of interactions will never amount to policy that is 'a single all-encompassing woven tapestry.'[44]

At the same time, in the reprint of their seminal book on the EU and human health policy and law, Hervey and McHale have come to the conclusion that, regardless of its precise nature, the existence of EU health law is an empirical fact, whether we agree with it or not.[45]

Politically the EU's increasing role in health is largely seen as the 'result of EU institutional actors' entrepreneurialism and ensuing Member State lobby, with very limited democratic feedback'.[46] The involvement of the EU in health develops in a 'closed

European Law Journal 3 (3) 210–29; on the relationship of the regulatory state and health policy, see further Chapter 2.

[38] J. Richardson (ed.) *Constructing a Policy-Making State? Policy Dynamics in the EU* (New York: Oxford University Press, 2012) at p. 12; also see S. L. Greer 'EU Healthcare Services Policy' in Richardson (ibid.). As a policymaking state the EU's political system is involved in the 'authoritative allocation' of values in regard to our health; ibid. at p. 15 and see further Chapter 2.

[39] G. Davies 'The Effect of Mrs Watts' Trip to France on the National Health Care Service' (2007) *King's Law Journal* 18 158–67; Greer (2006) supra note 33.

[40] See further Chapter 3.

[41] S. L. Greer *The Politics of European Union Health Policies* (Maidenhead/Philadelphia: Open University Press, 2009) (he goes on to say: 'as a result, health policy making for the EU is less a product if design than of translation and transplantation').

[42] Public health is a subfield of health policy with a focus on the health of the population at large; see further Chapter 2.

[43] M. McKee et al. 'Public Health Policies' in E. Mossialos et al. (eds) *Health Systems Governance in Europe: The Role of European Union Law and Policy* (New York: Cambridge University Press, 2010), at p. 232.

[44] See T. K. Hervey and B. Vanhercke 'Health Care and the EU: the Law and Policy Patchwork' in E. Mossialos et al. (ibid.) p. 133

[45] T. K. Hervey and J. V. McHale, *European Union Health Law: Themes and Implications* (Cambridge: Cambridge University Press, 2015).

[46] Greer (2009) supra note 41 at p. 160.

shop' of high level civil servants, EU officials and experts and many governance practices are particularly poorly integrated into domestic policy processes.[47]

Hence, generally, although there is no single theoretical explanation for the increasing expansion of the EU's role in human health, there seems to be ample opportunity for policymaking despite limited legislative competence for health specifically. However, as long as the responsibility to protect and promote human health remains legally with the Member States, the EU's role does not become explicit. Although the increasing role of the EU in human health issues is widely acknowledged, because EU health policy features in a number of different policies in the EU and escapes legal definition, its legitimacy has not explicitly been addressed before. Fundamental rights provide a powerful normative language for addressing the legitimacy of health policy.

3. Health Law: Rights and Functions

The EU's powers are silently increasing in a policy domain—EU health policy—on which we spend lots of public money,[48] and to which we sometimes literally owe our lives. Hence, the growth of the EU's role in the field of human health brings up the question of the nature of EU health law, both with respect to the protection of fundamental rights and vis-á-vis the functions of national health law. Health law generally functions to ensure the protection of fundamental rights in the context of health policy. It is seen as a legal discipline that '[i]ntends to create an environment in which the promotion of health goes hand in hand with the protection of individual rights and the general principles of equality and justice'.[49] Loosely defined, health law encompasses legal rules that regulate the provision of health care and the protection of human health.[50]

Fundamental rights in this context are of such central importance for the regulation of health that some scholars have defined health law as being part of fundamental

[47] Hervey and Vanhercke (2010) supra note 44 at p. 132. This problem of EU democratic deficit is widely acknowledged and also affects European public policy in other sectors. There is a long-standing debate on the EU's democratic deficit; see, among others, S. Hix *What's Wrong with the European Union and How to Fix It* (London: Polity, 2008).

[48] Funds for health programmes and health policies are very limited at EU level, whereas it 'is the second largest function of government spending, at 7.5 % of EU GDP in 2010 (14.7 % of total government expenditure)', Eurostat, available at <https://ec.europa.eu/eurostat/documents/3433488/5585032/KS-SF-12-033-EN.PDF/30f8523f-b9a9-4e3b-8e43-2bb983a4d472> accessed 9 November 2018.

[49] J. Legemaate 'Integrating Health Law and Policy: A European Perspective' (2002) *Health Policy* 60 101–10 at p. 102.

[50] The use of the term 'health law' here is deliberately not healthcare law, or medical law, as these terms refer more particularly to the regulation of healthcare arrangements rather than public health, whereas the term 'health law' here is taken to encompass both the regulation of public health and health care. See Hervey and McHale (2004) supra note 6 at p. 15 et seq. (provides a good overview of the different terminology); also see H. T. Greely 'Some Thoughts on Academic Health Law' (2006) *Wake Forest Law Review* 41 391–409 at p. 392 (Greely also includes public policy in his definition, and writes in the context of American health governance); H. J. J. Leenen et al. *Handboek Gezondheidsrecht, deel 1 rechten van mensen in de gezondheidszorg* 5 de druk (The Hague: Boom Juridische Uitgevers, 2011) at p. 19 (specifically refers to the horizontal cross-cutting character of health law, overarching other legal disciplines such as constitutional, private, administrative, and criminal law); see further A. P. den Exter *Health Care Law-making in Central and Eastern Europe* (Antwerp: Intersentia, 2002) at p. 56; H. J. J. Leenen 'Health Law in the Twenty-first Century' (1998) *European Journal of Health Law* 5 341–48 ('Essentially the role of health law in the future will not be different from the present one. The basic norms: humanity, human rights and equity have to be kept upright') at p. 348.

rights law.[51] And although there are many aspects to the governance of human health that may not have immediate fundamental rights implications,[52] health law as a discipline generally functions as a legal paradigm that safeguards fundamental rights in the activities of either the state or health professionals in relation to the human body and mind. This function is usually seen as the consequence of the historically ever-increasing power of the medical profession in the field of health care and the power of the state in human health.[53]

Hence, at Member State level health law functions to protect fundamental rights in relation to health policy. In the EU, the relevance of fundamental rights for health is also acknowledged through the adoption of a number of rights that take into account the special importance of health considerations in public policy.[54] However, if the EU's involvement in health is expanding in practice without a formal competence in the field, this could affect the level of protection fundamental rights receive at the national level, thus leaving a gap with respect to the responsibility for upholding fundamental rights in the context of health policy. In other words, EU health policy by its mere existence may '[i]ncidentally set fundamental rights standards and create mechanisms for their protection'.[55]

Therefore, if the growth of Union law and policymaking in the field of human health, 'with different degrees of visibility'[56] has implications for fundamental rights, this puts into question the legitimacy or even the constitutionality of the EU's role.[57] First, the involvement of the EU in health could have fundamental rights implications while at the same time going beyond the competences that are conferred by Member States to the EU in this regard. Second, if EU involvement in health is based on a competence other than health, the principle of subsidiarity, which holds that the

[51] 'The unifying legal theme is, to us, that of human rights. In our view, therefore, medical law is a subset of human rights law.' See I. Kennedy and A. Grubb *Medical Law* (London: Butterworths, 2000) at p. 3 (as the introduction states this textbook is 'firmly rooted' in English law and deals mainly with the legal relationships between doctors and patients); also E. Wicks *Human Rights and Health Care* (Oregon: Hart, 2007); but see J. K. Mason and G. T. Laurie *Law and Medical Ethics* (New York: Oxford University Press, 2006) at p. 41 (who put forward that too much emphasis on the human rights aspect of 'medical law' could lead to a problematic interpretation of the therapeutic relationships in health care, where paternalism or beneficence is an important pillar in conjunction with the safeguarding of patient autonomy); see further here S. Sheldonand M. Thomson (eds) *Feminist Perspectives on Health Care Law* (London: Cavendish Publishing, 1998) at p. 6 (who use the term 'health care law' in a reconstructive sense, expanding the scope of 'medical law' to include not only physicians, but also the myriad of healthcare workers that can impact on fundamental rights in the healthcare context). With regard to public health, human rights feature as an important balancing instrument in the 'state–patient' relationship; see Mason and Laurie (2006) ibid. On the relationship between (public) health and human rights, J. M. Mann et al. 'Health and Human Rights' (1994) *Health and Human Rights: An International Quarterly Journal* 1 (1) at p. 6 ('health and human rights are complementary approaches for defining and advancing human well-being'); also see L. O. Gostin and J. M. Mann 'Towards the Development of a Human Rights Impact Assessment for the Formulation and Evaluation of Public Health Policies' (1994) *Health and Human Rights: An International Quarterly Journal* 1 (1) 50–78; for a critical perspective on the development of health law and its connection to fundamental rights as a way of increasing the power of law and legal practice vis-à-vis the medical community, see K. Veitch *The Jurisdiction on Medical Law* (Aldershot: Ashgate, 2007).

[52] See H. E. G. M. Hermans and M. A. J. M. Buijsen *Recht en Gezondheidszorg* 2de druk (Amsterdam: Elsevier, 2010) at p. 45 (who take 'health' as an intrinsic value as the unifying principle for health law, not unlike the approach chosen in Mann et al. (1994) supra note 51).

[53] See e.g. Gostin (2000) supra note 30; Leenen (1998) supra note 50; Mann et al. (1994) supra note 51.

[54] See further Chapter 3.

[55] G. Davies 'Subsidiarity: The Wrong Idea, In the Wrong Place, at the Wrong Time' (2006) *Common Market Law Review* 43 63–84.

[56] See Muir (2014) supra note 15 at p. 223.

[57] See ibid. at p. 240.

EU should only act in cases where Member States themselves cannot achieve a particular objective sufficiently,[58] is not an apt tool to balance the importance of values that underlie fundamental rights with the level of governance at which these are best protected.[59] Last, if EU health policy impacts on fundamental rights as a result of non-legislative mechanisms or informal practices, neither the conferral nor the use of EU legislative competences can determine the legitimacy of the EU's role. Therefore, the rights-based approach to EU health policy can provide a powerful 'normative set of criteria' for establishing obligations for guaranteeing the rights of EU citizens in an area that is legally largely still within the autonomy of the Member States.[60] These values and rights, which are internal to health law, set the agenda for this book.

4. The Structure of the Book and Methodology of the Research

The approach that is chosen in this book for mapping the growth of EU power and its impact in terms of rights and values in the field of human health is largely legal. At the same time, European health policy is a matter of Union law, regulation, *and* empirical practices, and is not exceptional in this respect. With the increasing internationalization of law and legal rules—the decentralization of both government and the actors representing public power—law itself has become more diffuse. The legal sources that once delineated what the law is and how it evolves may no longer reflect the whole context in which law develops.[61] With respect to health policy: markets, the economy, developments in medical science, changing demands of patients, the political landscape, the social interactions of policymakers, and the involvements of agencies and other expert actors are all variables that shape the EU's involvement.[62]

Therefore, the current research goes beyond the 'formal sources of law' by including qualitative research data relating the accounts of civil servants working on health policy in the EU institutional context. Furthermore, as to the build-up of the EU institutional presence in health law and policy, many sources from the EU historical legislative archives have been used. In this respect the book is essentially multidisciplinary but based on the shared underlying assumption that law is not separate, but forms part of a social infrastructure and plays a role in the construction of the social world. Fundamental rights as expressions of shared values are an example of law as an expression with meaning beyond the narrower legal context. Legal methodology in this critical sense can be compared to social constructivism, as a particular school in the social sciences, with respect to its ontological approach: the law as a social construction

[58] Article 5(3) TFEU.

[59] Davies (2006) supra note 55 (subsidiarity as a tool for EU integration is a matter of assessing the effectiveness of law in view of a particular (legislative) objective, rather than balancing values).

[60] L. London, 'What is a Human Rights-Based Approach to Health and Does it Matter?' (2008) *Health and Human Rights* (10) 1, at p. 68. Also see V. Kosta, *Fundamental Rights in Internal Market Legislation*, PhD thesis on file at the EUI, Florence 2013 at p. 237. F. Scharpf 'Perpetual Momentum: Directed and Unconstrained?' (2012) *Journal of European Public Policy* 19 127–39; Muir (2014) supra note 15.

[61] R. Cryer et al. *Research Methodologees in EU and International Law* (Oxford: Hart, 2011) at p. 45

[62] G. Walt *Health Policy: An Introduction to Process and Power* 5th edn (Zed Books, London: 2001); also see Greer (2009) supra note 41.

is essentially value-laden.[63] In this regard, the choice to employ a qualitative research method for obtaining the insights of experts fits with the underlying assumptions of current legal research. These include the proposition that it is only possible to tell a convincing version of facts that correspond with a shared experience, such as the shared conviction that fundamental rights matter to us all.[64]

These underlying assumptions have certain consequences for the research design and the structure of the book. It is assumed that, to describe the growing power of the EU in health law and policy, reconstruction or interpretation needs to take place, much like the existence and 'finding' of law being a matter of legal interpretation.[65] However, a possible shared interpretation of social facts such as the role of law and policy in a particular field can make for a fairly convincing interpretation of this social construction.[66] In this sense a purely doctrinal legal approach—where only formal sources of law and their legal interpretation form the research material—would not take into consideration the contexts that shape the legal arrangements in EU health policy, or conversely the way that legal norms shape the social context in which this policy plays out. In sum, in this book, a broad conceptualization of EU power in the field of human health is developed, and coupled with a rights-based framework for analysis for two case studies, one on *public health* and the other on *health care*, that go beyond strictly legal norms.

4.1 Legal framework for analysis: fundamental rights beyond justiciability

In Chapter 2, a normative legal framework is outlined that is used for analysing the legitimacy of the involvement of the EU in human health. This framework is comprehensive in that it allows for an analysis of the promotion and protection of fundamental rights through EU health policy, but also extends to the implications of fundamental rights as an expression of shared values. In the current literature, the importance of the creation of a rights-based framework for addressing the legitimacy of the EU's involvement in health has been addressed and important contributions have been made in this respect.[67]

The framework of analysis developed in this book creates a broad scope that goes beyond fundamental rights that are justiciable in a 'formal' sense.[68] On one hand,

[63] D. della Porta and M. Keating 'How Many Approaches in the Social Sciences? An Epistemological Introduction' in D. della Porta and M. Keating (eds) *Approaches and Methodologies in Social Sciences: A Pluralist Perspective* (Cambridge:Cambridge University Press, 2008).

[64] Generally in quantitative research, realism is the assumption that we can know the world as such and that objective fact-finding as to our social existence is possible; see L. Snape and L. Spencer 'The Foundations of Qualitative Research' in J. Ritchie and J. Lewis (eds) *Qualitative Research Practice* (London: SAGE, 2003).

[65] A quantitative research design, however, is characterized by the use of variables, the proposition of neutrality towards the objective reality, deductive reasoning, testing hypotheses, probabilities, and prediction. As to methodology, in quantitative research one might use experiments, closed interviews, questionnaires, and experiments.

[66] See Snape and Spencer (2003) supra note 64 at p. 15.

[67] T. K. Hervey 'We Don't See a Connection: The "Right to Health" in the EU Charter and European Social Charter' in G. de Burca and B. de Witte (eds) *Social Rights in Europe* (Oxford: Oxford University Press, 2005); Hervey (2003) supra note 16; Hervey and McHale (2004) supra note 6; McHale (2012) supra note 14. Also see Kosta, supra note 60, who concludes that a rights-based approach for certain legislation would in practice not have made a big difference in its outcome.

[68] The particular scope of the framework for analysis in terms of fundamental rights as will be developed in this research will be addressed in detail in Chapter 3.

fundamental rights function as a benchmark in the analysis of the legitimacy of EU power in the field of health as a way of defining the rights of individuals and populations and the respective obligations at EU and Member State level. On the other hand, fundamental rights function to express shared European values in relation to health policy, to aid the analysis of the exercise of EU power in the field of health that may not create legal obligations; where fundamental rights may not necessarily be justiciable.

The subsequent chapters, 3 and 4, address the growth of EU power in the field of health. Chapter 3 looks at EU health law and policy substantively and Chapter 4 addresses the institutional expansion. Both chapters aim to, in the end, conceptualize EU health law and policy by use of legal and historical materials and through analysing and comparing a number of explanatory theories.

4.2 Case studies: public health and health care

In Chapters 5 and 6 two broad case studies are conducted: one in the field of EU public health and the other in the field of health care. The cases are chosen to explore the fundamental rights implications of the growing power of the EU in health policy, to do justice to the complexity of the 'real world' of European health policy.[69] The selected cases primarily illustrate the various ways EU health policy expands, and examine the relationship between EU health policy and fundamental rights. The use of case studies also gives the book a narrower focus regarding two functional areas of EU health policy and how these interlink with formal legislative procedures and legal rules.

Generally a case study is an appropriate tool for narrowing an otherwise broad scope for a research. A case study is a more 'intensive study of a single unit wherever the aim is to shed light on a question pertaining to a broader class of units'.[70] Accordingly, a case study is especially apt for exploring and describing a relatively newly defined policy area with some depth without attempting to be exhaustive,[71] particularly as it allows for the exploration of a 'unit' using a variety of data sources.[72] This means that beyond the narrower focus, case studies allow for the study of European health policy in an interdisciplinary manner without the assumption that there would be an exhaustive analysis of all EU health policy. In other words, in outlining two specific cases within the functional policy fields, the way European health policy is expanding both legally and empirically and what its impact is on fundamental rights can be explored in more detail.

A primary starting point for the book is to adopt a health 'policymaking' perspective, rather than a more strictly 'lawmaking' one through the formal legislative process. The underlying reason for this perspective is the puzzle that more is going on with respect to EU health policy than can be explained by the legislative competence in Article 168 TFEU. Therefore, the selected cases in Chapters 5 and 6 study examples of the different ways EU power, and the roles of institutional actors within it, is expanding in relation to human health. More specifically, the first (procedural) criterion for the selection of these case studies is their ability to illustrate different aspects of the (legal) practice of EU health policymaking. These different aspects include institutional actors

[69] R. K. Yin *Case Study Research: Design and Methods* (Thousand Oaks, CA: SAGE, 2003).

[70] J. Gerring 'What Is a Case Study and What Is It Good for?' (2004) *American Political Science Review* 98 (2) 341–54 at p. 344.

[71] J. Gerring *Case Study Research, Principles and Practices* (Cambridge: Cambridge University Press, 2007) at p. 39; Yin (2003) supra note 69 at p. 13.

[72] Gerring (2007) supra note 69.

involved in health policymaking at the European level, the legislative or policymaking processes involved, and the (legal) nature of the policy that is created. This criterion is important as fundamental rights function partly to legitimately limit public powers. In this regard the illustration with cases based on this criterion helps provide an understanding of the breadth of EU institutional involvement, where a rights-based analysis can provide insight into the legitimacy of EU health policy.

A second (substantive) criterion for the selection of the case studies is that the case illustrates an important aspect of health policy substantively with respect to its possible impact on fundamental rights. This second criterion is important, as the cases in this regard illustrate the other function of fundamental rights as input into legitimate objectives of the European political system. The rights-based analysis in this regard illustrates where rights and values are impacted as a result of EU health policy, both at EU and Member State level.

4.2.1 Public health: communicable disease outbreak

The case study in Chapter 5 on EU public health policy and law looks at the event of the outbreak of a communicable disease and the response to this outbreak at the European level. Specifically, the case focuses on the countermeasures taken to curb the spread of swine flu (influenza A H1N1) over the course of 2009–10. Communicable disease control is a classic and central aspect of public health policy generally.[73] At EU level, a variety of policy instruments come into play in a response to a public health emergency, particularly when responding to a communicable disease. In primary Union law, Article 168(1) TFEU establishes that the EU has a role to play in a public health response:

> Union action [. . .] shall cover the fight against the major health scourges, by promoting research into their causes, their transmission and their prevention, as well as health information and education, and monitoring, early warning of and combating serious cross-border threats to health.

This is translated into secondary Union law, and also involves the European Centre for Disease Control (ECDC). However, response to a disease outbreak at EU level also engages the European Medicines Agency (EMA) and particular provisions in the central regulation of medicines. At the same time, Member States tend to coordinate informally as well as in crisis meetings in the Council and under Commission auspices. Hence, the case study illustrates that a response to a public health emergency may create a basis for expanding EU health policy legally, through interlinking policy practices with law.

As to the second (substantive) criterion, the swine flu case shows the potential fundamental rights implications in terms of both the right to health and individual rights. In a public health emergency, public authorities generally have an obligation to 'do something' and safeguard the population. The provision in Article 168 TFEU cited above is an example of this. In general terms communicable disease control has the potential to touch on the right to health broadly, and the response to a public health emergency can touch on the right to access health care more specifically. An example where the right to access health care is implicated is when public authorities decide on what groups of the population are able to obtain access to particular life-saving

[73] S. Greer and P. Kurzer (eds) *European Union Public Health Policy: Regional and Global Trends* (New York: Routledge, 2013); also see G. Rosen *A History of Public Health* (Baltimore, MD: Johns Hopkins University Press, 1958).

medicines or treatment in the case of a pandemic. Furthermore, in order to protect the population, countermeasures such as mandatory vaccinations or quarantines can impact individual rights. Accordingly, the case of the swine flu outbreak illustrates the implications of EU health policy through a rights-based analysis of a response to a public health emergency.

4.2.2 Health care: access to medical care

The second case, in Chapter 6, illustrates legally how the course of a formal legislative process may provide a breeding ground for further policymaking and—eventually—law. In the field of EU health a prime example in this regard is the adoption of the Patients Rights Directive,[74] which presents the controversial case of creating access to health care at EU level. The creation of access to health care affects the delivery of care and the ability of a political system to make health care available to the population at large as a welfare entitlement, which is a highly charged political issue.[75] Health-care policy at Member State level involves the creation of access to doctors, hospitals, and other health-care services. The organization and management of social insurance and cost-containment strategies is what national health-care systems are all about.

In particular, Chapter 7 focuses on the processes and dynamics surrounding the adoption of the Patients Rights' Directive, on the involvement of different EU institutional actors, and on the policy mechanisms that were used. Therefore, with regard to the first (procedural) criterion for case selection, the case study of the EU's involvement in cross-border health care illustrates how a policy discourse can develop in the context of a formal legislative process. The chapter shows not just the legal aspects of access to cross-border health care as such, but also hones in on the institutional processes around the creation of access to health care at the European level. The adoption of the cross-border health-care directive includes a number of different Directorates General of the Commission, different (in)formal coordination groups of Member States under Commission auspices, and institutional actors within the Council.

In terms of the second (substantive) criterion, the cross-border health case shows generally that the legal possibilities of accessing and obtaining reimbursement for medical care can impact the right to access health care. However, in terms of quality and safety of medical care, the right to health could also be impacted by the adoption of a Cross-Border Healthcare Directive. Moreover, with respect to individual rights informed consent, human dignity, the right to life, and the right to privacy are of potential relevance in the context of the delivery of medical care.

4.3 Data sources: beyond law

The data sources in this book are standard to legal research.[76] They include legislative instruments, both primary and secondary EU legislation, as well as non-legislative Union acts and case law of the CJEU and the ECtHR, and policy documents of international organizations such as the WHO if relevant. In order to give as in-depth an

[74] Commission Proposal for a Directive of the European Parliament and of the Council on the Application of Patients' Rights in Cross-Border Healthcare (COM(2008)414 final).

[75] A. de Swaan *In Care of the State: Health Care, Education and Welfare in Europe and the USA in the Modern Era* (New York: Oxford University Press, 1988).

[76] M. McConville and W. H. Chui (eds) *Research Methods for Law* (Edinburgh: Edinburgh University Press, 2007); and see Cryer et al. (2011) supra note 61.

account as possible, other sources are policy studies of the EU agencies and other (national) actors, EU statistical information, Commission Communications, and Council deliberations, inasmuch as these are publicly accessible.

Additionally, data is included in the case studies from expert interviews as part of a qualitative social research method. Expert interviews provide a deeper insight into the context and processes that shape EU health policy.[77] The expert interviews aim to reconstruct specific specialized knowledge about a particular aspect of EU health policy. For the case studies the selected experts have the ability to contribute the kind of exclusive knowledge of EU health policymaking that is largely geared towards problem solution.[78] Hence, the selected respondents have specialized knowledge on a particular subject, which helps to understand the real world of health policymaking with respect to one of the case studies, but also because of their position in a particular institution or actor, so as to provide a broad representation of respondents across EU institutional actors. Therefore, the book includes the data of a number of experts in the Commission, the Council, Parliament, and the EU agencies. Preferably, the experts were true EU 'health specialists' able to talk on all of the case studies.[79]

5. Balancing Subsidiarity and Fundamental Rights

The concluding Chapter 7 brings together the different chapters as it analyses the expansion of EU power in the field of human health—both the case of health care and in public health—in terms of fundamental rights. in particular, it concludes that the EU is de facto balancing fundamental rights and values relating to health, *implicitly* taking on obligations for safeguarding fundamental rights in the field of health and affecting individuals' rights sometimes without an *explicit* legal competence to do so. This brings to light instances where EU health policy has implications for fundamental rights, as there is no possibility to challenge the exercising of EU power in human health.

The chapter also focuses our attention on the role of the EU principle of subsidiarity in dividing the tasks and functional powers of the EU Member States versus the EU. The legal function of the principle of subsidiarity in the Treaty stands in contrast with the expansion of de facto EU power in the field of human health, and the impact this has on health-related fundamental rights and values. This begs the question whether subsidiarity is still the most relevant legal principle for the division of powers and tasks between the Member States, particularly when EU policy and law involves politically sensitive areas such as health care and public health. This question defines the parameter for continuing the debate on the role of the European Union in promoting its own values and the wellbeing of its peoples,[80] in light of its ever-growing role in human health issues.

[77] The expert interview is a particular interview that has its own methodological purpose. Interviews with experts are geared for qualitative research in that it is their purpose to reconstruct particular 'knowledge stocks'. See B. Littig 'Interviewing Elites—Interviewing Experts: Is There a Difference? Methodological Considerations' in A. Bogner, B. Littig, and W. Menz (eds) *Expert Interviews* (London: Palgrave Macmillan, 2009).

[78] Ibid. [79] See further notes on interview protocol in the bibliography under sources.

[80] Article 2 TEU.

2

European Union Rights and Values in Human Health

> [T]he enjoyment of the highest attainable standard of health is one of the fundamental rights of every human being.[1]

Fundamental rights in the context of the regulation of human health have gained increasing importance in national and international legal institutional settings. This book looks at the impact of the expanding power of EU human health law and policy in terms of fundamental rights. The current chapter lays down the framework for this analysis. Law did not always have a central role to play in the context of medicine and health.[2] It grew after the Second World War and the Nuremberg Doctors Trials (1947), in which preventing the repetition of atrocities that were committed in the name of medicine became a guidepost for future law regarding patients' rights and bioethics.[3] In the period after the War, across the EU Member States, health law developed as a legal discipline in which a balance was struck in medicine and public health between law, bioethics, and fundamental rights.[4] The role of EU fundamental rights protections in the context of public health and health care developed in relation with the growth of multilevel governance and litigation (national, international, Council of Europe, and European Union).

1. Legitimizing the Use of Power in Human Health Policy and Law

A central focus of the book is the growing power of the EU to create health law and policy, and the impact on fundamental rights of the wielding of this power'. 'Power' is not an uncontested concept, particularly not in the EU. The classical conception of power put forward by Lasswell in the thirties is that it defines 'who gets what,

[1] Constitution of the World Health Organization, New York 22 July 1946 (Off. Rec. Wld Hlth Org. 2,100) entered into force on 7 April 1948.

[2] D. Giesen *International Medical Malpractice Law: A Comparative Study of Civil Responsibility Arising from Medical Care* (Tubingen: Mohr, 1988).

[3] J. K. Mason and G. T. Laurie *Law and Medical Ethics* (New York, Oxford: Oxford University Press, 2006). Andreas Frewer 'Human Rights from the Nuremberg Doctors Trial to the Geneva Declaration. Persons and Institutions in Medical Ethics and History' (2010) *Medicine, Health Care and Philosophy* 13 259.

[4] This chapter builds and reflects on A. de Ruijter 'The Impediment of Health Laws' Values in the Constitutional Setting of the EU' in T. K. Hervey, Calum Alasdair Young, and Louise Bishop (eds) *Research Handbook on EU Health Law and Policy* (Cheltenham: Edward Elgar, 2017) <http://www.e-elgar.com/shop/research-handbook-on-european-union-health-law-and-policy> accessed 28 March 2017.

EU Health Law & Policy: The Expansion of EU Power in Public Health and Health Care. Anniek de Ruijter © Anniek de Ruijter 2019. Published in 2019 by Oxford University Press.

when and how'.[5] In this conception, the manner in which value—that which is desired (rights, economic gain, protection, etc.)—is distributed is dependent on power. Public power, or 'public authority', is power that has its basis in a political process in a given political system. In order to capture the expansion of *EU* power in health, the EU political system can be seen as authoritatively allocating 'values' with respect to health. A 'political system', as described by the political scientist Easton, refers to the institutions and processes that are involved in this allocation of values in society.[6] The allocation of these values is the process by which public authority (public power) creates, grants, or denies these values. One of the ways to do this is by the process of adopting and adapting law and policy.[7]

Hence, referring to power in the context of the EU political system with regard to human health conceptualizes the EU's authority and ability to make law and policy that can change the (legal) position of individual Europeans with regard to human health. This includes the ability to influence, change, or limit the ability of Member States' health laws and policies *de jure* and *de facto*. The question is: How do we describe the impact of the EU's increasing power in the field of public health and health care? Here the link with fundamental rights in their constitutional role as a check on public power is pivotal.

In an EU Member State, public power is created by its Constitution. A Constitution generally grants and limits power, and determines the rights that protect individuals against the state. The European Union does not have a 'big C' constitution. Its composite legal order is constitutionalized, which means that over time the creation of EU law and policy has become guided by law and legal principles that have obtained a constitutional status.[8] A classical constitutional question that is central in health law is how to ensure the protection of health for the public at large while protecting the rights of individuals. Fundamental rights are central in this respect.[9] In other words: the general tenet in health law is that in assessing the legitimacy of the exercising of power (by public authorities or the medical profession) in this field, fundamental rights have a central role in balancing this with the protections of individual rights. Further, in the field of human health, bioethics guide clinical and public health practice. Bioethics are the basis for the articulation of legal and clinical principles that are often promulgated through law, but also in professional standards and in the organization of public health and health care.[10]

The use of the term 'fundamental rights' rather than 'human rights' is not intended to define one body of human rights as more 'fundamental' than the others. Rather, it

[5] H. D. Lasswell *Politics: Who Gets What, When, How* (New York and London: Whittlesey House/McGraw-Hill, 1936).

[6] These values may have material form, can come in the form of services, or may refer to ethical or metaphysical values. D. Easton 'An Approach to the Analysis of Political Systems' (1957) *World Politics* 9 (3) 383–400 at p. 384.

[7] Ibid.; also see G. Walt *Health Policy: An Introduction to Process and Power* 5th edn (Zed Books, London: 2001).

[8] Deirdre Curtin *Executive Power of the European Union, Law, Practices and the Living Constitution* (Oxford: Oxford University Press, 2009).

[9] J. M. Mann et al. 'Health and Human Rights' (1994) *Health and Human Rights: An International Quarterly Journal* 1.

[10] O'Neill *Autonomy and Trust in Bioethics* (Cambridge: Cambridge University Press, 2002) 73 (who explains that 'political legitimation is not enough for an ethical justification of fundamental rights'). But see S. Bagatur 'Toward a Democratic Conception of Human Rights' (2014) *Theoria and Praxis* 2(1) <http://theoriandpraxis.journals.yorku.ca/index.php/theoriandpraxis/article/view/39372> accessed 22 June 2016; T. L. Beauchamp and J. F. Childress *Principles of Biomedical Ethics* (7th edn, Oxford: Oxford University Press, 2012).

refers to rights with a similar objective but applicable as a matter of Union Law—in contrast with 'human rights', which could have a broader (international) or more abstract connotation.[11] For its purpose here, to speak in terms of 'rights' in the European Union context refers to the *praxis* of fundamental rights, in that these are used in balancing the legitimacy of the EU's policies with legal rights claims against the Member States, against institutions of the EU or in some cases even in horizontal, private relationships.[12] Fundamental rights are particularly important for the EU in that they not only legitimately limit the discretion of EU institutions but can also be seen as a possible raison d'être for the EU political and legal system.[13] Moreover, as particular aspects of EU integration are considered to be 'rights-based' rather than 'mere' market integration, fundamental rights protection and promotion could indicate a degree of 'constitutionalization' of the EU political system.[14]

1.1 Reciprocity of fundamental rights and health law and policy

Human health, which has been described as one of 'the most important conditions of human life and a critically significant constituent of human capabilities which we have reason to value', is directly impacted on by health policies.[15] Bioethical values intertwine in the application of fundamental rights in health contexts. And the protections given by health and fundamental rights can be seen as complementary in their aim to safeguard human wellbeing.[16] At the same time the protection of fundamental rights and policies to protect health can be at odds: health policy may affect fundamental health rights and, in turn, the (non-)protection of fundamental health rights may affect health. This intricate relationship needs careful balancing in both policy choices and individual cases. For this reason, some scholars consider health law a *lex specialis* of fundamental rights law.[17]

As introduced in Chapter 1, in the literature the link between fundamental rights and health became increasingly prominent over the course of the HIV/AIDS pandemic

[11] R. Alexy 'Discourse Theory and Fundamental Rights' in A. J. Menendez and E. O. Eriksen (eds) *Arguing Fundamental Rights* (Dordrecht: Springer, 2006) at p. 17.

[12] European Commission, *Report from the European Commission to the European Parliament, the Council, the European Economic and Social Committee and the Committee of the Regions, 2013 Report on the Application of the EU Charter of Fundamental Rights* (COM (2014) 224 final); C. Mak *Fundamental Rights in European Contract Law: A Comparison of the Impact of Fundamental Rights in Contractual Relationships in Germany, the Netherlands, Italy and England* (The Hague: Wolters Kluwer, 2008) at p. 6.

[13] A. von Bogdandy 'The European Union as a Human Rights Organisation? Human Rights and the Core of the European Union' (2000) *Common Market Law Review* 37 1307–38.

[14] A. Stone Sweet and K. Stranz 'Rights Adjudication and Constitutional Pluralism in Germany and Europe' (2014) *Journal of European Public Policy* 19 92–108; A. von Bogdandy et al. 'Reverse Solange: Protecting the Essence of Fundamental Rights Against EU Member States' (2012) *Common Market Law Review* 49 489–520; E. Muir 'Fundamental Rights: An Unsettling EU Competence' (2014) *Human Rights Review* 15 25–37; B. Rittberger and F. Schimmelfennig 'The Constitutionalization of the European Union: Explaining the Parliamentarization and Institutionalization of Human Rights' in S. Meunier and K. R. McNamara (eds) *The State of the European Union* (Oxford: Oxford University Press, 2007); C. Mak 'Europe-Building Through Private Law: Lessons from Constitutional Theory' (2012) *European Review of Contract Law* 2 326–41.

[15] A. Sen 'Why Health Equity?' in S. Anand et al. (eds) *Public Health, Ethics, and Equity* (Oxford: Oxford University Press, 2004) at p. 23.

[16] Mann et al. (1994) supra note 9.

[17] I. Kennedy and A. Grubb *Medical Law* (London: Butterworths, 2000); but see K. Veitch *The Jurisdiction on Medical Law* (Aldershot: Ashgate, 2007).

in the 1980s.[18] The connection between health and rights was initially put forward by Jonathan Mann and others, who observed that human rights infringements can be detrimental to human health, yet that at the same time the protection and improvement of human health could be viewed as a fundamental right in itself, leading to the 'hypothesis that promotion and protection of rights and health are inextricably linked and require […] much creative exploration and rigorous evaluation'.[19] The relationship between fundamental rights and health policy in this respect is reciprocal. On one hand the promotion, neglect, or violation of fundamental rights affects health—one only has to think of the involvement of physicians in torture practices. But there are also less immediate examples, such as discrimination against people with a particular disease, mental disorder, drug habits, or HIV/AIDS, and unequal access to public health programmes and restricted availability of medicines. On the other hand the relationship goes in the opposite direction, where health policy may have implications for fundamental rights protection. Obvious examples here are obligatory vaccination programmes or quarantines, but also how an inadequate healthcare system may affect fundamental rights under particular circumstances.[20]

Beyond legal scholarship, however, the connection between health policy and fundamental rights has been taken on and integrated into the law of numerous states and by a number of international organizations. E. D. Kinney and B. A. Clark's 2004 research found that 67.5 per cent of the world's constitutions have a provision addressing health or health care.[21] Health is also part of numerous international human rights instruments, including the 1948 Universal Declaration of Human Rights (in Article 25) and in the 1966 UN International Covenant on Economic, Social and Cultural Rights.[22] And although the mention of health in national constitutions may not always create a direct link between health and fundamental rights—in that some constitutions merely mention health as a public aspiration or a statement of public authorities' duty, rather than an individual right[23]— most states have at least committed

[18] S. Gruskin and D. Tarantola 'Health and Human Rights' in S. Gruskin et al. (eds) Perspectives on Health and Human Rights (New York: Routledge, 2005); J. M. Mann and D. Tarantola 'Responding to HIV/AIDS: A Historical Perspective' (1998) *Health and Human Rights: An International Quarterly Journal* 2 (4) 5–8; see Mann et al. (1994) supra note 9.

[19] See e.g. L. O. Gostin and J. M. Mann 'Towards the Development of a Human Rights Impact Assessment for the Formulation and Evaluation of Public Health Policies' (1994) *Health and Human Rights: An International Quarterly Journal* 1 (1) 50–78; Mann et al. (1994) supra note 9; A. Alfredsson and K. Tomasevski (eds) *A Thematic Guide to Documents on Health and Human Rights* (The Hague: Martinus Nijhoff, 1998); S. S. Fluss 'A Select Bibliography of Health Aspects of Human Rights 1984–1999' (1999) *Health and Human Rights: An International Quarterly Journal* 4 265–76; B. Toebes *The Right to Health as a Human Right in International Law* (Amsterdam: Hart/Intersentia, 1999); K. Tomasevski 'Health Rights' in A. Eide et al. (eds) *Economic, Social and Cultural Rights* (Dordrecht: Martinus Nijhoff, 1995); A. Hendriks 'The Right to Health in National and International Jurisprudence' (1998) *European Journal of Health Law* 5 389–408. For a comprehensive overview of this literature and the legislative and policy developments regarding the interconnection between health and fundamental rights, see Gruskin and Tarantola (2005) supra note 18.

[20] S. Gruskin et al. 'Health and Human Rights: History, Principles and Practice of Health and Human Rights' (2007) *The Lancet* 370 449–55; G. J. Annas 'Human Rights and Health: The Universal Declaration of Human Rights at 50' (1998) *The New England Journal of Medicine* 339 (24) 1778–81.

[21] E. D. Kinney and B. A. Clark 'Provisions for Health and Health Care in the Constitutions of the Countries of the World' (2004) *Cornell International Law Journal* 37 285–355 at p. 291.

[22] Universal Declaration of Human Rights (UDHR) United Nations General Assembly in Paris on 10 December 1948 General Assembly Resolution 217 A (III); United Nations, International Covenant on Economic, Social and Cultural Rights, General Assembly resolution 2200A (XXI) of 16 December 1966, entry into force 3 January 1976, Article 12; United Nations, Convention on the Rights of Persons with Disabilities (CRPD) New York, 13 December 2006.

[23] See Kinney and Clark (2004) supra note 21 at p. 290.

themselves to some version of the fundamental right to health through ratifying one or two international human rights treaties.[24] Table 2.1 gives an overview of the multitude of *international* human rights instruments and the rights they hold that may pertain to health.[25] Although some rights in this respect may overlap in different legal instruments, this does not mean they have a similar legal effect or status, as this depends on the type and the nature of the international organization and the implementation and enforcement mechanisms of that organization.

The recognition that violations of fundamental rights can be bad for health and that at the same time pursuing a health policy may have implications for fundamental rights leads to two possible ways of evaluation. In one way, fundamental rights may provide a framework for addressing the legitimacy of health policy. This focus considers the ways in which health policies promote or violate fundamental rights, either because of the way health policy is designed or the way it is executed. The other way examines how violations or lack of respect for fundamental rights can impact on health and well-being.[26]

In relation to health there are a number of fundamental rights that are especially relevant. As Table 2.1 shows, these rights include a number of 'negative' and 'positive' rights.[27] In the next section the different natures of the rights involved in health are discussed. The following categories or 'generations' of fundamental rights are simply intended as an approach for structuring the framework for analysis in the research. However, the underlying assumption for the framework is the indivisibility of fundamental rights, which is underlined by the generally broad scope of the catalogue of fundamental rights that is adopted by the EU, reflecting the notion that individual rights cannot be fully enjoyed if there are no related social rights that allow for their enjoyment.[28]

2. From 'Generations' towards the 'Indivisibility' of Rights in Human Health

2.1 First-generation rights and health policy

The first generation of fundamental rights most commonly recognized relates to basic liberties and non-interference rights, or 'negative' human rights. The negative health rights, including patients' rights, obtained legal recognition in the wake of the Second World War, after which they became an increasingly important safeguard for a patient

[24] World Health Organization and Office of the United Nations High Commissioner for Human Rights 'The Right to Health' (2004) *WHO Factsheet No. 31* at p. 1.

[25] Excluding the European Convention of Human Rights, given its particular importance in terms of its application to the EU, this instrument is included in Table 2.1.

[26] See Gruskin and Tarantola (2005) supra note 18.

[27] This is discussed further in the next section.

[28] T. K. Hervey 'The Right to Health in European Union Law' in T. K. Hervey and J. Kenner (eds) *Economic and Social Rights Under the Charter of Fundamental Rights* (Oxford: Hart, 2003) at p. 194 (Hervey argues that civil and political rights also impose economic burdens and in many ways have been underdetermined in substantive content); ibid. at p. 195; also see S. Douglas-Scott 'The European Union and Human Rights after the Treaty of Lisbon' (2011) *Human Rights Law Review* 11 (4) 645–82 at p. 651. Also see R. Alexy 'Discourse Theory and Fundamental Rights' in A. J. Menendez and E. O. Erkisen (eds) *Arguing Fundamental Rights* (Dordrecht: Springer, 2006); and see P. Alston and J. H. H. Weiler 'An "Ever Closer Union" in Need of a Human Rights Policy: The European Union and Human Rights' (1998) *European Journal of International Law* 9 658–723.

Table 2.1 International human rights instruments and provisions pertaining to health

Right/principle	UN provisions*	Health topics involved
Right to life	3 UDHR	Abortion End-of-life issues, euthanasia Protection of life through public health measures Duty to investigate deaths Environmental health threats
Dignity	1 UDHR	End-of-life issues, access to health care, care for the elderly and people with disabilities
Prohibition of torture and inhuman and degrading treatment	5 UDHR; CAT; 7 ICCPR; 15 CRPD	Confinement of persons with mental disabilities Access to health care for prisoners Rape, sexual abuse Undue delay of access to health care
Privacy and family life	12 UDHR; 17 ICCPR; 10 ICESCR; 16 CEDAW; 16 CRC; 12, 13 CRPD	Physical and psychological integrity, including personal autonomy in the context of medical interventions Protection of personal data, confidentiality of medical files Prohibition of compulsory use of contraceptives, non-voluntary sterilization, or abortion
Family life, founding a family	16 UDHR; 23 ICCPR; 5(d) (iv) CERD; 16 CEDAW; 8, 9 CRC	Prohibition of compulsory use of contraceptives, non-voluntary sterilization, or abortion Access to fertility treatments
Information and participation	19 UDHR; 19 ICCPR; 13, 17 CRC 13 MWC; 21, 29, 30CRPD	Access to health-related information Informed consent
Access to a remedy	8 UDHR; 13 CRPD	Medical negligence, accountability for failures or abuses in the health sector (supervision and inspection)
Health, including reproductive health	12 ICERSCR; 12 CEDAW; 24 CRC; 5 CERD; 28, 43, 45,MWC; 24 CSR; 25 ILO 169; 9, 25, 26 CRPD	Access to health care and other health-related (public) health services Access to preventive care Protection of public health Reproductive health Protection of environment as it affects public health Occupational health Rehabilitative care (re. disability)
Adequate standard of living	25 UDHR; 11 ICESCR; 27 CRC; 28 CRPD	Adequate access to food, housing, and clothes
Benefits of scientific progress	27 (2) UDHR; 15(2)(b), 15(3) ICESCR; WMA Declaration of Helsinki	Promotion of health research, including for vulnerable groups Development of affordable treatments

(continued)

Table 2.1 *Continued*

Right/principle	UN provisions*	Health topics involved
Social security	9 ICESCR; 13 CEDAW; 26 CRC; 24 CSR; 27 MWC	Social security as a social determinant of health
Protection of mothers, children, and the family	10 ICESSCR	Paid and sufficient maternity leave Social and family benefits Protection against violence against children
Food	11 ICESCR	Safe and nutritious food Food as a social determinant of health
Housing	11 ICESCR; 21 CSR; 19 CRPD	Housing as a social determinant of health Independent living with a disability
Education	12 ICESCR; 10 CEDAW; 28, 29 CRC; 30, 43, 45 MWC; 24 CRPD	Education as a social determinant of health Sex education as public health
Employment	6, 7 ICESCR; 11 CEDAW; 17 and 18 CSR; 27 CRPD; ILO Conventions 25, 38–71; MWC	Occupational health Employment as a social determinant of health

* The Universal Declaration of Human Rights (1948) (UDHR); UN Convention against Torture and Other Cruel, Inhuman or Degrading Treatment or Punishment adopted and opened for signature, ratification and accession by General Assembly resolution 39/46 of 10 December 1984, entry into force 26 June 1987 (CAT); United Nations, International Covenant on Civil and Political Rights (ICCPR) General Assembly resolution 2200A (XXI) of 16 December 1966, entry into force 23 March 1976 (1966); (2006) United Nations, International Convention on the Elimination of All Forms of Racial Discrimination (CERD), General Assembly resolution 2106 (XX) of 21 December 1965, entry into force 4 January 1969; United Nations, Convention on the Elimination of All Forms of Discrimination against Women (CEDAW) New York, 18 December 1979, entry into force 3 September 1981; United Nations, Convention on the Rights of the Child (CRC), General Assembly resolution 44/25 of 20 November 1989, entry into force 2 September 1990.

Source: Adapted from B. Toebes *The Right to Health and Other Health-Related Rights*, in *Health and Human Rights in Europe* (Cambridge: Intersentia, 2012) at p. 83.

vis-à-vis their physician.[29] Later patients became subject to the bureaucracies of ever-larger health-care systems and hospitals. In addition, the rights one has 'as a patient' became a major concern for medical ethics and bioethics, in response to major advances in medicine which over time became more proficient in its potential to intrude into the human mind and body.[30]

The central value underlying patients' rights is that of individual autonomy, balanced with a respect for the individual autonomy of others, such as that of the physician.[31]

[29] J. V. McHale 'Fundamental Rights and Health Care' in E. Mossialos et al. (eds) *Health Systems Governance in the EU: the Role of EU Law and Governance* (New York: Cambridge University Press, 2012).

[30] See H. J. J. Leenen 'Health Law in the Twenty-first Century' (1998) *European Journal of Health Law* 5 341–8; and see Anand et al. (eds) (2004) supra note 15 at p. 3.

[31] In medical ethics this balancing of the autonomy of the medical professional with the patient's autonomy is often couched in an ethical debate on autonomy versus paternalism, especially when it

Individual patients' rights address for instance the inviolability of the body, the right not to be treated against one's wishes, or the right to informed consent; they express rights to do with questions of individual health, life, and death.[32] The ethical basis of safeguarding individual rights as part of medical professional practice, however, goes back centuries. In Plato's *Laws*, the right to self-determination is already mentioned in that if a patient is a free man, a physician shall not provide medical treatment unless the patient consents.[33] The Hippocratic Oath from approximately the fifth century BC is another example where the interests of vulnerable patients vis-à-vis their physician are taken into consideration.[34] The adoption of the 1948 Nuremberg Code, however, marked the first step towards the notion of patients' rights as they are now recognized *legally* in most Member States. The Nuremburg Code lists principles on conducting biomedical research on humans, set out by the judges at the Nuremburg trial in response to the atrocious medical experiments carried out on people in concentration camps by Nazi doctors.[35]

Patients' rights are a particular subset of individual rights, but are not the only tie between fundamental rights and health.[36] Patients' rights primarily feature in the context of *health care*; by contrast, with respect to *public health* the impact on individual rights is often the result of the public health authority exercising its responsibilities, whereby the rights of the individual are balanced against the rights of the population as a whole.[37] Here 'the rights of the few' may be limited for the 'good of the many'.[38] This can impact on individual autonomy, for instance in the case of mandatory vaccinations against a communicable disease or when public authorities mandate quarantines.

2.2 Second-generation rights and health policy

The second generation of health rights relates to 'positive' obligations of assistance for the community and addresses the 'right to *be* a patient', particularly the right to access health (care).[39] However, social economic rights have been found not to be enforceable

concerns medical care for patients that are not capable of making their own decisions. See J. K. Mason and G. T. Laurie *Law and Medical Ethics* (New York: Oxford University Press, 2006) at p. 9. But also see this philosophical debate returning in case law, notably, ECtHR *Glass v. The United Kingdom* Application No. 61827/00 9 March 2004.

32 Anand et al. (eds) (2004) supra note 15; also see Mason and Laurie (2006) supra note 31 at p. 4 et seq.

33 Plato (360 BC) *Laws Book XI* available at <http://classics.mit.edu/Plato/laws.11.xi.html> and D. Giesen *International Medical Malpractice Law: A Comparative Study of Civil Responsibility Arising from Medical Care* (Tubingen: Mohr, 1988) at p. 3.

34 S. H. Miles 'Hippocrates and Informed Consent' (2009) *The Lancet* 374 (9698) 1322–3; also see A. de Ruijter 'Patient Autonomy in Europe' in J. Rutgers (ed.) *European Contract Law and the Welfare State* (Groningen: Europa Law Publishing, 2010).

35 See R. R. Faden and T. L. Beauchamp *A History and Theory of Informed Consent* (New York: Oxford University Press, 1986) at pp. 63, 155, and 186; also see M. R. Marrus 'The Nuremberg Doctors' Trial in Historical Context' (1999) *Bulletin of the History of Medicine* 73 (1) 106–23.

36 If only with regard to individual rights specifically, because there are also a number of examples when individual rights in the context of health do not pertain to 'patients', such as in case of abortion or sterilization; see H. J. J. Leenen et al. *The Rights of Patients in Europe* (Geneva: World Health Organization, Kluwer, 1993) at p. 2.

37 Gostin and Mann (1994) supra note 19.

38 Mann et al. (1994) supra note 9 at p. 15; also see ECtHR *Soering v. United Kingdom* Application No. 14038/88 7 July 1987 at para. 89; see too A. Muller 'Limitations to and Derogations from Economic, Social and Cultural Rights' (2009) *Human Rights Law Review* 9 (4) 557–601 at p. 559.

39 H. Nys and T. Goffin 'Mapping National Practices and Strategies Relating to Patients' Rights' in M. Wismar et al. (eds) *Cross-border Health Care in the European Union: Mapping and Analysing*

before a court. With respect to the right to access health care, for instance, it could be argued that given scarce resources, governments could never guarantee the entitlement to a right to health, which moreover would turn judges into policymakers and undermine the legitimacy of other fundamental rights.[40]

At the same time, as will be discussed in further detail, the right to access health care has in fact been recognized by courts, particularly by the European Court of Human Rights (ECtHR), which establishes a connection between individual rights and the right to access health care.[41] Moreover, outside the formal legal realm, the social right to health has been characterized as an assumption in liberal thinking about justice:

> [S]ince the fundamental problem of justice concerns the relations among those who are full and active participants in society [...] it is reasonable to assume that everyone has physical needs and psychological capacities within some normal range.[42]

This assumption has been translated not only into further theories on justice with regard to the right to access medical care,[43] but also in Member States' constitutions and fundamental rights instruments.[44] Therefore the assumption that social rights relating to health are simply non-justiciable is too limited.[45]

With respect to social rights, similarly to individual (patients') rights, there are also discrete *health care* and *public health* dimensions. The health care dimension is found in the right to gain access to hospitals and medical care providers, facilitated through means of social insurance. The public health dimension of the social right to access health care may be found in cases of access to preventive care or public health measures, such as vaccination in case of a serious communicable disease.[46] An important footnote for the assumption of social rights in relation to health, however, is that in this 'second-generation' approach, the right to access health care is seen as a *means* to achieve health. Consequently, questions of legitimacy or justice will focus on the equal

Practices and Policies (London: World Health Organization, European Observatory on Health Systems and Policies, 2011) at p. 160; M. San Giorgi *The Human Right to Access to Health Care* (Antwerp: Intersentia, 2012).

[40] R. C. Sunstein 'Against Positive Rights' in A. Sajo (ed.) *Western Rights? Post-Communist Application* (The Hague: Kluwer, 1995); but see R. C. Sunstein *Desigining Democracy: What Constitutions Do* (New York: Oxford University Press, 2001), particularly p. 222 et seq.; for an overview of this debate, see further San Giorgi (2012) supra note 39 at p. 80 et seq.

[41] The European Court of Human Rights in this respect does not make a strict division between individual and social economic rights, see ECtHR *Airey v. Ireland* Application No. 6289/73 9 October 1979 (addresses the effective right to fair trial through financial aid from the state) see particularly para. 25: 'fulfilment of a duty under the Convention on occasion necessitates some positive action on the part of the State; in such circumstances, the State cannot simply remain passive'; also see e.g. ECtHR *Powell v. the United Kingdom* Application No. 45305/99 4 May 2000 (on the negligent death of the Powells' son and the authorities' failure to investigate this matter) at p. 18: 'The Court accepts that it cannot be excluded that the acts and omissions of the authorities in the field of health care policy may in certain circumstances engage their responsibility under the positive limb of Article 2'; also see e.g. ECtHR *Calvelli and Ciglio v. Italy* Application No. 32967/96 17 January 2002 para. 48 et seq.; ECtHR *Nitecki v. Poland* Application No. 65653/01 21 March 2002 (on the right to access medicines).

[42] J. Rawls *Political Liberalism* (New York: Columbia University Press, 1993) at p. 172, also cited in Anand et al. (eds) (2004) supra note 15 at p. 3.

[43] N. Daniels *Just Health: Meeting Health Needs Fairly* (Cambridge: Cambridge University Press, 2008).

[44] McHale (2012) supra note 29.

[45] San Giorgi (2012) supra note 39.

[46] Toebes (1999) supra note 19; and see San Giorgi (2012) supra note 39.

distribution of access to health care.[47] In recent years, though, particularly with respect to public health, this view has been critiqued:[48]

> Nearly everything philosophers have written on justice and health is confined to issues of the allocation of health *care*. Yet social inequalities in health persist even when health care resources are more equitably distributed.[49]

From this perspective, the purely biomedical approach to public health and the right to *health care* as the principal solution for improving the health of a population is rejected.[50] Instead, health may be viewed as an essential capability and therefore the question of justice would address society securing the ability to achieve health as an objective in itself; the question of distribution of access to health care is secondary. In this view:

> [Q]uestions of justice emerge from the operation of the totality of social institutions' practices and policies that both independently and in combination have the potential for profound and pervasive impact on human wellbeing in all of its essential aspects.[51]

In the legal context, this view is translated in a 'third-generation approach' where the right to *health* encompasses a right to *health care*. The right to health in this respect is broader and usually seen as a right related to the right to a clean environment or the right to clean water or food.[52]

2.3 Third-generation rights and health policy

The *right to health* results in a broad approach to public health concerns.[53] Generally the acceptance of these third-generation (or third-'wave'[54]) health rights also links in with the growing development of 'evidence-based health policy', in that socio-economic inequalities and the outcomes of health policy and data that identify and affect health status in this view can be considered as facts that indicate whether a health policy is legitimate or not.[55] This view is reflected on different levels of (international) governance in a rights-based approach to health policy.[56]

[47] Daniels (2008) supra note 43.

[48] S. Marchand et al. 'Class, Health, and Justice' (1998) *The Milbank Quarterly* 76 (3) 449–67 at p. 450 (who identify that there is '... a preoccupation with the distribution of health *care* as opposed to the distribution of health' (emphasis in original)).

[49] See ibid. at p. 451 (emphasis in original).

[50] T. Mann 'Human Rights and the New Public Health' (1995) *Health and Human Rights: An International Quarterly Journal* 1 (3) 229–33.

[51] M. Powers and R. Faden *Social Justice: The Moral Foundations of Public Health and Health Policy* (Oxford: Oxford University Press, 2008) at p. 5 and World Health Organization and Office of the United Nations High Commissioner for Human Rights (2004) supra note 24.

[52] For a critical view on the use of a hierarchy in relation to human rights, see T. Meron 'On a Hierarchy of International Human Rights' (1986) *American Journal of International Law* 80 (1); Asbjorn Eide, The Right to Adequate Food as a Human Right (1987) United Nations Report prepared (E/CN.4/Sub.2/1987/23); Douglas-Scott (2011) supra note 28 at p. 651.

[53] Toebes (1999) supra note 19.

[54] See I. E. Koch *Human Rights as Indivisible Rights* (Martinus Nijhoff Publishers, Leiden: 2009) at p.27.

[55] See Toebes (1999) supra note 19T. L. Beauchamp 'Universal Principles and Universal Rights' in A. den Exter (ed.) *Human Rights and Biomedicine* (Antwerp: Maklu, 2010).

[56] The WHO 2006-2015 Global Health Agenda in a number of ways reflects this approach as a policy priority. See Toebes (1999) supra note 19. World Health Organization and Office of the United Nations High Commisisoner for Human Rights (2004) supra note 24 at p. 29; also see S. Gruskin

2.4 Towards indivisibility

The different generations of fundamental health rights illustrate the two-sided character of most commonly recognized rights, in that they express both the right to non-interference by public authority—to be left alone and not touched—whereas they also express a right to assistance. This indicates that the distinction between categories of rights that impose positive obligations and rights that require mere non-action from public authorities or medical professionals is an all-too simplistic divide. Many of the negative human health rights require some form of action, which importantly is also the general approach in international human rights practice.[57] For instance, the right to the inviolability of the human body also needs the backing of public authority to ensure the protection of such a right.

In this respect, the divide between positive and negative obligations with respect to all fundamental rights was challenged as early as the 1980s in that it was argued that all rights create obligations for states and public entities to 'respect' the underlying interests, 'protect' these interests against threats from non-state actors, and 'aid' or 'protect' those who are victims of deprivation of fundamental rights.[58] Notwithstanding the relativity of the divide between negative and positive rights, not all fundamental rights with a special bearing on health can easily serve as a basis for legal action.[59] For instance, the WHO has developed indicators for assessing whether a government is implementing a rights-based approach to health policy, through assessing availability, accessibility, acceptability, and quality;[60] however, holding a government liable under international human rights law for not providing this 'core content' of a rights-based policy is a different matter altogether, and may in many cases not be possible.[61] At the same time, using a rights-based framework for analysing a national, regional, or international health policy is a helpful tool in understanding and assessing the implications of this policy for individuals.[62]

3. The EU's Fundamental Rights Framework in Human Health

The first step in the evolution of EU fundamental rights took place in the form of the development of general principles in the case law of the CJEU, which drew on the common constitutional traditions of the Member States and from international sources of fundamental rights law that Member States participated in, with special

et al. 'Rights-based Approaches to Health Policies and Programs: Articulations, Ambiguities, and Assessment' (2010) *Journal of Public Health Policy* 31 (2) 129–45.

57 See generally M. Langford (ed.) *Social Rights Jurisprudence: Emerging Trends in International and Comparative Law* (Cambridge: Cambridge University Press, 2008); Sunstein (2001) supra note 40 at p. 222.

58 See Eide (1987) supra note 52; Toebes (1999) supra note 19; and see World Health Organization and Office of the United Nations High Commissioner for Human Rights (2004) supra note 24.

59 On justiciability of the right to health care, see e.g. San Giorgi (2012) supra note 39, chapter 5; on justiciability of the right to health, see Toebes (1999) supra note 19 chapter 6.

60 See generally Gruskin et al. (2010) supra note 56.

61 On international possibilities in this regard, see Toebes (1999) supra note 19 at p. 291 et seq.; but see Hervey (2003) supra note 28 at p. 200 (who argues that Toebes' 'core content' approach may be too narrow for the EU context).

62 L. London 'What is a Human Rights Based Approach to Health and does it Matter?' (2008) *Health and Human Rights: An International Quarterly Journal* 10 (1) 1–15.

significance for the European Convention on Human Rights (ECHR).[63] With the adoption of the Treaty of Maastricht in 1992, and subsequent Treaty revisions, these general principles were taken up in the Treaty on European Union (TEU). Currently they feature parallel to the fundamental rights as first proclaimed in December 2000 in the Charter of Fundamental Rights of the EU (CFREU),[64] which became legally binding following the entry into force of the Lisbon Treaty in 2009.[65] However, more recently the CJEU also refers to the CFREU itself, and directly to some provisions of the ECHR.[66]

Currently, beyond the general principles of Union law, the Charter of Fundamental Rights of the European Union ('the Charter') is a source of primary Union law,[67] the EU has a Fundamental Rights Agency and implementation mechanisms to monitor the 'mainstreaming' of fundamental rights in all EU policies.[68] In this regard the EU fundamental rights are a benchmark in determining the legitimacy of the EU political system and consequentially also for determining its policies.[69] First, fundamental rights in the EU can have a role in the process of policymaking in order to determine the legitimacy of a particular policy.[70] Second, fundamental rights can be used for judicial review of EU legislation or national law within the scope of Union law.[71] Third, outside their formal status in Union law and the scope of application of the Charter, fundamental rights have value and importance that 'extends beyond their formal judicial enforceability'.[72] They represent at minimum the values that are fundamental for a particular political system and offer a 'normative vocabulary' for framing questions of legitimacy in (quasi-) legal terms, depending on the legal nature of the policy that is under query.[73] In sum, fundamental rights form a primary starting point for analysing the legitimacy of EU policies, particularly when it relates to health policy, given its inextricable link with fundamental rights, which will be addressed below. In Table 2.2 this relationship between the values that are significant in the field of human health[74]—solidarity, equality, universal access, and human dignity—and the corresponding fundamental rights, and also the relationship with human health law and policy, is outlined:

[63] Case 29/69 *Erich Stauder v. City of Ulm Sozialamt* [1969] ECR 00419; Case 11/70 *Internationale Handelsgesellschaft mbH v. Einfuhr- und Vorratsstelle fur getreide und Futtermiddel* [1970] ECR 1125; J. G. Jacobs 'The European Convention on Human Rights, the EU Charter of Fundamental Rights and the European Court of Justice: The impact of European Union accession to the European Convention on Human Rights' in I. Pernice et al. (eds) *The Future of the European Judicial System in a Comparative Perspective* (Baden-Baden: Nomos, 2006); Case C-540/03 *European Parliament v. Council of the European Union (Family Reunification)* [2006] ECR I-5769.

[64] Charter of Fundamental Rights of the European Union (2000/C 364/01), 18 December 2000, *OJ* C 364/1.

[65] Article 6 TEU.

[66] See references to further case law C. Eckes 'EU Accession to the ECHR: Between Autonomy and Adaptation' (2013) *The Modern Law Review* 76 (2) 254–85 at p. 258.

[67] Article 6 TEU.

[68] Commission (2014) see supra note 12; D. Giesen *International Medical Malpractice Law: A Comparative Study of Civil Responsibility Arising from Medical Care* (Tübingen: Mohr, 1988)..

[69] F. Scharpf 'Perpetual Momentum: Directed and Unrestrained?' (2011) 19 *Journal of European Public Policy* 127–39; Stone Sweet and Stranz (2014) supra note 14.

[70] 'Mainstreaming' fundamental rights in EU policy, supra note 12.

[71] K. Lenaerts 'Exploring the Limits of the EU Charter of Fundamental Rights' (2012) *European Constitutional Law Review* 8 375–403.

[72] Hervey (2003) supra note 28 at p. 195.

[73] See reference to Case C-353/99 P *Council v. Hautala*, Opinion of A.G. Leger of 10 July 2001 by P. Eeckhout 'The EU Charter of Fundamental Rights and the Federal Question' (2002) *Common Market Law Review* 39 945–94; Hervey (2003) supra note 28 at p. 196.

[74] de Ruijter (2017) supra note 4.

Table 2.2 Values and corresponding rights

Value/human right	Fundamental right	European provisions	EU Health topics involved
Human dignity	Human dignity	1 CFREU	End-of-life issues, access to health care, long-term care
Human dignity (Respect for human life/ autonomy)	Right to life	2 CFREU	Access to abortion in another Member State End-of-life issues, euthanasia Protection of life through public health measures Environmental health threats
Human dignity	Informed consent	3 CFREU	Bodily integrity, inviolability of the human body, autonomy in medical decisions, the right to refuse medical treatment
Human dignity	Prohibition of torture and inhuman and degrading treatment	4 CFREU	Confinement of persons with mental disabilities Rape, sexual abuse Undue delay of access to health care
Human dignity	Privacy and family life, data protection	7,8 CFREU	Medical research Protection of personal data, confidentiality of medical files (ehealth) Medical files/psychological background Union civil servants
Human dignity	Information and participation	11 CFREU	Access to health-related information on services and public health Informed consent
Dignity, equality, solidarity	Education	14 CFREU	Education as a social determinant of health Sex education as public health
Equality	Protection of mothers, children, and of the family	24 CFREU	Paid and sufficient maternity leave Social and family benefits Equality directive, disabilities, gender, etc.
Equality, solidarity, and universal access	Non-discrimination	20-26 CFREU	Non-discrimination in access to health care services and preventive care
Equality, solidarity	Employment	32 CFREU	Occupational health Employment as a social determinant of public health
Solidarity and equality	Social security	33 CFREU	Social security as a social determinant of public health

(*continued*)

Table 2.2 *Continued*

Value/human right	Fundamental right	European provisions	EU Health topics involved
Equality, universal access	Right to health Right to access health care	35 CFREU	Access to health care and other (public) health services Access to preventive care Protection of public health Reproductive health Protection of the environment as it affects public health Occupational health Regulation of services of general interest Pharmaceuticals and medical devices

Source: A. de Ruijter 'The Impediment of Health Laws' Values in the Constitutional Setting of the EU' in T. K. Hervey, Calum Alasdair Young, and Louise Bishop (eds) *Research Handbook on EU Health Law and Policy* (Cheltenham: Edward Elgar, 2017) <http://www.e-elgar.com/shop/research-handbook-on-european-union-health-law-and-policy> accessed 28 March 2017.

3.1 The scope of application of fundamental rights to EU health policy

The above section outlined the significance of the relationship between the EU, fundamental rights, and health policy. This section addresses more specifically the possible scope of application of fundamental rights to EU health policy. Whereas there are a number of international legal instruments that protect health rights of individuals and populations vis-à-vis their nation state, the EU is not automatically bound to similar obligations. The EU has a rather particular political and legal system; moreover, the nature of EU health policy (-making) is in many respects of a different (legal) nature to that of its Member States. At the same time, the generations of fundamental health rights applicable to nation states in a broad sense, as outlined above, are mirrored in different legal instruments that may apply to the EU and its Member States.

3.2 The Charter and the European Convention on Human Rights

With respect to the European institutions, the CFREU and the ECHR are central legal sources in which applicable fundamental rights can be found.[75] With the entry into force in 2009 of the Lisbon amendments to the Treaty in Article 6(1) TEU:

> The Union recognises the rights, freedoms and principles set out in the Charter of Fundamental Rights of the European Union of 7 December 2000, as adapted at Strasbourg, on 12 December 2007, which shall have the same legal value as the Treaties [. . .].

[75] The ECHR is the central legal instrument, adopted by the Council of Europe from 1949 in the aftermath of the Second World War. The Council of Europe is explicitly a human rights organization, with the Strasbourg-based European Court of Human Rights able currently to hear individual complaints against states directly. The judgments of the Court are legally binding (Article 46 (2) ECHR). The introduction of the CFREU coincided with the Laeken Mandate of 2001. Presidency Conclusions

This article states that the Charter, which contains fifty-four provisions on fundamental rights, has the status of primary Union law.[76] Moreover, Article 6(2) TEU also refers to the fact that the EU will become party to the ECHR. Article 6(3) TEU holds that:

> Fundamental rights, as guaranteed by the European Convention for the Protection of Human Rights and Fundamental Freedoms and as they result from the constitutional traditions common to the Member States, shall constitute general principles of the Union's law.

The last Article reflects that although the EU itself is not in essence a human rights organization, in the context of economic integration the adherence to fundamental rights did develop over time in the case law of the CJEU.[77]

3.3 Scope of application of fundamental rights

The plurality of fundamental rights, from EU to international sources, applicable to the EU creates the potential problem of having too many rights, or no rights at all.[78] Yet with respect to health in the case law of the CJEU so far, there has not been a huge body of case law in which reference was made to fundamental rights in relation to health.[79] In the past, the case law of the CJEU on health issues was usually decided in relation to internal market law. In the context of the ECtHR however, there is more case law on the interplay between health policy and fundamental rights.

Currently, the Charter has become the main point of reference for EU fundamental rights. At the same time, the Court has repeatedly interpreted a fundamental right from the Charter as expressing an already existing principle.[80] Furthermore, as to interpretation of a particular right, another source is the case law of the ECtHR

of the Laeken European Council (14 and 15 December 2001): Annex I: Laeken Declaration on the future of the European Union in Bulletin of the European Union. 2001 No 12 pp. 19–23.

[76] At this point, the Treaty on European Union has not expressly been declared supreme. However, the declaration to the Lisbon Treaty on supremacy reiterates that in line with settled case law of the Court, EC law had supreme status, which will now apply to 'Union law'. As the declaration to the Lisbon Treaty refers to the case law on supremacy of Union law, it will, mutatis mutandis, also apply to the provisions of the Charter; for an in-depth analysis, see J. Dutheil de la Rochère 'The Protection of Fundamental Rights in the EU: Community of Values with Opt-Out?' in I. Pernice and E. Tanchev (eds) *Ceci n'est pas une Constitution—Constitutionalisation without a Constitution?* (Baden-Baden: Nomos, 2009) See Declaration 17 on primacy (or 'supremacy').

[77] See e.g. Case C-112/00 *Eugen Schmidberger, Internationale Transporte und Planzüge v. Republik Österreich* [2003] ECR I-5659 para. 71; Case C-36/02 *Omega Spielhallen- und Automatenaufstellungs-GmbH v. Oberbürgermeisterin der Bundesstadt Bonn* [2004] ECR I-9609 at para. 33; also see Case C-540/03 European *Parliament v. Council of the European Union (Family Reunification)* [2006] ECR I-5769 (which outlines that the Charter is meant as an affirmation of already existing fundamental rights as they are laid down in various international legal instruments and national constitutions as 'general principles of law'); also see Case C-303/05 *Advocaten voor de Wereld* [2007] ECR I-3633 (on the validity, in light of fundamental rights, of the transposition of a Directive on a European arrest warrant in Belgian law), para. 46; and see Case C-438/05 *International Transport Workers' Federation and Finnish Seamen's Union v. Viking Line ABP and OÜ Viking Line Eesti* [2007] ECR I-10779 (regarding the right to strike, which according to the Court is a general principle of Community (Union) law, which should be reconciled with the fundamental freedoms in accordance with the principle of proportionality) para. 43 et seq.; and see Case C-341/05 *Laval* [2007] ECR I-11767 paras 90–91.

[78] Douglas-Scott (2011) supra note 28.

[79] Unlike, perhaps problematically, references to 'solidarity'; see G. Davies 'The Price of Letting Courts Value Solidarity: The Judicial Role in Liberalizing Welfare' in M. Ross and Y. Borgmann-Prebil (eds) *Promoting Solidarity in the European Union* (Oxford University Press, Clarendon: 2010); but see Case C-270/99 *Z. v. EP, Opinion of A.G. Jacobs of 22 March 2001* [2001] ECR I-9197 particularly on Article 1 Charter on human dignity and informed consent in biotechnology.

[80] Lenaerts (2012) supra note 71.

in conjunction with Article 52(3) CFREU on interpretation and Article 6 TEU on the ECHR's binding force under Union law. With respect to EU health policy, there are three situations to consider. The first is when 'the institutions, bodies offices and agencies of the Union' are involved in health policymaking.[81] The second is when a Member State fulfils—or derogates from—an obligation imposed by Union law. The third situation that is relevant for health policy is when Union law imposes no obligation on Member States, yet Member States create policy at EU level, facilitated by EU institutions.

3.3.1 *Invoking fundamental rights against EU institutional actors*

The first situation—when institutional actors of the Union are involved in health policymaking—could trigger the application of fundamental rights, but there are several limitations.[82] Article 51(1) of the Charter in this regard outlines the principle of conferred competences; that 'provisions of the Charter shall not extend in any way the competences of the Union as defined in the Treaties'. Moreover, Article 51(1) provides for the application of fundamental rights to EU health policymaking activities of the Union institutions as long as it 'does not extend the field of application of Union law beyond the powers of the Union or establish any new power of task for the Union, or modify powers and tasks as defined in the Treaties'.[83] Therefore, the scope of application of fundamental rights to the EU is limited by the competences of the EU.[84]

Moreover, with respect to claims of individuals against the EU institutions, including EU agencies, Article 263 TFEU creates a high threshold for taking action, particularly when this concerns legislative measures. In that case individuals have to be able to show both direct and individual concern.[85] Private parties can challenge

[81] Article 51(1) CFREU.

[82] Institutions could be challenged before the general Court (Article 263 TFEU) or before a national court under an Article 267 TFEU procedure.

[83] Article 51(2) and also Article 6(1) TEU. Nevertheless, some Member States feared that the Charter would expand the scope of Union law, which led to some individual limitations in the run-up to the ratification of the Lisbon Treaty. This then led to a Czech declaration that stressed the Charter is only applicable when Union law is being implemented, and not when national law is being implemented and adopted independently of Union law. Poland has made a special exception as to social policy and social rights, and the UK has a limitation specifically with regard to the legal value of the Charter and its application. This provides that neither the ECJ nor any national tribunal can find laws, practices, or actions of these respective countries inconsistent with fundamental rights, freedoms, or principles, especially with regard to the solidarity title in the Charter, unless these rights are recognized under national law. However, this generally does not extend to those areas which do fall under the scope of the EU. This, taken together with the fact that the Charter is not the only source of fundamental rights, implies that in reality, the opt-out protocols will probably not have the levelling effect of derogating the general constitutional principle of adherence to fundamental rights within the European Constitution or Declaration no. 62 Lisbon Treaty; also see Declaration no 61; see further in this regard M. Dougan 'The Treaty of Lisbon 2007' (2008) *Common Market Law Review* (who refers to the opt-out protocols as a smokescreen obscuring the actual scope of the Charter for national constituents).

[84] Case C-309/96 *Annibaldi* [2007] ECR I-7493 (archaeological and nature park fell outside of the scope of Union law, therefore no application of the Charter); Case C-256/11 *Murat Dereci and Others v. Bundesministerium für Inneres* [2011] *ECR* I-11315 (para. 71: 'Accordingly, the Court is called upon to interpret, in the light of the Charter, the law of the European Union within the limits of the powers conferred on it'); also see D. M. Curtin and R. van Ooik 'The Sting is Always in the Tail. The Personal Scope of Application of the EU Charter of Fundamental Rights' (2001) *Maastricht Journal of European and Comparative Law* 8 102–13.

[85] 'Direct concern' relates to EU measures that directly affect the legal position of the individual, without requiring further implementation. 'Individual concern' can be established in a very limited

non-legislative acts of general concern (acts adopted other than through the Article 289 TFEU procedure) if they can show direct concern.[86] Given the generally limited EU competence for health in Article 168 TFEU, the above limitations on the application of the Charter would indicate a very narrow possibility for holding the EU legally responsible for breaching fundamental rights in the context of its health law and policy. However, fundamental rights can still be used to review the legality of EU health policy generally vis-à-vis the EU institutions and the Member States, either directly in front of the general court or through a preliminary reference on the basis of Article 267 TFEU.[87] Moreover, Member States can be held responsible in the second situation, where Member States are implementing or derogating from an obligation under Union law.

3.3.2 Invoking EU fundamental rights against Member States

In the second situation, the question of applicability of the Charter relates to the Member States when they are involved in EU health policy. The Charter is applicable to Member States' activity 'only when they are implementing Union law', [88] whereas general principles are applicable when Member States are 'acting in the scope of EU law'.[89] This provision has been the subject of much controversy as concerns the application of the Charter.[90] Particularly given that in the Explanations to Article 51 of the Charter, the Charter is deemed applicable when Member States act in 'the scope of (Union) law.'[91] In the recent *Åkerberg Fransson* case, where on the facts the Member States were allowed a wide margin of discretion in order to enforce an EU directive on VAT, the CJEU ruled that there was no distinction between Member State 'implementing' or 'acting in the scope of application [of]' Union law. What matters for the application of the Charter to a Member State is that it is acting under a Union obligation—in other words, that objectives of the EU are given effect by national laws.[92] This meant that:

number of cases when the litigant meets the Plaumann test, where the individual is: 'affected by reason of certain attributes which are peculiar to them or by reason of circumstances in which they are differentiated from all other persons and by virtue of these factors distinguishes them individually just as in the case of the person addressed.' See para. 31 of *Case 25/62 Plaumann & Co v. Commission [1963] ECR 95* but see later case law discussed in S. Peers and M. Costa 'Court of Justice of the European Union (General Chamber), Judicial review of EU Acts after the Treaty of Lisbon; Order of 6 September 2011, Case T-18/10 Inuit Tapiriit Kanatami and Others v. Commission & Judgment of 25 October 2011, Case T-262/10 Microban v. Commission' (2012) *European Constitutional Law Review* 8 82–104.

86 Case T-262/10 *Microban International and Microban (Europe) v. Commission* [2011] ECR. II-07697; Case T-18/10 *Inuit Tapiriit Kanatami and Others v. Commission* NYR [2011] (the Microban case involved an implementing act by the European Commission in order to protect public health).

87 Article 6 TEU, Article 263 TFEU, Article 52 (5) CFREU.

88 Article 51 (1) CFREU.

89 Case C-159/90 *Society for the unborn children of unborn children Ireland Ltd v. Stephen Grogan* [1991] ECR I-4685; but see on implementing Union law, Case 5/88 *Wachauf v. Federal Republic of Germany* [1989] ECR 2609; and on derogating from EU law, Case C260/89 *Elliniki Radiophoni a Tileorassi Anonymi Etairia v. Dimotiki Etairia Pliroforisis and Kouvelas (ERT)* [1993] ECR I-2925.

90 D. Sarmiento 'Who's Afraid of the Charter? The Court of Justice, National Courts and the New Framework of Fundamental Rights Protection in Europe' (2013) *Common Market Law Review* 50 1267–1304; Lenaerts (2012) supra note 71; Eeckhout (2002) supra note 73.

91 Explanations *Explanations Relating to the Charter of Fundamental Rights (2007/C303/02, 14-12-2007)* (2007); also see *Case C-112/00 Eugen Schmidberger, Internationale Transporte und Planzüge v. Republik Österreich [2003] ECR I-5659.*

92 Case C-617/10 *Åklagaren v. Hans Åkerberg Fransson* [2013] ECR I-0000 at paras 29, 30.

[a] rule giving effect to an EU obligation falls within the scope of Union law and triggers fundamental rights protection even if such a rule does not clearly flow from Union law.[93]

With regard to individuals invoking EU fundamental rights against Member States there are some additional difficulties, however, particularly with regard to the application of the Charter, which holds in Article 52(5) CFREU that:

The provisions of this Charter which contain principles may be implemented by legislative and executive acts taken by Institutions and bodies of the Union, and by acts of Member States when they are implementing Union law, in the exercise of their respective powers. They shall be judicially cognisable only in the interpretation of such acts and in the ruling on their legality.

This means that if a right in the Charter were to be interpreted as a 'principle' no direct action could be taken against the EU or the Member States with this right as a basis. However, a 'principle' could still be used for interpreting or reviewing EU legal measures giving expression to a principle.[94] This still creates significant limitations, especially for individuals. In the *AMS* case,[95] there was a directive that gave expression to a principle in the Charter. However, the national provisions could not be interpreted in line with the directive in question, as it would have resulted in a *contra legem* interpretation.[96] Therefore the Court considered, in line with an earlier case to this effect,[97] that individuals, so as to preclude the application of a national law that is not in conformity with the Directive, could invoke the Charter provision together with the Directive. In contrast to that earlier case, however, the Court ruled that, given that the underlying right in the Charter for the purpose of its justiciability could be considered a principle, individuals could not invoke it.[98] This means that, with regard to the *AMS* case, there would need to have been a secondary measure actually giving effect to a principle in order for individuals to invoke this principle in court—rather unlikely, given the fact that the principle itself cannot function as a source for legal action. Moreover, if national legislation is still needed to implement this measure, individuals, for interpretative use, can only invoke a principle when the national law is not *contra legem* the secondary Union measure. This still leaves open the matter of when a Member State derogates from Union law, which is often done on the basis of public health considerations in the context of internal market law.

Although the CJEU has not given a decisive judgment with regard to the derogations from Union law by Member States in light of the Charter,[99] the broad interpretation on the applicability of the Charter holds that the ability to derogate from Union law, for instance in order to protect public health, is provided for under Union law itself. Therefore, this would still be considered as 'acting in the scope' of Union law and would make the Charter applicable to derogations from Union law as well.[100] In this regard, the protection offered by the Charter, interpreted broadly, is considered

[93] E. Muir 'The Fundamental Rights implications of EU Legislation: Some Constitutional Challenges' (2014) *Common Market Law Review* 51 219–46 at p. 238.

[94] *Explanations Relating to the Charter of Fundamental Rights* (2007/C303/02, 14-12-2007).

[95] Case C-176/12 *Association de médiation sociale v. Union locale des syndicats CGT, Hichem Laboubi, Union départementale CGT des Bouches-du-Rhône, Confédération générale du travail (CGT)* [2014] NYR.

[96] Ibid. para. 39.

[97] Case C-555/07 *Seda Kücükdeveci v. Swedex GmbH & Co. KG [2010]* ECR I-00365.

[98] Case C-176/12 *Case Association de médiation sociale v. Union locale des syndicats CGT, Hichem Laboubi, Union départementale CGT des Bouches-du-Rhône, Confédération générale du travail (CGT)* [2014] NYR at para. 46.

[99] But see with regard to principles of Union law (Article 6 TEU); and see *ERT* case, supra note 89.

[100] A. Ward 'Article 51 Field of Application' in S. Peers et al. (eds) *The EU Charter of Fundamental Rights* (Oxford: Hart, 2014) at p. 1428, also see Lenaerts (2012) supra note 71 at p. 90.

similar to 'principles of Union law',[101] which are also considered by some to apply to derogations.[102]

Still, at the basis there needs to be an EU obligation, and in cases of EU health policy as a matter of non-legislation this may not always be present. However, the above-mentioned *Fransson* case does imply that, even when an EU obligation is a relatively technical matter and without specific reference to its relation with fundamental rights, the issue may well still fall within the EU's fundamental rights jurisdiction. However, in the *Fransson* case, and later cases in the context of family law and immigration, the Court had to find ways to limit the application of the Charter to Member States implementing measures in areas where fundamental rights application might expand the EU's competences.[103]

3.3.3 Application of fundamental rights without a Union law obligation

The third situation that is relevant for health policy is when Union law imposes no obligation on Member States, yet Member States create policy at EU level, facilitated by EU institutions. In this case there are two issues at stake. The first is whether this situation falls under the applicability of the Charter to actions of EU institutions and organs, or whether the Charter would apply to Member States in this situation. In the first case, the applicability of the Charter would depend firstly on whether the entity created at EU level by Member State cooperation can be considered as an 'institution' as listed in Article 51(1) CFREU,[104] and secondly on whether the EU has a legal basis for this policy. Given the relatively narrow EU competence for EU health policy, this could be a barrier to the application of the Charter to the involvement of EU institutional actors, particularly when the 'actor' in not an institutional actor as would fall, even broadly interpreted, under Article 51(1) CFREU. At the same time, however, in order to get around this restriction, EU health policy more often than not will find its legal basis in a number of different internal market objectives, which would bring it back to the realm of the applicability of the Charter.

The second issue here is the applicability of the Charter to the Member States. In an important 2012 case the CJEU outlined that Member State action under the heading of the Treaty establishing the European Stability Mechanism was not an implementation of EU law.[105] Hence the Charter would also not apply to the Member States when they create policy at EU level facilitated by EU institutions purely as a matter of international cooperation. Given the fact that this type of policy activity is basically either a matter of national responsibility or may possibly be seen as a collective

[101] Article 6 TEU.

[102] Opinion of A.G. Sharpston in Case C-427/06 *B. Bartsch v. Bosch und Siemens Hausgerate (BSH) Altersfursorge GmbHage* [2008] ECR I-07245; Muir (2014) supra note 93 and see Ward (2014) supra note 100 at p. 1429.

[103] Case C-400/10 PPU McB, EU:C:2010:582. Joined Cases C-570/07 and C-571/07José Manuel Blanco Pérez and María Del Pilar Chao Gómez v Consejería de Salud y Servicios Sanitarios and Principado de Asturias, ECR [2010]I-04629.

[104] See further a discussion on this issue by Ward (2014) supra note 100 at p. 1425

[105] Case C-370/12 *Thomas Pringle v. Government of Ireland, Ireland, the Attorney General* [2012] NYR, particularly para. 180:

> It must be observed that the Member States are not implementing Union law, within the meaning of Article 51(1) of the Charter, when they establish a stability mechanism such as the ESM where, as is clear from paragraph 105 of this judgment, the EU and FEU Treaties do not confer any specific competence on the Union to establish such a mechanism.

responsibility of the Member States, a more feasible judicial path would perhaps be to take a possible infringement of a fundamental right up to the ECtHR. However, although holding states collectively responsible before the ECtHR has been tried, the ECtHR to date has never found a collective violation by EU Member States.[106] This would mean that EU health policy may touch on sensitive issues and values that are fundamental to the EU political system, without possibilities for legal redress. In this regard, analysing the impact of EU health policy and law highlights a difficulty in effectuating particular obligations to promote or protect fundamental rights in this regard and demonstrates possible tensions in Member States' participation in EU policymaking activities.

3.4 Applicability of other fundamental rights instruments to EU health policy

An important aspect with regard to the applicability of other fundamental rights instruments is the fact that the EU may accede to the ECHR and ECtHR at some point. Although Article 263 TFEU together with Article 6(3) TEU provide for the applicability of the ECHR as general principles, the accession of the EU to the ECHR challenges the current status quo of fundamental rights protection of the EU, particularly in sensitive policy areas.[107] In this regard it is important take note of the particularities of the relationship between the Council of Europe and the European Union with respect to the different legal systems.[108] The Council of Europe (CoE) is essentially a human rights organization that has a diplomatic working method of adopting conventions and protocols under the aegis of international law at its basis.

Given the non-exhaustive nature of the recognition of fundamental rights in the EU context, there are a number of other CoE Conventions that come into play with respect to human rights and health.[109] However, although they have been ratified by a number of Member States, the EU is not a party to these covenants. For instance, there is the Convention on Human Rights and Biomedicine (1997) from the CoE ('Biomedicine Convention').[110] This instrument has had an important impact on the legal systems of the Member States with respect to health law.[111] Of the forty-seven countries that have ratified the ECHR, twenty-nine have ratified the Biomedicine Convention and six are signatories to it. Generally, from the perspective of the ECtHR, the rules of international law would preclude the EU from being bound to the Biomedicine Convention.[112] However, at EU level the Biomedicine Convention could be taken to apply indirectly to the European

[106] Although it has been tried numerous times, see further on this Eckes (2013) supra note 66 at p. 260.

[107] See ibid.; and see P. Craig 'EU Accession to the ECHR: Competence, Procedure and Substance' (2013) *Fordham International Law Journal* (36) 1114–50; also see Douglas-Scott (2011) supra note 28.

[108] Eckes (2013) supra note 66.

[109] Case C-112/00 *Eugen Schmidberger, Internationale Transporte und Planzüge v. Republik Österreich* [2003] ECR I-5659; Case C-36/02 *Omega Spielhallen- und Automatenaufstellungs-GmbH v. Oberbürgermeisterin der Bundesstadt Bonn* [2004] ECR I-9609; R. Herrmann et al. (2011) 'The European Union and Health and Human Rights' *European Human Rights Law Review* 4 419–36.

[110] Convention for the Protection of Human Rights and Dignity of the Human Being with regard to the Application of Biology and Medicine: Convention on Human Rights and Biomedicine (Oviedo: 4 April 1997).

[111] H. Nys et al. 'Patient Rights in EU Member States After the Ratification of the Convention on Human Rights and Biomedicine' in (2007) *Health Policy* 83 223–35.

[112] On personal scope, see also part II of Section 1, United Nations Vienna Convention on the Law of Treaties, 23 May 1969, United Nations Treaty Series, vol. 1155, p. 331.

Union institutions and Member States. The CJEU could find that the Biomedicine Convention gives evidence of a broad recognition of a particular health right by a majority of Member States, and creates a basis for finding the existence of a general principle of Union law.[113] This is particularly the case given that, outside of the possibility for the application of the Biomedicine Convention through Article 6(3) TEU, the indirect application of the Biomedicine Convention could be the result of the rules on interpretation of the Charter.

One interpretation of the provisions of the Charter, Article 52(3) outlines that if the rights in the Charter overlap with the rights in the ECHR, their meaning and scope are to be interpreted as similar to those in the Convention. However, a more extensive protection is permitted at EU level. The ECHR in this respect creates a baseline of rights. Yet, with respect to the case law, the CJEU has determined that for interpretation the jurisprudence of the ECtHR would be leading.[114] The Biomedicine Convention could then come into play through analogous interpretation of the Charter given the fact that the ECtHR also refers to it in its case law, for instance in difficult cases with regard to the status of the embryo and/or foetus in light of Article 2 ECHR 'right to life',[115] and with respect to the interpretation of the principle of informed consent (Chapter 2 of the Convention) in the context of Article 8 ECHR 'private and family life'.[116]

Similarly, application of another CoE instrument relevant for health, the European Social Charter (ESC), can result from the reference of the ECtHR in its case law to EU fundamental rights, especially as the Preamble to the TEU also speaks of the Member States' wish to confirm 'their attachment to fundamental social rights as defined in the European Social Charter signed at Turin on 18 October 1961'. The ESC, however, similarly to the Biomedicine Convention, has its own supervisory mechanism, which means the rights in these instruments could only became legally relevant for the EU if referred to by the ECtHR or if the CJEU deemed them evidence of general principles of EU law.[117] This possible dual or overlapping application of fundamental rights instruments applicable to EU institutions generally means that both ECHR and CFREU regimes could be applicable to a particular question intersecting fundamental rights and health (see Table 2.3).

[113] Article 6(3) TEU.

[114] Although increasingly the CJEU is solely referring to the Charter, see G. de Burca 'After the EU Charter of Fundamental Rights: The Court of Justice as a Human Rights Adjudicator?' (2013) *Maastricht Journal of European and Comparative Law* 20 (2) 168–84; Eckes (2013) supra note 66 at p. 258.

[115] See para. 84 of ECtHR *Vo v. France* Application No. 53924/00 8 July 2004:

> At best, it may be regarded as common ground between States that the embryo/foetus belongs to the human race. The potentiality of that being and its capacity to become a person—enjoying protection under the civil law, moreover, in many States, such as France, in the context of inheritance and gifts, and also in the United Kingdom [...]—require protection in the name of human dignity, without making it a 'person' with the 'right to life' for the purposes of Article 2. The Oviedo Convention on Human Rights and Biomedicine, indeed, is careful not to give a definition of the term 'everyone', and its explanatory report indicates that, in the absence of a unanimous agreement on the definition, the Member States decided to allow domestic law to provide clarification for the purposes of the application of that Convention.

[116] ECtHR *Glass v. The United Kingdom* Application No. 61827/00 9 March 2004.

[117] A Hendriks, 'The Council of Europe and Health and Human Rights', Health and Human Rights in Europe (Intersentia: Antwerp 2012) at p. 44 et seq.

Table 2.3 Overlapping rights between the ECHR and the CFREU

Right/principle	European provisions*	Health topics involved
Right to life	2 ECHR 2 CFREU	Abortion End-of-life issues, euthanasia Protection of life through public health measures Duty to investigate deaths Environmental health threats
Human dignity**	1 CFREU	End-of-life issues, access to health care, care for the elderly and for people with disabilities
Prohibition of torture and inhuman and degrading treatment	3 ECHR 4 CFREU	Confinement of persons with mental disabilities Access to health care for prisoners Rape, sexual abuse Undue delay of access to health care
Privacy and family life	8 ECHR 7, 10 Biomedicine Convention 7, 8 CFREU	Physical and psychological integrity, including personal autonomy in the context of medical interventions Protection of personal data, confidentiality of medical files Prohibition of compulsory use of contraceptives, non-voluntary sterilization, or abortion
Family life, founding a family	12 ECHR 9 CFREU	Prohibition of compulsory use of contraceptives, non-voluntary sterilization, or abortion; access to fertility treatments
Information and participation	8, 10 ECHR 5–9 Biomedicine Convention 11 CFREU	Access to health-related information Informed consent
Access to a remedy	13 ECHR	Medical negligence, accountability for failures or abuses in the health sector (supervision and inspection)
Non-discrimination	14 ECHR: Protocol 12 to ECHR 3 ECS; 1, 11, 14 Biomedicine Convention; 20–26 CFREU	Non-discrimination in access to health-care services and preventive care
Health, including reproductive health	11, 13 ESC 3 Biomedicine Convention 35 CFREU	Access to health care and other (public) health services Access to preventive care Protection of public health Reproductive health Protection of the environment as it affects public health Occupational health
Adequate standard of living	30 ESC	Adequate access to food, housing, and clothes

(*continued*)

Table 2.3 *Continued*

Right/principle	European provisions*	Health topics involved
Benefits of scientific progress		Promotion of health research, including for vulnerable groups Development of affordable treatments
Social security	12, 14, 16, and 23 ESC; 33 CFREU	Social security as a social determinant of health
Protection of mothers, children, and of the family	7, 8, 16, 17 ESC 24 CFREU	Paid and sufficient maternity leave Social and family benefits Protection against violence against children
Food	11 ESC	Safe and nutritious food Food as a social determinant of health
Housing	8 ECHR 31 ESC	Housing as a social determinant of health Independent living with a disability
Education	Protocol 1 ECHR 14 CFREU	Education as a social determinant of health Sex education as public health
Employment	1–4, 7–10, 18–22, 24–29 ESC 15, 31, 32 CFREU	Occupational health Employment as a social determinant of health

* Council of Europe, European Convention for the Prevention of Torture and Inhuman or Degrading Treatment or Punishment, Strasbourg, 26 November 1987 (ECPT); Charter of Fundamental Rights (2000) (CFREU); Convention on Human Rights and Biomedicine (1997) Council of Europe, European Convention for the Prevention of Torture and Inhuman or Degrading Treatment (Ref: CPT/Inf/C (2002) Strasbourg, 26 November 1987; Council of Europe, European Social Charter (Revised), 3 May 1996, ETS 163 (ESC).

** Human Dignity enters the legal realm of the ECHR through its case law and further protocols; C. McCrudden 'Human Dignity and Judicial Interpretation of Human Rights' (2008) *European Journal of International Law* 19, 655.

Besides the CFREU and the ECHR that are applicable to the EU,[118] the above outline of fundamental rights that can be affected by the adoption of health policy can also have significance for EU-level policymaking. In the context of interpreting 'general principles' of EU law, the CJEU has also made limited reference to UN human rights treaties.[119] Another avenue for international fundamental rights instruments to come into play is through reference to these instruments by the ECtHR and by the CJEU for interpreting the CFREU. A case in point could be the ECtHR case *OPUZ v. Turkey*, where the ECtHR extensively refers to the United Nations CEDAW convention on the rights of women, which also contains health-related provisions.[120] Albeit through a detour, the CJEU may use such a case in its interpretation of the CFREU and give relevance to rights contained in United Nations instruments and beyond. At

[118] As mentioned, the CJEU already refers directly to the ECHR in some cases; on this point, see further Eckes (2013) supra note 66 at p. 258.

[119] See e.g. Case C-540/03 *European Parliament v. Council of the European Union (Family Reunification)* [2006] ECR I-5769 (on the margin of appreciation of EU Member States with regard to a Directive setting out the right to family reunification for children); para. 37 particularly mentions the International Covenant on Civil and Political Rights.

[120] ECtHR *Opuz v. Turkey* Application no. 33401/02 9 June 2009 at para. 147.

the same time, international human rights instruments can also come into view as vehicles for policymaking. For instance, the EU Fundamental Rights Agency (established in 2007) in its reporting on the status of fundamental rights protection by the EU and its Member States explicitly refers to UN human rights treaties.[121]

Another non-EU legal instrument that can find application to the EU, especially given the fact that clinical trials are regulated at EU level with respect to pharmaceuticals, is the World Medical Association Declaration of Helsinki—Ethical Principles for Medical Research Involving Human Subjects,[122] particularly as these principles are generally accepted by the medical profession and in Member States' health law.[123] The Helsinki Declaration in many ways is already incorporated in Union Law. The Helsinki principles for protecting patients in a clinical trial setting are contained in Union law and applied through guidelines for good clinical practice, for instance by the committee at the EMA that is responsible for preparing opinions on questions concerning medicines for human use, the Committee for Medicinal Products for Human Use (CHMP).[124]

4. EU Fundamental Rights in Public Health and Health Care

Thus far, this chapter has outlined the role of fundamental rights in creating the limit to the use of power in the context of health policy and law. The fundamental rights that are particularly relevant in relation to human health are found both in the spheres of individual rights and of social and economic rights. In the EU these 'generations' of rights are codified in the Charter and in related legal instruments, which apply to the EU as well as the Member States, but their application cannot expand the relatively limited legal power (competence) the EU has in the field of health (Art. 168 TFEU). The last part of the chapter outlines two branches of fundamental rights that will be used in describing the implications of the expansion of EU power in health care and public health. These branches follow roughly the second part (social rights) and the first part (dignity and freedoms) of the Charter. However, health policy more often than not may have implications for multiple fundamental rights (see Figure 2.1). Therefore, each branch allows for overlaps and linkages of several rights in relation to health policy.

[121] European Agency for Fundamental Rights (2009), *Housing Conditions of Roma and Travellers in the European Union: Comparative Report*, 12–14; and see further United Nations (2010) *The European Union and International Human Rights Law*, UN Office of the United Nations High Commissioner for Human Rights, Brussels.

[122] World Medical Association Declaration of Helsinki (1964)—Ethical Principles for Medical Research Involving Human Subjects, adopted at the eighteenth WMA General Assembly, Helsinki, Finland ('Helsinki Declaration').

[123] R. V. Carlson et al. 'The Revision of the Declaration of Helsinki: Past, Present and Future' (2004) *British Journal of Clinical Pharmacology* 57 (6) 695–713.

[124] Directive 2001/20/EC of the European Parliament and of the Council of 4 April 2001 on the approximation of the laws, regulations, and administrative provisions of the Member States relating to the implementation of good clinical practice in the conduct of clinical trials on medicinal products for human use (OJ L 121/34, 01-05-2001); Commission Directive 2005/28/EC of 8 April 2005 (laying down principles and detailed guidelines for good clinical practice as regards investigational medicinal products for human use, as well as the requirements for authorization of the manufacturing or importation of such products (L 91/13, 09-04-2005)).

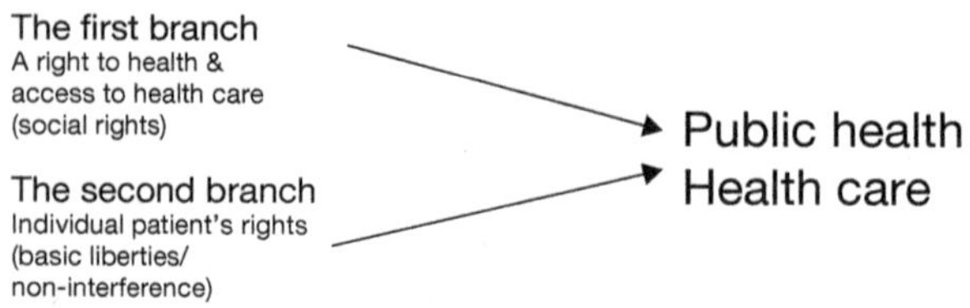

Figure 2.1 Two branches of fundamental rights, implications for public health and health care.

4.1 The first branch: right to health in health care and public health

In 1946 the WHO Constitution recognized that 'the enjoyment of the highest attainable standard of health is one of the fundamental rights of every human being'.[125] The central precept of a right to health is that public authorities have a certain responsibility for health.[126] With respect to *public health*, this has long been recognized.[127] In all Member States there is also a recognized 'right *to health care*' that, for example, guarantees at minimum access to the national health-care system.[128] The legal discussion with respect to these rights is not so much on their existence as on their scope and application.[129] 'A right to health' is a right no public authority is able to guarantee. Disease and infirmity are not factors under anyone's absolute control—that is, there is no right to be healthy.[130] Moreover, public authorities and health-care systems have limited resources. Hence, the right to health is deemed notoriously difficult to enforce before a court.[131] ESC (CoE) Article 11 outlines that in order to ensure the right to the protection of health, contracting parties should take steps:

(1) to remove as far as possible the causes of ill-health;
(2) to provide advisory and educational facilities for the promotion of health and the encouragement of individual responsibilities in matters of health;
(3) to prevent as far as possible epidemic, endemic, and other diseases.[132]

However, the Union is not a party to the ESC. Therefore, if accession takes place, the ECtHR would be unlikely to apply this article to the EU. Moreover, given the fact that the ECHR contains neither social rights nor the right to health, the CJEU would also not be able to make reference to Article 11 ESC. In the European policy context however, Article 11 ESC together with Article 35 CFREU (the right to health), for

[125] Constitution of the World Health Organization (1946).

[126] B. Toebes *The Right to Health and Other Health-Related Rights*, in *Health and Human Rights in Europe* (Cambridge: Intersentia, 2012) at p. 86.

[127] Sanitation, clean water, and other public health policies have been around for centuries, see G. Rosen *A History of Public Health* (Baltimore: Johns Hopkins University Press, 1958).

[128] Council Conclusions on Common values and principles in European Union Health Systems (2006/C 146/01) (OJ 146/1).

[129] Hendriks (1998) supra note 22; also see Toebes (1999) supra note 19; San Giorgi (2012) supra note 39; M. Langford (ed.) *Social Rights Jurisprudence: Emerging Trends in International and Comparative Law* (Cambridge: Cambridge University Press, 2008); Muller (2009) supra note 38.

[130] See UN general comment 14, para. 8, UN Committee on Economic, Social, and Cultural Rights, General Comment 14 on the Right to the Highest Attainable Standard of Health, UN Doc. E/C.12/200/4, 11 August 2000.

[131] See Hervey (2003) supra note 28; also see Toebes (1999) supra note 19; but see ECtHR *Nitecki v. Poland* Application No.65653/01 21 March 2002; and further in what follows.

[132] Table 2.3 outlines other sources where the right to health is expressed in international law. The Universal Declaration of Human Rights (1948) famously outlines in Article 25 that: 'Everyone has the right to a standard of living adequate for the health and well-being of himself and his family, including food, clothing, housing and medical care and necessary social services .'

instance as a matter of pre-policy-adoption 'impact assessment', could be used to assess the fundamental rights impact of European health policy, particularly given that the ESC is reaffirmed in the preamble of the TEU.[133]

At the same time there are a number of individual rights in the CFREU that could come into play with regard to the right to health and EU health policy. However, the application of these rights is context related. For instance, Article 21 CFREU on non-discrimination is important as a matter of equal access to health care, or with respect to public health in a case where policy may affect particular risk groups, for instance when a disease is tracked or isolation measures are taken in order to curb the spread of disease.[134] Combining a social right to (access) health (care) may be seen as a 'social rights-plus' approach that could be used to strengthen the justiciability of social rights.[135] Article 35 of the CFREU holds that:

> Everyone has the right of access to preventive health care and the right to benefit from medical treatment under the conditions established by national laws and practices. A high level of human health protection shall be ensured in the definition and implementation of all Union policies and activities.[136]

Generally, then, the right to health in the EU refers to the rights to *access health care services* and to the *protection of health*.[137] Article 35 CFREU mirrors these two aspects of the right to health. However, the legal scope of this article, as outlined, is not undisputed, as the Charter sets out 'an unfortunate distinction' between *principles* and *rights* in Article 52(5) CFREU.[138] This means that a 'right' in an article of the Charter may be interpreted as a principle, which has the consequence that it does not create directly enforceable rights, but instead is 'judicially cognisable only in the interpretation of such acts[[139]] and in the ruling on their legality'.[140]

4.1.1 The right to health: public health

The second paragraph of Article 35 mirrors Article 9 and 168 TFEU in that it mainstreams health concerns in all Union activities, and creates the possibility for judicial review of the legality of 'legislative and executive acts' generally with respect to health.[141] Hervey refers to this as a 'super mainstreaming' provision that forms the basis for health as a fundamental foundation for all EU public policy.[142] Hence, on one hand this provision can be seen as a 'touchstone against which Community [Union] ... action can

[133] Communication from the Commission, Strategy for the effective implementation of the Charter of Fundamental Rights by the European Union (COM(2010) 573 final).

[134] For instance in the case of the HIV/AIDS epidemic in the eighties, public health policy was soon aimed at homosexual men. S. Michalowski 'Health Care Law' in S. Peers and A. Ward (eds) *The EU Charter of Fundamental Rights: Politics, Law and Policy* (Oregon: Hart, 2004) at p. 291.

[135] Hervey (2003) supra note 28 at p. 204.

[136] The paragraph on access to preventive care and the right to benefit from medical treatment echoes similar articles in the CoE ESC Arts. 11 and 13.

[137] Hervey (2003) supra note 28.

[138] Douglas-Scott (2011) supra note 28.

[139] Article 51(5) CFREU speaks of: 'legislative and executive acts taken by institutions, bodies, offices and agencies of the Union and by acts of Member States when they are implementing Union law'.

[140] Article 52(5) CFREU); see the recent case on the application of the Charter in a dispute between private parties, where Article 27 CJEU was deemed to not confer rights on individuals at para. 48 Case C-176/12 *Association de médiation sociale v. Union locale des syndicats CGT (CGT)* [2014] NYR.

[141] Article 52(4) CFREU.

[142] See further on this point Hervey (2003) supra note 28 at p. 202; also see Michalowski (2004) supra note 134 at p. 291.

be tested'.[143] On the other hand, a more controversial question would be whether this paragraph might also be read as a directly enforceable right, particularly as it may be difficult to establish what constitutes a 'high level of health protection'.[144]

Considering the involvement of the EU in public health with regard to food, medical devices, tobacco, pharmaceuticals, blood, a safe environment, communicable diseases, and in the context of public health programmes, it is not unlikely that, if a Union act is deemed invalid by the Court on the basis of Article 35 CFREU, this declaration could affect enforceable rights that existed under the Union act in question. However, this right would then come about on the basis of the individual rights that existed or were affected by that particular Union act.[145] At the same time, say Article 11 ESC is recognized as a general principle, if we take the more specific positive obligations of the state parties that Article 11 ESC imposes on governments,[146] it is questionable that these obligations would be individually justiciable at EU level, even though Article 35(2) CFREU implies the imposition of comparable obligations on the EU.[147] In this regard there are a number of limitations. For one, Article 35 CFREU is more a procedural instruction for legislation. In order to bring a suit against an institution of the Union the legislation under question would need to be of direct and individual concern to the individual in question or, in the case of a regulatory act, the act needs to be of direct concern to the individual and not entail an implementing act (Art. 263 TFEU).[148] These preconditions make the justiciability of Article 35 CFREU more difficult, given that it is directed at the population at large rather than individuals.[149] Moreover, Article 263 TFEU restricts judicial review to 'legally binding acts', which means that a lot of the 'preparatory' work of EU agencies would fall outside the scope for litigation.[150]

Another question is whether Article 35 CFREU in combination with a directly enforceable right could be constructed as a right in terms of the CFREU ('social right-plus approach'). In this regard, reference to positive obligations of public authorities that have been deemed justiciable with regard to public health in the CoE context

[143] K. Lenaerts and P. Foubert 'Social Rights in the Case-Law of the European Court of Justice: The Impact of the Charter of Fundamental Rights of the European Union on Standing Case-Law' *Legal Issues of Economic Integration* (2001) 28 (3) 267 at p. 271.

[144] For general information on under what circumstances in Union law a conferral of an individual right is in question, see Case T-13/99 *Pfizer Animal Health SA v. Council of the European Union* [2002] ECR II-3318, particularly para. 81 et seq. and in para. 88:

> [T]he Court observes that natural or legal persons may claim that a measure of general application is of individual concern to them only if they are affected by reason of certain attributes which are peculiar to them or by reason of circumstances in which they are differentiated from all other persons.

Also see further case references here, restrictively e.g. Case 25/62 *Plaumann v. Commission* [1963] ECR 95 at para. 77.

[145] Article 263 TFEU.

[146] Reiterating Article 11 ESC, to take appropriate measures: '(1) to remove as far as possible the causes of ill-health; (2) to provide advisory and educational facilities for the promotion of health and the encouragement of individual responsibilities in matters of health; (3) to prevent as far as possible epidemic, endemic and other diseases.'

[147] See O. de Schutter 'Article 52 in Commentary of the Charter of Fundamental Rights of the European Union' in the EU Network of Independent Experts on Fundamental Rights (ed.) (Brussels: European Union, 2006) at p. 407.

[148] Another route would be to ask a preliminary question on the basis of Art. 267 TFEU. However, this route vis à vis EU institutions would also be limited by the Art. 263 TFEU 'test'. See Case C-370/12 *Thomas Pringle v. Government of Ireland, Ireland, The Attorney General* [2012] NYR.

[149] But see Case T-13/99 *Pfizer Animal Health SA v. Council of the European Union* [2002] ECR II-3318 with regard to the 'precautionary principle'.

[150] See for further references on this Ward (2014) supra note 100 at p. 1426.

could provide an interpretational background for Article 35 CFREU (Article 52(3) CFREU) only to the extent that such a positive obligation is construed through reference to an individual right that is protected both by the CFREU and the ECHR, such as the right to life. In a recent case where the CJEU addressed the applicability of the CFREU between individuals, the Court iterated that the Charter is applicable in 'all situations governed by European Union Law'.[151] The prevention of loss of life is of particular importance in this context, where it would be more likely that the EU has competence given its involvement in a broad array of safety and risk regulation in relation to public health.

In this regard the ECtHR has on occasion accepted that the right to life can be interpreted as an obligation on the public authorities to undertake steps to prevent avoidable loss of life. The general ECtHR doctrine with regard to positive obligations on public authorities in this context is that the right to life 'must be interpreted in a way which does not impose an impossible or disproportionate burden on the authorities'.[152] However, in a later case, the ECtHR also acknowledged that the right to life would impose a positive obligation on states to prevent human life being avoidably put at risk. In this case the UK exposed military personnel to dangerous levels of radiation, which created a risk to their offspring. The daughter of a former catering assistant of the British air force brought the case; she had developed childhood leukaemia, which turned out to be linked to her father's exposure to radioactive material. The Court rejected the application on the basis of the information available at the time on the link between childhood leukaemia and exposure to radiation.[153]

A relevant preventive measure in this regard that the EU may be obliged to undertake in light of the right to health is to *warn* the general public about public health risks. In the ECtHR case *Oneryildiz v. Turkey* the right to health created an obligation to inform the public of public health risks. The case involved the death of thirteen members of the Oneryildiz family as a result of a methane gas explosion in the municipal rubbish tip of Ümraniye (Istanbul). Ten slum dwellings situated below the mountain of waste were buried as a result of the landslide caused by the explosion. Thirty-nine people in total died. The ECtHR in this case accepted that the right to life includes an obligation of the public authorities to warn the public about public health risks.[154]

Taking preventive measures beyond the Member States, after accession to the ECHR the EU could also be held liable in a similar case for not ensuring the right to health,

[151] Case C-176/12 *Association de médiation sociale v. Union locale des syndicats CGT (CGT) [2014]* NYR at para. 42

[152] ECtHR *Osman v. United Kingdom* [1998] EHRR 101 28 October 1998 (the judgment denied the right-to-life claim under Article 2 ECHR in a case where there was an alleged failure to appreciate the threat an individual posed towards the life of Mr Osman).

[153] ECtHR *L.C.B. v. the United Kingdom* (14/1997/798/1001) 9 June 1998; ECtHR *Calvelli and Ciglio v. Italy* Application No. 32967/96 17 January 2002.

[154] See para. 63:

> Although not every presumed threat to life obliges the authorities, under the Convention, to take concrete measures to avoid that risk, the position is different, *inter alia*, if it is established that the authorities knew or ought to have known at the time of the existence of a real and immediate risk to the life of an individual or individuals and that they failed to take measures within the scope of their powers which might have been expected to avoid that risk.

Chamber Judgment ECtHR Case of *Oneryildiz v. Turkey* Application No. 48939/99 18 June 2002 and see Grand Chamber Judgment ECtHR Case of *Oneryildiz v. Turkey* Application No. 48939/99 30 November 2004 paras 87–90.

possibly linked with an individual right. The EU is in charge of numerous surveillance and response mechanisms that enable the trade of products that may have possible public health risks. In the *Pfizer* case, which dealt directly with the level of public health protection at EU level, the CJEU iterated that:

> [T]he Community institutions are entitled, in the interests of human health to adopt, on the basis of as yet incomplete scientific knowledge, protective measures which may seriously harm legally protected positions, and they enjoy a broad discretion in that regard.[155]

This means that a positive obligation could exist for the *EU institutions* to prevent the loss of life and ensure the right to health. At the same time, in cases where the *Member States* enjoy a wide discretion, the recent *Association Mediation Sociale* and *Fransson* cases seem to indicate that, regardless of a wide discretion allowed to the Member State to give effect to EU law, as long as there is a connection to an EU obligation the Charter would need to be observed. Arguably, the Member States in such a case could be also be obliged to uphold the right to life in terms of positive obligations (the right to health).

4.1.2 The right to health: access to health care

The right to access *health care* in Article 35 CFREU is a 'principle' which, strictly in the legal context of the Charter, would imply that this article does not entail an individual right. Similarly to the 'right to health', theoretically it might be possible to adopt a 'social rights-plus' approach to the right to health care, by which the right to health care becomes justiciable when it *also* impacts on an individual right, such as the right to life, the right to dignity, or the right to non-discrimination.[156] In this regard it is important that the right to equal treatment in Article 21 CFREU, which has been deemed to confer an individual right,[157] specifically refers to for instance genetic aspects and disabilities. Hence in theory Article 21 CFREU could be invoked with respect to equal access to health care.[158]

The right to life in relation to the right to health care in Article 2 CFREU (and also in Article 2 ECHR) could be invoked.[159] In the CoE context, this right in relation to health has been made explicit in a number of cases.[160] Even though the EU has limited competence with respect to the provision of health care,[161] in light of the fact that these ECtHR cases address provisions in the ECHR that are analogous to provision in the CFREU, through interpretation the CJEU may also be asked to rule on such highly delicate health-care issues in the future. Patients may seek abortion or reproductive treatments in another Member State, and indeed patients travel for euthanasia; in

[155] Case T-13/99 *Pfizer Animal Health SA v. Council of the European Union* [2002] ECR II-3318 at para. 170.

[156] Hervey (2003) supra note 28 at p. 196

[157] Case C-555/07 *Seda Kücükdeveci v. Swedex GmbH & Co. KG* [2010] *ECR* I-00365.

[158] Also see Article 14 of the ECHR and Article 11 of the Biomedicine Convention.

[159] See Case C-467/10 *Baris Akyüz v. Germany* Judgment of the Court (Second Chamber) [2012] OJ C 328, where Germany invokes the right to life to protect the public against unsafe drivers.

[160] ECtHR *Powell v. the United Kingdom* Application No. 45305/99, 4 May 2000; ECtHR *Calvelli and Ciglio v. Italy* Application No. 32967/96, 17 January 2002; particularly ECtHR *Cyprus v. Turkey* Application No. 25781/94, 10 May 2001 (where the Court outlines in para. 219 that a Contracting State puts an individual's life at risk by not granting access to health care that is available to the rest of the population); see further San Giorgi (2012) supra note 39 at p. 104.

[161] Art 168 (7) TFEU.

those cases, there are possible implications in terms of the right to life, or the right to family life in combination with the right to access health care.[162]

Another theoretical claim could be made when Article 35 EUCFR on the right to health care is read in relation to Article 4 CFREU on the infliction of inhuman or degrading treatment.[163] In this situation, a patient who is in pain or disabled and is made to wait for health care in his or her home state, while access to cross-border health care is denied, could claim the infliction of inhuman or degrading treatment in combination with a right to health care. Interestingly, in the case law of the CJEU the right to access health care—which could come into direct conflict with Article 168(7) TFEU that restates the autonomy of the Member States with respect to organizing the health care systems—has never been recognized as such. However, in a recent case the Advocate-General found, on the basis of the free-movement rules, that:

> [A]lthough the case-law takes as the main point of reference the fundamental freedoms established in the Treaty, there is another aspect which is becoming more and more important in the Community sphere, namely the right of citizens to health care, proclaimed in Article 35 of the Charter of Fundamental Rights of the European Union since 'being a fundamental asset' health cannot be considered solely in terms of social expenditure and latent economic difficulties. This right is perceived as a personal entitlement unconnected to a person's relationship with social security and the Court of Justice cannot overlook that aspect.[164]

Although the Court did not consider the case in light of Article 35 CFREU, the quote illustrates the potential 'constitutional struggle' that a rights-based approach to the involvement of the EU in health policy may bring to light. It shows that the right to access health care at EU level facilitated by the Treaty, on the basis of free movement together with a possible claim to Article 35 CFREU in combination with an individual right, collides with the autonomy that Member States claim in order to effectuate the right to access health care at the national level. Yet another important aspect of the right to access health care (Article 35 CFREU) is that it also creates a legal standard for assessing the legality of Union acts. This may even consist in a claim that the involvement of the EU in a particular area of health policy infringes on the right to access health care by affecting a Member State's autonomy to manage and sustain a national health-care system. For example, the effectuation of the right to access medicines at EU level, through making available particular subscriptions cross-border, could infringe on Member States' autonomy to manage the costs of health care.[165] The rationing of health-care entitlements is a primary element in the creation of universal access to health care at the national level.

For the purpose of analysing the implications of European health policy in light of the right to health, specifically with respect to public health and health care, making the connection between the right to health and individual rights may give more weight

[162] See generally McHale (2012) supra note 29 at p. 306 et seq.

[163] On the connection between the prohibition of torture and inhumane treatment and health care, see San Giorgi (2012) supra note 39 at p. 104 et seq. (referencing a number of ECtHR cases addressing the application of Article 3 ECHR in cases of the lack of health care in prisons—with respect to people suffering from a disease, being expelled, and with respect to mentally disabled persons); also see Hendriks (2012) supra note 22.

[164] AG R.-J. Colomer Opinion Case C-44/05 *Aikaterini Stamatelaki v. NPDD Organismos Asfaliseos Eleftheron Epangelmation (OAEE)* AG Opinion [2007] ECR I-3185 at para. 40.

[165] See ECtHR *Nitecki v. Poland* Application No.65653/01, 21 March 2002; also see European Commission (2013) Impact assessment roadmap 'Implementing measures for improving the recognition of prescriptions issued in another Member State' under Article 11 para. 2 of the Directive on the Application of Patients' Rights in Cross-Border Healthcare (CBHC)

and procedural strength if the EU institutions are ever challenged in court. However, for the purposes of analysing the fundamental rights implications of EU health policy more broadly and also as a matter of values, and analysing from a standpoint of fundamental rights as a matter of (internal to the EU legal system) legitimacy, the right to health as recognized by EU law gives plentiful points of reference for the institutions of the EU to take into account in the context of adopting health policy.[166]

4.2 The second branch: individual (patients') rights

The Charter protects a number of individual rights that are particularly important in the health context. At the same time, the legal significance of these rights may be diminished by the scope of application of the Charter, which is not to exceed established EU competences in a particular policy field. The provision of medical care, and specifically the patient–medical professional relationship, is not an area of general competence for the EU. Individual rights play a role in this relationship in that patients may want to protect their physical integrity. However, this can also be the case in a public health setting, where the relationship is characterized by the imposition of public power on the individual, often to protect a public health objective, such as curbing the spread of a particular communicable disease. In the public health setting, examples where individual rights provide important safeguards include forced psychiatric interventions, such as the mandatory administration of particular drugs, body searches, forced taking of blood samples or DNA swabs, and so on. In the following outline of individual rights that can come into play with respect to EU health policy, specific attention is paid firstly to the right to informed consent in connection with the right to human dignity and integrity of the person, and secondly to the right to data protection and privacy. This is done to create a more streamlined framework for analysis, while recognizing—as the explanation on the right to health showed—that other individual rights such as the right to life, the right to equal treatment, and the prohibition of torture, in combination with the right to health and the right to access health care, can create a basis for finding a fundamental rights implication of EU health policy.

4.2.1 Informed consent in public health and health care

Article 1 CFREU on human dignity lies at the basis of all elements of law and involvement in health, and can thus be taken as the foundation for a number of specific patients' rights.[167] At EU level, however, the question of what human dignity requires is essentially left up to the Member States.[168] But the question of human dignity could also become a European issue; Article 3 CFREU on the integrity of the person is closely related to the principle of human dignity.[169] Human dignity in this regard can

[166] T. K. Hervey 'We Don't See a Connection: The "Right to Health" in the EU Charter and European Social Charter' in G. de Burca and B. de Witte (eds) *Social Rights in Europe* (Oxford: Oxford University Press, 2005).

[167] See McHale (2012) supra note 29.

[168] See Case C-36/02 *Omega Spielhallen und Automatenaufstellungs-GmbH v. Oberbürgermeisterin der Bundesstadt Bonn* [2004] ECR I-9609 and see Douglas-Scott (2011) supra note 28.

[169] Case C-377/98 *The Netherlands v. European Parliament and Council of the European Union* [2001] ECR I-07079; see paras 77 and 78 on the basis of human dignity for not allowing patentability of elements of the human body.

refer both to the individual in terms of personal integrity and to protecting society at large. The principles outlined in Article 3 CFREU are generally also part of the ECHR, except for informed consent, which has only been developed in the case law of the ECtHR on the basis of Article 8 ECHR.[170] The second paragraph of Article 3 CFREU specifically outlines that informed consent must be respected in the field of medicine and biology and that eugenic practices, particularly those aiming at the selection of persons, making the human body and its parts a source for financial gain, and reproductive cloning of human beings, are prohibited.[171] The prohibition of reproductive cloning is not an individual right as such, but the provision in itself could come into play with respect to EU health policymaking, for instance with regard to the regulation of clinical trials at EU level or even the appropriation of funds for medical research from the EU.[172]

Article 3 CFREU could also be invoked when considering the European regulation of medicines. For instance, take the authorization on gene therapy with respect to regulation of pharmaceuticals at EU level. In 2013, the European Commission approved the medicine Glybera. This medicine uses a virus to deliver DNA encoding a lipid-processing enzyme to patients that lack this gene mutation. Gene therapy alters the human genetic code; the question is how this is different from a 'eugenic practice' and to what extent this should affect the authorization of these therapies at EU level.[173]

Furthermore, with respect to informed consent, Article 3 of the Charter can have implications in both health-care and public health contexts. In the context of health care, the right to informed consent and the integrity of the human body is part of the medical professional's legal obligation to protect the patient's right to self-determination.[174] Since the Nuremburg trials, informed consent has been one of the central legal underpinnings of the doctor–patient relationship in the different Member States.[175] In practice, liability for informed consent becomes an issue when something goes wrong in the provision of information and the outcome of medical treatment is negative. Patients can then say that they would never have consented had they been in possession of the right information. As such, 'informed consent' refers mainly to the duty to provide information, given that consent comprises information.[176] Only if

[170] See ECtHR *Tysiąc v. Poland* Application No. 5410/03, 20 March 2007, ECtHR *K.H. and others v. Slovakia* Application no. 32881/04, 28 April 2009, ECtHR *R.R. v. Poland* Application No. 27617/04, 26 May 2011 (these are some of the more recent ECtHR cases on the forced sterilization of Roma women and in the context of abortions for medical reasons).

[171] Article 3(2)(d) CFREU; these are also prohibited in the UN declaration on the Human Genome and Human Rights and in Directive 98/44 on the legal protection of biotechnological inventions (OJ L213/13, p. 123).

[172] An example here is case C-377/98, *Kingdom of the Netherlands v. European Parliament and Council of the European Union* [2001] ECR I-7149, where although an appeal to human dignity is accepted, nevertheless the plea with respect to informed consent is rejected given that 'The purpose of the Directive is not to replace the restrictive provisions which guarantee, outside the scope of the Directive, compliance with certain ethical rules which include the right to self-determination by informed consent'; see para. 80.

[173] See ibid.; to interpret this provision as an individual right would probably involve reference to human dignity.

[174] G. Dworkin *The Theory and Practice of Autonomy* (Cambridge: Cambridge University Press, 1988) at p. 54.

[175] There is often a knowledge gap between the two parties in the doctor–patient relationship. The provision of information is designed to balance out this power difference; see further de Ruijter (2010) supra note 34.

[176] The Biomedicine Convention refers to 'informed consent' in Article 5, whereas the French text merely refers to 'consentment'; see Mason and McCall (2005) at p. 233.

patients have enough information on possible medical treatments and on the implications of a particular treatment can they make an autonomous decision.[177]

In the *public health* context, the right to informed consent and human dignity is particularly salient as the interests of the population as a whole often need to be balanced against the rights of individuals, or in other words the collective good against individual rights. For instance, in the case of a public health emergency, the enforcement of quarantine and compulsory immunizations is not unlikely and has occurred in the past.[178] These situations can create an exception to the protection of informed consent and patients can be forced to undergo medical treatment, involuntary testing, or medical examination against their will if mandated by public authorities.[179] However, here also the EU has little room to manoeuvre, so individual rights being implicated in the context of extraordinary public health measures is in practice still generally a matter for the Member States.

At the same time, there are examples where the EU may be involved in particular issues of security policy where health issues come into play. One example is the screening of airline passengers. The use of screening devices and the particular health risks involved in this are quite intricately regulated at EU level on the basis of internal market law and transport.[180] However, the scanners used for screening passengers may involve a health risk from ionizing radiation technology, and therefore the EU regulates what scanners may be used and under what circumstances. This presents an example of where EU health policy, particularly with respect to the protection of public health, has fundamental rights implications with respect to bodily integrity and even informed consent.[181]

In the ECHR context, as mentioned before, the right to informed consent is made explicit in the Covenant, but in the case law of the ECtHR it is usually grounded on the right to private life of Article 8 ECHR. In the ECtHR case *Pretty v. UK* the Court made it explicit that the right to life could not 'be interpreted as conferring the diametrically opposite right, namely a right to die'.[182] However, with regard to the right to family life, the court explicitly made informed consent part of the scope of Article 8 ECHR.[183] There are a number of cases from the ECtHR with respect to the right to informed consent; however, these cases all play out in a national medical care context,

[177] See further de Ruijter (2010) supra note 34.

[178] S. Mounier-Jack and R. J. Coker 'How Prepared is Europe for Pandemic Influenza? Analysis of National Plans' (2006) *The Lancet* 367 (9520) 1405–11.

[179] See e.g. Article 19 of the International Covenant on Civil and Political Rights (ICCPR) (which allows the public good to take precedence over individual rights in a number of situations, including when there are threats to public health and the range of public health exceptions to EU free-movement rules); also see S. Gruskin 'Is There a Government in the Cockpit: A Passenger's Perspective, or Global Public Health: The Role of Human Rights' (2004) *Temple Law Review* 77 313–34; also see Nuffield Council on Bioethics (2007) 'Public Health: Ethical Issues' available at: <http://nuffieldbioethics.org/wp-content/uploads/2014/07/Public-health-ethical-issues.pdf> (last visited February 2014).

[180] European Commission, Commission Regulation (EU) No. 185/2010 of 4 March 2010 laying down detailed measures for the implementation of the common basic standards on aviation security (OJ L 55 05-03-2010, p. 1).

[181] European Commission, Commission implementing Regulation (EU) No. 711/2012 amending Regulation (EU) No 185/2010 laying down detailed measures for the implementation of the common basic standards on aviation security as regards the methods used for screening persons other than passengers and items carried, 3 August 2012 (OJ L 209/04-08-2012); European Commission, Scientific Committee on Emerging and Newly Identified Health Risks SCENIHR, Health effects of security scanners for passenger screening (based on X-ray technology), 26 April 2012.

[182] ECtHR *Pretty v. United Kingdom* Application No.2346/02, 29 April 2002 at para. 39.

[183] See ibid. at para. 63; also see ECtHR *X and Y v. the Netherlands* Application No. 8978/80, 26 March 1985.

where the EU in principle has no competence.[184] Yet in this respect there is potential for future developments. For instance, questions surrounding a right to assisted suicide may put into question the scope of Article 7 CFREU, which mirrors Article 8 ECHR. However, whereas Article 8 ECHR allows for a public policy exception, Article 7 CFREU does not contain such an exception. The case law of the ECtHR essentially holds that patients have the right to determine their own death on the basis of Article 8(1) ECHR.[185] Consequently, it is theoretically possible that patients would seek life-ending treatment in another Member State beyond the freedom-of-movement principles with reference to right to a private life. If the right to end one's life is regulated differently in these Member States (e.g. Belgium and the Netherlands) and the home state wanted to refuse authorization of cross-border health care, on the basis of the CFREU no public policy exception would be available. This situation makes it harder for Member States to regulate a morally highly charged issue such as euthanasia.[186]

4.2.2 Privacy and confidentiality in public health and health care

The right to private life in Article 7 CFREU also includes respect for family life. This also relates to the information that is gathered and stored about an individual, such as the collection of medical data and medical records. Moreover, with respect to the right to privacy, a physician's duty to secrecy about the patient's medical and mental well-being might also come to mind. These privacy issues could apply to the EU institutions, for instance in situations where physicians may be under obligation to report instances of communicable disease that are determined at the EU level,[187] yet the confidentiality of health information is recognized as crucial to preserving patients' confidence in the medical profession and health services in general.[188] Patients may be inclined not to report a particular communicable disease to their physician if this would easily override patient–doctor confidentiality and consequentially prompt a patient to be subject to public health measures (immunizations, quarantine, etc.).

Nevertheless, public health grounds may limit the right to have one's personal data protected. More to point in this regard is Article 8 CFREU on the right to protect personal data that is accessible or may be accessible to third parties (as can certainly be the case in the exchange of public health information), including when health-care providers interchange medical data about a patient across national borders.[189] In this regard, the right to protection of personal data and the right to protection of a patient's health status are explicitly protected at EU level.[190]

[184] See Hendriks (2012) supra note 22.

[185] ECtHR *Pretty v. United Kingdom* Application No.2346/02, 29 April 2002.

[186] Hendriks (2012) supra note 22.

[187] Decision No. 1082/2013/EU of the European Parliament and of the Council of 22 October 2013 on serious cross-border threats to health and repealing Decision No. 2119/98/EC (OJ L 293/1, 05-11-2013); it is important to note in this regard that the International Health Regulations also prescribe an obligation to report; see particularly Articles under part II IHR.

[188] R. Reintjes et al. 'Benchmarking National Surveillance Systems: A New Tool for the Comparison of Communicable Disease Surveillance and Control in Europe' (2007) *European Journal of Public Health* 17 375–80; S. Gainotti et al. 'Ethical Models Underpinning Responses to Threats to Public Health: A Comparison of Approaches to Communicable Disease Control in Europe' (2008) *Bioethics* 22 466–76.

[189] Decision No. 1082/2013/EU of the European Parliament and of the Council (2013) supra note 187.

[190] Case C-404/92 *X v. Commission of the European Communities* [1994] ECR I-04737. In this case Article 8 ECHR is interpreted as a 'general principle' of community law, protecting the right to

In cases where EU health policy has implications for individual rights, this would without question be a matter over which the European institutions could be challenged in court. However, a large volume of EU legislation generally is directed at Member States rather than individuals. At the same time—as the example of the screening of airline passengers showed—the effects of EU health policy can sometimes be found in relatively low-level implementing legislation that is directly applicable in Member States. To stay with the example of screening, this can be where the EU gives very clear guidance on how, under what circumstances, and with what machines European citizens should be screened. Although it may be difficult to hold the EU responsible in court for potential fundamental rights implications in this regard, this does not preclude rights, such as the bodily integrity and dignity of European citizens, being implicated in such cases.

5. Fundamental Rights: Beyond a Legal Framework

The two branches of EU fundamental rights form a framework for analysing the expansion of EU power in the field of human health in terms of its impact on EU fundamental rights. As the first part of this chapter outlined, using a rights-based framework for assessing health policy is seen as a recognition of a health policy's potential to impact on fundamental rights. Moreover, this framework recognizes that the violation of fundamental rights in the context of health policy can be viewed as a 'dignity violation',[191] which can strike the very core of a society's efforts to promote well-being.[192] In other words, beyond their role in the legal praxis of determining the legitimacy of policy *ex ante* in the policymaking process, and *ex post* in litigation, fundamental rights have value and importance that surpass their formal judicial enforceability. They can also offer a framework for discussing legitimacy as it is conceived internal to a particular political system (in this case the EU political (and legal) system) beyond their justiciability in a concrete case. This broader scope in particular helps in taking into consideration the breadth of EU health policy, including the situation discussed where Member States may engage in health policymaking facilitated by EU institutions, outside a formal competence to legislate.[193]

In sum, the rights-based framework for analysing EU health policy creates a legal 'benchmark' with respect to EU health policy that is based on EU competence to legislate with respect to both the EU institutions and the Member States. As outlined, the legal scope of application of fundamental rights to EU policy is limited by the EU's powers and tasks defined in the Treaties. EU health policy may be based on explicit EU legislative competence or on another legislative basis in the Treaty, for example in the context of agriculture or the internal market. In these cases EU health policy is a matter covered by EU law, and EU fundamental rights would be applicable both to EU institutions and to the Member States when they are 'implementing' Union law in a broad sense. Even with respect to provisions in the Charter that contain 'principles'

informed consent of a civil servant of the Commission not to undergo a blood test for HIV/AIDS; it also protects the right to privacy with regard to having medical records sent to another physician without the patient's consent); also see Case C-62/90 *Commission v. Germany* [1992] ECR I-2575.

[191] Mann et al. (1994) supra note 9. [192] Article 3 TEU.

[193] L. O. Gostin 'Public Health, Ethics, and Human Rights: A Tribute to the Late Jonathan Mann' (2007) *Journal of Law, Medicine and Ethics* 29 (2) 121–30 (on the importance of narrowing the analytical framework when addressing the relationship between health and human rights).

rather than 'rights', acts of the EU institutions and of the Member States can be used in the interpretation of these acts and in ruling on their legality.

Given the recent case law, as discussed, a rights-based framework for analysing the legitimacy of EU health policy in terms fundamental rights already casts a wide net. Outside the EU institutions being bound by fundamental rights, in the area of health there is generally a relatively large discretion for Member States to give effect to EU law. Yet, regardless of this wide discretion for the Member States, EU fundamental rights have to be observed even when there is only a relatively weak link to an EU obligation to act. Moreover, although there is no decisive case law on this matter, given that the possibility to derogate from EU law on public health bases is founded on EU law itself, arguably Member States also have to observe EU fundamental rights law when derogating from EU law.

There are also, however, limitations to the legal framework for analysis, particularly with respect to EU institutions when EU health policy is a matter of implementing acts, or when it is unclear if the EU actor involved in health policymaking is an institution, body, office, or agency of the EU. With respect to the Member States and EU institutions, other important limitations of the legal framework are the situations where Member States engage in health policymaking facilitated by EU institutions, outside a formal competence to legislate. For these situations, a rights-based approach for analysing EU health policy should be employed that goes beyond a strictly legal framework, allowing for a 'normative language' that takes into consideration that fundamental rights are an expression of important shared values in the context of the European Union.[194]

Moreover, the perspective of EU fundamental rights can demonstrate possible tensions caused by EU health policy: implications in terms of fundamental rights can show how highly sensitive national policy issues may be affected by the Member States' participation in EU policymaking activities. Accordingly, this research examines the expansion of EU power in the field of human health in light of its implications for EU fundamental rights. Specifically, the right to (access) health (care) and individual patients' rights form the two branches of the framework of fundamental rights that will be used to analyse the implications of European health law and policy.

[194] Article 2 TEU.

3

EU 'Public Health' and 'Health-care' Law and Policy

> A high level of human health protection shall be ensured in the definition and implementation of all Union policies and activities.[1]

Taking into consideration the above provision in the Treaty, which forms the basis for the involvement of the EU in human health, it could be inferred that EU public health and health-care policy and law is either non-existent as an autonomous policy area, given that it is mainstreamed in all other policies, or that it is basically everything, in that all EU public policy is also health policy. This puzzle forms the starting point for this chapter, which aims to describe the nature of EU power in the field of human health currently. The chapter first, as an initial exploration, questions the existence of a European authoritative concept of 'health'. Second, the chapter takes into consideration the nature of EU policymaking in general and regarding health in particular and develops a concept of EU health law and policy. Last, to draw out the scope of EU health policy more specifically, a historical overview is given of the involvement of the EU in health.

1. Human 'Health' in the EU

The first step to describing the nature of EU power in the field of human health is to consider: what is 'health', and is there an authoritative European concept of health? Health,[2] in the end, is the determining factor for defining the scope of the law and policy content where this book is aiming to grasp the role of the EU. At the same time, it is unlikely that any conceptualization of health will be beyond critique, since what we mean by it can vary in cultural and historical contexts.[3] The debate about what defines 'health' goes back centuries and has philosophical, religious, cultural, political, and legal ramifications.[4] Moreover, conceptualizing health can also have normative social or political implications ('normative' in the sense that ill health is a deviation from a norm, the norm being the condition of 'a fictional person whom one considers to be

[1] Article 168 TFEU.

[2] Health is discussed here as a 'concept', not as a 'right'; see Toebes (2012) at p. 15.

[3] See K. Jaspers *General Psychopathology* (Baltimore, MD: Johns Hopkins University Press, 1997) at p. 780 ('What sick in general may mean depends less on a doctor's judgment than on the judgment of the patients and the prevailing conceptions of the contemporary culture'); also see J. Bircher 'Towards a Dynamic Definition of Health and Disease' (2005) *Medicine, Health Care and Philosophy* 8 335–41; and see K. Bergdolt *Wellbeing: A Cultural History of Healthy Living* (Cambridge: Polity Press, 2008) (describing the shift in Western medicine from the traditional holistic conception of health as personal responsibility in finding a balance in healthy living to the current more technical concept of health in the context of evidence-based medicine).

[4] Bergdolt (2008) supra note 3.

EU Health Law & Policy: The Expansion of EU Power in Public Health and Health Care. Anniek de Ruijter © Anniek de Ruijter 2019. Published in 2019 by Oxford University Press.

in a state of normality'[5]). For example, female hysteria used to be a recognized illness that in the nineteenth century was claimed to affect about a quarter of all women. Although the disease was ascribed to a number of different symptoms, generally the deviation from the norm that diagnosed female hysteria was 'unfeminine' behaviour. Female hysteria would often prevent women from participating in public life.[6] Hence, that which counts as 'normal functioning' of the species may be a (normative) societal construction of what *should* count as normal.[7]

In the European Union there is no authoritative legal text that defines human health. The United Nations' World Health Organization defines health as: 'a state of complete physical, mental and social well-being, and not merely the absence of disease or infirmity.'[8] This definition has received some criticism,[9] particularly with regard to its political rather than descriptive nature: 'The WHO definition risks turning all of social philosophy and social policy into health care.'[10] The WHO concept is viewed as too broad, and the adoption of a more biomedical conception of health would give health a more positivist scientific meaning. A biomedical conception of health uses scientific biomedical judgement to determine whether a condition is a deviation from the normal functioning of the (human) species; normative judgements as to whether this dysfunction is a 'health need' would only be a next step.[11] A biomedical conception of health then refers to the 'soundness of body; that condition in which its functions are duly and efficiently discharged'.[12]

However, at the level of biomedical sciences there can also be heated debate of the distinction between pathology and normal functioning.[13] An example is female sexual dysfunction (FSD), which is often said to be a constructed dysfunction, created by the pharmaceutical industry in an attempt to create a market for new pharmaceuticals that mirrors the profits made from selling Viagra to men with 'erectile dysfunction'.[14]

[5] Quote by L. A. Quetelet 1869, Belgian physician cited in ibid. at p. 277.

[6] Another example here is the Harvard president Edward Clarke who argued against women's education in 1873. He claimed that the blood demanded by the brain for studying would prevent the reproductive system from developing properly, see L. Briggs 'The Race of Hysteria: "Overcivilization" and the "Savage" Woman in Late Nineteenth-Century Obstetrics and Gynecology' (2000) *American Quarterly* 52 (2) 246–73 at p. 248.

[7] N. Daniels *Just Health: Meeting Health Needs Fairly* (Cambridge: Cambridge University Press, 2008) at p. 40 (Norman Daniels has developed a theory of justice for health linking health and opportunity on the basis of John Rawls's theory of justice as fairness).

[8] See WHO Preamble to the Constitution of the World Health Organization as adopted by the International Health Conference New York, 19–22 June 1946; signed on 22 July 1946 by the representatives of sixty-one States (Official Records of the World Health Organization no. 2 at 100) and entered into force on 7 April 1948.

[9] M. Huber et al. 'How Should We Define Health?' (2011) *British Medical Journal* 343 (4163); Editorial 'What Is Health? The Ability to Adapt' (2009) *The Lancet* 373 (781); J. S. Larson 'The Conceptualization of Health' (1999) *Medical Care Research and Review* 56 123–36; A. R. Jadad and L. O'Grady 'How Should Health be Defined?' (2008) *British Medical Journal* 337.

[10] N. Daniels *Just Health: Meeting Health Needs Fairly* (Cambridge: Cambridge University Press, 2008) at p. 37.

[11] Ibid. in this regard speaks of 'alleviating the effect of the natural lottery' at p. 42. The concept of the 'natural lottery' refers to the 'biologically given partial potential of individuals which initially results from their genetic constitution and from their prenatal development. Consequently, it varies from person to person, part of the injustice of biology'; Bircher (2005) supra note 3 at p. 337.

[12] See J. Simpson and E. Weiner (eds) *The Oxford English Dictionary* (Oxford: Clarendon Press, 1989) definition of health, and see Daniels (2008) supra note 10 at p. 37.

[13] Daniels (2008) supra note 10 at p.42.

[14] R. Moynihan 'The Making of a Disease: Female Sexual Dysfunction' (2003) *British Medical Journal* 326 (7379) 45–7; L. Tiefer 'Female Sexual Dysfunction: A Case Study of Disease Mongering and Activist Resistance' (2006) *PLoS Medicine* 3 (4).

Moreover, beyond health as a biomedical standard, health is also a subjective experience that has something to do with an 'individual being in tune with himself'.[15] In this sense health is undisputedly a positive thing:

> What is desired is life, long life, the ability to procreate, physical capacity, strength, little fatigability, absence of pain, a lasting state in which the body, apart from pleasurable feelings of its existence, is disregarded as much as possible. (Jaspers 1883–1969)[16]

And from a sociological perspective 'health is the result of a complex and dynamic interaction of three factors: fate representing the biological and the social lottery; personal responsibility; and support from the social setting'.[17] Health is not only a biomedical assessment and an individual experience. It can also be ascribed to populations (public health). In this regard the social circumstances of the population can impact upon one's health, and one's individual health can impact upon the population:

> Without minimum levels of health, people cannot fully engage in social interactions, participate in the political process, exercise rights of citizenship, generate wealth, create art, and provide for the common security. A safe and healthy population builds strong roots for a country's governmental structures, social organizations, cultural endowment, economic prosperity, and national defense. Population health becomes a transcendent value because a certain level of human functioning is a prerequisite for activities that are critical to the public's welfare—social, political, and economic.[18]

For example, obesity affects the health of an individual. At the same time it can be a problem for the health of a population, and moreover it can impact upon a person's wellbeing and mental health way beyond the physical problems that may result from being overweight.[19] The WHO definition in this respect rightly puts the focus on the importance of human health in contributing to general *wellbeing*,[20] for what we mean by health may go beyond the physical soundness of the individual human body. Also, in the EU health contributes to wellbeing as one of its central objectives.[21] Still, health is not synonymous with wellbeing, as personal happiness and social wellbeing can exist separate from being healthy.[22] Moreover, for the purpose of conceptualizing *European Union* health policy, we need greater conceptual focus. If one of the central objectives of the European Union is to contribute to the *wellbeing* of its peoples, and we take the WHO definition of health as 'complete wellbeing' as the defining standard, or even

[15] Bergdolt (2008) supra note 3.

[16] Jaspers (1997) supra note 3 at p. 780, and see further Bergdolt (2008) supra note 3.

[17] Bircher (2005) supra note 3 at p. 338.

[18] L. O. Gostin 'A Theory and Definiton of Public Health Law' (2007) *Journal of Health Care Law and Policy* 10 1–12 at p. 2.

[19] Not to mention the societal stigmatization that may come with obesity.

[20] The term wellbeing here refers generally to a broader concept than health. It includes aspects such as subjective wellbeing, which may be a matter of luck, genetics or personality, self-sufficiency or income, access to public services, education and intellectual development, health and nutrition, leisure, relationships, cultural or spiritual activities, mobility, a clean environment, and other aspects that impact quality of life; see European Commission, Communication from the Commission to the Council and the European Parliament, GDP and beyond: Measuring progress in a changing world (COM(2009) 433 final); also see European Commission 'Wellbeing Aggregate Report' (2011) *Eurobarometer Qualitative Studies* (Brussels). The term wellbeing also has an important philosophical use in that it is often used in virtue ethics and related philosophies as referring to some version of the Aristotelian concept of eudaimonia; see generally J. L. Jost and R. A. Shiner (eds) *Eudaimonia and Well-Being, Ancient and Modern Conceptions* (Kelowna BC: Academic Printing and Publishing, 2003).

[21] Article 3(1) TEU and Article 9 TFEU.

[22] D. Callahan 'The WHO Definition of "Health"' (1973) *Hastings Center Studies* 1 (3) 77–87 and ibid.

Article 168 TFEU quoted at the beginning of this chapter, *all* EU public policy could well fall within the concept of European health policy.

1.1 Legal sources defining health in the EU

There is no European authoritative (legal) text that defines a European concept of health in the manner of the WHO Constitution.[23] Although there is much to say for adopting a biomedical concept of health in terms of conceptual narrowness, in the European policy context there is evidence that health is taken to be something beyond the 'normal functioning' of a (human) species. The best example for this is the indicator of healthy life years (HLY) that Eurostat, the statistical office of the EU, uses to measure the health of Europeans each year.[24] HLY is an indicator for human health that not only includes statistics on mortality and morbidity/disability, but also data on self-perceived health.[25] On the basis of the combined data on mortality, morbidity/disability, and self-perceived health, the number of expected life years in good health is estimated. The inclusion of data on self-perceived health in the European policy context admits that health is actually almost impossible to establish, given the fluidity of the concept itself: 'health expectancy is a combination of life expectancy and a concept of health; there are potentially as many health expectancies as there are concepts of health.'[26]

In the Treaty, references are made to both 'human health' and 'public health'. According to Ellen Vos, public health and human health in the Treaty refer to different things: Vos distinguishes between the protection of *public health*, as Title 14 in Article 168 TFEU articulates, and *human health*, as it is used in the free movement provisions, in the sense that Article 36 TFEU refers to the protection of 'life and health of humans' and Article 114 (3) TFEU refers 'health and safety'.[27] According to Vos, public health is more narrowly understood in the European context in that it refers to a notion that aims at such objectives as the prevention of disease and combating drug dependence.[28] However, the Treaty does not support the idea that 'human health' and 'public health' refer to different notions. Articles 45 and 52 TFEU refer to *public health* as an exception to the free movement of workers and the right of establishment, which are also provisions that feature relatively centrally in the context of Union free movement law.

[23] In one of the first comprehensive law books on the role of Union law for national health law, by Hervey and McHale, the biomedical concept of health, or what they call the 'engineering model' of health—in line with Montgomery—is taken as the conceptual scope. The 'engineering model' of health refers to a concept of health that defines a well-functioning human machine, which when it is broken needs to be fixed; T. K. Hervey and J. V. McHale *Health Law and the European Union* (Cambridge: Cambridge University Press, 2004) at p. 10; and see their discussion of J. Montgomery *Health Care Law* 2nd edn (Oxford: Oxford University Press, 2002) at pp. 2–4, 7.

[24] The EU generally gathers a large number of other public health statistics, such as on the protection against communicable diseases, the impact of social-demographic background on health, etc. See Regulation (EC) 1338/2008 of the European Parliament and of the Council on Community statistics on public health and health and safety at work (OJ L354/70, 31-12-2008).

[25] Self-perceived health is a well-accepted indicator for health in a broad body of social science (and public health) research on health and public health. See S. M. Hunt and J. McEwen 'The Development of a Subjective Health Indicator' (1980) *Sociology of Health & Illness* 2 (3) 231–46.

[26] See methodological annex to HLY, Healthy life expectancy based on self-perceived health, available at <http://appsso.eurostat.ec.europa.eu/nui/show.do?dataset=hlth_silc_17&lang=en> (last accessed January 16, 2013).

[27] Vos refers to the EC Treaty in this regard. However, given the fact that the text with respect to health has not changed in these particular Articles after subsequent Treaty amendments, the references here are made to the equivalent Articles in the TFEU.

[28] See E Vos, *Institutional Frameworks of Community Health and Safety Regulation: Committees, Agencies and Private Bodies* (Hart Publishing 1999 at p. 18.

Moreover, Article 9 TFEU, which has been introduced into the Treaty with the adoption of the Treaty of Lisbon, refers to the protection of *human health*. Article 3(p) of the EC Treaty used to refer to the protection of *human health* as well, which was an area of shared competence of the Member States and the European Community.[29] The current Article 4 TFEU on shared competences, however, refers to *public health*.

At the same time, the new Article 6(a) TFEU refers to an additional competence of the EU to complement Member States' actions with regard to the improvement of *human health*. So, while references to human health and public health appear throughout the Treaty, the terms are used interchangeably, in both cases referring to the protection of the *health of the population* as a legitimate objective for public policy in the context of Union law. This objective is fully in line with the classical notion of public health in that it refers to the health of a population at large.[30] In contrast with the assertion of Ellen Vos, the role of the EU in the area of the health and safety provisions for products and food is a classic matter of public health protection regardless of the fact that there are different (regulatory) *ways* through which the EU is involved in this respect.[31]

The CJEU also uses the terms 'human health' and 'public health' interchangeably in the case law on the free movement of goods.[32] More substantively, as to what is meant by the Court by the concept of health, both when it refers to public health and also when it refers to the health of an individual in cases concerning access to health care, there are indications that biomedical evidence should be a guideline for assessing infringements of Union law.[33] At the same time, the Court accepts that there can

[29] 'Competence' in the EU legal paradigm refers to the legal bases in the Treaty that give EU institutions the power to adopt legal measures, and the delimitations of that power; for a broad overview, see P. Craig and G. de Búrca *EU Law: Text, Cases, and Materials* (Oxford: Oxford University Press, 2008) at p. 83et seq.

[30] Public health is usually seen as a separate field of science, where epidemiology is of central importance. However, it is also seen as a separate field of public policy and law, in that it largely involves the legal relationships between public authorities and the individual. See L. O. Gostin *Public Health Law: Power, Duty, Restraint* (Berkeley, CA: University of California Press, 2000) at p. 3 et seq.

[31] The counterargument here is that public health exceptions in the Treaty and developed in EEC/EC/EU case law are often used instrumentally to harmonize national public health barriers in order to free movement and create EU markets. However, the fact that provisions may help to build a market for particular goods as well as protect the health of the population does not take away from these regulatory arrangements at EU level needing all the technical, scientific expertise that public health provisions typically require. Moreover, the duality of objectives—market building and public health protection—is also present in 'typical' public health activities of the EU that are not adopted in the legal context of the internal market. For instance, in most EU public health programmes the connection is made between a healthy workforce and economic growth. The latest proposal, for a public health programme 2014–2020, outlines that: 'Health is not just a value in itself—it is also a driver for growth. Only a healthy population can achieve its full economic potential.' See European Commission, Proposal for a Regulation of the European Parliament and of the Council establishing a Health for Growth Programme, the third multi-annual programme of EU action in the field of health for the period 2014–2020 (COM (2011) 709 final) at p. 1.

[32] Vos (1999) at supra note 28 p. 18.

[33] In the field of public health, the area of the free movement of goods is exemplary. In case 272/80 *Frans-Nederlandse Maatschappij voor Biologische Producten* [1981] ECR 3277 it was decided that unless there is (international) scientific evidence to the contrary, the Member States may decide on the degree of the protection of health that is necessary and meets the requirements of the free movements (proportionality). On the point of individual health see Case C-157/99 *B.S.M. Geraets-Smits v. Stichting Ziekenfonds VGZ and H.T.M. Peerbooms v. Stichting CZ Groep Zorgverzekeringen* [2001] ECR I-5473 (where the Court states in para. 108 that medical treatment abroad cannot be denied prior authorization by the national health insurance authorities if this treatment is 'normal in the professional circles concerned'; here 'normal' is to be read as 'sufficiently tried and tested by *international* medical science' emphasis added).

be disagreement at the level of biomedical science on whether a good or a service is harmful or beneficial to health. Therefore the Court leaves discretionary room for the Member States to show that particular health exceptions to the freedom of movement are necessary.[34] Certainly the Court in these cases does not conceptualize health, but rather recognizes that the ways of pursuing health may differ, not only as a matter of scientific disagreement but also as a matter of national differences.

1.2 Beyond a biomedical concept

Accordingly, on the basis of the general use of 'health' in the context of some authoritative sources for policymaking in the EU, there is no one single evident EU concept of health. As the HLY indicator's inclusion of self-perceived health implies, it is accepted that health in the EU context refers to more than a purely biomedical concept. This is also the gist of CJEU case law. In other words, in the European (legal/policy) context—at least implicitly—the Court and policymakers do seem to accept that the lived experience of (public) health may vary across the EU, depending on individual and social (national) backgrounds. For example, across EU Member States the take on pregnancy is vastly different—it is viewed as a form of 'normal functioning', but also an 'abnormal state' of the human body that is in need of medical attention.[35]

In this regard the biomedical concept of health alone is too narrow to do justice to the use of the concept of health in the European policy context, which also takes into consideration physical and mental wellbeing in a subjective and social sense. And although there is no authoritative reference to a concept of health, the concept exists in the EU policy context, given the fact that it is used in many different legal instruments, in policy documents, and by a large number of institutional actors. A first starting point then for defining human health in the EU is the biomedical approach as 'normal functioning' of the human body. Internationally recognized evidence-based medicine is a key aspect herein, as shown by the often-emphasized need to ground EU activity regarding health on sound scientific data.[36] However, there are also indications that in the EU public policy domain it is accepted that a European concept of health allows for subjective and social aspects that characterize its use in particular contexts. Accordingly, the concept of human health in the EU policy and legal context refers to the normal functioning of the (human) species and also to a more subjective expression

[34] Case 178/84 *Commission v. Germany* ECR [1987] 1227 and Case 174/82 *Officier van Justitie v. Sandoz* BV ECR 2445; see further discussion in Craig and de Búrca (2008) supra note 29 at p. 702 et seq.

[35] D. Lupton *Medicine as Culture: Illness, Disease and the Body* 3rd edn (London: SAGE, 2012) at p. 155 et seq.

[36] Evidence-based medicine (EBM) refers to 'The clinical, and epidemiological research in the management of patients, with particular attention to the balance of benefits, risks, and costs of diagnostic tests, screening programs, and treatment regimens, taking account of each patient's circumstances, including baseline risk, co-morbid conditions, culture, and personal preferences' in M. A. Porta *Dictionary of Epidemiology* 5th edn (New York: Oxford University Press, 2008) at p. 87. In the EU the most prominent reference here is the overarching EU health strategy, as it aims to bring together and apply to all EU activities relating to health; European Commission, Together for Health: A Strategic Approach for the EU 2008-2013 (COM (2007) 630 final) at. p. 3; but see also European Centre for Disease Prevention and Control *Evidence-based Methodologies for Public Health – How to Assess the Best Available Evidence When Time is Limited and There is Lack of Sound Evidence* (Stockholm, 2007); and see in the area of pharmaceuticals the European ban on non-evidence-based pharmaceuticals Directive 2004/24/EC, amending, as regards traditional herbal medicinal products, Directive 2001/83/EC on the Community code relating to medicinal products for human use (OJ L 136/85, 31-03-2005).

of a (social) state of physical and mental wellbeing, depending on individual and social (national) backgrounds.[37]

1.3 Differentiating EU 'public health' and 'individual health (care)'

In EU law and policy, there are numerous authoritative references made to 'public health' or the protection of 'human health' regarding the protection of the public from particular health hazards that may result from economic activities within the EU common market. In this regard, 'public health' in the EU policy context can be distinguished from 'individual health'. This distinction is not new in health policy generally, given that it matters legally, since in the sphere of public health legal relationships are usually public (government v. individual), whereas in the sphere of individual health the relationships are usually private (patient v. physician or hospital v. (private) insurance, etc.).[38] Therefore, future references in the EU legal context to 'health' for the purpose of the current research will also make this distinction and refer to either 'public health' or 'individual health', and the distinction will be drawn—based on the context in which the term is used—between addressing the health (protection) of the population at large or in terms of (access to) individual health (care). Of course this is not a neat distinction; the health complex in many Member States and certainly in the EU is intricate, with many overlaps between public health and individual health arrangements.

In sum, the concept of 'health' in the EU policy context refers to the normal functioning of the (human) species, which is not only defined by biomedical determination, but is also influenced by more subjective descriptions of a state of physical and mental wellbeing, depending on individual and social (national) backgrounds. At the same time health in the EU public policy context can either refer to 'public health' or 'individual health', and the distinction is found in the context in which the term is used, either as addressing the health (protection) of the population at large, or in terms of (access to) individual health (care).

2. EU Power: Policy and Law in Human Health

The concept of health in the EU policy context is a first element in determining the scope of EU power in human health. Hence, in order to conceptualize 'European Union health policy', a first marker for this policy is that in general terms it is geared towards achieving some measure of physical (and mental) wellbeing for the individual and the population at large.[39] Health policy is a particular kind of public policy, and the nature of decision-making in health, involving life and death, moral and ethical choices, sets health policy apart from other social issues. With respect to individual health arrangements, most people are in contact with the health-care sector at least one point in their lives, which can be an event of deep significance. The health-care sector is a large part of Member States' economy; it employs a large number of workers,

[37] See Callahan (1973) supra note 22 who also refers to 'physical wellbeing' in narrowing the WHO definition.

[38] Gostin (2007) supra note 18.

[39] G. Walt *Health Policy: An Introduction to Process and Power* 5th edn (London: Zed Books, 2001).

absorbs a vast amount of the national resources, and plays a central role in knowledge and innovation competition.[40]

At the same time, health policy generally is a cross-cutting policy area in that it is highly affected or shaped by other sectors of public policy such as environmental policy, social policy, economic regulation, and internal and foreign security policy. The same holds true for EU policy geared towards achieving health, in that it can be developed in the context of, for instance, EU internal market policy, agriculture, and environmental policy, or as part of employment strategy. However, in the words of the political scientist Richardson: 'health, at the heart of the welfare state, has been one of the slowest [sectors] to become Europeanized'.[41] This seems to contrast with the large volume of regulatory activity aimed at addressing health at EU level. How to make sense of this puzzle?

2.1 Human health as part of the EU regulatory state

One explanation is that regulation as a form of EU public policy cuts straight through the involvement of the EU in health, where on one hand Europeanization has been able to take place as a result of regulation,[42] especially in the area of public health, whereas on the other hand the EU has only marginally affected (re-)distribution of entitlements by impacting individual access to health-care arrangements.[43] Majone's concept of 'social regulation' refers to the idea that a central instrument for social change in the EU is regulation that aims to fix 'market failures', rather than redistribution of resources, the latter being key for social change in the Member States. In this respect the EU has been called a 'regulatory state' rather than a 'welfare state'.[44] In other words, the EU has been able to take over or share the Member States' powers regarding health,

[40] On average the EU Member States spend about 8 per cent of their GDP on health care. See ibid. at p. 10; T. Stahl et al. (eds) *Health in all Policies: Prospects and Potentials* (Brussels: European Observatory on Health Systems and Policies, Finnish Ministry of Social Affairs and Health, 2006); and see generally W. H. Reinicke *Global Public Policy: Governing Without Government?* (Washington, DC: Brookings Institution Press, 1998) at p. 222.

[41] J. Richardson 'The Onward March of Europeanization: Tectonic Movement and Seismic Events' in J. Richardson *Constructing a Policy-Making State? Policy Dynamics in the EU* (Oxford: Oxford University Press, 2012) at 337; (Richardson here uses the term 'Europeanization' not only in terms of top-down domestic adaptation to the EU, but also as a merging of EU and national policy styles (venue shift)) at p. 5. Europeanization relates to 'the processes by which the key decisions about public policies are gradually transferred to the European level (or for new policy areas, emerge at EU level); see Richardson (ed.) (2012) at p. 4; and see Greer (2012).

[42] D. S. Martinsen 'The Europeanization of HealthCare: Processes and Factors' in T. Exadaktylos and C. M. Radaelli (eds) *Research Design in European Studies: Establishing Causality in Europeanization* (Basingstoke: Palgrave MacMillan, 2012) (which looks at this process in top-down modus, but in relation to health-care provisions).

[43] European Commission (2013), Impact asssessment roadmap 'Implementing measures for improving the recognition of prescriptions issues in another Member State under Article 11 para. 2 of the Directive on the Application of Patients' Rights in Cross-Border Healthcare (CBHC).

[44] G. Majone 'The European Community Between Social Policy and Social Regulation' (1993) *Journal of Common Market Studies* 31 153–70. The EU's role in regulation of health, rather than in welfare issues related to health, is seen as increasing the credibility or the legitimacy of the role of the EU in this area. Delegation to specialized, non-majoritan bodies such as EU agencies allows for credible commitment to long-term goals of importance, for instance food safety etc., taking these matters out of the risky and uncertain realm of electorates and politicians. Also see e.g. S. Krapohl 'Risk Regulation in the EU Between Interests and Expertise: The Case of BSE' (2003) *Journal of European Public Policy* 10 (2) 189–207; G. Permanand and E. Vos 'EU Regulatory Agencies and Health Protection' in E. Mossialos et al. (eds), *Health Systems Governance in Europe: The Role of EU Law and Governance* (New York: Cambridge University Press, 2010); Vos (1999) supra note 28.

without necessarily noticeably redistributing any welfare arrangements for EU citizens individually. This aspect of EU power has been critiqued as creating a 'constitutional asymmetry between policies promoting market efficiencies and policies promoting social protection and equality. National welfare states are legally and economically constrained by European rules of integration',[45] yet there is very limited legislative room to recreate the welfare state at EU level.

This picture of constitutional asymmetry can be illustrated with regard to health by the fact that beyond the general principle of subsidiarity in the Treaty,[46] the Member States have felt it important to restate that they do not consider the EU to have the required competence to organize health-care systems in Article 168(7) TFEU, which amounts to a double rejection of legislative competence for the EU in this respect. Hence, the EU has no authority for substantial redistribution of access to individual health-care arrangements through social insurance, welfare rights, or otherwise. However, that Member States still deemed it important to create the double rejection highlights the power of the EU in health through other channels than its own legislative health basis, such as through EU regulatory activity and through legislation based on other public policy objectives and through more or less non-legislative pathways.[47]

Hence, regardless of the EU's relative limited ability to redistribute welfare entitlements with regard to health, it is still highly involved in health issues through various policymaking strategies. At the same time, these various ways for EU institutions to pursue health and health objectives do not comprise regulatory activities alone, which means that the regulatory state as a concept cannot capture the whole story of the EU's powers in the field of human health.[48] Regulation of (public) health risks may constitute the major instrument for impacting health issues at EU level,[49] but there are a number of other policymaking strategies used by the EU institutions that fit within a 'redistribution' function of public policymaking.[50] In a number of bottom-up activities, Member States coordinate with one another at EU level, sometimes facilitated by the European Commission or in the context of the Council.[51] Moreover, there are numerous financial incentives created at EU level geared towards pursuing health objectives, either through public health programmes, structural funds, the European Social fund, or funding for research.[52]

[45] See F. Scharpf 'The European Social Model: Coping with Challenges of Diversity' (2002) *Journal of Common Market Studies* 40 (4) 645–70 at p. 645.

[46] The principle of subsidiarity (Article 5 TEU) in the EU holds that the EU does not act outside the limits of conferred competences unless the Member States cannot sufficiently achieve the objectives of the proposed action.

[47] Hervey and McHale (2004) supra note 23.

[48] Majone distinguishes three functions of government: the redistribution function, the stabilization function, and the regulatory function, whereby the EU engages primarily in regulation, which is aimed at increasing the 'allocative efficiency of the market' rather than to 'transfer resources from one group to another (redistribution) or the 'preservation of economic growth' (stabilization); see G. Majone 'The Rise of Statutory Regulation in Europe' in G. Majone (ed.) *Regulating Europe* (London: Routledge, 1996) at p. 54.

[49] Ibid. at p. 57.

[50] See ibid. and see Majone (1993) supra note 44.

[51] Notable examples include Presidency Conclusions, Gothenburg European Council, 15 and 16 June, 2001; Council Conclusions on Common values and principles in European Union Health Systems (OJ C 146/1, 2006); also see L. Trubek et al. 'The Construction of a Healthier Europe: Lessons from the Fight Against Cancer' (2008) *Wisconsin International Law Journal* 26 (3); and see A.-M. Farrell (2005) 'The Emergence of EU Governance in Public Health: The Case of Blood Policy and Regulation' in M. Steffen (ed.) *Health Governance in Europe: Issues, Challenges and Theories* (New York: Routledge, 2005).

[52] European Commission (2013) supra note 43.

2.2 Authority: policymaking and power

In order to capture the involvement of EU power in health, and to characterize the result of this involvement as 'policy', the EU political system can be explained as at the very least authoritatively allocating 'values' with respect to health. A 'political system', as described by the political scientist Easton, refers to the institutions and processes that are involved this allocation of values in society.[53] These values may have material form, can come in the form of services, or may refer to ethical or metaphysical values.[54] The allocation of these values is the process by which public authority creates, grants, or denies these values. One of the ways to do this is by the process of adopting and adapting law and policy.[55]

Richardson in this respect describes the EU as a 'policy-making state',[56] going beyond yet including its role in regulatory policy. The policymaking state does not refer to the EU in the sense of its 'state-ness' but rather in its ability to create and adopt a wide range of policymaking strategies that are able to authoritatively effect social change in a variety of ways, including through regulatory strategies.[57] Whereas the concept of a 'regulatory state' *legitimizes* a particular function of the EU political system, the concept of a 'policymaking state' *describes* the central function of the EU political system. For instance, the fact that the EU is highly involved in *regulating* to keep our food safe creates value (food safety) through the authoritative allocation of this policy in the EU political system. Another example is the authoritative determination of the focus on primary care as a health-care gateway for patients across the EU to curb the costs of public expenditures.[58] This relatively low-level policy with respect to human health is allocated through the policymaking processes (in the context of economic policy coordination, i.e. creating policy consensus) of the European political system. Hence, without making any specific characterizations of the nature of the EU, its political system is authoritatively allocating value with respect to health, through a variety of policymaking strategies and instruments such as regulation, incentive measures, and a number of coordination and non-legislative practices.[59]

In light of this 'policymaking' perspective for describing the exercise of power of the EU, European Union health policy can be conceptualized as referring to authoritative allocations of value through the European Union political system that are aimed at the protection and promotion of human health. This concept is broad, in that it includes both a wide range of institutional practices in the EU and also a relatively broad concept of health. At the same time the above conceptualization of EU health policy is able to distinguish and describe health policy that is pursued in the context of other European policies, rather than subsuming all EU public policy under health policy. For example, if EU agricultural policy aims to create a European market for milk, it is

[53] D. Easton 'An Approach to the Analysis of Political Systems' (1957) *World Politics* 9 (3) 383–400 at p. 384.

[54] Ibid. [55] Ibid.; also see Walt (2001) supra note 39.

[56] Richardson (ed.) (2012) supra note 41.

[57] Europeanization in this regard is described as 'the processes by which the key decisions about public policies are gradually transferred to the European level (or for new policy areas, emerge at EU level)'; Richardson (ed.) (2012) supra note 41.

[58] European Commission and the Economic Policy Committee (AWG) *Joint Report on Health Systems*, European Economy, Occasional Papers 74.

[59] T. A. Birkland *An Introduction to the Policy Process: Theories, Concepts and Models of Public Policy Making* 2nd edn (New York: M. E. Sharpe, 2005) at p. 17; See T. Stahl et al. (eds) (2006) supra note 40; also see K. Lee et al. (eds) *Health Policy in a Globalising World* (Cambridge: Cambridge University Press, 2002) at p. 10; also see I. Crinson *Health Policy: A Critical Perspective* (London: SAGE, 2009) at p. 9.

agricultural policy. However, European Union health policy is adopted when—within the context of creating a market for milk—mandatory testing for bovine tuberculosis is implemented at the European level, given the concept of EU health policy as developed here.

2.3 Differentiating EU 'health-care' and 'public health' policy

Although a conceptualization of European Union health policy is helpful in delineating its scope and content, at the same time, finding the locus of European health policy is not as clear-cut as going to the website of a Member State Health Department to find a national health policy.[60] To complicate the picture, beyond the different modes of policymaking that are used in the EU for creating health policy, the European political system also facilitates the involvement of international agencies, NGOs, and private interest lobbies.[61] How is EU health policy discerned, taking into account its legally (and sectorally) fragmented nature? Generally, 'public policies contain designs recognizable in the text and the practices through which they are conveyed and have consequences'.[62] This means that public policies are not just contained in laws or regulations. Once a law or rule is made, policies continue to be made and developed through implementation, and as decisions are made regarding who will benefit from policies and who will bear the costs.[63] Therefore, a second key in discerning EU health policy is to look beyond the formal legal structure and EU competences, and take into account what goes on below the surface of EU policymaking in the context of non-legislative practices as part of implementation mechanisms or in the form of coordination between Member States.

Besides discerning European Union health policy, this policy can be differentiated into two broad and different categories. These two categories refer to the duality of public health and individual health found when conceptualizing a European Union understanding of 'health'. This duality in relation to EU health policy relates to its addressees, objectives, and legal instruments. On one hand EU health policy has the objective of managing collective health risks and preventing major disease scourges; this can be called public health policy.[64] Law, as an instrument in this field of health policy, is usually public law, in that it regulates the relations between holders of public authority and citizens.[65] On the other hand, EU health policy addresses objectives relating to the provision of medical care and individual health. Here the addressees are primarily private individuals. Objectives include creating universal access to health care, which means regulating the medical field in general, and allowing access to medicinal

[60] Although one might find that locating a national health policy is also not as clear-cut as the constitutional settlement of responsibility for health policy in health departments might suggest. In many Member States health policy is fragmented and compartmentalized by sharing responsibilities, public–private partnerships, etc.

[61] See S. L. Greer et al. 'Mobilizing Bias in Europe: Lobbies, Democracy and EU Health Policy-Making' (2008) *European Union Politics* 9 (3) 403–33; also see S. L. Greer (2009); also see S. L. Greer 'Choosing Paths in European Union Health Services Policy: A Political Analysis of a Critical Juncture' (2008) *Journal of European Social Policy* 18 (3) 219–31.

[62] A. L. Schneider and H. M. Ingram *Policy Design for Democracy* (Lawrence, KS: Kansas University Press, 1997).

[63] See T. A. Birkland *An Introduction to the Policy Process: Theories, Concepts and Models of Public Policy Making* 3rd edn (New York: M. E. Sharpe, 2005) at p. 18.

[64] J. Orme et al. (eds) *Public Health for the 21st Century: New Perspectives on Policy, Participation and Practice* 2nd edn (Open University Press, 2007). (In this area of policymaking, the EU has been able to establish its competence relatively strongly in Article 168 TFEU).

[65] Gostin (2000) supra note 30.

products, health-care professionals, and health insurance.[66] In this area of health policy, the legal relations are predominantly arranged in contractual agreements: between hospitals and doctors, between doctors and patients, between insurance institutions and hospitals, etc. However, importantly, these legal relationships change when a health-care system is more centrally organized through the government.[67] Nevertheless, this area of 'health-care policy', private law, or the public regulation of private relations is often an instrument for policymaking. In the European context, this is the area of health policy that is generally regulated through different modes of market regulation without having its own legislative 'health-care' basis.[68]

Neither of these policy areas—public health policy or health-care policy—operates separately from the other. An example might be the European market in pharmaceuticals. On one hand, this is a highly important sector in terms of market regulation. There is a public health factor: a batch of unsafe medicines on the market can have a disastrous effect in terms of public health.[69] On the other, access to medicines through health professionals, reimbursements of the costs of medicines by the health insurers, public procurement of medicines, and so on are all subject to European health-care policy.[70] In this sense, EU activities in public health and health-care policy form two relatively differentiated categories of European health policy.[71]

In sum, European Union health policy is conceptualized as authoritative allocations of value through the European Union political system, the aim being to protect and promote human health. In order to discern EU health policy, given its relatively broad conceptualization, one would need to look beyond the formal legal structure and EU competences and take into account what goes on below the surface of formal EU policymaking. Lastly, EU health policy encompasses public health and health-care policy, which are seen as differentiated yet overlapping areas of policy within it.

3. EU Public Health Policy and Law

In this part of the chapter, the concept of EU health policy forms the basis for tracing the evolution of the EU's involvement in health and the various pressures responsible for this. This section will concentrate on the growing involvement of the EU in *public health policy* over the years. Section 4 will turn to the evolution of EU involvement in *health-care policy.* The involvement of the EU in health goes back to the European Coal and Steel Community (ECSC 1951), which included provisions for the safety and health of coalminers and steelworkers.[72] Article 69 ECSC created a

[66] Montgomery (2002) supra note 23.

[67] The core examples here being the UK National Health Service and the centralized Eastern European 'shemasko' health-care systems.

[68] Hervey and McHale (2004) supra note 23 at p. 18.

[69] An example here are the thalidomide tragedies of the sixties, which prompted some of the first public health regulation on the European level in Directive 65/65/EEC of 26 January 1965 on the approximation of provisions laid down by law, regulation or administrative action relating to medicinal products (OJ 2, 09-02-1965).

[70] See generally L. Hancher 'The EU pharmaceuticals Market: Parameters and Pathways' in E. Mossailos et al. (eds) *Health Systems Governance in Europe: The Role of European Law and Policy* (New York: Cambridge University Press, 2010) at p. 635 et seq.

[71] See Articles 9, 114, and 168 TFEU; also see Charter of Fundamental Rights of the European Union (OJ C 364/01, 18-12-2000) especially Article 35.

[72] This is essentially the 'cradle' of EU occupational health and safety policy, which will be addressed further in what follows. D. Gagliardi et al. 'Occupational Safety and Health in Europe: Lessons from the Past, Challenges and Opportunities for the Future' (2012) *Industrial Health* 50 7–11.

public health exception to the obligation to remove restrictions on the free movement of steelworkers, with paragraph 4 of that article determining that in order to ensure the free movement of workers, social security arrangements should be made.[73] Over time, European law and policy increasingly began to impact upon the health arrangements of the Member States, and the number of health considerations grew across law and policy at the European level.

With the industrial revolution and the rise of cross-border commerce, public health progressively became more a matter for international politics. In the middle of the nineteenth century the first International Sanitary Conference was held in Paris, which was a response by European societies to the threat of cholera.[74] Arguably, this conference can be seen as the birth of international public health.[75] An important aspect of international public health is that it provides for agreements on the restriction of free movement (i.e. quarantines) of people and goods if this poses a public health threat, for instance in case of a communicable disease.[76] In this regard, the Treaties of Rome in 1957 likewise provided for restrictions to free movements on account of public health. Articles 36, 48, and 56 of the EEC Treaty (1957) created exceptions to the free movement of persons, goods, and services on the basis of public health considerations. Perhaps paradoxically, these exceptions have been key in the increased involvement of the EU in public health over time. Another crucial aspect has been the introduction of a Common Agricultural Policy (CAP) on the basis of title 2 (Article 38 et seq.) of the EEC Treaty.

3.1 Public health in the Common Agricultural Policy

In the CAP, the first truly supranational policy of the European Economic Community, public health became an important policy area.[77] In 1964, with the adoption of the first directives addressing public health in the CAP, the Commission expressed the role of health as follows:

> Harmonization of legislation must also take into account the need to work out Community rules to safeguard the health and life of humans and animals. One of the major difficulties of

[73] See the Treaty establishing the European Coal and Steel Community (OJ, unpublished); see S. Guerrieri 'The Evolution of the European Parliament's Role before Direct Elections' in D. Preda and D. Pasquinucci (eds) *The Evolution of the EEC/EU Institutions and Policies* (Brussels: Peter Lang, 2010) at p. 205; also see European Community Information Service (1966) Social Policy in the ECSC 1953–1965 Community Topics 20.

[74] In Britain 61,000 people died of cholera in 1848–9 and 26,000 people in 1853–4; in Paris 20,000 people died in 1849; see M. Liverani and R. Coker 'Protecting Europe from Diseases: From the International Sanitary Conferences to the ECDC' (2012) *Journal of Health Politics, Policy and Law* 37 (6) 913–32; G. Rosen *A History of Public Health* (Baltimore, MD: John Hopkins University Press, 1958) at p. 267.

[75] Rosen (1958) supra note 74 in this regard points out several previous efforts that were made in an international setting to come to public health agreements between countries, at p. 267 et seq.; also see Liverani and Coker (2012) supra note 74 at p. 914.

[76] The WHO provides a number of provisions for the event that quarantine measures would need to be taken; World Health Organization *International Health Regulations 2005* 2nd edn (2008). At EU level, legislation to this effect has also already existed since 1964: Council Directive 64/221/EEC of 25 February 1964 on the co-ordination of special measures concerning the movement and residence of foreign nationals which are justified on grounds of public policy, public security or public health (OJ 56, 04-04-1964) at pp. 850–7.

[77] S. Hix 'The EU as New Political System' in D. Caramani (ed.) *Comparative Politics* (Oxford: Oxford University Press, 2008); E. Rieger 'Agricultural Policy: Constrained Reforms' in H. Wallace et al. (eds) *Policy-Making in the European Union* 5th edn (Oxford: Oxford University Press, 2005) at p. 574.

harmonization has in fact been the reconciliation of these two aims—liberalization of trade and protection of health.[78]

The focus on health in the context of CAP was not only in the area of food safety, but extended to classic public health safeguards in the area of sanitary supervisions and the combating of communicable diseases. A key example is the harmonization of mandatory testing for tuberculosis in meat and milk. Tuberculosis (TB) posed a major threat to public health at that time, and bovine TB often spread to humans and across borders in unpasteurized milk or meat.[79] The CAP in many respects was one of the first EU policies that was not only involved in the removal of barriers to trade (negative integration), but also introduced regulation at a supranational level (positive integration).[80] In relation to public health, positive integration, under the heading of agriculture policy, entailed regulation on food safety, sanitary supervision, and animal health, with particular importance in the reduction of zoonotic animal diseases.[81]

3.2 EU public health to promote the free movement of goods

The public health exceptions to the free movement of goods prompted the adoption of a large volume of legal public health provisions at the European level.[82] However, a crucial difference between international public health's *creation* of barriers to trade and the EU's involvement in public health is that at the European level public health was often instrumental in *removing* barriers to free trade.[83] One example of this is the regulation of pharmaceuticals, which became subject to EU public health efforts initially as a response to the thalidomide tragedy. Thalidomide was given to women to reduce the symptoms of morning sickness during pregnancy. In the early sixties it became apparent that this drug was causing severe limb deformities and other birth defects in children.[84] However, even though public health protection was a crucial precondition, Directive 65/65/EEC especially aimed to create a European market in pharmaceuticals.

[78] EEC Commisison (1964) 'Veterinary Matters: Harmonisation of Legislation, and other Activities' *Newsletter on the Common Agricultural Policy No. 24* at p. 2.

[79] Case 6/64 *Flaminio Costa v. ENEL* [1964] ECR 584, 593; Council Directive 64/432/EEC of 26 June 1964 on animal health problems affecting intra-Community trade in bovine animals and swine (OJ L 121, 29-07-1964). (These directives were the first to address animal health as a precursor for human health. They dealt for example with the health conditions for the marketing and production of fresh meat and harmonized the rules in Member States on testing for tuberculosis).

[80] Especially in the sense that the CAP created individual entitlements for EU farmers, see further Rieger (2005) supra note 77; negative integration and positive integration are terms that generally refer to market-creating and market-correcting policies; F. W. Scharpf 'Negative and Positive Integration in the Political Economy of European Welfare States' in G. Marks (ed.) *Governance in the European Union* (London: SAGE, 1996) at p. 18. However, the terms are also often used in the sense of the elimination versus the formation of new policies; see Vos (1999) supra note 28 at p. 14 and J. H. H. Weiler 'The Community System: The Dual Character of Supranationalism' (1982) *Yearbook of European Law* 1 (267).

[81] These are diseases that may transfer from animals to humans; see supra note 79.

[82] Currently, implementing measures on the basis of EU secondary law in the area of public health make up the second-highest number in regulatory output of the European Commission, Report from the Commission in the Working of Committees during 2009 (COM (2010) 354 final) p. 6. The highest number of implementing measures is taken in the area of agriculture, which also includes a number of committees and working groups that work on issues of public health in relation to food.

[83] In the sense that public health measures have been an important instrument to remove 'negative externalities' to the expansion to the European internal market. See Hix (2008) supra note 77 at p. 584.

[84] G. Permanand *EU Pharmaceutical Regulation: The Politics of Policy-making* (Manchester: Manchester University Press, 2006).

The directive required all pharmaceuticals marketed for the European Community to have a marketing authorization from a Member State competent authority.[85]

The involvement of the EU in safeguarding the public's health in relation to pharmaceuticals has grown exponentially since the initial directive adopted in the sixties.[86] Currently the European market for pharmaceuticals is highly regulated. Most medicinal products are authorized at the European level through the EMA,[87] which manages the approval of medicines for the European market and a system for pharmacovigilance.[88] At the same time, in terms of *access* to medicines, procurement, price, and controlling the profits, the Member States are still firmly in control of the market.[89]

More generally in the area of goods, over the course of the seventies, an increasing number of provisions for the protection of public health were adopted. Whereas EEC legislative activity over the course of the sixties into the seventies was hampered by the Luxembourg compromise,[90] the pressure to harmonize public health standards remained, arguably as the result of the logic of functional spillover.[91] The logic of spillover is one of neo-functionalist theory's central explanations for increased integration in the EU over time.[92] It holds that if integration is initiated in one policy area, this in itself will create pressure for expanding the scope of integration to other policy

[85] In 1975 the Committee for Proprietary Medicinal Products (CPMP) was set up, to assess the public health risks of new medicines to be authorized for the European Market in order to facilitate the already existing system of mutual recognition; see Council Directive 65/65/EEC of 26 January 1965 on the approximation of provisions laid down by law, regulation or administrative action relating to medicinal products (OJ L 22, 09.02.1965) amended by Directives 66/454/EEC, 75/319/EEC, 83/570/EEC; also see Hervey and McHale (2004) supra note 23 at p. 49. The next chapter will give a more in-depth overview of the institutional actors involved in health in the EU over time. With respect to institutional actors in the field of pharmaceuticals more specifically see e.g. Vos (1999) supra note 28; also see Hancher (2010) supra note 70; McKee et al. 'Public Health Policies' in E. Mossialos et al. (eds) *Health Systems Governance in Europe: The Role of European Union Law and Policy* (New York: Cambridge University Press, 2010); and Permanand (2006) supra note 84.

[86] At this point all medicinal products for human and animal use have to be authorized either at the Member State or at Community level, see Directive 2011/62/EU of the European Parliament and of the Council of 8 June 2011 amending Directive 2001/83/EC on the Community code relating to medicinal products for human use, as regards the prevention of the entry into the legal supply chain of falsified medicinal products (OJ L 174/74,01-07-2011).

[87] This agency was established in 1994 to evaluate the quality, safety and efficacy of medicinal products, which undergo an authorisation procedure Regulation (EC) No 726/2004.

[88] There is a special compilation of all EU legislation and guidelines in the area of pharmaceutical published called 'Eudralex' in order to make the dense volume of Union law in this area more manageable; see further: Eudralex, available at: <http://www.ec.europa.eu/health/documents/eudralex/index_en.htm> also for the latest amendments.

[89] Hancher (2010) supra note 70.

[90] The Luxembourg compromise in January 1966 as a result of the empty chair crisis in the late months of 1965 allowed the Council to block measures by veto if they felt it touched a vital interest. The threat of a veto had a particular impact on the Commission's entrepreneurialism in putting forward legislative proposals in the following years. See for example J. Palayret et al. (eds) *Visions, Votes and Vetoes: The Empty Chair Crisis and the Luxembourg Compromise Forty Years On* (Brussels: P.I.E. Peter Lang, 2006); K. Neureither 'Transformation of a Political Role: Reconsidering the Case of the Commission of the European Communities' (1972) *Journal of Common Market Studies* 10 (3) 233–48.

[91] In the period politically and legislatively most marked by the Luxembourg compromise, Article 235 EEC was used relatively infrequently and restrictively, yet in the area of food safety and the freedom of movement of goods, if measures were clearly an extension of an expressly granted power in the Treaty, public health measures were based on Article 235 EEC; See J. H. H. Weiler 'The Transformation of Europe' (1991) *The Yale Law Journal* 100 (8) 2403–83 at p. 2444.

[92] E. Haas *The Uniting of Europe: Political, Social, and Economic Forces, 1950–1957* (Stanford, CA: Stanford University Press, 1958).

areas in order to reach the initial policy objectives.[93] An example in this regard is the harmonization of safety measures in the area of medical devices. The EEC Treaty did not provide any legal basis for public health measures.[94] However, the realization of a market in technological products, including products for the sterilization of medical devices and electro-medical equipment, called for a way to address public health considerations.[95] At the same time, pressure for more EU activity in the area of public health also increased following the CJEU's broad interpretation in the *Dassonville* case of when Member States' regulations could be considered barriers to free trade.[96] Unless there was harmonizing legislation at the European level, Member State public health measures could remain in place, even if this discriminated against goods from other Member States.[97] *Harmonization* of public health provisions at the European level thus became an important instrument for building the common market.[98]

3.3 Mutual recognition

The establishment of the principle of mutual recognition in the 'landmark' case *Cassis de Dijon* at the end of the seventies also gave impetus—with respect to the creation of a common market—to address public health at the EU level, rather than leaving this to Member States. The judgment held that Member States must allow a good that was lawfully marketed in another Member State onto their own markets, unless mandatory requirements such as public health would provide a legitimate 'rule of reason'.[99] Hence,

[93] Ibid.; and see M. A. Pollack 'Creeping Competence: The Expanding Agenda of the European Community' (1994) *Journal of Public Policy* 14 (2) 95–145; also see Hix (2008) supra note 77 at p. 577.

[94] Competence in the European legal order is a central prerequisite for European institutions' formal legal power to act. The founding treaties, the Treaty on the Functioning of the EU and the Treaty on European Union, only grant this power to act in specific areas; cf. Craig and de Búrca (2008) supra note 29 at p. 98.

[95] This could be viewed as a form of positive integration as well as in terms of market-correcting policy; Commission of the European Communities, Information Memo: New proposals by the Commission to eliminate obstacles to intra-Community merchandise trade resulting from technical regulations, Brussels, July 1968 (P-47/68); Commission Des Communautes Europeennes, Note d'Information: Le Conseil des Ministres adopte 12 directives concernant l' élimination des entraves techniques, Brussels, December 1972 (P-54/72).

[96] The Court in this regard at times has been the jump-start for deepening integration of the internal market. See generally J. H. H. Weiler (1991) supra note 91; A.-M. Burley and W. Mattli 'Europe before the Court: A Political Theory of Legal Integration' (1993) *International Integration* 47 (1) 41–76; and see further A. J. Obermaier, *The End of Territoriality? The Impact of ECJ Rulings on British, German and French Social Policy* (Farnham: Ashgate, 2009) at p. 41; also see K. A. Armstrong and S. J. Bulmer, *The Governance of the Single European Market* (Manchester: Manchester University Press, 1998) at p. 47 et seq. for a clear description of the different interpretations of the role of the CJEU in the integration of the EU by legal scholars and political scientists. In Case 8/74 *Procureur du Roi v. Dassonville* [1974] ECR 837, the Court determined that 'measures having equivalent effect to quantitative restrictions' (Article 36 TFEU) are 'all trading rules enacted by Member States which are capable of hindering, directly or indirectly, actually or potentially, intra-Community trade.' (Herewith the Court significantly broadened the interpretation of Member State measures that could be considered prohibited barriers to free trade.)

[97] Article 36 EEC (currently Article 36 TFEU) precludes prohibitions or restrictions from Article 34 EEC that were justified—among other grounds—by protecting the health and life of humans.

[98] Recourse to Article 36 was also restricted however; in *Simmenthal* the Court determines that: 'Article 36 [...] permits national law to derogate from the principles of free movements of goods to the extent to which such derogation is and continues to be justified for the objectives referred to in that Article'; see Case 35/76 *Amministrazione delle Finanze dello Stato v. Simmenthal [1976] ECR 1871.*

[99] Rule of Recognition para. 14 Case 120/78 *Rewe-Zentrale AG v. Bundesmonopolverwaltung fur Branntwein* [1979] ECR 649, para. 8 (emphasis added):

Cassis de Dijon not only broadened the scope of Article 34 TFEU regarding Member State measures that were non-discriminatory (yet harmful to intercommunity trade), but also expanded the ways for legitimating an exception to this prohibition. With regard to health the Court in *Cassis* mentions 'public health' explicitly, even though the protection of health is already ground for exception in Article 36 EEC/TFEU.[100]

Hervey and McHale argue that the principle of mutual recognition reduced the need for harmonized public health measures at EU level.[101] However, there are indications that pressure to harmonize public health provisions also remained, especially given the fact that public health was often used by Member States as an exception to the application of Article 34 TFEU in ensuing court cases, and that the Court took a cautious approach to striking down these exceptions.[102] With the 'new approach' to harmonization in the mid-eighties, positive integration of public health measures in the area of goods really began to take off: in the eighties, the case law on free movement of goods and the increasingly detailed and slow pace of harmonization led to increased pressure by transnational businesses on governments to build on the internal market.[103] Harmonization based on Article 100 EEC with regard to the establishment and functioning of the internal market and/or Article 235 EEC had to be adopted unanimously and was deemed very detailed without being able to keep up with changes in the respective markets.[104]

With the relaunch of the internal market project,[105] a new approach to public health harmonization measures was adopted. This new approach meant that only 'essential health and safety requirements' would from now on be subject to harmonization; for all non-essential elements the *Cassis* mutual recognition principle would suffice.[106] This new approach refocused the regulatory activity at EU level on public health.[107]

> Obstacles to movement within the Community resulting from disparities between the national laws relating the marketing of the products in question must be read in so far as these provisions may be recognized as being necessary in order to satisfy mandatory requirements relating in particular to the effectiveness of fiscal supervision, the protection of *public health*, the fairness of commercial transactions and the defence of the consumer.

[100] See further on the extensive discussions of this case law, Craig and de Búrca (2008) supra note 29 at p. 680 and further references mentioned there. (It is unclear why public health is mentioned explicitly as a ground for the application of the rule of reason in *Cassis*, other than that it was under debate specifically in that case or that the Court merely gave an example of a number of legitimate grounds.) See P. J. G. Kapteyn et al. *Introduction to the Law of the European Communities: After Maastricht* (Deventer: Kluwer, 1995) at p. 396 (where it is explained that the President of the Court later admitted that mentioning public health again in the context of the Rule of Reason had been a 'slip of the pen'; many thanks to Professor A. A. M. Schrauwen for drawing my attention to this reference).

[101] See Hervey and McHale (2004) supra note 23.

[102] See Vos (1999) supra note 28 at p. 18.

[103] See W. Sandholtz and J. Zysman '1992: Recasting the European Bargain' (1989) *World Politics* 42 (1) 95–128 at p. 104 et seq. (who explain the recasting of the European integration project at the end of the eighties as a result of technological changes and shifts in international market, such as the rise of Japan, and how this influenced business elites and the European Commission in the course of the eighties); for a broad discussion on these and other factors that spurred the development of the single market from several political science perspectives, also see Armstrong and Bulmer (1998) supra note 96 at p. 35 et seq.

[104] The 'old approach' to harmonisation was tuned to the meet the requirements of each individual product category (detailed harmonisation); see Council Resolution of 7 May 1985 on a new approach to technical harmonisation and standards (OJ C 136/01, 04-06-1985).

[105] European Commission, White paper from the Commission to the European Council, Completing the Internal Market (COM (1985) 310 final).

[106] However, the white paper emphasizes the need to create common health standards to enable the free movement of goods; see ibid. at paras. 39–43;

[107] Craig and de Búrca (2008) supra note 29 at 621.

Particularly in combination with the introduction of Article 100a EEC (now Article 114(3) TFEU) with the Single European Act, this article for the first time allowed for the adoption of public health protection measures in the context of the functioning and the establishment of the internal market, subject to a qualified majority voting in the Council.[108]

The new approach allowed for the adoption of harmonization measures at EU level that would give broad indications of the public health requirements that needed to be met for a particular class of products, whereas the intricate details of health standards could be left to standardization bodies.[109] At the same time, in sensitive public health areas the role of committees, already existing around since the sixties, became more important and led to a deepening of regulation, importantly in the area of food.[110] But the growing importance of agencies after the Single Market programme was launched also resulted in deepened regulation of public health matters at the European level.[111] In this regard the revolutionary growth of the EU's involvement in public health in the context of building a modern European market is a typical public health matter in that it involves

> what we, as a society, do collectively to assure the conditions for people to be healthy. This requires that continuing and emerging threats to the health of the public be successfully countered. These threats include [...] the toxic by-products of a modern economy [...].[112]

However, the flood of EU public health regulation also created tensions, given that it required that:

> The acceptability of risks must be weighed against normative values which are often strongly rooted in national traditions and cultures; a delicate process explaining the political sensitivity of the Member States as regards health and safety regulation.[113]

[108] At the same time, Article 100(4) allowed for a procedure through which Member States could still adopt national provision to protect public interests mentioned in Article 36 EEC (including public health); however, this rule, which may be seen as an attempt of Member States to retain some of their earlier 'Luxembourg powers', failed after being challenged in Court; see Weiler (1991) supra note 91 at p. 2459.

[109] The Medical Device Directives are adopted on the basis of this regime; see Council Directive 90/385/EEC of 20 June 1990 on the approximation of the laws of the Member States relating to active implantable medical devices (OJ L 189/17, 20-07-1990); also see Council Directive 93/42/EEC of 14 June 1993 concerning medical devices (OJ L 169, 12-07-1993); and Directive 98/79/EC of the European Parliament and of the Council of 27 October 1998 on in vitro diagnostic medical devices (OJ L 331/1, 07-12-1998). The harmonized standards are voluntary, which means that they do not have to be complied with by producers of medicinal products. The essential requirements are set out in the annexes of directives, but the special technical specifications for products are drawn up by European Standards Organizations (ESOs) that are competent in the areas in question, enabling them to take into account the current stage of technological knowledge.

[110] The role of Committees will be further addressed in the next chapter; see E. Vos 'The Rise of the Committees' (1997) *European Law Journal* 3 (3) 210–29; and see Vos (1999) supra note at p. 136; also see Communication from the Commission to the Council and the European Parliament on the completion of the internal market: Community legislation on foodstuffs (COM (1985) 603 final); for a critical view, see O. Brouwer 'Free Movement of Foodstuffs and Quality Requirements: Has the Commission Got It Wrong?' (1998) *Common Market Law Review* 25 237–62.

[111] Permanand and Vos (2010) supra note 44; Vos (1999) supra note 28.

[112] See Institute of Medicine *The Future of Public Health* (Washington, DC: National Academy Press, 1998) at p. 1; also cited in Gostin (2000) supra note 30 at p. 13.

[113] Vos (1999) supra note 28.

3.4 Tensions between internal market and public health objectives

With the expansion of the EU's role in protecting public health, the tension between market objectives and public health protection grew. After the Paris Summit in 1972, the Heads of States and Governments decided to revive the common European market project by making more use of Article 235 EEC, which provided a legal basis for legislation that was not explicitly the competence of the EEC.[114] At the same time it was agreed that health and consumer protection constituted a 'basic right'.[115] Although characterized as a 'side game' at the time,[116] the Paris Summit marked the birth of the consumer and health protection programme that still plays an important role today.[117] Nevertheless, even though Article 2 of the EEC Treaty formulated raising the standard of living as one of the Community objectives, for a long time there was no legislative basis to make public health policy on the European level.

Regardless of this lack of legislative basis, beyond the 'story of bureaucratic, neoliberal expansion' of public health provisions in the context of the free movement of goods,[118] from the seventies onwards Europe also became involved in communicable disease control, a classic aspect of public health. The first involvement in communicable disease monitoring outside of what was already taking place in the context of agriculture developed in the context of an exchange of letters with the WHO in 1972.[119] And over the course of the seventies European surveillance networks were set up for a number of communicable diseases, such as HIV/AIDS, tuberculosis, legionella, and influenza.[120] Eventually a European public health research programme was launched in 1984 on the serious spread and thread of HIV/AIDS.[121] This programme led to one of the first European public health programmes: the 'Europe Against AIDS Programme', which promoted measures for safe blood, training, and information exchange.[122]

[114] Weiler (1991) supra note 91 at p. 2445 et seq.

[115] See Council resolution on the preliminary programme of the EEC for a consumer protection and information policy (OJ 92/1, 25-04-1975).

[116] Weiler (1991) supra note 91 at p. 2449.

[117] However, the health and consumer programmes as they stand have been separated; for the current consumer programme see Communication from the Commission to the European Parliament, the Council, the European Economic and Social Committee and the Committee of Regions to the European Parliament, the Council, the Economic and Social Committee and the Committee of the Regions, A European Consumer Agenda—Boosting confidence and growth (COM (2012) 225 final); for the public health programmes see what follows. These programmes are also an example of positive integration in the sense of a 'market correcting' policy; Vos (1999) supra note 28 at pp. 18–20.

[118] Trubek et al. (2008) supra note 51 at p. 804.

[119] Exchange of letters between the European Communities and the World Health Organization laying down the procedure for cooperation between the two organizations; Memorandum defining the arrangements for cooperation between the World Health Organization and the European Communities (72/725/ECSC, EEC, Euratom) (OJ L 300, 28-10-1982, p. 20-22).

[120] Liverani and Coker (2012) supra note 74; also see L. MacLehose et al. 'Responding to the Challenge of Communicable Disease in Europe' (2002) *Science* 295 2047–50; the surveillance of diseases in the EU is currently disseminated through a scientific, peer-reviewed publication, *Eurosurveillance*, available at: <https://www.eurosurveillance.org/>.

[121] Community Programme of Research into AIDS (OJ C 46, 20-02-1984).

[122] Hervey and McHale (2004) supra note 23 at p. 337, and see for example Resolution of Representatives of the Governments of Member States meeting within the Council of 29 May 1986 on AIDS (OJ C 184/21, 23-07-1986); Proposal for a Decision of the Council and the Ministers for Health of the Member States meeting within the Council adopting a plan of action in the framework of the 1991–1993 'Europe against AIDS' programme (COM (90) 601 final); Programme 1991 to 1993 Europe Against AIDS. Report from the Commission on the implementation of the plan of action in 1991–1992 (COM (93) 42 final); Communication from the Commission concerning a Community action programme on the prevention of AIDS and certain other communicable diseases within the framework for action in the field of public health. Proposal for a European Parliament and

This programme was able to achieve a relatively 'high force' of convergence between Member States programmes with respect to agreements on methods and data.[123]

3.4.1 HIV/AIDS programme and blood products

However, the concern over HIV/AIDS created tension with European internal market objectives. At the end of the seventies, the structure of trade in blood in Europe started changing into a mixed public–private market: whereas 'pure' blood would come from local, voluntary unpaid donors, *blood products*, such as plasma and medicines made from blood, came from both paid and unpaid donors, within and outside of Europe.[124] In the eighties there were a number of scandals over HIV-contaminated blood transfusions.[125] These scandals, together with the fact that there was already collaboration between Member States on a European market for blood products, led to the European Community's involvement in the public health safety of blood products, and at the end of the eighties a directive was adopted as part of the European market for pharmaceuticals.[126]

At the time, no legal basis for public health was available in the EC Treaty and blood itself was impossible to regulate at the European level. Although the Single European Act in 1986 provided in Article 100a(3) EEC that a 'high level of protection of health' should be considered when proposing internal market measures, if a directive regarding blood were to have been based on Article 100a(3) EEC, the only public health legal basis available at the time, this would have made blood a commodity.[127] The commoditization of human blood or parts of the human body was seen as ethically highly problematic by virtually all Member States.[128] At the same time, the pressure to 'do something' at the European level increased.[129] Over the course of the nineties

Council Decision adopting a programme of Community action on the prevention of AIDS and certain other communicable diseases within the framework for action in the field of public health (COM (94) 413 final).

[123] For further references, see Hervey and McHale (2004) supra note 23 at p. 340, who outline that there were also a number of implementation problems with the programme, but that on the whole it was deemed relatively effective.

[124] A.-M. Farrell 'Is the Gift Still Good? Examining the Politics and Regulation of Blood Safety in the European Union' (2006) *Medical Law Review* 14 155–79 at 161; and see P. Hagen *Blood: Gift or Merchandise? Towards an International Blood Policy* (New York: A. R. Liss, 1982); P. Hagen *Blood Transfusion in Europe: A White Paper* (Strasbourg: Council of Europe Press, 1993).

[125] Farrell (2005) supra note 51.

[126] Council Directive 89/381/EEC of 14 June 1989 extending the scope of Directives 65/65/EEC and 75/319/EEC on the approximation of provisions laid down by Law, Regulation or Administrative Action relating to proprietary medicinal products and laying down special provisions for medicinal products derived from human blood or human plasma (OJ L 181, 28-06-1989) pp. 44–6.

[127] R. Titmuss *The Gift Relationship: From Human Blood to Social Policy* (London: reprinted by the New Press, LSE Books, 1997) (this seminal study showed that in the United States, where blood banks would often pay blood donors, the blood was more dangerous (for contamination with hepatitis) that in the UK, where blood was voluntarily donated. This finding was and still is of major importance as an argument against the commoditization of blood).

[128] Hervey and McHale (2004) supra note 23; and see T. K. Hervey 'Mapping the Contours of European Union Health Law and Policy' (2002) *European Public Law* 8 (1) 60–105.

[129] Given the lack of public health controls on blood that came from the developing world, there were mainly calls for the EC to become self-sufficient in regard to blood. See inter alia J. Leikola 'Achieving Self Sufficiency in Blood across Europe' (1998) *British Medical Journal* 316 489–90 and see Hervey and McHale (2004) supra note 23 at p. 345 et seq., and see Blood self-sufficiency in the European Community, Communication from the Commission to the Council, the European Parliament and the Economic and Social Committee (COM (93) 198 final); Communication from the Commission Blood safety and self-sufficiency in the European Community(COM (94) 652 final).

a number of non-binding recommendations were adopted regarding the safety of donated blood, as the public fear over contaminated blood could only really be addressed at the European level.[130]

This particular tension between internal market objectives and public health objectives eventually led to an amendment to the EC Treaty with the Treaty of Amsterdam that allowed for the possibility to adopt measures on the 'setting of high standards of quality on the safety of organs and substances of human origin, blood and blood derivatives', which is also the legal basis for the Blood Directive.[131] In this area of involvement in public health, therefore, the EU currently has a relatively strong legislative basis, comparable to that in the area of the internal market, but singularly grounded in the objective of public health protection—rather than needing a dual objective, as in the case of the protection of public health with respect to the safety of goods in Article 114(3) TFEU (formerly Article 100a EEC/Article 95 EC).

With respect to the other communicable diseases that had become subject of surveillance networks in the eighties, in 1994 the heads of national communicable disease surveillance centres established a Charter Group (later called the Network Committee)[132] to create a unified framework for the surveillance of communicable diseases and training for epidemiological intervention (EPIET) under the auspices of the European Commission.[133] This led to the adoption of Decision 2119/1998, which streamlined the surveillance structures of several communicable diseases into one network, setting up an early-warning and response system (EWRS) and ensuring its workings by formalizing the Network Committee for Communicable Diseases into the comitology process.[134] In a 2004 the EU's work on communicable diseases was further consolidated with the establishment of the European Centre for Disease Control (ECDC).[135]

3.4.2 Constitutional tensions over tobacco advertising

Taking a step back in history again, the market–public health tension really became a constitutional battleground over the scope of the European internal market as a result of the Europe Against Cancer programme of the eighties. After the Chernobyl disaster, and with help of the political pressure of cancer experts—notably of Professor Maurice Tubiana, close friend of Francois Mitterand, then President of France—cancer rose on the agenda as a public health problem that needed European-wide attention. In 1986 a public health programme was launched on cancer,[136] which covered issues such as the

[130] Farrell (2006) supra note 124; Hagen (1993) supra note 124.

[131] Directive 2002/98/EC of the European Parliament and of the Council of 27 January 2003, setting standards of quality and safety for the collection, testing, processing, storage and distribution of human blood and blood components and amending Directive 2001/83/EC (OJ L 33, of 08-02-2003).

[132] J. Giesecke and J. Weinberg 'A European Centre for Infectious Disease?' (1998) *The Lancet* 352 (9136) 1038.

[133] J. Weinberg et al. 'On Behalf of the Charter Group: Establishing Priorities for European Collaboration in Communicable Disease Surveillance' (1999) *European Journal of Public Health* 9 (3) 236–40.

[134] Decision No. 2119/98/EC of the European Parliament and of the Council of 24 September 1998 setting up a network for the epidemiological surveillance and control of communicable diseases in the Community (OJ L 268/1, 03-10-1998).

[135] Regulation (EC) No 851/2004 of the European Parliament and of the Council of 21 April 2004 establishing a European Centre for Disease Prevention and Control (OJ L 142/1, 30-04-2004); Liverani and Coker (2012) supra note 74.

[136] A Programme of Action of the European Community Against Cancer (OJ C184, 23-07-1986).

prevention, screening, and treatment of cancer. From the very outset, the programme put major emphasis on an anti-smoking campaign to curb the incidence of cancer. These activities, rather than as a result of the entrepreneurialism of the Commission and the Court, find their explanation in the 'bottom-up' dynamics of policy communities at Member State level, seeking out one another at the European level in order to generate new ideas and best practice.[137]

The 'Europe Against Cancer' programme, similar to the HIV/AIDS programme, had to be based merely on the 'Treaty establishing the EC', given that there was no legislative public health basis.[138] In the late eighties a proposal for a Directive on Tobacco Advertising was prepared by the European Experts on Cancer Committee as part of the Europe Against Cancer Programme. This directive, based on Article 100a EEC (Article 114 TFEU), imposed partial restrictions on tobacco advertising. At the same time, the foundational rationale of the directive was explicitly aimed at curbing the incidence of cancer.[139] In 1989 the Council of Health Ministers meeting approved the Tobacco Advertising Directive with a qualified majority.[140] The tension was, in the words of Weiler, that

> Member States here thus face not only the normativity of measures adopted often wholly or partially against their will, but also the operation of this normativity in a vast area of public policy.[141]

Moreover, under pressure from the European Parliament, the directive was amended and a total ban on tobacco advertising was created.[142] The fact that the directive prohibited tobacco advertising altogether generated an immense lobby ('Goliath') from the tobacco industry.[143] This lobby instigated a debate on the legal basis of the directive, in that a total ban could in no way benefit the functioning of the internal market or have an economic aim at all.[144] Thus the argument was that the adoption of the directive would overstep the legislative authority of the European Community.

This controversy led to a stalling of the qualified majority voting procedure by Member States for many years. When the directive was finally adopted,[145] it was challenged in Court by Germany, with the main legal argument offered that it was vested on the wrong legal basis.[146] As a defence, the European institutions put forward that

[137] Trubek et al (2008) supra note 51 at pp. 811–12.

[138] See The Europe Against Aids Programme, Decision 91/317/EEC of the Council of Ministers of Heath of the Member States (OJ L 175/26, 04-07-1991); and see Hervey and McHale (2004) supra note 23 at p. 73.

[139] Proposal for a Council Directive on the Authorized Advertising of Tobacco Products in the Press and by Means of Bills and Posters (OJ C 124, 19-5-1989).

[140] See S. Boessen and H. Maarse 'The Impact of the Treaty Basis on Health Policy Legislation in the European Union: A Case Study on the Tobacco Advertising Directive' (2008) *BMC Health Services Research* 8 (77).

[141] See Weiler (1991) supra note 91 at p. 2463.

[142] Amended Proposal for a Council Directive on the Authorized Advertising of Tobacco Products in the Press and by Means of Bills and Posters (COM (90)147 final).

[143] Boessen and Maarse (2008) supra note 140; N. Gray 'Tobacco Industry and EC Advertising Ban' (2002) *The Lancet* 359 (9314) 1264–5; M. Hall 'EU Lawmakers Ready to Confront Tobacco Industry "Goliath"' (2013) *Euractiv*; M. Neuman et al. 'Tobacco Industry Strategies for Influencing European Community Tobacco Advertising Legislation' (2002) *The Lancet* 359 (9314) 1323–30.

[144] Neuman et al. (2002) supra note 143.

[145] As a result of the change of government in the UK, where Labour under Blair had just come into power, committed to a national ban on tobacco advertising; for an elaborate overview of the subsequent litigation and political controversy, see Hervey and McHale (2004) supra note 23 at p. 97 et seq.

[146] Case C-376/98 *Germany v. Parliament and Council (Tobacco Advertising)* [2000] ECR I-8419, Case C-380/03 *Federal Republic of Germany v. European Parliament and Council of the European Union* [2004] ECR I-08419.

Article 114 TFEU (by then Article 95 EC) also permitted regulation of the internal market even when this regulation did not have the objective of liberalizing the market. The Court, however, rejected this argument, and for the first time ruled that as it was vested on the wrong legal basis, the directive as a whole had to be annulled, as leaving it intact would 'vest in the Community legislature a general power to regulate the internal market' which would be incompatible with the subsidiarity principle.[147] This tension and the 'tug of war' between internal market on one hand and public health objectives on the other also characterize the growing presence of public health objectives in the Treaty. Paradoxically, over time the competences for public health in the Treaty grew as a way for Member States to legally determine their scope and in order to curb further 'competence creep' of the European Union in health. Whenever the Treaty basis for public health was introduced or expanded it resulted in broadening EU public health policy, rather than limiting its growth.[148]

3.5 Treaty bases for public health: reconciling different objectives

With the increasingly strong role of the EU in public health in relation to the free movement of goods and the controversies surrounding the HIV/AIDS and cancer programmes, when the Treaty of Maastricht was negotiated in the early nineties, a formal arrangement for public health was made with the inclusion of Article 129 in the EC Treaty.[149] Whereas some Member States may have seen the inclusion of Article 129 EC as a way to curb competence creep, other Member States saw it as an opportunity to formalize the involvement of the EU in public health.[150] Article 129 EC Treaty provided:

> The community shall contribute towards a high level of human health protection by encouraging corporation between Member States and, if necessary, lending support to their action.[151]

[147] Ibid., paras 78, 83. After the first Tobacco Advertising Directive was annulled, a new directive was adopted. In the litigation that followed the adoption of this new directive, the Court outlined that legislation based on Article 114 TFEU does not need to have internal market as its core aim, but it must *also* have the objective of creating a well-functioning market, next to taking possible public health measures, Case C-380/03 *Federal Republic of Germany v. European Parliament and Council of the European Union* [2004] ECR I-08419, at para. 62.

[148] Hervey and McHale (2004) supra note 23 at p. 104; also see Opinion of Advocate General Geelhoed in Case C-491/01 *BAT and Imperial Tobacco v. Secretary State of Health* [2002] ECR I-11453; also see T. K. Hervey 'Community and National Competence in Health after Tobacco Advertising' (2001) *Common Market Law Review* 38 (6) 1421–46; for a legal perspective on competence creep see S. Weatherill 'Competence Creep and Competence Control' (2004) *Yearbook of European Law* 23 (1) 1–55 (which argues that the legal arrangement of EU competences should not take away from the fact that ultimately the law here is to facilitate a reasonably flexible political process); in the political science literature Pollack (1994) supra note 93 explains the occurrence of competence creep as dependent on the 'type' of regulation (regulatory, redistributive, or distributive) under deliberation by the institutions or the Member States; however, he also adds that institutional rules on the legislative process are decisive in each of the policy types.

[149] The Treaty on European Union (TEU) signed in Maastricht on 7 February 1992, entered into force on 1 November 1993 (OJ C 191/1, 1992).

[150] See Hervey and McHale (2004) supra note 23; also see M. McKee et al. 'The Influence of European Law on National Health Policy' (1996) *Journal of European social policy* 6 (4) 263–86. These different objectives are not necessarily mutually exclusive.

[151] The actions of the EU were to be directed to specific areas such as major health challenges, research into these diseases and their transmission, and the provision of information and education on health. These areas of activity outline that action on the basis of Article 129 EC was mostly to be directed towards public health rather than health-care entitlements for individual citizens.

Article 129 EC also provided for a 'mainstreaming' of health into other policy areas. This meant that the Community had to take into consideration public health in all its activities. This proposition forms the basis of the later development of a 'Health in all Policies' (HiaP) approach, first proposed under the Finnish presidency.[152] The purpose of this policy approach is to examine the health determinants that improve health but are controlled in other policy sectors. HiaP is currently a central feature in the recent 'EU health strategy' and also features in the 'Renewed EU Social Agenda', the EU's Economic Strategy (2020), and as part of the EU's Cohesion Policy.[153] However, although a methodology—Health Impact Assessment (HIA) and Health Systems Impact Assessment (HSIA)—has been developed in order to support the mainstreaming of HiaP, the actual effectiveness of this mechanism seems to be low, both at the level of Commission Services and at Member State level.[154]

3.6 Redistributing through public health programmes

At the same time Article 129 EC excluded any harmonization of public health provisions of the Member States.[155] Nevertheless, after the adoption of the treaty text it needed to be translated into a 'policy text'. This resulted in the series of public health (disease) programmes that, while the exchange of research was an important aspect, provided for actual policy mechanisms such as training and education, running information campaigns, and health monitoring.[156] However, these programmes only had modest budgets and were adopted in a piecemeal fashion.[157] In 1998, the Commission

[152] Giesecke and Weinberg (1998) supra note 132; Stahl et al. (eds) (2006) supra note 40.

[153] See European Commission, White paper: Together for Health, A Strategic Approach for the EU 2008-2013 (COM (2007) 630 final); Communication from the Commission to the European Parliament, the Council, the European Economic and Social Committee and the Committee of the Regions of 2 July 2008—Renewed social agenda: Opportunities, access and solidarity in 21st century Europe (COM (2008) 412 final); Communication from the Commission, EUROPE 2020, A strategy for smart, sustainable and inclusive growth (COM(2010) 2020 final); See Health investments in Structural Funds 2000–2006: learning lessons to inform regions in the 2007–2013 period (EUROREGIO III), available at: <http://www.ec.europa.eu/eahc/projects/database.html?prjno=20081218> which allocates about 5 billion euros for investment in health projects.

[154] See European Commission, Impact Assessment Board Report for 2012, at p. 27:

> Despite the Board's previous recommendations to thoroughly assess social impacts the Board notes that there has been no progress in the initial assessments of these impacts. While this may also reflect a slightly different mix in the types of impact assessments being submitted (with higher percentage of impact assessments dealing for example, with health, consumer or justice issues), the need to strengthen the quality of the analysis for social impacts remains.

See also M. Wismar 'Is HIA Effective? A Synthesis of Concepts, Methodologes and Results' in M. Wismar et al. (eds) *The Effectiveness of Health Impact Assessment. Scope and Limitations Supporting Decision-making in Europe* (Copenhagen: European Observatory on Health Systems and Policies, World Health Organization, 2007) (where the overall effectiveness of HIA in the Member States remains relatively inconclusive, given the variety of cases where it may be used as a factor in the decision-making process).

[155] Article 129 EC formally granted the Commission the power to recommend and promote measures for coordination. The Council and the Parliament were given the power to formulate 'incentive measures' in accordance with the co-decision procedure, or they could make recommendations on the basis of a proposal of the Commission; see Article 152 EC, ex Article 129 EC.

[156] Resolution of the Council and the Ministers for Health, meeting within the Council of 27 May 1993 on future action in the field of public health (OJ C 174, 25-06-1993).

[157] First an action programme for promotion, information, and education in the field of public health was adopted. Later HIV/AIDS was added, and then cancer, drug dependence, and health promotion. Health monitoring was added in 1997 and in three later programmes injury prevention, rare diseases, and pollution-related diseases were also added. Moreover, consecutive European public

proposed streamlining all the different programmes into one public health programme.[158] Following this first integrated public health programme, currently a third cycle has been adopted.[159] The programme is executed under Commission auspices through a 'programme committee'. In 2004, the Commission set up the Executive Agency for the Public Health Programme (as it was then called) to manage the Public Health Programme 2003–2008. This agency currently has a broader scope and is called the Consumers, Health, Agriculture, and Food Executive Agency.[160]

These public health programmes are an example of positive integration at EU level that actually *redistributes* funds in the area of social welfare. And although the public health programmes over the years have had to make do on very low budgets,[161] they have links with the much larger budget of the EU research programme that allocates over 6 billion euros for health. The priorities defined in the Programme Committee for the public health programme filter through in the funding priorities that are chosen in the Programme committee of the health programme under the heading of Directorate General Research.[162] Moreover, much of the public health budget is distributed through co-funding, which means any activity or action usually needs at least 40 per cent funding from other sources. Another aspect that plays into this is that the EU public health programmes play a role in the distribution of EU structural funds, in that objectives of the public health programmes are mirrored with respect to the budget for health priorities in the structural funds.[163]

3.7 The Treaty gives and the Treaty takes: legislative basis

The initial prohibition of harmonization in former Article 129(4) EC of public health provisions in the Treaty is puzzling, given the fact that in Article 95(3) EC (now Article 114 TFEU) harmonization of public health provisions was already allowed.

health programmes also play a role here in terms of coordination and financing Communication from the Commission to the Council, the European Parliament, and the Economic and Social Committee on the framework for action in the field of public health in the European Community (COM (93) 559); see for example the First Programme of Community action in the Field of Public Health (2003–2008); the Second Programme of Community Action in the Field of Health 2008–2013.

[158] Programme on the basis of three aspects, improving information for the development of public health, reacting rapidly to public health threats and addressing health determinants through health promotion and disease prevention. The programme was still small in size, only 312 million euros and it ran from 2003 to 2008.

[159] Third Health Programme (2014–2020) Regulation 282/2014/EU for the third Health Programme (OJ L 86, Vol. 57 of 21 March 2014).

[160] Commission Decision of 15 December 2004 setting up an executive agency, the 'Executive Agency for the Public Health Programme', for the management of Community action in the field of public health—pursuant to Regulation (EC) No.58/2003 (2004/858/EC) (OJ L 369/73, 16-12-2004); and see the amending decision to include the consumer programme into the work of the public health agency Commission Decision of 20 June 2008 amending Decision 2004/858/EC in order to transform the 'Executive Agency for the Public Health Programme' into the 'Executive Agency for Health and Consumers' (2008/544/EC) (OJ L172/27, 03-07-2008).

[161] Averaging 300 to 500 million euros.

[162] This link with research and health at EU level goes back to the fifties since the ECSC funded research programmes in the area of occupational diseases. Over the course of the seventies and especially in the eighties, research into communicable diseases was also funded by the Community; this was mainly in the context of the common market and agriculture. However, in the field of research and technology biomedical research became funded at the European level. Commission of the European Communities, Biology and Health Protection Prgramme, Research Programme 1976–1980 (COM (75) 351 final).

[163] J. Watson *Health and Structural Funds 2007–2013 (2013) Country and Regional Assessment (Hungary)* (2009) EUREGIO III Project for DG SANCO.

This paradoxical give and take was the result of Member States' initiatives to make sure the EC would not creep from public health activities that were market-creating to public health activities that would cause Member States to lose autonomy over national budgets. This reconciliation of different objectives, together with a number of public health crises, marks the further development of the public health provision(s) in the Treaty.

In the early nineties, the UK's role in covering up the fact that BSE (bovine spongiform encephalitis) in cows could cause Creutzfeldt–Jacob disease—which it did by virtually taking over European veterinary safety committees—prompted the adoption of a critical report by the European Parliament on the role of the European executive in taking public health measures.[164] As a result, with the adoption of the Treaty of Amsterdam in 1997, the public health article was amended to allow for harmonization of Member States' regulations of the quality and safety of organs and substances, veterinary and phytosanitary measures which have as their direct objective the protection of public health.[165] At the same time, with respect to individual health the involvement of the EU was also growing—this will be outlined in more detail in section 4 of this chapter—and as the total ban on harmonization of purely public health measures was abandoned, a new paragraph was added, reasserting the autonomy of the Member States regarding the organization of access to individual health care.[166]

The latest amendments to the Lisbon Treaty are a response to the public health crisis in the area of communicable diseases and the threat of bioterrorism. What is now Article 168 TFEU includes—on top of improving public health, and preventing physical and mental illness and diseases—monitoring and early warning, and combating cross-border health threats. The focus on public health threats has come about as a result of a sequence of crises where Member States made attempts to coordinate responses.[167] The first were the anthrax threats after 9/11, and later the SARS and avian flu threats. In practice this brings the EU's involvement in public health into the realm of common foreign and security policy.[168]

With the ratification of the Treaty of Lisbon, public health in Article 9 TFEU is added. Article 9 TFEU presents public health as an overarching objective of the Union, which should be taken into account when defining or implementing EU policies or activities. This means that public health is no longer supplementing internal market provisions alone; it has become a self-standing objective for all Union policies. In this sense it reaffirms that not only internal market measures but all Union activities can

[164] Resolution of the European Parliament on the report of the Temporary Committee instructed to follow up the recommendations on BSE (19 February 1997) (R4-3135/97). The European Parliament even considered dismissing the European Commission entirely. Jacques Santer, then president of the European Commission, in turn promised that from now on public health would be at the 'forefront of development of Europe'.

[165] After the Amsterdam amendments, Article 152(4) (a) (b) EC; See H. D. C. Roscam Abbing 'Public Health in the Treaty of Amsterdam: An Analysis' (1998) *Journal for Health Law* at pp. 75–80.

[166] The new paragraph 5 of Article 152 (Article 129 renumbered after the Treaty of Amsterdam) reads: 'Community action in the field of public health shall fully respect the responsibilities if the Member States for the organization and delivery of health services and medical care.'

[167] This article was first introduced in the 2003 deliberations in the Constitution for Europe, Conference of the Representatives of the Governments of the Member States, Naples Ministerial Conclave: Presidency proposal CIG 52/03 addendum to the Presidency Note, Brussels, 25 November 2003, upon requests of the Commission, the French and Scandinavian delegations.

[168] A. de Ruijter, 'EU External Health Security Policy and Law' in S. Blockmans and P. Koutrakos (eds), *Research Handbook, The EU's Common Foreign and Security Policy* (Cheltenham: Edward Elgar, 2018).

have a public health impact. However, it still remains to be seen what practical impact this objective may have.[169]

Altogether, the involvement of the EU in public health currently is the result of continuous reconciliations. On one hand, the Member States have desired to curb the role of the EU in this area. Paradoxically the instrument for doing so—the creation of a Treaty competence for the Union including provisions restating the limitations of this competence—seems to have had the opposite effect over time. On the other hand, Member States have also sought each other out to respond to public health crises at EU level, and EU public health policy has expanded continuously as a market-making instrument. At the same time, woven through these opposing pressures are the 'bottom-up dynamics of policy specialists' that seek out one another at the EU level as a result of the internationalization of medical and epidemiological expertise, aiming to come up with solutions for shared problems. Furthermore, in the face of major health threats and communicable diseases the Member States have created European alliances in order to respond to and come up with policy solutions for major diseases such as cancer and HIV/AIDS. Another aspect of EU public health policy is the development of public health programmes, where the EU is able to show its 'social face' by distributing funds to particular public health objectives. And although these programmes have been relatively limited over the years, the fact that they interlink with larger budgets in the area of EU research programmes, the structural funds, or the European Social Fund still amounts to a more significant redistribution of funding for EU public health policy.

4. EU Health-care Policy and Law

EU health-care policy addresses objectives relating to the provision of medical care and individual health. Importantly, health-care policy often impacts on social insurance and benefits, which are central to the welfare state arrangements and redistribution of value, particularly because all Member States in the EU adhere to the principle of universal access.[170] With the amendments to the Lisbon Treaty, Member States reasserted their autonomy with respect to access to individual health care. Article 152(4) EC initially read:

> Union action in the field of public health shall fully respect the responsibilities if the Member States for the organization and delivery of health services and medical care.

However, in the Lisbon Treaty the following is added into the (renumbered) Article 168(7) TFEU:

> The responsibilities of the Member States shall include the management of health services and medical care and the allocation of resources assigned to them.

The question is: how did EU health-care policy evolve to lead to it being felt necessary to reaffirm Member State autonomy in this field? There is no EU legal basis for the regulation of access to health care or with respect to social security generally,

[169] As outlined, since the inclusion of Article 129 the 'mainstreaming' of public health in all EU policies has been an objective in the Treaty; however, the implementation of Health Impact Assessment in EU policies remains limited, see supra note 58.

[170] Council Conclusions, 'Council Conclusions on Common Values and Principles in European Union Health Systems(2006/C 146/01) (O.J. 146/1)' <https://eur-lex.europa.eu/LexUriServ/LexUriServ.do?uri=OJ:C:2006:146:0001:0003:EN:PDF>.

and the Council has to act unanimously on the social security and social protection of workers.[171] Moreover, harmonization is excluded from the modernization of social protection systems.[172] The political importance of access to individual health care can hardly be overestimated. Health care is a matter of vast public expenditure and complicated distributive national social insurance schedules. As will be outlined in what follows, the involvement of the EU has come about mostly as a result of private litigation in the context of the free movement of persons and the very strong role of the CJEU in this respect.[173] At the same time, public procurement law and European competition law have affected the regulation of health care in the Member States to such an extent that special rules have been adopted at the European level in order to recognize the special nature of health-care services. Moreover, as a result of 'soft' macroeconomic policy at EU level, access to individual health care has become part of governance mechanisms such as the open method of coordination (OMC).

4.1 Cross-border health care: angry letters and private litigation

The adoption of the Treaty of Rome in 1958 establishing the European Economic Community (EEC) formed the basis for a legal instrument on the creation of social security measures. Regulation No. 3 (1958) provided rights to social security for employed migrant workers and pensioners and their dependants in conjunction with the establishment of the common market and the provision for freedom of movement for workers in Article 51 EEC Treaty.[174] Soon this Regulation became important in allowing migrant workers access to health-care insurance across borders.[175] At the start of the seventies, Regulation 1408/71 replaced Regulation 3.[176] Regulation 1408/71 established a mechanism by which Europeans could obtain access to health care in another Member State. However, the regulation was not meant to provide for an actual common scheme of social security; or in other words, it was meant to coordinate access to Member State social security systems, rather than harmonize them.[177]

Not long after the adoption of this Social Security Regulation in the seventies, calls came for its reform. The procedural scheme set out in this regulation to allow access to cross-border health care was limiting and in practice mostly dependent on the authorization of the health authority of the Member State of affiliation.[178] In fact this

[171] Article 153(1)(c) TFEU with Article 153(2)(b) para. 2 TFEU.

[172] Article 153(2)(a) TFEU.

[173] A. P. Van der Mei *Free Movement of Persons within the European Community: Cross-Border Access to Public Benefits* (Oxford: Hart, 2003).

[174] Regulation No. 3 of the Council on Social Security for Migrant Workers (OJ 30/561, 25-09-1958, p. 561).

[175] European Commission, Medical expenses incurred during temporary residence in another country of the European Economic Community, Information Memo P-39/64, 1964; Commission Administrative pour la Securite Sociale des travaileurs migrants, Assurance maladie-maternité des travailleurs immigrant aux Pays-Bas avec leur famille, Guide no 1 (1961); Commission Administrative pour la Securite Sociale des Travailleurs Migrants, Assurance maladie-maternité des membres de la famille residant au Luxembourg alors que le travailleur est occupe dans un autre pays de la Communaute Guide No 5 (1961).

[176] Council Regulation (EEC) No. 1408/72 on the Application of Social Security Schemes to Employed Persons, to Self-Employed Persons and to Members of their Families Moving within the Community (OJ L149, 05-07-1971).

[177] Case C 100/78 *Claudino Rossi v. Caisse de Compensation pour Allocations Familiales des Regions de Charleroi et Namur* [1979] ECR 831.

[178] As are the E110 (for international road haulers), E119 (for unemployed/job seekers), and E128 (for students and workers in another member state). See inter alia the Administrative Commission on Social Security for Migrant Workers (CASSTM) of 18 June 2003 aimed at introducing a European

Regulation generated the highest influx to the Commission of angry or anxious letters from European citizens, around 1,800 every year, which is about 25 per cent of the total complaints under review by the Commission.[179] However, social security legislation turned out to be the most difficult sector for legislative reform. For most of the EU's history, access to cross-border social security was subject to unanimous voting in the Council.[180] In the end it took almost forty years for the current version of the new 'Social Security Regulation' (or 'Regulation 883/2004')[181] to become effective, without adding significant changes in the Regulation from the seventies regarding health-care access.[182] With the final adoption of a new Social Security Regulation in 2004, a European Health Insurance Card was implemented in 2005. This provided new procedural tools for the European social security scheme of the new Regulation 883/2004.[183]

Arguably, as evidenced by the number of citizens' complaints, the very slow reform of the European social security scheme created pressure for European patients to seek access to cross-border health care outside the Social Security Regulation on the basis of primary European law on free movement in the Treaty through the Court.[184] Over the years there have been a number of proceedings for the CJEU in which the health benefits scheme on the basis of the Social Security Regulation was further explicated. In the

health insurance card replacing the forms necessary for the application of Council Regulations (EEC) No. 1408/71 and (EEC) No. 574/72 as regards access to health care during a temporary stay in a Member State other than the competent state or the state of residence (OJ L 276, 27-10-2003); Decision No. 190 of the Administrative Commission on Social Security for Migrant Workers (CASSTM) 18 June 2003 concerning the technical specifications of the European health insurance card (OJ L 276, 27-10-2003); Decision No. 191 of 18 June 2003 concerning the replacement of forms E 111 and E 111 B by the European health insurance card (OJ L 276, 27-10-2003).

179 Jerome Vignon (Director DG Employment Social Affairs and Equal Opportunities) Speech, 'From Old to New Social Security Regulation', at the conference on European Citizenship, Free Circulation and Social Protection, Brussels, 20–1 November 2008.

180 With the amendments of the Lisbon Treaty, Article 48 on the freedom of movement for workers and social security is now subject to qualified majority voting in the Council. However, a special referral procedure to the European Council is possible in case one of the Members of the Council feels a draft legislative act would affect important aspects of its social security system; the scope, costs, or financial structure or the financial balance of that system (Article 48(b) TFEU).

181 Regulation 883/2004 and 'Social Security Regulation' will be used interchangeably.

182 As early as 1992, the European Council in Edinburgh 11–12 December 1992 (DOC/92/8, 13-12-1992), in anticipation of a complete scan of European secondary legislation in the context of the subsidiarity principle adopted with the Maastricht Treaty, called for reform of Regulation 1408/71. This was confirmed five years later in the context of the 1997 action plan for the free movement of workers by the Commission, in relation to the adoption of the Treaty on European Union in Maastricht; see: An action plan for free movement of workers—Communication from the Commission (COM (1997) 586 final). However, no significant advancement had been made by the time of the Presidency Conclusions, European Council Meeting in Laeken, 14 and 15 December 2001 (SN 300/1/01 REV 1) at para. 29, but here again it was decided that the social security rights should be transferable across the European Union. At the Barcelona Council in 2002 the Member States renewed their resolve to reform the Regulation in the context of the Lisbon Agenda to improve competitiveness by creating a flexible labour market. The new Regulation was to be adopted before the end of 2003 Presidency: Conclusions, Barcelona European Council 15 and 16 March 2002 (SN 100/1/02 REV 1). Moreover, at the Barcelona Council the European Council formulated a number of policy initiatives in the area of health-care policy. The focus is on the interconnection between transferability of social security measures and a flexible labour market, to which end a European Health Insurance Card was to become available for Europeans. Presidency Conclusions, Barcelona European Council 15 and 16 March 2002 (SN 100/1/02 REV 1) para. 34.

183 It meant that complicated procedures with separate forms for health benefits for different categories of persons moving across borders became simplified; see references in supra note 175.

184 See D. S. Martinsen 'The Europeanization of Welfare: The Domestic Impact of Intra-European Social Security' (2005) *JCMS* 43 (5) 1027–54.

Pierik cases in the late seventies, the Court adopted an extensive interpretation of the legal definition of a 'worker' and the related rights for workers on the basis of the Social Security Regulation.[185] However, Member States in turn reasserted control over the scope of social insurance entitlement in subsequent amendments to Regulation 1408/71.[186] Nevertheless, the access to cross-border health care for Europeans in relation to the Social Security Regulation was challenged soon enough. Already in the *Luisi and Carbone* (1984) case (on limiting currency exchange for the purpose of buying health care abroad in a Member State) and in the *SPUC v. Grogan* (1991) case (on access to health care in another Member State for the purpose of terminating a pregnancy), the Court established that health care falls within the ambit of the freedom to provide and receive services.[187]

4.1.1 Medical tourism or medical need?

Over the course of the nineties, patients increasingly began to effectuate access to cross-border health care through the Court. These cases on cross-border health care have been controversial for their perceived potential to undermine Member States' territorial and financial autonomy to regulate their own health-care systems. A key aspect in this context is the limited right to access cross-border health care, given the fact that 'prior authorization' is needed from the competent health institution in the home state(s) in order to travel abroad for health care and have costs covered under the health insurance scheme.[188] For a long time, Member States were able to use prior authorization as a way to limit access to cross-border health care. They would argue that cross-border health care was medical tourism, rather than that there was a medical need to create access to health care in another Member State.

However, the Court changed the rules of the game when it started using primary provisions in the Treaty directly to carve out a European right to health care. It has even been argued that the Court in this respect has adopted a 'patients-centred' and 'needs-based' approach.[189] In the *Grogan* case in 1991, the Court determined that the medical termination of a pregnancy is a 'service' within the meaning of the freedom to provide services under Union law. In this case, officers of Irish student associations were offering information to pregnant women regarding the availability of abortion beyond national borders. Ireland had prohibited abortion first by common law and then

[185] Case 177/77 *Bestuur van het Algemeen Ziekenfonds Drente-Platteland v. G. Pierik* (*Pierik I*) [1978] ECR 825; Case 182/78 *Bestuur van het Algemeen Ziekenfonds Drenthe-Platteland v. G. Pierik* (*Pierik II*)[1979] ECR 1977.

[186] V. Hatzopoulos 'Health Law and Policy: the Impact of the EU' in G. de Búrca (ed.) *EU Law and the Welfare State: In Search of Solidarity* (Oxford: Oxford University Press, 2005).

[187] Joined cases C 283/82 and C 26/83 *Luisi and Carbone v. Ministero del Tesoro* [1984] ECR-377; Case C-159/90 *Society for the Protection of Unborn Children (Ireland) Ltd v. Stephen Grogan* [1991] ECR I-4685.

[188] For a thematic overview of all ECJ case law relating to health-care services, see V. Hatzapoulos *Briefing note for the European Parliament The ECJ Case Law on Cross-Border Aspects of Health Services* (2007) (IP/A/IMCO/FWC/2006-167/C3/SC1).

[189] G. Davies 'The Effect of Mrs Watts' Trip to France on the National Health Care Service' (2007) *King's Law Journal* 18 158–67 at 160; although it may be more likely that the Court here adopted its usual 'market-driven' approach in order to 'secure a level playing field in an area of free movement', see S. Douglas-Scott 'The Problem of Justice in the European Union' in J. Dickson and P. Eleftheriadis (eds) *Philosophical Foundations of European Union Law* (Oxford: Oxford University Press, 2012) at p. 416.

by statute.[190] However, the Court's judgment held that in principle Irish citizens could not be prohibited from accessing medical services offered in another Member State.[191] This particular case on abortion was controversial, not only because it determined that health care was a 'service' within the meaning of the Treaty (what is now Article 57 TFEU),[192] but especially because it determined that a citizen of any EU Member State is in principle allowed to travel freely to another Member State for medical services, unhindered by legislative and possible moral obstacles. This early case sparked the debate on the use of Union law to circumvent national legislation based on ethical and moral considerations, for instance 'reproductive tourism' and 'end-of-life tourism'.[193]

When in 1994 a fifty-nine-year-old woman travelled from the UK to receive IVF treatment in Italy, calls came for the EU to ban this type of free movement.[194] However, the response at EU level was 'conspicuous in its absence'.[195] Instead, in subsequent cases the Court has taken a market-driven approach to health care. In the 1998 *Kohll* case, the Court determined that the prior authorization procedure, through which Member States had strengthened their autonomy by limiting the access to cross-border health care, could be in direct breach of primary treaty law. The case dealt with a Luxembourg national who sought the reimbursement of the costs of dental treatment received in Germany by his daughter without seeking prior authorization as per the Social Security Regulation. The Court explains: '[T]he special nature of certain services does not remove them from the ambit of the fundamental principle of the freedom of movement.'[196] This meant that the requirement of prior authorization was in breach of the freedom to provide services.[197] In a judgment delivered on the same day, the ECJ determined the same with respect to goods, in the *Decker* case, which concerned a Luxembourg national who had purchased a pair of spectacles in Belgium.[198] After these cases a number of other cases were brought before the Court over the course of the nineties and beyond. In many of these cases the autonomy for Member States to determine the reach and accessibility of their health-care systems was limited. However, the Court also determined that the maintenance of the balance of a social security system may provide reason to override the application of the freedom-of-movement principles.[199]

[190] See Case C-159/90 *Society for the Protection of Unborn Children (Ireland) Ltd v. Stephen Grogan* [1991] ECR I-4685.

[191] Nevertheless, the distribution of information on the availability of these services could be prohibited under national law.

[192] Apparently, although Article 49 EC (now Article 57 TFEU) only referred to the provision of services, this article also extends to the freedom to *receive* services. See Case C-204/90 *Hanns-Martin Bachmann v. Belgium* [1992] ECR I-149.

[193] Hervey and McHale (2004) supra note 23 at p. 144 et seq.; also see R. L. Lee and D. Morgan *Human Fertilisation and Embryology: Regulating the Reproductive Revolution* (London: Blackstone Press, 2001). Medical tourism generally is of course also a global issue, see I. G. Cohen (ed.) *The Globalization of Health Care: Legal and Ethical Issues* (New York: Oxford University Press, 2013).

[194] R. Watson 'Focus: Brussels, Which "Europe" Should Deal With Ethical Issues?' (1994) *British Medical Journal* 308 (362).

[195] Hervey and McHale (2004) supra note 23 at p. 149.

[196] Case C-158/96 *Raymond Kohll v. Union des caisses de maladie* [1998] ECR I-1931 at para. 10.

[197] Article 57 TFEU.

[198] Case C-120/95 *Nicolas Decker v. Caisse de maladie de employes prives* [1998] ECR I-1831.

[199] See inter alia Case C-158/96 *Raymond Kohll v. Union des caisses de maladie* [1998] ECR I-1931 at para. 41; also see Case C-157/99 *B.S.M. Geraets-Smits v. Stichting Ziekenfonds VGZ* and *H.T.M. Peerbooms v. Stichting CZ Groep Zorgverzekeringen* (*Smits* and *Peerbooms*) [2001] ECR I-5473 at para. 73; also see Case 368/98 *Abdon VanBraekel and Others v. Alliance nationale des mutualités chrétiennes (ANMC)* ECR I-5363 [2001] at para. 47.

4.1.2 Health professionals and health services in Union law

Although the Member States in negotiations on primary Treaty texts have maintained that the EU has no role in the governance of health-care systems, there are a number of other ways the EU has become involved nonetheless. EU involvement in access to health care grew indirectly with respect to the application of Union law to health professionals and health services. When a health professional moves abroad, Union Law regulates the recognition of medicinal professional qualifications.[200] Whereas in the nineties at EU level the special nature of the qualifications for the medical profession were to some extent taken into consideration,[201] currently qualifications for the medical profession are a matter of mutual recognition, in respect of both the establishment and the provision of (temporary) services in another Member State. Article 53(2) TFEU, which deals with freedom of establishment, specifically addresses the medical profession and makes the abolition of restrictions on the freedom of establishment dependent on coordination in the various Member States. The general system of mutual recognition has created a number of challenges, however, especially with respect to the quality of health care and the possibility for undermining the system of self-regulation in many Member States with respect to medical disciplinary law.[202]

Another avenue of EU involvement in health care is through the setting up and development of Centres of Reference, focused specifically on developing networks and facilities for rare diseases requiring specialized care.[203] The idea behind these centres in hospitals across the EU is that this way the EU can contribute to an economy of scale, and help to focus on treatment and research in the area of rare diseases. This type of EU involvement, though, is purely based on soft coordination of Member States'

[200] M. A. Garcia-Perez et al. 'Physicians Migration in Europe: An Overview of the Current Situation' (2007) *BioMEd Central Health Services Research* 7. Professional qualifications are mutually recognized across the EU. For many of the medical sectors there are specific national guidelines as to the minimum standard of training required for particular health-care professionals. However, once those qualifications are met, a physician is automatically qualified to work anywhere within the European Union; see Directive 2005/36/EC of the European Parliament and of the Council of 7 September 2005 on the recognition of professional qualifications (L 255/22, 30-09-2005), replacing the more specific Council Directive 93/16/EEC of 5 April 1993 to facilitate the free movement of doctors and the mutual recognition of their diplomas, certificates, and other evidence of formal qualifications (OJ L 165, 07-07-1993, pp. 1–24); see further Hervey and McHale (2004) supra note 23 at p. 197; also see J. Irwin 'Migration Patterns of Nurses in the EU' (2001) *Euro Health* 7 (13). At the same time, general EU measures in the area of employment law do not take into consideration the specificities of the medical profession, which has created notable problems in the context of the Working Time Directive Directive 2003/88/EC of the European Parliament and of the Council of 4 November 2003 concerning certain aspects of the organisation of working time (OJ L 299, 18-11-2003, pp. 9–19), which was amended to allow for exceptions to the working time of doctors in training, in Article 17 (4) Working Time Directive, after a number of Court cases, notably Case C-303/98 *Sindicato de Medicos de Asistencia Publica v. Conselleria de Sanidad y Consumo de la Generalidad Valenciana* (*SIMAP v. CSCGV*) [2000] ECR I-7963 and Case C-151/02 *Landeshauptstadt Kiel v. Jaegar* [2003] ECR I-08389. Measures with regard to allowing Member States to ask medical professionals to take an oath or solemn declaration before being able to practice medicine; and measures with regard to exchanging information regarding disciplinary, administrative, or criminal actions taken against a medical professional, were established, (see the cases in n 200).

[201] See Editorial 'Doctors' training and the European Working Time Directive 375' (2010) *The Lancet* 375 (9732) at p. 2121.

[202] See further for a detailed overview of the current law and case law M. Peeters et al. 'EU law and Health Professionals' in E Mossailos et al. (eds) *Health Systems Governance in Europe: The Role of European Union Law and Policy* (Cambridge: Cambridge University Press, 2010).

[203] Overview of current Centres of Reference for Rare Diseases in Europe: State-of-the-art in 2006 and recommendations of the Rare Diseases Task Force to the The High Level Group on Health Services and Medical Care (December 2006) available at: <http://www.ec.europa.eu/health/ph_threats/non_com/docs/contribution_policy.pdf> (last accessed February 2014).

health specialists and hospital representatives. Currently the Centres of Reference have found their way into the recently implemented Patients' Rights Directive;[204] however, the setting up and management of these Centres is governed through coordination in this context also.

In the area of e-Health, too, the EU is involved in health-care policy through soft coordination and incentive measures. Through this mode of governance the EU aims to develop e-Health and telemedicine within a broader 'digital agenda'. The idea here is that rather than the physician moving abroad to treat patients, if necessary the patient is treated across the border on the basis of images or through 'telesurgery'.[205] Another branch of e-health relates to the digitalization of patient records and the interoperability of these systems across European borders, and the e-prescription of pharmaceuticals.[206] Policy here is aimed at developing a European 'e-Health Area'.[207] e-health is also a policy area that depends on softer forms of cooperation and implementation mechanisms. There is a particular inter-sectoral subgroup within the Commission that works on e-Health across Commission Directorates. However, Member State representatives from telecommunications departments within national ministries, health authorities, doctors' and nurses' associations, and industry, as well as patient and citizen groups, also work within this framework.[208]

4.1.3 Special consideration for health care in competition and procurement law

For the autonomous governance of national health-care systems, the European rules on public procurement represent a highly salient issue with respect to the possibility to (re-)distribute welfare. If all health-care arrangements are subject to EU public procurement law then health-care systems would need to operate to some extent as a market, regardless of whether the buyer of health care is the government or a private insurance company. As EU rules on the prohibition of state aid prevent public authorities interfering with the market, the rules on public procurement prescribe that public contracts are awarded in accordance with specific rules that allow for competition. Directive 2004/18 on public procurement gives special recognition to the importance of individual health considerations.[209] Annex II B of the directive specifically mentions

[204] Directive 2011/24/EU of the European Parliament and of the Council of 9 March 2011 on the application of patients' rights in cross-border healthcare (OJ L 88/45, 04-04-2011).

[205] Communication from the Commission to the European Parliament, the Council, the European Economic and Social Committee, and the Committee of the Regions on telemedicine for the benefit of patients, health-care systems and society (COM/2008/689 final); also see <http://www.ec.europa.eu/information_society/activities/health/policy/telemedicine/telemedicine2/index_en.htm> for an overview of the current active work plan on telemedicine. Communication from the Commission to the Council, the European Parliament, the European Economic and Social Committee, and the Committee of the Regions: e-Health—making health care better for European citizens: an action plan for a European e-Health Area (COM(2004)0356 final); also see Commission Recommendation on cross-border interoperability of electronic health record systems (COM (2008) 3282).

[206] Ibid.; also see European Commission Directorate General Information Society study, Study on the Legal Framework for Interoperable eHealth in Europe (SMART 2007/0059).

[207] See Conclusions of the European Council 25/26 March 2010 (EUCO 7/10); also see Commission Communication, EUROPE 2020 A strategy for smart, sustainable, and inclusive growth (COM (2010) 2020).

[208] See further the website of the EU's Digital Agenda 2020: <http://www.ec.europa.eu/digital-agenda/>.

[209] Directive 2004/18/EC of 31 March 2004 on the coordination of procedures for the award of public works contracts, public supply contracts, and public service contracts (OJ L 134, 30-04-2004, pp. 114–240).

health services, outlining that 'nothing in this directive should prevent the imposition or enforcement of measures necessary to protect public policy, public morality, public security, health [...]'.[210]

However, other than this public policy exception, the Directive *does* apply to health care. For this reason, much is still unclear as to how Europe rules on public procurement would apply in legal practice. What, for instance, will constitute grounds for exception? When does an undertaking have enough ties to the state or a public body to be a contracting authority in the sense of Article 1(9) of the Directive?[211] The Treaty confers exclusive legislative powers on the Commission in particular areas with regard to competition law. For instance, Article 106 TFEU grants the Commission the exclusive right to issue directives relating to public works, to ensure that these comply with the Treaties. Using this exclusive right, the Commission can also decide to allow for exceptions to the general Treaty regime relating to public undertakings, especially with regard to state aid and the applicability of EU competition rules. With regard to health care, the Commission has indeed created such an exception with regard to public funding for hospitals.[212] Competition law and public procurement obviously link to financial schemes in health care. Ways to curb the costs of medical services and goods are closely linked and can have all kinds of consequences in the different health-care systems. In this respect, these areas of economic law interlink with creating access to health care, how hospitals are financed, and access to medicinal products and devices.

4.1.4 EU involvement through 'soft' governance tools

Finally, there are a number of non-legislative ways—facilitated by the European Commission—through which Member States work together on health care. One of these is through an 'open method of coordination'.[213] This form of governance lacks command-and control-techniques and uses instead methods of shared learning, peer review, benchmarking, and the outlining of best practices,[214] and these techniques help

[210] See ibid. at rec. 6.

[211] See V. Hatzopoulos 'Public Procurement and State Aid in National Health Care Systems' in E. Mossailos et al. (eds) *Health Systems Governance in Europe: The Role of European Union Law and Policy* (Cambridge: Cambridge University Press, 2010) at p. 379.

[212] See Commission Decision 2005/842/EC of 28 November 2005, on the application of Article 86(2) of the EC Treaty on State Aid in the form of public service compensation granted to certain undertakings entrusted with the operation of services of general economic interest (notified under document number C (2005) 2673) (OJ L 312, 29-11-2005), at para. 16.

[213] The open method of coordination (OMC) is in principle an implementation mechanism that constitutes a flexible form of cooperation, based on commonly agreed indicators or benchmarks, which are not binding but allow for changes in preferences. The OMC engages at least four levels of European policymakers. First, the European Council agrees on the general objectives and outlines general guidelines hereto. Second, the Council of Ministers selects more specific, quantitative and qualitative indicators for the evaluation of national practices. These are selected on the basis of proposals of the Commission or by—and with—other independent bodies and agencies. Third, the adoption of measures at the national or regional level follows in National Action Plans, which allows local particularities to be taken into consideration. Last, the process is completed with mutual evaluation and peer review between Member States and the Council. See M. A. Pollock 'Theorizing EU Policy-Making' in H. Wallace et al. (eds) *Policy-Making in the European Union* (Oxford: Oxford University Press, 2005); K. Armstrong and C. Kilpatrick 'Law, Governance, or New Governance? The Changing Open Method of Coordination' (2007) *Columbia Journal of European Law* 13 649–79.

[214] As such some also recognize the potential of the OMC to create policy networks, through which information can be exchanged and policy can be made without putting pressure on the process due to hierarchical relations. See T. K. Hervey 'The European Union's Governance and the Welfare Modernisation Agenda' (2008) *Regulation and Governance* 2 (103–20) at p. 103; also see E. Szyszczak

'the EU to promulgate authoritative frameworks and oversee their enforcement'.[215] In the Lisbon amendments to the Treaty, Article 168(2) specifically refers to this type of governance as initiatives by the Commission are welcomed in order to facilitate co-ordination between Member States' health policies that aims at the 'establishment of guidelines and indicators, the organisation of exchange of best practice, and the preparation of the necessary elements for periodic monitoring and evaluation'. The OMC on health and long-term care, however, was already launched in 2003 in the context of the 'Lisbon Agenda' (2000).[216]

The Open Method of Coordination is often seen as a way to overcome legislative deadlocks in sensitive policy areas such as health care.[217] However, the reality is that there is currently no indication that the OMC has been able to overcome what Scharpf has called the 'constitutional asymmetry' of the EU's involvement in health-care policy.[218] Scharpf proposes that the institutional and legal constraints at EU level that create 'market-correcting policies' favour economic liberal interests and policies, which in turn constrain Member States to pursue welfare goals at national level. Another constraint to EU-level policy which Scharpf points out is the immense diversity of social systems.[219] In order to overcome this limitation, which came to the fore particularly when the European Commission proposed making health care subject to the Services Directive,[220] the Commission set up another 'soft policy' mode through the High Level Group on Health Services and Medical Care. Over the first years of the new millennium, this high-level group worked mostly on exchanging information on how health-care systems across Member States, and also discussed and exchanged information on complex policy issues. Although currently some of these working groups still reside at Commission level, the main participants in the High Level Group have been moved to the Council, where they have been subsumed under the governance mechanism of

'Experimental Governance: The Open Method of Coordination' (2006) *European Law Journal* 12 (4) 486–502 at p. 491.

[215] See C. Sabel and J. Zeitlin 'Learning from Difference: The New Architecture of Experimentalist Governance in the EU' (2008) *European Law Journal* 14 (3) 271–327 at p. 276 (analysing new governance forms, such as the open method of coordination in occupational health and safety, as an architecture that allows for 'experimentation' with regulation processes and implementation of policy through mutual learning and adaptation, as a matter of authority rather than coercion).

[216] See A. de Ruijter and T. K. Hervey 'Healthcare and the Lisbon Agenda' in P. Copeland and D. Papadimitriou (eds) *The EU's Lisbon Strategy: Evaluating Succes, Understanding Failure* (New York: Palgrave MacMillan, 2012). Also see Opinion of the Social Protection Committee on the Commission's Communication on 'Modernising social protection for the development of high-quality, accessible and sustainable health care and long-term care: support for the national strategies using the open method of coordination', endorsement (12410/04).

[217] T. K. Hervey and L. Trubek 'Freedom to Provide Health Care Services Within the EU: An opportUnity for a Transformative Directive' (2007) *Columbia Journal of European Law* 13 (3) 623–49.

[218] de Ruijter and Hervey (2012) supra note 216. See F. Scharpf 'The Asymmetry of European Integration, or Why the EU Cannot be a "Social Market Economy"' (2009) *KFG Working Paper Series* 6.

[219] See F. Scharpf 'The European Social Model: Coping with Challenges of Diversity' (2002) *Journal of Common Market Studies* 40 (4) 645–70 at p. 645:

> European integration has created a constitutional asymmetry between policies promoting market efficiencies and policies promoting social protection and equality. National welfare states are legally and economically constrained by European rules of integration [...] whereas efforts to adopt European social policies are politically impeded by the diversity of national welfare states, differing not only in levels of economic development and hence their ability to pay for social transfers and services but, even more significantly, in their normative aspirations and institutional structures.

[220] Directive 2006/123/EC of the European Parliament and of the Council of 12 December 2006 on services in the internal market (OJ L 376/36).

the 2007 Health Strategy. This Strategy aims to bundle European health policies under one coordinating mechanism, that also 'borrows' from some of the principal methods of the OMC in order to implement and mainstream health-care policy in adjacent European public policy.[221]

4.1.5 Pressures and constraints for EU health-care policy

The involvement of the EU in health-care policy takes place between reciprocal pressures and constraints. On one hand there is limited legislative competence to create health-care policy, and there have been numerous attempts by Member States to limit both the EU's inroads into the organization of their health-care systems and the creation of rules regarding European-level health-care entitlements. A further constraint is created by the vast differences between health-care systems and cultural differences in terms of the level and quality of care and the nature of medical services provided in each Member State. On the other hand, pressures for more EU involvement in health-care policy have come from patients seeking access to cross-border health care through the CJEU. Pressures also result not only from European internal market policies in the area of public procurement and competition law, but also from the mutual recognition of the qualifications of medical personnel. A future pressure that can be expected comes from the EU's increasing role in managing national budgets, which has occurred due to the financial crisis. It is very possible that in the EU review of national budgets, cuts and priorities based on EU-level health-care priorities may enter into the debate on what entitlements exist under the national health-care systems.

However, the pressures and constraints also stand in reciprocal relation. As the soft policy mechanisms such as the OMC in the area of health-care policy show, Member States often seek each other out to discuss policy options at the European level, even in areas constrained by a lack of legislative competence. These softer mechanisms may tie into harder regulation and take place in response to outside pressures. A notable example in this regard is the High Level Group for Medical Services and Health Care, launched under Commission auspices as a response to the Court cases in the area of health care. This mechanism for Member State cooperation is was subsumed under the 2008–13 Health Strategy, and created part of a new institutional pathway for creating EU health-care policy.

4.2 Overlapping EU public health and health-care policy

The discussion of EU health policy so far seems to provide for a neat public-health-versus-health-care policy divide. Whereas the EU has some legislative competence for public health, there is no legislative competence with respect to health-care policy. However, in more than one way, the divide between the involvement of the EU in public health policy and individual health is not as clear-cut as it might seem. An important example in this respect is occupational health, which on one hand has the objective of protecting the public and workers from work-related health hazards, while on the other may create individual health-care entitlements to particular treatments.[222]

[221] Together for Health: A Strategic Approach for the EU 2008-2013 (COM (2007) 630); T. K. Hervey 'The European Union and the Governance of Health Care' in G. de Búrca and C. Scott (eds) *New Governance and Constitutionalism in the EU and the US* (Oxford: Hart, 2006).

[222] Seefor example Communication from the Commission to the European Parliament, the Council, the European Economic and Social Committee and the Committee of Regions, Improving

The EU has a long history of involvement in occupational health. In the ECSC (1951), studies were commissioned on the health and safety of steel workers' and miners' diseases. Similarly, in Chapter 3 of the Euratom Treaty the protection of workers' health from the danger of ionizing radiation was addressed.[223] Over the years, these initial research programmes led to the current action programme at the European Union level, which is backed up by a number of (framework) directives.[224] The EU in this respect has been called the 'cradle of occupational health', in that its regulation of the field in many ways has gone beyond what Member States would have been able to achieve.[225]

Research, another grey area as to the functional divide, is important for both public health and health-care policy. The EU provides funding for a large volume of research on public health issues and individual health. Moreover, it creates the baseline for how this research should be conducted through the Clinical Trials Directive.[226] European concern for ethical issues involved in medical research on human subjects ties in with European history and more specifically the Nuremberg Code of 1949.[227] Another relevant part of the background context here is the development of a single European Research Area in health. The activities for this policy objective take place for instance by funding European medical research by the DG for Research. These policy activities have been taking place since the eighties and have led to the establishment of several programmes and committees in the area of clinical research. An important advisory body in this respect has been the Group of Advisors on the Ethical Implications of Biotechnology.[228] This Group has contributed to setting up guidelines of which type of research would receive funding and which would not.[229]

These types of coordination measures have the potential to create commonly agreed European values underpinning health policy in the area of clinical research; for instance, Article 3 CFREU specifically prohibits eugenics and cloning.[230] The scope of

quality and productivity at work: Community strategy 2007–2012 on health and safety at work (COM(2007) 62 final).

[223] Article 30 Euratom Treaty.

[224] Some versions here are amended; see for example Council Directive 89/391/EEC of 12 June 1989 on the introduction of measures to encourage improvements in the safety and health of workers at work (OJ L 183, 29-06-1989, p. 1); Directive 99/92/EC—risks from explosive atmospheres of 16 December 1999 on the minimum requirements for improving the safety and health protection of workers potentially at risk from explosive atmospheres (15th individual Directive within the meaning of Article 16(1) of Directive 89/391/EEC) (OJ L 23, 28-01-2000, p. 57); Directive 89/656/EEC—use of personal protective equipment of 30 November 1989 on the minimum health and safety requirements for the use by workers of personal protective equipment at the workplace (third individual directive within the meaning of Article 16 (1) of Directive 89/391/EEC) (OJ L 393, 30-12-1989, p. 1); Regulation (EC) No 596/2009 of the European Parliament and of the Council of 18 June 2009 (O.J. L 188, 18-07-2009).

[225] Majone (1993) supra note 44; Gagliardi et al. (2012) supra note 72.

[226] Directive 2001/20/EC of the European Parliament and of the Council of 4 April 2001 on the approximation of the laws, regulations and administrative provisions of the Member States relating to the implementation of good clinical practice in the conduct of clinical trials on medicinal products for human use (OJ L 121/34, 01-05-2001).

[227] See for example J. K. M. Gevers 'Medical Research and the Law: A European Perspective' (1995) *European Journal of Health Law* 2; also see ibid.

[228] See M. W. Bauer and G. Gaskell *Biotechnology: The Making of a Global Controversy* (Cambridge: Cambridge University Press, 2002) at p. 136.

[229] See for instance Hervey and McHale (2004) supra note 23 at p. 247, and see Council Decision 2002/834/EC of 30 September 2002 adopting a specific programme for research, technological development and demonstration: 'Integrating and strengthening the European Research Area' (2002-2006) (OJ L294/1, 29-10-2002), specifically outlining that medical research on human cloning would not be funded and eugenics and therapeutic cloning would not be allowed.

[230] Hervey and McHale (2004) supra note 23 at p. 247.

the Directive is limited in that it only covers trials of medical products in the sense of Directive 65/65/EEC:

> [A]ny substance or combination of substances presented for preventing disease in human beings or animals [and] any substance [...] which may be administered to human beings or animals with a view to making a medical diagnosis or restoring, correcting or modifying functions in human beings or in animals.

However, in Article 3(7) of the Clinical Trials Directive some advanced medical therapies are exempted from the application of the Clinical Trials Directive under the 'hospital exemption'.[231] This means that at this point a group of cutting-edge areas in clinical research, such as psychological research and medical devices or embryo research, fall outside the scope of the Directive. However, in the area of clinical trials for the authorization of pharmaceuticals, very precise guidelines are published by the EMA.[232] With respect to medical devices, European standards and guidelines are made by European standards organizations such as the CEN (European Committee of Standardization) and CENELEC (European Committee of Electronic Standardization).[233]

4.2.1 *Divides in EU health policy*

Although in functional terms EU public health and health-care policy may have overlaps, in terms of objectives the two policy areas are still generally distinguishable as separate, yet connected. Looking more closely, however, there is another aspect that muddles any clear divide within European health policy. This relates to those EU activities that impact the redistribution of health as a welfare entitlement in the Member States. Access to individual health care is a matter of complex and expensive public welfare distributions, which is arguably the reason that the EU's role remains limited, whereas a large portion of European public health policy has often been a matter of centralizing institutional arrangements through regulation. However, the divide between European public health policy and European health-care policy is not as simple as the former being regulatory and not redistributive and the latter being redistributive in nature.

For example, with respect to vaccinations policies, which are fairly standard *public health* provisions, the EU has no powers, at least not with respect to their procurement, given that vaccination policy is costly and subject to planning and distribution. Moreover, it is a welfare entitlement that is laden with cultural beliefs about what is good policy and what is not.[234] So the case is rather that redistribution takes place

[231] Directive 2001/20/EC (2001) supra note 226; see further J. P. Griffin et al. (eds) *The Textbook of Pharmaceutical Medicine, 7th Edition* (London: Wiley Blackwell, 2013) at p. 488.

[232] The EMA inspects the harmonization and coordination of good clinical practice activity at EU level. This is mainly done through the work of an Inspectors Working Group. This group prepares guidance on good clinical practice. See European Medicines Agency, Mandate, Objectives and Rules of Procedure for the GCP inspectors Working Group, London, 27 July 2007 (EMEA/INS/GCP/239486/2007); also see Communication from the Commission, Information from European Union Institutions, Bodies, Offices and Agencies—Detailed guidance on the request to the competent authorities for authorisation of a clinical trial on a medicinal product for human use, the notification of substantial amendments and the declaration of the end of the trial (CT-1) (2010/C 82/01).

[233] CEN/CELENEC draws up European standards and guidelines. Moreover, CEN/CELENEC has to ensure that national standards institutes of the EU transpose the European Standards into their national framework as national standards or refrain from introducing any diverging national standards; see European Commission, CEN, CENELEC, and the European Free Trade Association, General Guidelines for Cooperation, 28 March 2006.

[234] G. A. Poland 'The 2009–2010 Influenza Pandemic: Effects on Pandemic and Seasonal Vaccine Uptake and Lessons Learned for Seasonal Vaccination Campaigns' (2010) *Vaccine* 28 (4) D3–D13.

within both EU public health policy, for instance through financing particular public health programmes, and through European health-care policy, for instance through redistribution of entitlements by creating access to health care across borders.

5. EU Power in Health Law and Policy

The objective for this chapter has been to describe the power of the EU in public health and health care. The reference to Article 168 TFEU seemed to suggest that EU health policy could be conceptualized as either being in all EU public policy or as being completely non-existent. However, taking a European Union conceptualization of 'health' as a central feature, EU power in the field of human health can be seen as authoritative allocations of value through the European Union political system with the object of protecting and promoting human health. This conceptualization draws out the scope of policy that will be the central focus for the following chapters.

Important in this respect is that, as a consequence of the relatively wide scope of the concept, in order to discern EU health policy one needs to look beyond the formal legal structure and EU competences and take into account that what goes on below the surface of EU formal policymaking in health is that it encompasses separate yet overlapping policy areas of public health and health care: *EU public health policy* has the objective of managing collective health risks and preventing major disease scourges. Law, as an instrument in this field of health policy, is usually public law, in that it regulates the relations between holders of public authority and citizens. The objectives of *EU health-care policy* relate to the provision of medical care and individual health, including creating universal access to health care, which means regulating the medical field in general, allowing access to medicinal products, health-care professionals, and health insurance. Here the addressees are primarily private individuals. In health-care policy generally, the legal relations are predominantly arranged in contractual agreements: between hospitals and doctors, between doctors and patients, between insurance institutions and hospitals, and so on. Importantly, however, these legal relationships change when a health-care system is more centrally organized through the government.

Tracing the involvement of the EU in both health-care and public health policy outlines that there were different pressures and constraints that created the involvement of the EU. With respect to public health policy, the involvement of the EU in public health is the result of continuous reconciliations. The Member States have tried to curb the role of the EU in this area but have also sought each other out to respond to public health crises at EU level, and EU public health policy has expanded continuously as a market-making instrument. At the same time, over the course of the evolution of European public health policy European alliances have been forged to respond to and come up with policy solutions for major diseases such as cancer and HIV/AIDS. This led to the development of public health programmes, where the EU is able to show its 'social face' by distributing funds to particular public health objectives.

In EU health-care policy, the major pressures for policymaking are the result of patients seeking access to cross-border health care through the CJEU. Pressures also result from European internal market policies in the area of public procurement and competition law, and from the mutual recognition of medical qualifications. At the same time, the further development of European health-care policy is constrained by limited legislative competence, the insistence of Member States on limiting the inroads of the EU into the organization of their health-care systems, and the creation of rules regarding European-level health-care entitlements. A further constraint is created by the vast differences between Member States' health-care systems, and cultural differences in terms of the level and quality of care and the nature of medical services provided in each Member State.

Although EU public health and health-care policy may be seen as two differentiated policy areas within EU health policy, they are also intrinsically connected and overlapping in a number of ways. Moreover, in both policy areas the role of the EU becomes most controversial when its involvement could affect possible welfare redistributions of the Member States. Yet in both policy areas redistribution at the European level does take place, for instance through financing particular public health programmes, or by creating access to health care across borders.

Hence the conceptualization of EU health policy as developed in this chapter allows for its identification, even when this policy is promulgated in other policy contexts. The question then is not whether a particular EU public policy has as its main objective the protection or improvement of health, given that health concerns generally permeate all aspects of our life when they affect us personally, and similarly infuse all public policy. Health concerns that are addressed as part of another policy are in themselves no reason to maintain that this not a distinguishable policy objective, for the following reason. Health policy affects an aspect in our life that comes before many, if not most other things that we care about, which is why a number of fundamental rights are recognized at EU level that have particular importance for health and the way health policy is pursued.

4

Institutional Build-up of EU Health Actors

> Making a list of all health committees and groups that exist is a completely impossible task. Half of them are sleeping but have never really been abandoned. Often it is impossible to find what the legal basis has been, [...] and a committee never really shuts down, but they may not meet for two or three years.[1]

The growth of substantive EU public health and individual health policy and law is matched by a historic build-up of EU institutional actors.[2] The institutional expansion has increased the EU's capacity for law- and policy-making in the field of health and as such the possibility for the growth of EU power in this area. The current chapter traces the evolution and growing presence of EU institutional actors in human health. First, the relevance of the growing institutional capacity for creating EU health law and policy is described. Second, a sketch of the emergence of the EU institutional involvement in health policy is outlined—while taking into consideration the advice of the Member State representative cited above that it may not be possible to create an exhaustive overview of all health actors involved at the EU level.

1. Expanding EU Institutional Power

In describing institutional developments and the growth of EU institutional health actors, the EU 'legal' institutions as these are outlined in the Treaty on European Union form the baseline in this chapter for defining the actors and the rules by which these actors have to behave.[3] The Treaty in this respect creates the basis for rules regarding the attribution as to who is to be included in the institution; what the competences of the institution are; and what instrument can be used to reach the particular aims, including what sanctions can be imposed by the institution.[4] The development of specific institutional actors signifies that there is a collective capacity for creating health policy and law. This means that there is the possibility for facilitating policy change and the possibility of sanctions or action that can be taken to enforce policies and laws. Another manner of describing this development is through the theoretical frame of 'Europeanization' which in this particular instance would refer to

> the emergence and development at the European level of distinct structures of governance, that is, of political, legal, and social institutions associated with the problem-solving that formalize

[1] Respondent 4 (MS Representative Working Party on Public Health in the Council, 2010).

[2] Parts of this chapter form the basis of and are published in a previous publication A. de Ruijter 'Mapping the Institutional Consolidation of EU Human Health Expertise' (2017) *Comparative European Politics* 15 370 (which traces the increasing development of expertise within the EU institutions with regard to human health).

[3] A. Heritier *Explaining Institutional Change in Europe* (Oxford: Oxford University Press, 2007) 7.

[4] Ibid. 8.

EU Health Law & Policy: The Expansion of EU Power in Public Health and Health Care. Anniek de Ruijter © Anniek de Ruijter 2019. Published in 2019 by Oxford University Press.

interactions among the actors, and of policy networks specializing in the creation of authoritative European rules.[5]

In this regard, without delving into the different explanation on the driving forces that are behind increased EU institutionalization and the build-up of policy- and law-making capacity, what is important to note is that authority and the power of these institutional actors is not only expressed in the ability to coerce or use sanctions or force. Börzel has outlined that the exercising of authority at EU level through its institutions is also possible in the shadow of hierarchy and without the use of formal compliance mechanisms: 'the supranational institutions of the EU Treaty provide ample possibility for hierarchical co-ordination. Supranational centralization reigns where supranational actors have the power to make legally binding decisions without requiring the consent of the member states.'[6] Hence, centralization of institutional capacity and the rules under which institutions organize cooperation and deliberation on policies matter a great deal with respect to illustrating an increased power of the EU to impact health law and policies in the Member States, even if substantive formal competence for creating legislation is still limited.

The structure of the chapter in describing this institutional expansion now follows the 'ordinary' legislative path through the institutions on the basis of Article 294 TFEU. It starts with the EU's executive body, the European Commission, followed by the European Parliament. Next, the chapter turns to health actors in the setting of the Council, representing the Member States. Lastly, the chapter concentrates on the actors that are especially important in the implementation phase, such as the comitology committees and EU agencies.[7]

2. Health Policy in the European Commission

At its inception the European Commission was designed as an 'administrative' technocratic body of experts, rather than a 'political' executive institution.[8] The Commission had to ensure that the interests of the Community were represented and at the same time initiate legislative proposals. The exclusive right to initiate legislative proposals,[9] in exception to its initial 'administrative nature', from the very beginning also gave the Commission a political tool for keeping the process of European integration in motion.[10] At the same time, the Commission not only initiates legislation and policy, but also oversees their implementation.[11] The Commission is composed of a college of Commissioners, each being responsible for a particular policy sector. At the same time, it has bureaucratic services comparable to national ministries, organized in Directorates-General, each addressing particular EU policies. More recently, the

[5] M. Green Cowles, J. A. Caporaso, and T. Risse-Kappen *Transforming Europe: Europeanization and Domestic Change* (Ithaca, NY: Cornell University Press 2001) 3. Also see J. A. Caporaso and J. Wittenbrinck 'The New Modes of Governance and Political Authority in Europe' (2006) *Journal of European Public Policy* 13 471.

[6] T. Börzel 'European Governance: Negotiation and Competition in the Shadow of Hierarchy' (2010) *Journal of Common Market Studies* 48 191, 198.

[7] Although these actors are also important in the phase when legislation is drafted or proposed by the Commission.

[8] See D. M. Curtin *Executive Power of the European Union: Law, Practices and the Living Constitution* (Oxford: Oxford University Press, 2009) at p. 63 et seq.

[9] Article 17 (2) TEU.

[10] See Curtin (2009) supra note 8.

[11] Article 17 (1) TEU.

Commission has been described as a more-or-less 'normalized executive' of the EU, with an increasingly important political autonomy and function, including with respect to politically sensitive and new EU policy sectors.[12] This changing role of the Commission can be illustrated by its role in brokering cooperation and legislation in health, a particularly sensitive policy area, as the case studies in the following chapters will show.

2.1 The early days

Historically, health was dispersed across different Commission services and commissioners. Over time, however, the Commission services became increasingly specialized with respect to health. Sometimes this was the consequence of pragmatic considerations, and sometimes a result of crisis (political or health crises). In the early days, the 'High Authority', the administrative executive institution in the ECSC, dealt with all sectors of policy activity. However, soon its members began to specialize and by the end of 1953 there were six Working Parties, including one on Social Problems.[13] Health aspects of these social problems were the working conditions in the coal and steel industries that led to occupational health hazards, such as black lungs and explosions in mines.

In order to perform administrative tasks, the High Authority instituted services or 'divisions'. One of these was the Division on Work-Related Problems.[14] This division had a sub-unit on social security and another on security and hygiene at work.[15] In 1960 these divisions were streamlined into Directorates-General. The 'Division on Work-Related Problems' became a Directorate-General, which contained two Directorates instead of the six sub-units it held previously: the Directorate for Preparation and Study and the Directorate on Operational Tasks.[16] The issue of occupational health and social security was initially divided between these directorates. However, three years later in 1963, a third Directorate was added, the Directorate on Safety and Occupational Health, which may arguably have been because specialized knowledge was needed to address occupational health issues.[17]

2.1.1 Euratom 1958: occupational public health

With the adoption of the Euratom Treaty in 1958 the Euratom Commission immediately established the Directorate-General on Health Protection, which drafted policy for the protection of health in the context of radioactive health risks, prescribed by part III of the Euratom Treaty.[18] In 1959, an expert Scientific and Technical Committee

[12] Curtin (2009) supra note 8 at p. 98.

[13] Rules of procedures and general organizational rules, 5 November 1954 (OJ 21 24-11-1954, pp. 515–17).

[14] *Division Problèmes du Travail.*

[15] Remuneration and social security and safety and health at work, see Rules of Procedure (1954) supra note 13. This structure was created by the High Authority at its meeting on 1 October 1952 and presented by the High Authority at the General Assembly meeting of 6 January 1953, Exposé sur la situation de la Communauté, January 1953 at p. 14.

[16] On the reorganization of the administration of the High Authority on 20 April 1960, see the Rules of Procedures (OJ 03-05-1960).

[17] *Sécurité et médecine du travail,* see Rapport général sur les activités de la Communauté (La structure interne des sept directions générales elle-même a été adoptée le 1er juillet) CECA: Luxembourg, 1960, point 1; (the 'secteur principal' becomes 'division').

[18] See De Commissie van de Europese Gemeenschap voor Atoomenergie, Eerste Algemeen Verslag over de werkzaamheden van de gemeenschap (January 1958–September 1958) at pp. 8 and 30.

advised on the adoption of the first Euratom directives, with the aim of protecting workers and the general public from health threats that could arise from ionizing radiation.[19] However, the Euratom Commission and the High Authority of the ECSC also worked together on aspects such as 'industrial medicine' that dealt with the training and status of medical officers in the workplace.[20]

2.1.2 *EEC Treaty 1958: free movement of workers*

With the adoption of the EEC Treaty in 1958, the EEC Commission established a Working Group on Social Affairs that was manned by two commissioners, comparable to the first Working Parties of the ECSC Commission. In terms of administrative services there was Directorate V on Social Affairs, which had four directorates. Two of these directorates worked on health issues and also on social security and social services.[21] The EEC at the time focused on the removal of limitations to the freedom of movement of workers and the reduction of waiting time for authorization of free movement for workers for reasons of public health.[22] However, in other EEC Commission services health became topical in the context of the free movement of goods. With respect to pharmaceuticals for instance, a first proposal was submitted to the Council in 1962.[23] At the same time, in the area of agriculture, additives in food and hygiene and safety of food production were also considered.[24]

The Commissions and the High Authority of the three communities also deliberated on health issues that affected all three communities.[25] The nature of the communities' executives' work was mainly focused on research and bringing together expertise.[26]

[19] Directives laying down the basic standards for the protection of the health of workers and the general public against the dangers arising from ionizing radiation (OJ 221/59, 20-02-1959).

[20] Nowadays 'industrial health' would probably fall under the term 'occupational health'. See Bulletin of the European Economic Community, Brussels, December, Third Year (no 10, 1960) at p. 43.

[21] First General Report on the Activities of the Community (January 1, 1958–September 17, 1958) at p. 17.

[22] See ibid. p. 79 PV 39; also see Communication from Giuseppe Petrilli, 24 November 1958 (COM (58) 257).

[23] See Draft Council Directive on the harmonization of laws and regulation governing pharmaceutical products, proposal submitted to the Council by the Commission on 5 November 1962 in Supplement to Bulletin of the European Economic Community (No. 12, 1962) at p. 2.

[24] See Voorstel van de Commissie aan de Raad ingediend op 23 Juni 1962 Ontwerp richtlijn van de Raad tot regeling van sanitaire vraagstukken op het gebied van handelsverkeer in vers vlees binnen de gemeenschap, Supplement van het Bulletin van de Europese Economische Gemeenschap (No. 11, 1962) at p. 3; and see Proposal submitted by the Commission to the Council on 15 February 1963 for a Council Directive relating to the approximation of the laws of Member States concerning preservatives which may be used in foods, Supplement to Bulletin of the European Economic Community (No. 4, 1963) at p. 1.

[25] See Proposal Council Directive Preservatives in Food (1963) at p. 30; also see EEC Bulletin February 1961 no. 2, Fourth Year, Brussels (1958) at p. 4; also see First General Report on the Activities of the Community (1 January 1958–17 September 1958) at p. 30; p. 91 (In the area of occupational health, the Communities wanted to create a uniform detailed list on occupational diseases to allow Member States to report on these diseases. In order to do so, the Commission of the EEC called in February 1960 summoned a group of experts on lead poisoning, occupational cancer, and rheumatism and arthritic conditions to provide information on the legislative and administrative ways in which these diseases were dealt with in the Member States at that time. The idea of the Commission was to harmonize this list across the community members).

[26] See Hoge Authoriteit, 15 de Algemeen verslag van de EGKS (1967) paras 493, 495, and 505; and see Commissie van de Europese Gemeenschappen Het Eerste Algemeen Verslag over de werkzaamheden van de Gemeenschappen in 1967 (E.G. Pub. bl. 1/68) at p. 287 (in the area of research, there were research streams adopted for a five-year programme called 'Physiopathology and clinics' which was mostly directed towards chronic emphysema and bronchitis, but also covered trauma

For instance, in the area of industrial hygiene, medicine, and safety the Commissions would work on studies regarding hygiene in enterprises and the social and economic aspects of occupational health.[27] These studies were done in collaboration with specialized European and international agencies such as the ILO.[28]

2.2 Fragmentation of health policy in the Commission

As far as the Commission *services* are concerned, in the seventies health policy in the context of Euratom was part of DG XV on Energy and Safety. In DG V Social Affairs, access to health benefits was regulated, and DG VI Agriculture addressed public health considerations.[29] In 1973 the internal structure of the Commission services was reconfigured, but the health policy actors remained fragmented and divided over multiple services, such as a DG V on Social Affairs, DG VI for Agriculture, DG XI for the Internal Market, and DG XII for Research. However, health policy was also addressed in the 'Service for living environment and consumer interests', which was not a full DG but had developed from an expansion of the former DG III on Industry, Technology, and Sciences which addressed human environmental issues, and of the administrative unit which dealt with consumer interests at DG IV.[30]

2.2.1 1967 Merger Treaty: health in the CAP

Over the course of the sixties, as the European agricultural policy agenda increased, public health considerations in the area of food and hygiene grew as well. By the time the communities and services merged in 1967, health policy had become fragmented among Commission services.[31] The Commission from 1967 to 1970 had fourteen Commissioners, but no special Commissioner on health. From the seventies to the end of the nineties, health was for the most part included in the portfolio of the Commissioner on consumer protection or environment. It was not until the 1999

and revalidation); see 15de Algemeen verslag EGKS nr. 495; also see the series Hoge Authoriteit EGKS, Reeks arbeidshygiëne en arbeidsgeneeskunde nr. 5, Symposium Bronchitis-Emfyseem (Stresa, 21–22 april 1966) Luxembourg; see further Hoge Authoriteit (1967) at p. 289.

[27] There was a Permanent Committee for the health and safety of coal mines, which was to exchange research findings and advise the Commission on legislation. It would research accidents in mines and had working groups on emergencies and mine fires. There was also an expansion of the responsibilities of the permanent committee for health promotion, which had a special working group on health in coal mines. In the area of Euratom studies were also carried out on radiation therapies and the role of radiation for cancer development and therapies. There was a monthly bulletin on the documentation and studies on the protection of health. For the start of this programme, see Negende Verslag Hoge authoriteit van de Europese Gemeenschap voor Kolen en Staal over de werkzaamheden van de gemeenschap (1 februari 1960–31 januari 1961) at p. 396.

[28] See Bulletin of the European Economic Community (Third Year) No. 3, 1960 (Brussels, March–April) at pages 40–1, and see further the follow-up of this activity in the Bulletin of the European Economic Community 10 (1960) at p. 3.

[29] See Vierde algemeen verslag over de werkzaamheden van de gemeenschappen 1970 (Februari 1971) at p. 413.

[30] See Zevende Algemeen verslag over de werkzaamheden van de Europeesche gemeenschappen in 1973 Februari 1974 at p. 67 and p. 534 et seq.

[31] For instance, there was a coordination of national labour inspection services for occupational health, whereby legislation was being prepared for harmonization of national measures in the field. In the context of the ECSC there had been coordination and exchange regarding the dust in coal mines; in the steel industry there was also policy for the prevention of inhalation of particulate gases in the steel factories. There was a special commission for the safety of steel, which had seven working groups; see supra note 26, Commissie van de Europese Gemeenschappen (1967).

Prodi Commission that the first Commissioner for Health and Consumers, David Byrne from Ireland, was appointed.[32] Since then there has always been a commissioner either for health and consumers, or—as a result of political pragmatism—an individual commissioner for consumers and one for health.[33]

2.3 DG SANTE: the EU department for health

Currently health policy largely resides with DG SANTE (health and food safety 'DG Health'), previously DG SANCO. DG SANTE is a relatively young DG, constituted in 1997 as DG XXIV (at the time Consumer Policy and Consumer Health).[34] An important impetus for its inception was the BSE crisis under the Santer Commission in the 1990s. In 1996, the UK government admitted that the consumption of beef that was infected with bovine spongiform encephalopathy (BSE) could lead to a condition damaging to the human brain called Creutzfeldt–Jakob disease.[35] The Medina Report of the temporary committee of the European Parliament, set up to investigate the role of the European institutions in the BSE affair,[36] severely criticized the EU system for public health safety. These criticisms especially concerned the fact that there was no independent public health agency or institution responsible for the public health implications of the European internal market, and that there was no institutional framework in place to ensure that scientific risk assessment would take place independently of market (management) considerations.

In response to this report, the President of the Commission, Jacques Santer, outlined a reform of the Commission services, especially with respect to the system of scientific consultation and the organization of public health actors (such as the Food and

[32] In the 1977–81 Jenkins Commission, Richard Burke from Ireland held the health portfolio, and was the Commissioner for Consumer Affairs; in the 1981–5 Thorn Commission Karl-Heinz Narjes from West Germany was responsible for health, and was also the Consumer Affairs Commissioner. Under the 1985–8 Delors Commission I, Stanley Clinton Davis (UK), as part of his responsibilities for the environment, and Grigoris Varfis from Greece as part of Consumer Protection; Delors Commission I 1989–92, Karel Van Miert from Belgium (as part of Consumers) and Christiane Scrivener from France (Consumers and Trade) for the Delors Commission II 1992–4. In the Santer Commission 1995–9, Emma Bonino (Italy) held the portfolio in the context of Consumer Policy and fisheries. In 1997 her portfolio was specifically widened to include health protection and food safety.

[33] Markos Kyprianou (Cyprus) 2004–8 and from 2008–10 Androulla Vasiliou for the Barroso Commission I (Health only), and in double function, the appointment of Meglena Kuneva (Bulgaria) 2007–10 for the Barroso Commission I (consumer protection only); John Dalli for Malta, 2010 onwards, Barroso Commission II, who resigned due to his possible role in taking bribes from the tobacco industry trying to influence a new proposal for a Tobacco Products Directive, see European Commission, Press statement on behalf of the European Commission—MEMO/12/788 (16-10-2012); the current outgoing Commissioner for Health is Tonio Borg.

[34] See DG XXIV annual report 1997, available at <http://aei.pitt.edu/85932/1/1998_Annual_Report.pdf> (last visited 9 November 2018).

[35] See ibid.; further see S. Krapohl 'Risk Regulation in the EU Between Interests and Expertise: The Case of BSE'(2003) *Journal of European Public Policy* 10 (2) 189–207; E. Vos 'EU Food Safety Regulation in the Aftermath of the BSE Crisis' (2000) *Journal of Consumer Policy* 23 227–55; G. R. Chambers 'The BSE Crisis and the European Parliament' in C. Joerges and E. Vos (eds) *EU Committees: Social Regulation, Law and Politics* (Oxford: Hart, 1999).

[36] Report of the Temporary Committee of Inquiry into BSE set up by the Parliament in July 1996 on the alleged contraventions or maladministration in the implementation of Community law in relation to BSE without prejudice to the jurisdiction of the Community and the national courts of 7 February 1997 (A4-0020/97/A, PE 220.544/fin/A).

Veterinary Office).[37] At the same time however, the Commission blamed the Member States:

> [D]id the Commission put market before public health? [. . .] I would add in this connection that a number of Commission proposals designed to strengthen the health pillar of the single market were not adopted. The Member States rejected them.[38]

It was one of the first times in EU history that the effect of the single market on health was emphasized so explicitly. As a result, DG SANTE was to take on a more central role in health policy, since 'the time has come to put health to the fore in Europe'.[39]

In its current organizational structure there is an internal divide within DG SANTE between the Directorates that work on public health issues and those working on health-care issues.[40] Moreover, most of the activities of DG SANTE are now singularly health-policy related, as much of its legislative activity in the area of consumer law has moved to DG Justice and Home Affairs and DG MARKT (Directorate-General for the internal market and services); and pharmaceuticals and medical devices were moved from DG Enterprise to DG SANTE. When the newly appointed Juncker Commission outlined the new portfolios of Commissioners, Juncker tried to move the pharmaceutical, medical devices, and health technology units back to DG Enterprise.[41] This move caused a wave of criticism in the public health community, given that it appeared Juncker was downplaying the primarily public health aspects of the respective industries.[42] Now, following pressure from health groups and the European Parliament, these industries will remain the responsibility of DG SANTE. This does not mean DG SANTE has come to complete stability, as in 2018 rumours did circle that DG SANTE might again become disbursed, including a fragmentation of health policies and law across other Commission services.

2.4 The role of the European Commission in human health

The European Commission plays an entrepreneurial role in European health policy, as it does in other policy areas, in that it initiates legislation and policy. However, what characterizes the growth of the role of the Commission in health is its initial institutional fragmentation towards increasing consolidation and centralization.[43] This

[37] And the scientific committees were to be placed under the authority of the expanded Health and Consumers DG. Thus a new unit specifically involved in the assessment of public health risk assessment was also installed under the new DG.

[38] Speech by Mr Jacques Santer on the Commission Programme for 1997 to the European Parliament, Strasbourg, 22 October 1996 (SPEECH/96/260 22-10-1996).

[39] See ibid.

[40] See Organisational Chart DG SANCO 2014, available at <https://ec.europa.eu/info/sites/info/files/organisation_charts/organisation-chart_dg-rtd_en_0.pdf> (last visited 9 November 2018).

[41] See European Commission Press Release 'The Juncker Commission: A strong and experienced team standing for change' (IP/14/984) 10 September 2014.

[42] See the opinion piece of E. Woodward, secretary general of European Public Health Alliance 'Why Juncker should backtrack and keep pharma policy health portfolio in *EUractiv* 18 September 2014 available at <http://www.euractiv.com/sections/health-consumers/why-juncker-should-backtrack-and-keep-pharma-policy-health-portfolio>.

[43] See Respondent 11 (Representative DG Research) 2010. Besides SANCO, many other Commission services remain involved in health policy as well. For example: DG Environment (chemicals, pesticides, soil, air, water pollution, biodiversity, nature reserves); DG Employment and Social Affairs (health and safety at work, combating discrimination and poverty, maternity and parental leave); DG Internal market (recognition of professional qualifications); DG Competition (approving mergers, e.g. pharmaceutical and medical care companies); DG Development (the EU is the world's largest source of overseas aid, i.e. global health); DG Trade (TRIPS, GATS, access to medicines); DG Research (scientific research on genomics, food safety, causes of diseases, environmental health); DG

goes for DG SANTE itself but also extends to the whole Commission. For instance, through the 'health in all policies approach', which is a policy mechanism used across political systems to address public health issues in a comprehensive manner,[44] the EU Commission has set up an inter-service group on public health. This group works on health across EU policies in the different Commission departments. Over twenty departments are represented in this group, which also addresses subjects such as health systems, health and the environment, and HIV/AIDS in particular sub-groups.[45]

Hence, while other services also address health concerns, the primary tenet is that health has solidified institutionally as a more-or-less autonomous policy within the context of the European Commission—particularly in light of the fact that major aspects of the EU's health policy, such as the regulation of pharmaceuticals and medical devices, food safety, and animal health, have been moved to DG SANTE over the years and the non-health aspects of consumer protection have for the most part been moved to other Commission services. At the same time, DG SANTE is still characterized as a politically 'weak' DG.[46] This is not surprising: 'Health departments are generally the weakest link in government. There is no reason this should be different within a College [of Commissioners].'[47] Despite its political weakness, DG SANTE has become more than an entrepreneur with respect to policy as such, but the DG is also an entrepreneur with regard to policymaking mechanisms. On a number of highly sensitive health policy questions DG SANTE has invented new, informal ways of creating a policy narrative with the Member States outside of formal legislative procedures. A key recent example is the Health Security Committee, where high-level Member State representatives coordinate on public health emergencies.[48] Another example, in the area of health care, is the high-level Group on Health Services and Medical Care that hosts a number of working groups on particularly sensitive aspects of national health-care entitlements and policies.[49] The Commission hence engages a number of policy forums

Transport and Energy (energy generation, rail transport, road safety, passenger screening); DG Tax and Customs (excise duties on tobacco and alcohol); and DG Agriculture (public health effects of agriculture policies).

[44] S. Kahlmeier et al. 'Health in All Policies in Practice: Guidance and Tools to Quantifying the Health Effects of Cycling and Walking' (2010) *Journal of Physical Activity and Health* 7 (1) 120–5 on addressing the benefits of cycling and walking for public health within transport and infrastructure policies.

[45] See http://www.ec.europa.eu/health/health_policies/coordination/index_en.htm.

[46] S. L. Greer *The Politics of European Union Health Policies* (Maidenhead/Philadelphia: Open University Press, 2009) at p. 27.

[47] Respondent 13, High level representative Commission Services, DG SANCO (2010).

[48] Decision No. 1082/2013/EU of the European Parliament and of the Council of 22 October 2013 on serious cross-border threats to health and repealing Decision No. 2119/98/EC (OJ L 293, 15-11-2013).

[49] High Level Group on Health Services and Medical Care—information from the Commission (15190/04, Brussels); European Commission HLG Work of the High Level Group on health services and medical care during 2005 (HLG/2005/16); European Commission HLG Work of the High Level Group in 2006 (HLG/2006/08 FINAL, 2006); European Commission, High level process on Patient Mobility and Healthcare Developments in the EU, Outcome of the reflection process (HLPR/200316, December 2003). With the adoption of the 2007 Health Strategy this process moved to the Council, where a 'new' coordination method was adopted. However, the working group on patient safety, European reference networks, and the working group on health workforce still remain active. The work done here feeds into the Council Working Party on Public Health at Senior Level, which was newly created as part of the EU Health Strategy's 'strategic cooperation' mechanism; see Council Conclusions on a cooperation mechanism between the Council and the Commission for the implementation of the EU Health Strategy 2,876th EPSCO Council meeting (Luxembourg, 10 June 2008).

and experts in numerous working groups, which allows national experts opportunities for promoting their vision on the EU stage.[50] Greer comments in this regard:

> Engagement in the Commission forum on an interesting topic, such as the reduction of obesity, will not just promote good policymaking. It will also attract policy advocates who are more interested in substance than constitutions.[51]

DG SANTE is particularly good at creating these more or less informal cooperation structures for the exchange of policy ideas and approaches. The process of involving national experts and scientific communities is an archetype of EU policymaking, and is particularly salient with regard to health. One may argue that in terms of the quality of policy (scientific footing) this is a welcome role for the EU. At the same time, the EU Commission's involvement in this regard can be seen as controversial, given the possible danger of 'expert knowledge' or 'science' replacing legal, social, or political considerations.[52]

3. Health Policy in the European Parliament

At its inception as the Common Assembly in the 1952 ECSC Treaty, the European Parliament was not meant to exercise legislative powers. It was purely intended as a consultative and supervisory body.[53] Yet as European integration deepened, the role of the European Parliament expanded. After direct elections were called and after subsequent amendments to the Treaty, the Parliament gained important legislative powers[54] and currently has a significant impact on European Union public policy.[55] Historically, different aspects of health policy became divided between a number of European Parliamentary committees. In the following overview of the institutional landscape in the setting of the European Parliament, the main focus lies on the development of the Committee on Environment, Public Health and Food Safety (ENVI Committee), currently the principal committee involved in health policy. However, other actors involved will also be discussed.

[50] See Greer (2009) supra note 46 at p. 25 and see C. Shore *Building Europe: The Cultural Politics of European Integration* (New York: Routledge, 2000).

[51] See Greer (2009) supra note 46 at p. 25.

[52] C. Joerges 'Law, Science and the Management of Risks to Health at the National, European and International Level—Stories on Baby Dummies, Mad Cows and Hormones in Beef' (2001) *Columbia Journal of European Law* 7 (1–19) at pp. 2–3. Joerges poses this controversy as a dilemma:

> [T]o what degree should, could, or does 'expertise' replace legal, political and ethical criteria? Judgments on the social acceptability of risks require a balancing of benefits and costs, which cannot be meaningfully performed without the help of scientific advice. On the other hand, such judgments must also pay due regard to normative, political and ethical considerations. Suffice it here to restate the problem as a dilemma: the 'law' cannot resolve the cognitive dimension of risks; 'science' cannot provide answers to the normative dimensions.

See also M. Weimer 'Risk Regulation, GMOs, and the Challenges to Deliberation in EU Governance: Politicization and Scientification as Co-Producing Trends' in C. Joerges and C. Glinski (eds) *The European Crisis and the Transformation of Transnational Governance* (New York: Hart, 2014); M. Weimer and A. de Ruijter (eds) *Risk Regulation in the EU: The Co-Production of EU Expert and Executive Power* (New York: Hart, 2017).

[53] P. Craig and G. de Búrca *EU Law: Text, Cases and Materials* (Oxford: Oxford University Press, 2008).

[54] Ibid.

[55] S. Hix and B. Hoyland 'Empowerment of the European Parliament' (2013) *Annual Review of Political Science* 16 171–89.

3.1 The early days: health policy across parliamentary committees

In 1953, in the early days of the Common Assembly of the ECSC (the predecessor of the current EP), the Common Assembly set up seven committees. One of these, the Social Affairs Committee, focused mainly on social policy for miners and steelworkers. Occupational health thus was the primary focus.[56] After the 1957 signing of the Treaties of Rome (EEC, Euratom), the new 'Parliamentary Assembly' installed thirteen committees. With regard to health it installed the Committee on Security, Work Hygiene, and Health Protection. This committee was to focus on public health policy, whereas the Social Affairs Committee, which remained in existence, was to focus on social security aspects, such as access to sickness benefits for migrant workers.[57]

In 1962, the Committee on Security, Work Hygiene, and Health Protection was renamed the Committee for the Protection of Health.[58] The renaming was a consequence of the changing role of the health committee that was to take on more general health policy issues, including those that had come up in the context of EEC social policy.[59] Over the course of the sixties this committee expanded its policy domain: in the early part of the decade, the Committee for the Protection of Health principally discussed health and safety related to the work in Euratom and the ECSC.[60] By the end of the decade it had developed to be able to address public health issues in relation to food safety in the context of the Common Agricultural Policy. With respect to social affairs it advised on occupational health alongside the Social Affairs Committee, and it discussed health-care issues in the context of the internal market, for example in relation to pharmaceuticals.[61] In 1967, due to institutional reshuffling in relation to the adoption of the Merger Treaty, the Committee was dissolved and the policy agenda was added to the Committee for Social Affairs, which was renamed the Committee for Social Affairs and Health.[62]

56 EPA Debates—Sitting of 20 March 1958 at p. 48; also see Archive and Documentation Centre (CARDOC) Directorate General for the Presidency *the European Parliament 50 Years Ago*, CARDOC Journals No.2 March (2008) at p. 13; and see D. Preda and D. Pasquinucci (eds) *The Evolution of the EEC/EU Institutions and Policies* (Brussels: Peter Lang, 2010) at p. 205.

57 Commission de la Securité, de hygiene du travail et de la protection sanitaire (Commission Permanente) Resolution (OJ 1 20-04-1958) at p. 5; also see Europees Parlement, resolutie nopens de samenstelling en de bevoegdheden van de commissies nodig voor de goede verloop van de werkzaamheden der vergadering (OJ 4/58 20-04-1958); also see Europees Parlement, Commissie voor de bedrijfsveiligheid, voor de arbeids hygiene en voor de bescherming van de gezondheid, Notulen van de constitutieve vergadering van vrijdag 9 januari 1959 (PE/CSH/PV59-1).

58 Europees Parlement, Zittingdocumenten 1961–1962, Verslag namens de Commissie voor Juridische aangelegenheden, voor het Reglement en Immuniteiten, nopens de benaming van de Commissies van het Europese Parlement, 24 Februari 1961, Document No. 2 at para. 11.

59 Ibid.

60 Europees Parlement, Commissie voor de bescherming van de gezondheid, notulen van de constitutieve vergadering, gehouden op 23 maart 1964, (PE 11.549) at para. 7.

61 It headed, for instance, a resolution of the European Parliament to install a permanent committee to advise the EEC Commission on questions relating to protecting the health of workers; see Europees Parlement, Commissie voor de bescherming van de Gezondheid, Nota betreffende het programma van werkzaamheden van de commissie voor de bescherming van de gezondheid tijdens het dienstjaar september 1964 – juli 1965 (PE12.467 - B). It dealt with directives on dangerous substances, issues relating to occupational health, and in the area of food safety, but also with clean air and air pollution; moreover, the European Parliament then also adopted a resolution regarding regulation for the protection of the health of the population, see Europees Parlement, Commissie voor de bescherming van de gezondheid, Nota inzake het Programma van werkzaamheden van de Commissie voor de bescherming van de gezondheid in het jaar september 1965 – juni 1966 (PE 14462) at p. 9.

62 Europees Parlement, commissie voor de bescherming van de gezondheid, notulen van de vergadering gehouden op dinsdag 7 maart 1967, (PE67-4 - PE17.198) at para. 9; also see Europees Parlement, Notulen van de Vergadering van 2 Februari 1967, Resolutie nopens de samenstelling van commissies van het Europees parlement (EEC OJ 449/67, 17-02-1967).

The first enlargement in 1973, with the United Kingdom, Ireland, and Denmark as new Member States, again led to a reassignment of the policy domains amongst committees. In 1973 the Commission on Public Health and the Environment was constituted. Aspects of occupational health and social security remained the remit of the Commission for Social Affairs and Employment, and the Agriculture Committee dealt with food safety.[63] In 1976 its name was changed in line with its increased focus on individual Europeans under the heading of 'consumer protection', to the Committee on the Environment, Public Health, and Consumer Protection (ENVI Committee).[64]

3.2 The ENVI Committee: expanding power

In 1992 the scope of legislation where co-decision could be used was broadened with the adoption of the Treaty of Maastricht.[65] This expansion of competences especially benefitted the ENVI Committee, as much of the power to co-legislate fell within the scope of its policy domains. Over the course of the nineties the committee became an increasingly powerful negotiating forum for more contentious issues.[66] By the end of that decade, the industry and business lobby around the ENVI Committee increased and in the fifth parliament (1999–2004) 29 per cent of co-decision procedures were negotiated in the ENVI Committee, compared to 18 per cent for the next-busiest co-decision Committee.[67] In 2004, the name and functions of the ENVI Committee changed again, which indicated institutional reconfiguration: consumer protection was excluded and food safety included. This mirrored similar developments in the Commission where, after the BSE crisis, food safety was moved from Directorate-General (DG) Agriculture to DG SANCO (Health and Consumers). Consumer protection moved to the newly constituted Committee on the Internal Market and Consumer Protection (IMCO), whereas the ENVI Committee became more focused on public health.

The ENVI Committee currently has a central role in the areas of both health-care and public health policy. However, the environment is also part of its policy agenda. In the field of the environment, the committee deals with pollution of water and air and waste management among other things. In the area of health, the committee discusses cross-border health care, pharmaceuticals, patients' rights, and health threats related to bioterrorism and public health generally. In the area of public health specifically, the committee also works on food safety such as labelling and veterinary legislation

[63] Minutes of the constituent meeting held on 13 March 1973 (PE/VIII/PV/73-1) (Resolution published in OJ C 19, 12-04-1973); also see Resolution of the European Parliament on the number of Committees of the European Parliament and their membership (OJ C19/14, 12-04-1973), including annex (OJ C19/14, 12-04-1973).

[64] Minutes of the constituent meeting held on 9 March 1976 (OJ C 28, 09-02-1976).

[65] Legislation where the Parliament was needed for its adoption. Treaty on European Union, amended by the Maastricht Treaty (Consolidated version, 1992 OJ C 224, 31-08-1992).

[66] J. Lambert and C. Hoskyns 'How Democratic is the European Parliament?' in C. Hoskyns and M. Newman (eds) *Democratizing the European Union: Issues for the Twenty-first Century* (New Brunswick, NJ: Transaction, 2007) at p. 99.

[67] European Parliament, ENVI Committee, Activity Report of the Committee on the Environment, Public Health and Consumer Policy 1999–2004 Parliament (DT\537810EN.doc) at p. 9:

> The Environment Committee has continued to be the busiest legislative Committee during the 1999–2004 Parliament, being responsible for drawing-up reports on 146 legislative proposals and opinions on 120 others. Most of the Committee's areas of competence entail codecision and the Committee's share of codecision legislation has been 117 proposals out of a total of 403 [. . .] Finally, the Committee has also been responsible for 40 of the 88 proposals ending up in conciliation, 46 % of the total.

as it affects risks to human health and the safety of food production.[68] At this point, the Committee has sixty-four members and thus is one of the largest parliamentary committees.[69]

A particular feature of the ENVI committee is the involvement of its rapporteurs in legislative implementation.[70] Given the technical complexity of some of the legislative issues under consideration in ENVI, there are implementation sessions, where a member of the committee can submit a written question to the Commission on the state of implementation of particular legislation. This needs to be done ten days in advance of the implementation deadline. Then there is a session if there are a number of implementation questions. During a session the Commission is usually represented by someone at staff level who is the head of the infringements unit of the relevant DG. The idea is that rapporteurs who have specialized knowledge remain involved in the implementation of the legislation they adopted.[71]

Although the majority of EU health policy issues are currently addressed in the context of the ENVI Committee, a number of key issues are still taken up in other Committees. The Committee on the Internal Market and Consumer Protection (IMCO) was instituted in 2004 in order to 'raise the profile of the internal market'. This coincided with an emphasis on competitiveness and enlargement in the context of the Lisbon Agenda.[72] However, there have been similar parliamentary committees dealing with the internal market since the early years of the Communities.[73] Its responsibilities lie in coordinating national legislation in the area of the internal market, particularly the free movement of goods, including the harmonization of technical standards, the right of establishment, the freedom to provide services, and the promotion of consumer interests except when this relates to public health.[74] With respect to consumers, the issue of health and food safety is explicitly removed from the responsibility of IMCO (chapter 3 of Rules of Procedures EU Parliament) as this is part of the ENVI Committee's remit. However, especially in relation to health-care policy—which in the EU context is often addressed as a matter of internal market law—IMCO has been able to play an important role.[75]

Another actor in the context of the EP is the Committee on Employment and Social Affairs (EMPL), which addresses issues relating to social security for workers, including professional qualifications and health and safety in the workplace. The EMPL Committee has, in some shape or form, also been around since the early days of the

[68] See European Parliament, 7th Parliamentary term, Rules of Procedure February 2014, Annex VII.

[69] Lambert and Hoskyns (2007) supra note 66.

[70] A 'rapporteur' in the European Parliament is the main Parliamentary member in charge of overseeing a particular legislative proposal and its amendments, see Parliament (2014) supra note 68.

[71] See on the details of this arrangements, ENVI Committee (2004) at p. 11; also see European Parliament (2004) 'European Parliament, Delegations to the Conciliation Committee, Activity Report, 1 May 1999 to 30 April 2004 (5th Parliamentary term) (DV\530227EN.doc, PE 287.644), and see European Parliament resolution on the Commission's 21st and 22nd Annual reports on monitoring the application of Community law (2003 and 2004) (2005/2150(INI)) at para. 3.

[72] European Parliament, Committee on the Internal Market and Consumer Protection, Activity Report (June 2004–May 2009).

[73] Ibid. [74] See Parliament (2014) supra note 68.

[75] A recent example is its role in the exclusion of the health provision from the Services Directive, which would have made the rules of the internal market directly applicable to health services. On 23 May 2007, after it had played a pivotal role in excluding health services from the Services Directive, the European Parliament (IMCO) adopted the Vergnaud report on health services; see European Parliament resolution of 23 May 2007 on the impact and consequences of the exclusion of health services from the Directive on services in the internal market (2006/2275(INI)); also see European Parliament (2009) supra note 72 at p. 40.

ECSC, and has been involved especially in the area of social security.[76] Other committees that have a corollary role are for instance the Committee on Legal Affairs, with regard to pharmaceutical legislation relating to intellectual property law[77] and with regard to ethical questions on new technologies, which may feature with respect to health care.[78]

3.3 The role of the European Parliament

The entry into force of the Lisbon Treaty in 2009 led to the expansion of the number of policy areas where the 'normal legislative' procedure can be followed. Whereas a number of public health issues already became subject to co-decision with the Treaty of Maastricht, and therefore became subject to the power of the European Parliament, many of these issues remained limited to the involvement of the EU in the regulation of public health risks. However, with the amendments of the Treaty of Lisbon, the issue of the coordination of national social security systems (Article 48 TFEU) has also become subject to the ordinary legislative procedure. This has potentially increased the power of the European Parliament not only in strictly regulatory aspects, but by extending this to a potentially distributive aspect of EU health (care) policy. At the same time, Article 48 TFEU is also subject to an 'emergency brake' procedure with respect to qualified voting in the Council of Ministers of the EU, which can be suspended and referred to the European Council if a Member State considers that its social security system is threatened. This procedure significantly limits the powers of the European Parliament on social security coordination vis-à-vis the Council.

All in all, health policy has become a more autonomous and specialized policy field in the European Parliament and even within the ENVI Committee. For instance, in 2002 the ENVI Committee set up the 'Health Working Group', initially to follow the implementation of the EU public health programme.[79] In 2004 this working group was given additional mandate by the coordinators' meeting to discuss any health issues that could not be discussed in the full committee (due to time constraints) and bring issues to the attention of the full committee. The mandate of the Health Working Group was renewed at mid-term and still exists to date.[80] In fact the Health Working Group, albeit an informal configuration, deals with a myriad of health policy issues,

[76] See Hoge Authoriteit, 15 de Algemeen verslag van de EGKS (1967).Interestingly, for the Directive 2011/24/EU of the European Parliament and of the Council of 9 March 2011 on the application of patients' rights in cross-border health care (OJ L88/45, 04-04-2011) the principal reporting committee was the ENVI committee and the secondary advising Committee was IMCO, whereas really this directive is the consequence of social security regulations that historically have been the policy domain of Committee of Social Affairs.

[77] Regulation (EU) No 1257/2012 of the European Parliament and of the Council of 17 December 2012 implementing enhanced cooperation in the area of the creation of unitary patent protection (OJ L361/1, 31-12-2012); as of 2014 the London division of a Unified Patent Court is addressing legal questions relating to patents in the field of pharmaceuticals, see Agreement on a Unified Patent Court and Statute (document 16351/12, 11-01-2013).

[78] See for instance: European Parliament legislative resolution of 21 November 2013 on the proposal for a regulation of the European Parliament and of the Council establishing Horizon 2020—The Framework Programme for Research and Innovation (2014–2020) (COM(2011)0809 -C7-0466/2011 – 2011/0401(COD)), with a special exception for the funding of stem cell research in para. 31.

[79] Decision No. 1786/2002/EC of the European Parliament and of the Council of 23 September 2002 adopting a programme of Community action in the field of public health (2003-2008) (OJ 271/1, 09-10-2002).

[80] European Parliament, ENVI Committee Co-ordinators Meeting Results, 27 February 2008 (PHS 1A02).

such as the first and second public health programmes, the impact of the financial crisis on national health systems, the added value of EU health policies for national health systems, tackling antibacterial resistance, the quality of medicines, influenza pandemic preparedness, and more.[81]

4. Health Policy in the Council of the European Union

The Council of the European Union was originally formed as a body of executive representatives of the Member States. However, it has grown beyond its original intergovernmental nature. Generally, the Council is the EU's legislative forum. Yet within the Council, too, administrative and political executive powers coexist and interplay. The Council itself plays a political role, but at the same time an administration is developing, particularly in the General Secretariat of the Council and within the work of working groups and committees.[82] Over time, the Council has developed specialized configurations according to policy domains,[83] where the European Council, the assembly of the EU Heads of State, performs the generalist role with respect to Member State representation. The European Council only recently became a formal institutional actor in the EU with the Treaty of Lisbon, albeit without any formal legislative powers. However, in terms of policymaking, the European Council historically has been important for the involvement of the EU in health, given the fact that it can give impetus to the development of new policy.[84] Therefore the European Council can more easily set the EU agenda with respect to subjects that are not foreseen to be part of the EU's competence in the Treaties.[85]

4.1 At the level of ministers: the EPSCO Council

From the early days of the ECSC the Council was a single institutional entity. At first only the foreign affairs ministers would be represented. However, over time it became difficult for the foreign affairs council to deal with increasingly specialized agendas. Therefore, the Council started meeting with the Member State ministers of more specialized departments. Social policy was one of the first policy sectors in which a specialized Council configuration would meet.[86] Over the years, an increasing number of sectoral councils were established and with each new community competence a new sectoral council would emerge.[87] In the field of health, however, the first specific Council meeting took place in 1977.[88]

[81] European Parliament, Activity Report of the Committee on the Environment, Public Health and Food Safety 2004–2009 Parliament.

[82] See Curtin (2009) supra note 8 at p. 58. Other classifications of the functions of the Council can be found in F. Hayes-Renshaw and H. Wallace *The Council of Ministers* 2nd edn (Basingstoke: Palgrave MacMillan, 2006) at p. 322 et seq. (who identify legislative, executive, a steering committee, and a forum for coordination national policies); another classification is made by N. Nugent 'Tobacco Industry Strategies for Influencing European Community Tobacco Advertising Legislation' (2010) *The Lancet* 359 (9314) 1323–30 at p. 1327 (here a threefold classification identifies the Council as executive, legislator, and mediator).

[83] M. Westlake and D. Galloway (eds) *The Council of the European Union* 3rd edn (London: John Harper, 2004) at p. 44.

[84] Article 4 TEU.

[85] See Greer (2009) supra note 46 at p. 29.

[86] The second time this happened, in 1960, it was a meeting of the Social Affairs Council on 10–11 May 1960, Bulletin of the European Economic Community 10 (1960).

[87] Westlake and Galloway (eds) (2004) supra note 83 at p. 44.

[88] Secretariaat Generaal van de Raad der Europeesche gemeenschappen, Vijfentwintigse Overzicht der Werkzaamheden van de Raad (1 januari – 31 december 1977) at p. 12.

At the end of the seventies, there was no legal competence for creating health policy. In November 1978 this specific configuration came together for the second time. The main issues at the table were the economic aspects of health.[89] Generally, by the late seventies and the beginning of the eighties, health was mainly discussed in conjunction with other policies.[90] Therefore it took some time before the health ministers met again,[91] this time in response to the action taken in the context of the Fontainebleau European Council of 25 and 26 June 1984: the low participation in the election of the European Parliament prompted a policy on strengthening and promoting the relationship between Europeans and Europe. An ad hoc committee comprised of Heads of States and Governments under the chairmanship of Pietro Adonnino was set up to work out ideas for a 'People's Europe'.[92] This Committee developed two reports. The second report was submitted to the Milan European Council of 28 and 29 June 1985. In this report, health was put forward as an important issue for the creation of this People's Europe, especially because in a public opinion survey that carried out in 1983, 58 per cent of Europeans considered health to be most important when they were asked about wellbeing, and 81 per cent placed it first when they were asked about a range of items covering family, relationships, money, and leisure.[93] The Adonnino report further advised the Health Council to come together more intensively than it had previously, in order to 'enlarge the scope of common [European] activities in an opportune matter'.[94]

The European Council adopted the suggestions of the committee and especially emphasized the launch of a programme on cancer.[95] The meetings of the Health Council now became more frequent, yet many health-related issues were still discussed in other council configurations. In 1992, Article 146 TEC inserted by the Maastricht Treaty

[89] The subjects for debates were on pharmaceutical products, specialized personnel, and harmonization of health statistics across Member States. Moreover, the Council agreed on funding for two programmes, one on disease prevention and the other on health-care costs; see Secretariaat Generaal van de Raad der Europeesche gemeenschappen, zesentwintigste overzicht der werkzaamheden van de Raad, (1 januari – 31 december 1978) at p. 103; also see Commission of the European Communities *Cooperation at Community level on Health Related Problems* (COM (1984) 502 final) at p. 2.

[90] See General Secretariat of the Council of the European Communities, *Thirty-second review of the Councils work* (1 January–31 December 1984) at p. 3.

[91] They met informally on 1984 under the Irish presidency, see ibid. at p. 241. They met again informally in Venice on 2 and 3 May in response to health in the agenda for a 'People's Europe'. At this meeting it was emphasized that the EU had no responsibility for health matters; see p. 177 of General Secretariat of the Council of the European Communities, *Thirty-third review of the Councils work* (1 January–31 December 1985).

[92] One of the suggestions of EU Council meeting was, for example, to adopt measures to combat drug abuse; Conclusions of the Fontainebleau European Council (25 and 26 June 1984) (Bulletin of the European Communities June 1984, No. 6 Luxembourg).

[93] See General Secretariat of the Council of the European Communities, supra note 90; Commission of the European Communities (1984) supra note 89 at p. 2.

[94] Otherwise the report proposes for ministers of health to create policy on dialysis for kidney patients and a programme of action on toxicology for health protection. Also discussed are subjects like cooperation on handicapped persons; encouragement in the area of medical research and technology related to cancer, for instance; the issuing of cross-border health-care and access, as it concerns the citizens' agenda; an Emergency Health Card (on which medical information is stored); and cooperation on the problems of drug addiction. See A People's Europe, Reports from the Ad Hoc Committee, Chairman Pietro Adonnino, Bulletin of the European Communities (Supplement 7/85) at p. 18 para. 1.4.

[95] European Council Conclusion Milan 28 and 29 June 1985 (2740/1/85) at p. 31. See the resolutions adopted by the health council in response to this programme and the different strands of public health programmes, for example on HIV/AIDS, cancer, epidemiological data, chemicals, prevention of smoking, and so on. See Secretariat of the Council of the European Communities Thirty-fourth review of the Councils work (1 January–31 December 1986) at p. 197.

read: 'the Council shall consist of a representative of each Member State at ministerial level authorized to commit the Government of that Member State.'[96] However, as the number of specialized Council configurations grew, at the Helsinki European Council meeting in 1999 the number of Council configurations was reduced to sixteen in view of the enlargement of the Union.[97] In 2002 this number was cut back even further. Currently there are nine configurations. As a result of this cut-back, the Health Council became part of the EPSCO Council, which is the Council on Employment, Social Policy, Health, and Consumer Affairs. The addition of health to the EPSCO configuration, however, is seen as somewhat 'artificial' and usually the Health Council meets separately on the second day of the EPSCO Council meeting.[98] At the same time, health-related issues still appear on the agenda of other Council configurations. In this regard the Economic and Financial Affairs (ECOFIN) Council is especially important, where in view of public expenditures, for instance, the efficiency of health-care systems or matters of prioritization have featured on the agenda.[99]

4.2 Lower-level Member State representatives for health in the Council

'Governing in the shadow' by preparing the Council's work[100] is the Committee for the Permanent Representatives of the Member States (COREPER). COREPER originates in the 1951 ECSC 'Commission de coordination du Conseil des Ministres (COCOR)', instituted to prepare the work for the ministers of foreign affairs. In 1957 it was decided that similar preparatory bodies would be installed for the new communities, which would reside permanently in Brussels.[101] In the 1965 Merger Treaty these committees became more formalized.[102] COREPER is composed of the heads (COREPER II) and the deputies (COREPER I) of the Member State permanent representatives in Europe. They meet weekly to agree on items on the Council's agenda.[103] The deputy permanent representatives take on the more specialized policy agendas. COREPER I therefore usually prepares the Health Council meetings. Although the EPSCO Council institutionally is one council, on the level of COREPER I many permanent representations, similar to the ministerial level, have a specialist available to prepare the Health Council meetings.[104]

[96] Article 16(6) TEU in conjunction with Article 236 TFEU.

[97] See the Annex to the Presidency Conclusions Seville European Council 21 and 22 June 2002 (European Council – DOC/02/13 – 24-06-2002).

[98] With respect to this configuration there is a feeling that it does not do justice to the policy contents, see Hayes-Renshaw and Wallace (2006) supra note 82 at p. 45.

[99] See for example (ECOFIN) Council conclusions, Report on budgetary challenges posed by ageing populations, Brussels 6 November 2001 (SN 4406/1/01 REV 1); also see 3054th Council meeting Economic and Financial Affairs Brussels, 7 December 2010 (17447/10); see further EPC Commission, Joint report on health systems (16940/10) Brussels, 29 November 2010.

[100] See Curtin (2009) supra note 8 at p. 87.

[101] Ibid. at p. 75; also see Provisional Rules of Procedure of the Council of the European Economic Community (EEC) 18 March 1958 in Communauté économique européenne (1958) pp. 1–8.

[102] Article 4 Merger Treaty.

[103] See further on the role and functions of COREPER e.g. Curtin (2009) supra note 8 at p. 61 et seq.; also see M. J. Johnston 'European Council and the Council of the European Union' in P. van der Hoek (ed.) *Hand of Public Administration and Policy in the European Union* (Boca Raton: Taylor & Francis, 2005); Hayes-Renshaw and Wallace (2006) supra note 82, particularly chapter 12.

[104] Respondent 2 (Deputy Permanent Representative for Health in the Council, 2010); but see S. L. Greer 'Standing Up for Health? Health Departments in EU Health Policy Formulation' 2010 *Social Policy & Administration* 44 (2) 208–24 (which indicates that the political weight brought to the table in EU health policymaking is highly dependent on the level of centralized coordination in

4.2.1 *The Council Working Party on Public Health*

The creation of the nine Council formations in 2002 led to a streamlining of the Council Working Parties.[105] The working parties for the Council reside under COREPER and usually consist of attachés to the permanent representations. They prepare the work for COREPER and are generally classified according to the Council formations.[106] There has been a working party on health since the 1958 Treaty of Rome.[107] After the entry into force of the Treaty of Maastricht, which introduced a specific legal basis for health policy, a 'working party on health questions' was put in place. This working party was later renamed the 'Working Party on Public Health' following the adoption of a COREPER agreement in 2000.[108] There are also other working parties involved in aspects of health policy,[109] such as the Working party on Pharmaceuticals and Medical Devices; under the heading of agriculture there are multiple working parties that work in relation to certain kinds of produce that have specific public health policy implications.[110]

4.2.2 *The Working Party on Public Health at senior level*

As outlined, as a consequence of a series of Court cases on access to cross-border health care over the course of the nineties and early 2000s, different processes under Commission auspices were launched to find common ground among the Member States to respond to this case law.[111] By the time health was excluded from a proposal to add a general provision on health services in the proposal for a services directive,[112] many of these ad hoc fora in which national representatives and health experts were involved had become established under the heading of DG SANTE.[113] In 2007, however, with

the Member State government and the general power of the Health department. Thus the level and nature of representation at EU level also varies across Member States); a similar opinion was voiced by Respondent 3 (MS Representative Working Party on Public Health in the Council, 2010).

105 Presidency Conclusions (2002) supra note 97.

106 See Article 19 of the Council Decision 2009/937/EU of 1 December 2009 adopting the Council's Rules of Procedure (OJ L 325/35, 11-12-2009) (Annex).

107 Council Rules of Procedure (1958) supra note 101.

108 See Trumpf-Piris Report, Operation of the Council with an enlarged Union in prospect (10 March 1999), Report by the working party set up by the Secretary-General of the Council, Operation of the Council with an enlarged Union in prospect, presented on 10 March 1999 in accordance with the conclusions of the Vienna European Council held from 11 to 13 December 1998.

109 Under the heading of Agriculture there is a Working Party on Public Health, and besides the Working Party for Public Health under the heading EPSCO there is also the Working Party on Pharmaceuticals and Medical Devices and the Working Party on Foodstuffs. See General Secretariat to the Delegations, List of Council Prepatory Bodies, Brussels 14 January 2014 (5312/14).

110 Such as on tobacco and alcohol, the use of pesticides in foods, and animal health (whereas in the context of the Commission, animal health is part of DG SANCO; not Agriculture), see ibid.

111 V. Hatzopoulos 'The ECJ Case Law on Cross-Border Aspects of Health Services' (2007) *Briefing to the European Parliaments' Committee on Internal Market and Consumer Protection* European Commission; European Commission 'The Internal Market and Health Services' *Report of the High Level Committee on Health* (Brussels, 17 September 2001); European Commission Proposal for a Joint Report: Health Care and Care for the Elderly: Supporting National Strategies for Ensuring a High Level of Social Protection (COM (2002) 774 final).

112 Directive 2006/123/EC of the European Parliament and of the Council of 12 December 2006 on services in the internal market (OJ L 376/36); Respondent 10 (Representative Commission Services DG MARKT, 2010). The exclusion of health care from the Services Directive created a new impetus for DG SANTE to try and regain the driver's seat on health care with its high-level Process of Reflection, European Commission HLPR (2003).

113 This eventually led to the creation of the more formalised High Level Group in Health Services and Medical Care. This forum brought together senior national representatives in different working

the launch of the first 'European Health Strategy', these high-level Member State representative groups were moved and reshaped under Council auspices in order 'to give the Member States a better sense of ownership over the European Health Strategy'.[114] The High Level Group itself was suspended in 2009, and the implementation of the European Health Strategy became the responsibility of the Council Working Party on Public Health convening at senior level. This means that, instead of the health attachés to the permanent representations, usually Member States convene at a higher level in that someone is sent from the national capitals, such as the director-general of the national health departments or ministries.[115]

Whether this new 'strategic' policy mechanism is effective, however, remains unclear. Relatively recent working methods under this mechanism were adapted in order to improve the communication of its conclusions to the agendas of consecutive Council Presidencies.[116] Generally this working party at senior level produces opinion papers and conclusions and gives political advice to the Commission on the implementation of the health strategy, which is a rather broad, overarching policy framework. This type of coordination is not new in health, however; although the high-level group was formed under Commission auspices, a proposal for an Advisory Committee on public health had already been discussed at the meeting of the Council in 1978. In 1984 a group of senior officials of Member States with responsibilities in the health field (at that time especially public health) met with Commission officials in order to determine priorities and actions to be taken.[117]

4.3 The role of the Council

All in all, although the formal role of the Council is primarily legislative and executive, in practice the Council also has a role in *policy*making more generally in health, particularly at the lower level of representative groups and committees that prepare legislation.[118] Moreover, although there is no formal Health Council, in practice health is usually addressed as a particular or special issue in the Council context, in need of specialized groups and expert policymakers.

> It's obvious that all ministers have considered it absolutely necessary to have their own people on health [....] [N]ormally these are people like me, former directors of ministries, senior officials, that know exactly how things work in the ministry, and what the policy agenda is and what the main stakeholders are, and know the field of health. This is quite good to be effective here in the Brussels arena in order to negotiate all the legislative and non-legislative work that is presented by the Commission in that area.[119]

Importantly, this COREPER representative also emphasizes the growing importance of being involved in non-legislative policy activities in the area of health in the

groups. See European Commission HLG (2005) supra note 49; European Commission HLG (2006) supra note 49.

[114] Respondent 12 (Representative Commission Services DG SANCO, 2010).

[115] Respondent 2 (Deputy Permanent Representative for Health in the Council, 2010); Respondent 1 (Representative of the Council General-Secretariat, 2010).

[116] Respondent 1 (Representative of the Council General-Secretariat, 2010).

[117] Commission of the European Communities (1984) supra note 89.

[118] Curtin (2009) supra note 8 at p. 87.

[119] Respondent 2 (Deputy Permanent Representative for Health in the Council, 2010) (this also reflects that in most Member States there is a special ministerial department for health).

context of the Council.[120] This is particularly salient given the fact that for health there is only a limited legal basis to create formal legislation. The institutional setting of the Council then also facilitates lower-level policymaking and even administrative involvement, particularly in the context of the General Secretariat, which offers administrative support to the Council.[121] This secretariat houses a specific directorate for public health, consumers, and food legislation. Compared to DG SANTE, the administrative capacity of the directorate for health within the General Secretariat of the Council is limited in that its main role is to provide logistical support. However, the General Secretariat becomes more politically involved with respect to setting the political agenda for the rotating Council presidencies.[122] This is especially the case when the presidency is headed by a Member State that has less experience or is in any way weaker (fewer resources) in the political setting of the Council.[123]

5. Health Policy in Committees, Expert Groups, and Fora

The importance of the role of committees and expert groups for the development of European health policy can hardly be overestimated.[124] The different groups and committees of scientific experts principally are a 'functional demand' of the institutions' need for scientific information in order to create policy and law.[125] On one hand, a number of 'expert bodies' are involved before the Commission initiates a legislative proposal or policies. On the other, there are a number committees involved in health after legislation is adopted; that is, in the implementation phase.[126] These committees are a particular feature of EU governance in that they 'check' the executive powers delegated from the Council to the Commission.[127] Historically, expert groups and working groups that are used at the inception phase of European health policy have been particularly important in the area of food safety.[128] An intricate typology of the different committees and expert groups can be made with respect to their powers and function.[129] However, given the sheer breadth of these committees and groups, for our purposes a simple line is drawn between *independent* 'scientific committees' and committees with a more-or-less *political* role.[130]

[120] See Curtin (2009) supra note 8 at p. 88; and see Hayes-Renshaw and Wallace (2006) supra note 82.

[121] See Nugent (2010) supra note 82 at p. 147.

[122] See Respondent 1 (Representative of the Council General-Secretariat, 2010).

[123] See Respondent 4 (MS Representative Working Party on Public Health in the Council, 2010); and Respondent 1 (Representative of the Council General-Secretariat, 2010).

[124] With respect to public health arrangements, Vos describes the role of Committees as the 'first regulatory model' by which the EU regulates health; see S. Nicholas 'The Challenges of the Free Movement of Health Professionals' in M. McKee et al. (eds) *Health Policy and European Union Enlargement* (New York: Open University Press/McGraw-Hill, 2004); Vos (1999) supra note 35 at p. 110.

[125] Curtin (2009) supra note 8 at p. 109; and see Joerges (2001) supra note 52 and Vos (1999) supra note 35.

[126] See Curtin (2009) supra note 8.

[127] G. J. Brandsma *Controlling Comitology: Accountability in a Multi-level System* (Basingstoke: Palgrave MacMillan, 2013).

[128] Although these committees are often also used in the comitology process. See E. Vos 'The Rise of the Committees' (1997) *European Law Journal* 3 (3) 210–29; Vos (1999) supra note 35.

[129] Keeping in mind that it is not a clear dichotomy—Weimer and de Ruijter (n 52). See further Vos (1999) supra note 35 at p. 114 et seq.

[130] Ibid.

5.1 Independent scientific committees

After the BSE crisis, the importance of independent scientific advice as a basis for policy and law was emphasized for the first time, given that the lack thereof was found to be an important reason why the European health governance mechanism failed to safeguard the general public from health risks.[131] Accordingly, in 1997 a Scientific Steering Committee and eight scientific committees were set up by a Commission decision.[132] In 2003 these committees moved under the auspices of the European Food and Safety Agency (EFSA).[133]

However, although the scientific committees have been moved to the EFSA as far as food is concerned, currently within DG SANTE there is still a separate Directorate for risk assessment. Hence, in 2008 a Scientific Risk Assessment Advisory Structure was created within DG SANTE. This structure facilitates the advice of the Scientific Committee on Consumer Safety (SCCS), the Scientific Committee on Health and Environmental Risks (SCHER), and the Scientific Committee on Emerging and Newly Identified Health Risks (SCENIHR), which have adopted their own rules of procedure to ensure the advice they give is independent.[134]

5.2 Committees and groups with a political role, and private interests lobby

Beyond the more formal structure of 'risk regulation' within DG SANTE, however, there are a number of expert groups and scientific committees that have a more political role in the sense that scientific independence is less emphasized. These groups and committees advise on policy proposals and legislation or coordinate on Member State health policies.[135] An important aspect is that DG SANTE manages these committees, which are made up of Member State representatives, and there is generally no strong legislative basis for EU supranational law-making in the health issues these committees address. For instance, there is the High Level Group on Nutrition and Physical Activity, a group of government representatives which liaises at EU level with the 'EU platform for action on diet, physical activity and health'. In this platform a number

[131] Commission Communication on Consumer health and food safety (COM(1997) 183 Final).

[132] Commission Decision setting up Scientific Committees in the field of consumer health and food safety 97/404/EC of 10 June 1997 (OJ L 169 27-06-97).

[133] A Scientific Steering Committee was also set up to replace the 1996 Multi Disciplinary Steering Committee, alongside the Scientific Committee on Food, the Scientific Committee on Animal Nutrition, the Scientific Committee on Animal Health and Animal Welfare, the Scientific Committee on Veterinary Measures Relating to Public Health, and the Scientific Committee on Plants, as well as the Scientific Steering Committee's responsibilities on scientific advice on BSE/TSE. See Regulation (EC) No 178/2002 of the European Parliament and of the Council of 28 January 2002 laying down the general principles and requirements of food law, establishing the European Food Safety Authority and laying down procedures in matters of food safety (OJ L 31 01-02-2002 p. 1-24). There is also an advisory Group particularly in relation to food, which represents consumers and business and meets twice a year, and also has working groups on particular technical issues.

[134] Commission Decision 2008/721/EC of 5 August 2008 setting up an advisory structure of Scientific Committees and experts in the field of consumer safety, public health and the environment and repealing Decision 2004/210/EC (OJ 241/21 10-09-2008); the Committees adopted their own rules of procedure in order to ensure their independent workings (latest publication April 2013) Scientific Committees on Consumer Safety (SCCS) Health and Environmental Risks (SCHER) Emerging and Newly Identified Health Risks (SCENIHR).

[135] S. L. Greer 'The Changing World of European Health Lobbies' in D. Coen and J. Richardson (eds) *Lobbying the European Union: Institutions, Actors and Issues* (Oxford: Oxford University Press, 2009).

of European-level organizations are represented, ranging from the food industry to consumer protection NGOs.[136] This platform has its own system for monitoring the commitments of its members.[137]

There is an older but similar initiative in the area of cancer, which also uses its own method for measuring progress and brings together a wide range of actors at EU level, including Member State representatives, experts, health-care professionals, NGOs, patient groups, civil society representatives, and industry representatives. This initiative builds on more formal EU law and activities (e.g. in the area of tobacco regulation), and European Reference Networks that are facilitated through the Cross Border Healthcare Directive; moreover, with respect to research the cancer initiative creates a link with the Clinical Trials Directive.[138] Another example is the Committee of Experts on Rare Diseases, which brings together representatives of national governments, patients' organizations, pharmaceutical industry representatives, the EMA, the European Centre for Disease Control, and relevant international organizations.[139]

As a common denominator, private interest also has access to all these committees, which may make these policy initiatives the bedrock for lobbying the Commission and Member States' representatives directly at the EU level. In this respect, these committees—beyond the fact that they are meant to impact health policies that are largely within the competence of the Member States—have a more explicit political role in the formation of policy initiatives at EU level. In this regard there is also the EU Health Policy Forum, which represents private interests at EU level and is allowed to give input into EU health policy generally; notably there is the Health Forum, which brings together stakeholders in both public health and health care. Currently about fifty Brussels-based organizations come together in this forum.[140]

5.3 Lower-level legislation through committees in health

Whereas some of the expert groups and committees already mentioned in the context of policy initiation can have a political role, many of them, especially the more formalized groups, are supposed to give expert, independent scientific advice on health risks. In this regard, over time the EU has 'become a "true" regulator of intricate health and safety aspects'.[141] The health committees primarily involved in the implementation

[136] EU Platform on Diet, Charter, Physical Activity and Health, Diet, Physical Activity and Health—a European Platform for Action, 15 March 2005, avaliable at: <http://www.ec.europa.eu/health/archive/ph_determinants/life_style/nutrition/platform/docs/platform_charter.pdf> (last accessed March 2014).

[137] EU Platform on diet, Physical Activity and Health (2006) Monitoring Framework, available at: <http://www.ec.europa.eu/health/archive/ph_determinants/life_style/nutrition/platform/docs/eu_platform_mon-framework_en.pdf> (last accessed: March 2014).

[138] Commission Communication from the Commission to the European Parliament, the Council, the European Economic and Social Committee and the Committee of the Regions on Action Against Cancer: European Partnership (COM(2009) 291/4).

[139] Article 3,Commission Decision 2009/872/EC of 30 November 2009 establishing a European Union Committee of Experts on Rare Diseases (OJ L 315, 02-12-2009, pp. 18-21); also see Communication from the Commission to the European Parliament, the Council and the European Economic and Social Committeee and the Committee of Regions on rare diseases: Europe's challenges (COM(2008) 679 Final); Rare Disease Task Force, Health Indicators for Rare Diseases I—Conceptual Framework and Development of Indicators from Existing Sources, Final Report, April 2010, available at <http://www.eucerd.eu/?post_type=document&p=1211> (last accesssed: March 2014).

[140] See The European Health Forum, The Forum's Renewed Mandate, January 2009.

[141] See E. Vos 'EU Committees: the Evolution of Unforeseen Institutional Actors in European Product Regulation' in C. Joerges and E.Vos (eds) *EU Committees: Social Regulation, Law and Politics* (Oxford: Hart, 1999) at p. 30.

phase of EU policy and regulation are those involved in what used to be the comitology process, which have a more formal place in the EU institutional design as a 'check' on EU legislation. The use of these committees goes back to the 1960s.[142] Article 155 in the Rome Treaty provided for the implementation of rules on how the Commission should exercise the powers conferred by the Council.[143] The Council further obliged the Commission to consult committees made up of national representatives, especially in the area of agricultural policy, which required a higher level of specialization for implementation measures.[144] By the time these committees became institutionalized, they had become envisioned as 'management committees that were being used in the context of Agricultural Market Organizations' for the purpose of the Common Agricultural Policy.[145]

By the eighties, committees had proliferated in other health-related fields, including those outside of the CAP. However, many of these committees may not have been primarily concerned with health. At that time there were, for instance, a Committee of Senior Officials on Public Health to oversee the application of directives on the mutual recognition of medical and related diplomas;[146] an advisory committee on the training of the health profession; a committee on health and safety at work; and many expert committees on food safety, cosmetology, pesticides, and toxicology, which were all considered matters related to health. Various groupings also existed beyond the Community institutions by then. There was a hospital committee of the EEC, which existed in a semi-official capacity, drawing financial support from hospital organizations in Member States. Moreover, the chief medical officers would meet to exchange views, and other professionals were represented in various ways.[147]

The institutional EU health policy setting, however, also facilitated private self-regulation in some areas.[148] One actor in this regard, formed at first without formal legal status, is the Medical Device Expert Group. This body of experts in the area of medical devices, chaired by the Commission, is composed of delegates from Member States' competent authorities and European standards organizations.[149] Although a

[142] As early as 1957, for instance, the Standing Committee for Operational Safety and Health Protection in Coal Mining and in other mineral extracting industries was established. This committee was to support the Commission in the area of legislation initiatives. Commission de la Securité (1958) EGKS Commissie (1958). In 1974 the Advisory Committee on Safety, Hygiene and Occupational Health Protection at Work was established. Its task is to support the European Commission in the process of developing and implementing measures that relate to health and to facilitate cooperation between national authorities and employers' organizations. This committee has tripartite parity with members of the governments, employees' organizations, and employers' representatives of all Member States, as well as the Commission. Mostly it has a role in the area of policy formation rather than implementation. Commission of the European Communities, Biology and Health Protection Programme, Research Programme 1976–1980 (COM (75) 351 final).

[143] P. Craig *EU Administrative Law* (Oxford, Oxford Unversity Press, 2012) at p.103.

[144] If the committee did not adopt an implementing measure with a qualified majority, the measure could be sent back to the Council, which could then take an alternative decision within a month. See Council Regulation 19/62/EEC of 4 April 1962 On the Progressive Establishment of a Common Organisation of the Market in Cereals (OJ 1962 30/933) Articles 25 and 26; see further Craig (2012) supra note 143 at p. 105.

[145] Committee on Animal Feed, Food stuffs and Veterinary measures, Establishment of permanent committees for the approximation of agricultural legislation (Information Memo P-38/67, June 1967).

[146] Council Decision of 16 June 1975 setting up a Committee of Senior Officials on Public Health (75/365/EEC) (OJ 167/19, 30-06-1975); also see Nicholas (2004) supra note 124.

[147] Commission of the European Communities, Communication from the Commission to the Council, Cooperation at Community level on Health Related Problems (COM (84) 502 Final).

[148] Vos (1999) note 35.

[149] Similarly to the CEN/CENELEC, NB-MED and NBOG form the umbrella group for other working groups in the field and coordinate and oversee their activities. See Council Directive 83/189/

form of private regulation, this group currently creates authoritative standards and guidelines in the area of medical devices: the MEDDEV guidance documents.[150] These guidance documents on medical devices confront medical professionals with Europeanized professional standards related to clinical practice, which are usually maintained either at national, regional, or hospital-specific level.[151] Over time, there have been a number of 'comitology decisions' laying down the procedures and working methods of comitology committees.[152] Under the TFEU, 'delegated acts', which are quasi-legislative measures, no longer require the use of a committee.[153] Article 291 TFEU refers to 'implementing acts', which are to be used in order to create uniform conditions for the implementation of Union acts. In order to further specify the way these powers are to be exercised a new regulation was adopted in 2011.[154]

5.4 The role of committees and experts in EU health policy

The incredible breadth and variety, or 'types', of committees and groups involved in health policy in the EU institutional context is telling with regard to the depth of the EU's involvement, but also as to how difficult it is to 'grasp' or conceptualize this involvement. There are about sixteen main comitology committees directly concerned with the implementation of legislation that is health-related; however, many of these committees have sub-committees or 'sections' on more specialized issues.[155] These

EEC Laying down a Procedure for the Provision of Information in the Field of Technical Standards and Regulations (OJ L 109, 26-04-1983, pp. 8–12); also see General Guidelines for cooperation between the Commission of the European Communities (CEC), the European Free Trade Association (EFTA), and the European Standards institutions the European Committee for Standardization (CEN) and the European Committee for Electrotechnical Standardization (CENELEC) (CEN/CELENEC Guide 4:2001/01) at p. 16; S. Frank *A New Model for European Medical Device Regulation: A Comparative Legal Analysis in the EU and the USA* (Groningen: Europa Law, 2003); also see Vos (1999) note 30.

[150] These documents are adopted by consensus and initially drafted by the Commission. The MEDDEVs are currently published on the website of DG SANCO. They are regularly updated, revised, and redefined. On clinical trials, see MEDDEV 2.7.1 CEN reference: Clinical investigation of medical devices for human subjects—Part 1: General requirements CEN/TC 258 (ISO 14155-1:2003) (OJ C 153 24-06-2005); and see European Commission <http://ec.europa.eu/growth/sectors/medical-devices/guidance_en> (last visited 9 November 2018).

[151] MEDDEV 2.7/4 (2011) 'MEDDEV 2.7/4 Clinical investigation of medical devices for human subjects—Good clinical practice (ISO 14155: 2011)'.

[152] For an overview of the development of the procedures of comitology committees, see Craig (2012) supra note 143 at p. 99 et seq.; also see Vos (1997) supra note 128.

[153] Article 290 TFEU.

[154] Regulation (EU) No 182/2011 of the European Parliament and of the Council of 16 February 2011, laying down the rules and general principles concerning mechanisms for control by Member States of the Commission's exercise of implementing powers (OJ L 55/13 28-02-2011). In case a comitology committee does not deliver an opinion, it is the general rule that the Commission may adopt the implementation measure; however, there is an exception when this measure concerns the health and safety of humans, animals, or plants (Article 5 (4)(a) of the Regulation). In this case, when a comitology committee does not deliver an opinion and the measure concerns health, the Commission cannot adopt the act unless the chair amends the implementing act and presents the act to the committee again, or otherwise directly brings it to the appeal committee, where the final vote would take place (see Article 5(4)(a) Regulation 182/2011). When a simple majority rejects the proposal, a special consultation procedure applies in which the appeal committee plays a central role (Article 5(5) Regulation 182/2011). This means that in case of doubt or opposition in the committee, a more thorough procedure needs to be followed, rather than relying or falling back on the baseline of trust in the Commission that was indicated with the conferral of powers in the Union act. In other words, especially when it concerns health, Member States are less willing to let the reins go.

[155] Tobacco Products Regulatory Committee, Tissues and Cells Committee, Standing Committee on Zootechnics, Standing Committee on Veterinary Medicinal Products. Some of the committees have subdivisions, such as the Standing Committee on the Food Chain and Animal Health Section

committees are mainly managed by DG SANTE and although it is not necessarily the majority of committees that are active in the area of health, meetings on health are the second most numerous, following agriculture: over the year 2016 there were 116 meetings on health and 436 written procedures, more than in any other policy area.[156] Also, in terms of *output*, the committees involved in health adopted almost as many implementing measures as those in the area of agriculture. These figures are to some extent an indication of the intensity of the work that is delegated to the Commission in this area, and also of the intensity of managing this policy sector.[157]

The varied and diverse nature of the involvement of committees and expert groups in health illustrates the build-up of institutional actors involved in health. One dynamic that is obviously at work is that the evolution of increased market-making has proliferated EU institutional activity in the field of health. With each category of products or economic activity that becomes subject of the EU internal market come linked health concerns that are addressed in a multifarious manner across EU economic activity. However, looking over time, beyond health as a by-product of market concerns, the limited legislative power for health, rather than limiting the institutional proliferation of actors in health, seems to invite an enormous institutional creativity for developing new mechanisms and actors to enable deliberation on health concerns.

6. Health Policy in European Agencies

One of the first agencies to take up public health in the EU was the European Foundation for the Improvement of Living and Working Conditions ('EUROFOUND') in 1975. EUROFOUND aimed to provide information on the improvement of living and working conditions.[158] However, particularly in the nineties, the 'agency phenomenon' grew as a consequence of the expansion of the EU's involvement in technical and scientific policy issues.[159] An additional explanation for the growth of the role of agencies in

Toxicological Safety of the Food Chain, Section Phytopharmaceuticals Pesticide Residues; Section Phytopharmaceuticals Legislation; Section on Genetically Modified Food and Feed and Environmental Risk; Section General Food Law; Section Controls and Import Conditions; Section Biological Safety of the Food Chain; Section Animal Nutrition; Animal Health and Animal Welfare; Standing Committee on the Food Chain and Animal Health; Standing Committee on Plant Health; Standing Committee on Medicinal Products for Human Use; Regulatory Committee on the Quality and Safety of Blood; Committee on the Decision to Set Up a Network for the Epidemiological Surveillance and Control of Communicable Diseases; Committee on the Approximation of the Laws of Member States relating to Medical Devices; Committee on Cross-Border Health Care; Committee of the Second Programme of Community Action in the Field of Health; Committee for the Directive on General Product Safety; Committee for the Adaptation to the Technical Progress of the Directives on the Removal of Technical Barriers to Trade in Colouring Matters which may be added to Medicinal Products; Committee for the Adaptation to Technical Progress and Implementation of the Directive on the Deliberate Release into the Environment of Genetically Modified Organisms; Committee on the Recognition of Professional Qualifications; Committee of Senior Officials on Public Health; Committee for the Technical Adaptation of Legislation on the Minimum Safety and Health Requirements for Improved Medical Treatment on board Vessels; Committee for the Technical Adaptation on Legislation in the introduction of Measures to Encourage Improvements in the Safety and Health of Workers at Work.

[156] Report from the Commission on the Working of Committees during 2016 (COM(2017) 594 final) at p. 6.

[157] See ibid.

[158] Council Regulation (EEC) No. 1365/75 of 26 May 1975 on the creation of a European Foundation for the Improvement of Living and Working Conditions (OJ L 139 30-05-1975).

[159] M. E. Busuioc *The Accountability of European Agencies: Legal Provisions and Ongoing Practices* (Utrecht: Eburon, 2010) at p. 15.

EU regulation is that they provide for 'credible commitment' to long-term policy goals such as the protection of public health and safety, beyond the short-term political influence of Member States or other political interests.[160] Legally the powers of agencies are limited by the 'Meroni principle' which holds that no powers can be delegated to an agency that requires a wide margin of discretion, as this would displace the responsibility of the delegating institution to the agency.[161] Particularly with regard to health, which can be a sensitive and high-risk field of regulation, EU agencies have been given tasks relating to the safety of food, medicines, occupational disease, drug abuse, and communicable disease, to name but a few.

6.1 Agencies for health policy

In the EU about one third of all agencies are involved in health policy to some extent. At the EU level in total there are over thirty agencies (depending on the classification used) that either gather and disseminate information; manage the implementation of a particular public policy programme; perform operational tasks and facilitate policy cooperation; make decisions that may be binding on individuals or perform decision-making powers; or perform (quasi-)regulatory tasks by adopting draft rules of general application.[162] These agencies each have a different history, different functions, and different powers. Moreover, in some agencies health is the principal objective, whereas in other agencies it may be an important consideration for the particular objectives of the agency. The latter is certainly true for the first agency to emerge in the European context that had bearing on health, the Euratom Supply Agency. This agency is to aid the implementation of the provisions regarding health and risks to public for workers and citizens.[163] The main aim of the agency is to regulate the functioning of a common nuclear market; however, an important aspect is the protection of human health with respect to threats to the public; health protection for workers at power plants; and the development of medicines, for instance radiation therapies for cancer treatment.

In 1975 the Council set up the aforementioned EUROFOUND.[164] This agency's scope is fairly wide in the area of social security with respect to gathering and

[160] G. Majone 'The Rise of Statutory Regulation in Europe' in G. Majone (ed.) *Regulating Europe* (London: Routledge, 1996) (where the author puts forward a normative theory that regulation should only take place to correct market failures rather than to redistribute wealth. Delegation to non-majoritarian independent agencies takes the regulation of market failures beyond the 'political' realm of short-term national Member State interests); however, see S. Krapohl 'Credible Commitment in Non-Independent Regulatory Agencies: A Comparative Analysis of European Agencies for Pharmaceuticals and Foodstuffs' (2004) *European Law Journal* 10 (5) 518–38.

[161] Case C-9/56 and 10/56 *Meroni v. High Authority* [1957/1958] ECR 133.

[162] E. M. Busuioc *European Agencies: Law and Practices of Accountability* (Oxford: Oxford University Press, 2013).

[163] Article 2b Euratom 1957. The Euratom Supply Agency was established by the Euratom Treaty. It became operational on 1 June 1960, in accordance with the principles in Title II, Chapter VI of the Treaty. See Decision of the Commission fixing the date on which the Euratom Supply Agency shall take up its duties and approving the Agency Rules of 5 May 1960 determining the manner in which demand is to be balanced against the supply of ores, source materials, and special fissile materials (OJ 32 11-05-1960 at p. 776) (at this point legislation on this subject has also been adopted on medical applications, research, the maximum permissible levels of radioactive contamination in food, and the health protection measures to be taken in the event of a radiological emergency); also see Title III on Health and Safety in the old Euratom 1957 Article 31, Articles 34, 35, et seq. (where there is already reference to a Scientific and Technical Committee that is to advise the Commission, made up of public health experts of the Member States).

[164] Regulation (EEC) No. 1365/75 of the Council of 26 May 1975 on the creation of a European Foundation for the improvement of living and working conditions (OJ L 139, 30-05-1975 at p. 1).

dissemination of information. However, it does not have health as its principal objective. Health is part of its working sphere inasmuch as it touches on more general social security considerations. Another information-providing agency in the area of health is the European Agency for Safety and Health at Work.[165] The agency is particularly involved in the field of occupational health for workers. It provides the institutions and the Member States with technical scientific and economic information to use in the area of safety and health at work, using national information networks and national focal points in its operations. Also, the European Monitoring Centre for Drugs and Drug Addiction (EMCDDA) was established in 1993. This agency exists to provide the EU and its Member States with a factual overview of European drug problems and evidence to support (anti-)drugs policy; in this sense its main function is also the dissemination and gathering of information.[166]

The relatively young European Centre for Disease Prevention and Control (ECDC) was established in 2004. It does more than provide information. During its short existence, this agency has been able to create a central role for itself in the area of public health. It has operational powers,[167] with representatives operating on the ground in events that have the potential to create Europe-wide public health implications.[168] This agency works on the framework against infectious diseases[169] and on emerging health threats in general,[170] which includes a system of surveillance and early warning and response.[171] The Executive Agency for Health and Consumers (EAHC) (formerly the Public Health Executive Agency) is a 'management agency' in that it was specifically installed in 2005 order to implement the EU Health Programme; in 2008, the Consumer Programme and Better Training for Safer Food initiative were added.[172]

The EMA is a quasi-regulatory agency in that it is responsible for the market authorization of medicinal products for human and veterinary use.[173] Formally, it 'merely' gives scientific advice on the evaluation of the quality and safety and efficacy of medicinal products. However, given the highly specialized knowledge necessary to assess medicines, in most cases the EMA's advice is followed when the Commission decides

[165] Regulation (EC) No. 2062/94 of 18 July 1994 establishing a European Agency for Safety and Health at Work (OJ L 21,20-08-1994, pp. 1–8).

[166] Busuioc (2013) supra note 162.

[167] S. L. Greer 'The European Centre for Disease Prevention and Control' (2012) *Journal of Health Politics, Policy and Law* 37 1001–1030.

[168] Respondent 26 (High level representative ECDC, 2010). Central objectives for the ECDC are to: (a) search for, collect, collate, evaluate, and disseminate relevant scientific and technical data; (b) provide scientific opinions and scientific and technical assistance including training; (c) provide timely information to the Commission, the Member States, Community agencies, and international organizations active within the field of public health; (d) coordinate the European network of bodies operating in the fields within the Centre's mission, including networks arising from public health activities supported by the Commission, and operating the dedicated surveillance networks; (e) exchange information, expertise, and best practices, and facilitate the development and implementation of joint actions.

[169] Decision No. 1082/2013/EU (2013) supra note 48.

[170] Article 3 of the ECDC Regulation.

[171] It also works on antimicrobial resistance and health care-associated infections; emerging and vector-borne diseases; food- and waterborne diseases and zoonoses; STIs, including HIV and blood-borne viruses; influenza; tuberculosis; and vaccine-preventable disease.

[172] Commission Decision 2008/544/EC of 20 June 2008 amending Decision 2004/858/EC in order to transform the 'Executive Agency for the Public Health Programme' into the 'Executive Agency for Health and Consumers' (L173/27 03-07-2008).

[173] Regulation (EC) No. 726/2004 of the European Parliament and of the Council of 31 March 2004 laying down Community procedures for the authorization and supervision of medicinal products for human and veterinary use and establishing a European Medicines Agency.

on the authorization of medicines for access on the European market.[174] The EMA is also responsible for pharmacovigilance; however, in this respect some of its working sphere overlaps with the work of the ECDC. Hence, it could be argued that the EMA could, or should, accept 'supervision' with respect to pharmacovigilance from the ECDC, which has a broader perspective on protecting public health. According to an ECDC representative, the EMA does not have enough incentive in this respect, as it does not want to undercut its own previous advice to the Commission.[175]

Another quasi-regulatory agency in the area of health is the European Food Safety Agency (EFSA). The EFSA advises on risks in the area of food and feed safety. The agency was set up in 2002 in response to a number of food crises over the course of the nineties,[176] such as BSE. The work of the EFSA feeds into the scientific committees on risk assessment that reside under auspice of DG SANTE. This is separate from the work of the Food and Veterinary Office (FVO), which inspects and controls the food and feed chain in order to make sure food legislation is implemented and applied.[177]

6.2 The role of EU agencies

About one third of European agencies are involved in health policy and DG SANTE currently makes use of the work of more agencies than any other DG.[178] Although reducing the workload of the Commission is often cited as a principal rationale for the creation of agencies, there is no evidence that the workload of the Commission's administrative services has actually reduced.[179] Moreover, as mentioned, agencies are meant to depoliticize and legitimize the Commission's work, given the fact that they are independent bodies with their own legal personalities, separate from the EU's institutions.[180] However, a central constitutional problem concerning agencies, which is particularly salient for health given the fact that there is limited legislative competence, is that through the outsourcing of certain tasks to an agency, the Commission may delegate away or create more powers than it actually has.[181] Agencies are merely there to 'assist' the Commission in carrying out its executive and administrative tasks. However, assigning a particular task to an agency has also become a way for the Commission to engage in 'creating new executive and operational tasks at the EU level and tasking newly created actors in that regard'.[182]

174 P. Craig and G. de Burca *EU Law, Text, Cases and Materials* (Oxford: Oxford University Press, 2008) at p. 156; also see Busuioc (2013) supra note 162.

175 Respondent 26 (High level representative ECDC, 2010).

176 Regulation (EC) No. 178/2002 (2002) supra note 133.

177 The Food and Veterinary Office is not an agency as such, but a somewhat more independent Commission (DG SANCO) service.

178 About ten of the thirty EU agencies.

179 Busuioc (2013) supra note 162.

180 See ibid. at p. 17 and reference to Krapohl (2004) supra note 160.

181 D. M. Curtin 'Delegation to EU Non-Majoritarian Agencies and Emerging Practices of Public Accountability' in D. Gerardin et al. (eds) *Regulation through Agencies in the EU: A New Paradigm of European Governance* (Cheltenham: Edward Elgar, 2005). The Commission can only delegate tasks to agencies that do not entail the power to adopt secondary legislation nor the power to formulate rules for implementing legislation; for further discussion of this issue, see Curtin (2009) supra note 8 at p. 146 et seq.

182 Curtin (2009) supra note 8 at p. 145 and see D. M. Curtin 'Holding (Quasi-) Autonomous EU Administrative Actors to Public Account' (2007) *European Law Journal* 13 (4) 523–41; the legal baseline for delegation was created by the Court of Justice in Case C-9/56 and 10/56 *Meroni v. High Authority* [1957/1958] ECR 133 which provided guidelines to limit the delegation not to exceed the principle of conferred powers.

The expansion of the role of agencies for EU public policymaking generally also expands EU policymaking in health, as many agencies are involved with health policy—particularly as there is research that indicates that in a sensitive policy area such as health, credible commitment or depoliticization through the use of agencies may not always be effective.[183] This makes it all the more important that agencies, and the policies that are given effect through them, are analysed for their legitimacy as well.[184] Agencies may engage health policymakers from national health authorities at the European level. Many of the civil servants in this regard are public health experts, epidemiologists, etc. These experts may be more interested in engaging on a particular health policy topic than being concerned with institutional divisions and legislative powers. However, what they may take home, or contribute to at EU level—be that in the context of an agency, a committee or an expert group—could still entail an authoritative allocation of value, facilitated by their participation in EU policy mechanisms.

7. Growing Institutional Capacity to Make EU Health Policy and Law

This chapter has illustrated the build-up and increasing coherence of the institutional capacity to address health policy at EU level through policymaking, beyond legislation. Mapping an overview of the institutional landscape of actors involved in EU health policy shows that over time, health has become the responsibility of increasingly specialized actors rather than generalists, and that specialization and centralization went hand in hand with expanding powers or increased policy activity relating to the field of health. In the administrative services of the European Commission, health has solidified institutionally as a more-or-less autonomous policy—particularly in light of the fact that over the years major aspects of the EU's health policy have been moved to DG SANTE.

In the context of the European Parliament, the actors involved in health policy have also become more specialized, and institutionally health policy has become more integrated, even within the ENVI Committee. Since 2002 there has existed a special 'Health Working Group' that has a mandate to discuss any health issues not discussed in full committee and to bring issues to the attention of the full committee. At ministerial level in the Council, formally health is a matter discussed in the EPSCO Committee. However, in practice here, too, the discussion of health issues has become consolidated and in fact the health ministers have a separate meeting, usually the day after the meeting of the social affairs ministers. At the same time, in the Council health sometimes also appears on the agenda of the ECOFIN Council when it deals with matters involving national budgets. At the lower level, with respect to working groups under the auspices of the Council, the institutional setting of Member States' EU health policy specialists and bureaucrats amongst each other actually facilitates policymaking and soft coordination and exchange. The High-Level Health Working Group is a prime example thereof.

Hence, the EU engages health policymakers in all the core institutional actors. Furthermore, beyond their formal roles as legislators, the Parliament, Commission, and Council all have several forums in which they can engage in health policy outside

[183] Krapohl (2004) supra note 160; Krapohl (2003) supra note 35.
[184] Busuioc (2013) supra note 162, who looks at accountability in this regard.

of legislative activity. With regard to the Commission this is not very surprising perhaps; however, the European Parliament for instance has the special working group and created a mechanism to stay involved in the implementation of health policy. In the Council there is also a special mechanism to coordinate health policies through the Working Group and at Senior Level. At the same time, the incredible variety of types of committees and groups (more or less informal) involved in health policy in the EU institutional context illustrates the depth of the EU's involvement. With about one third of all EU agencies involved in health policy, and with DG SANTE currently making use of the work of more agencies than any other DG, the actual depth of EU involvement in health policy is clear.

Taking the long view, this chapter illustrates the growing variety of institutional actors and the expanding number of ways these engage in health policymaking. Moreover, the chapter shows various ways that EU institutional involvement in health is continuously expanding and changing. It also illustrates that there is ample opportunity for formal actors with legislative or regulatory powers to be involved in more informal coordinating policy processes, in the shadow of hierarchy. The growing institutional presence of the EU in health policy, and the possible shift in power to the EU this can entail, again confront us with the pressing issue of its legitimacy. This makes it all the more important to address the implications of EU health policy in terms of its impact on fundamental rights.

5

EU Public Health: Countermeasures to Swine Flu

> Countermeasures [to public health emergencies] may restrict movement of people, animals, plants, food, water, goods, energy flows and may have implication on data privacy protection. Those countermeasures should be momentary, ad hoc and subject to the subsidiarity principle when they affect social and economical life, or generate judicial consequences. Their implementation is necessary but difficult to grasp in a legal act before the event occurs.[1]

This chapter examines a case study on the EU's response to a public health emergency in the form of countermeasures.[2] More specifically, the scope of the case study is the involvement of the EU in the response to the outbreak of swine flu (influenza A H1N1) in 2009–10. The main objective for the chapter is to explore and map legally the manner by which health policymaking can become strengthened through intertwining with more formal rules and the impact this may have for EU fundamental rights and values. The case study illustrates the growth and impact of EU health policy beyond legislative powers. Where Member State engagement in EU health policymaking may have an impact beyond what is envisioned in law. The chapter first addresses how measures to counter a public health emergency can be taken at EU level, particularly focusing on the institutional actors. Second, the countermeasures taken at EU level to combat the swine flu pandemic are identified. Third, we look at the ways informal health policy intertwines with more formal regulation, sometimes even deliberately staged to do so by the European Commission. Lastly, the impact of EU health law and policy in this particular case is analysed in terms of fundamental rights.

1. The 2009 Outbreak of Swine Flu and the EU Response

In April 2009 a new strain of influenza virus first became apparent in Mexico.[3] The strain originated in pigs from Asia that were transported to North America (hence the name 'swine flu' or 'Mexican flu').[4] Public health officials were worried: in the

[1] European Commission Interim Document Technical guidance on preparedness planning for public health emergencies April 2005.

[2] Elements (such as the institutional tables) of this chapter have been used previously in A. de Ruijter, 'Mixing EU Security and Public Health in the Health Threats Decision' in A. de Ruijter and M. Weimer (eds), *EU Risk Regulation, Expert and Executive Power* (Oxford: Hart, 2017).

[3] See M. Lacey and D. G. McNeil 'Fighting Deadly Flu, Mexico Shuts School ' (2009, 24 April) *New York Times*.

[4] The 'flu is a mutation of four types of influenza: one that is found in humans, one in birds, and two strains that are more common in pigs. See European Centre for Disease Control Threat Assessment Human cases of swine influenza without apparent exposure to pigs, United States and

EU Health Law & Policy: The Expansion of EU Power in Public Health and Health Care. Anniek de Ruijter © Anniek de Ruijter 2019. Published in 2019 by Oxford University Press.

case of the 2003 SARS (Severe Acute Respiratory Syndrome) outbreak in Asia, 774 of the 8,096 people infected died.[5] This is a large percentage (about 10 per cent); by comparison, the Spanish flu outbreak of 1918–19 killed millions, but had an actual mortality rate of only 2.5 per cent.[6] The fear was that influenza A H1N1 would be comparable in mortality rate to bird flu (influenza A H5 N1), which has a mortality rate of about 60 per cent.[7] On 11 June 2009 the WHO declared that there was a pandemic spread of 'swine flu', raising the threat level to phase 6 (the highest level). However, as of 21 March 2010, more than 213 countries and territories worldwide reported over 16,931 deaths due to influenza A H1N1.[8] Although the EU has a role in the surveillance and early warning of public health events,[9] the management and containment of public health emergencies through countermeasures is largely still a matter for Member States. The amendments of the Treaty of Lisbon entered in to force in 2009 and circumscribe the EU's role with respect to health crises as follows:

> Union action, which shall complement national policies, shall be directed towards improving public health, [...]. Such action shall cover the fight against major health scourges, by promoting research into their courses, their transmission and their prevention, as well as health information and education, and monitoring, early warning of and combating serious cross-border threats to health.[10]

Generally, countermeasures to a public health disaster can restrict movement of people and goods; they have a direct impact on social and economic life and in many ways can have a legal impact—especially when one considers that these measures could include quarantine, selective immunization of a predefined group, and the requisition of property and medical facilities.[11] Countermeasures can even warrant law-enforcement actions in order to implement public health measures.[12] These measures then immediately affect the fundamental and constitutional balance between the protection of the population at large and the rights of the individual. It is now discussed how, and by whom, countermeasures can be taken at EU level.

Mexico of 24 April 2009; also see K. Bradsher 'The Naming of Swine Flu, a Curious Matter' (2009, 28 April) *New York Times*.

[5] See WHO Communicable Disease Surveillance and Response, *Severe Acute Respiratory Syndrome (SARS): Status of the Outbreak and Lessons for the Immediate Future*, 20 May 2003 at p. 3; also see WHO, Severe Acute Respiratory Syndrome (SARS)—multi-country outbreak—Update 6 March 2003.

[6] See V. Wiwanitkit *Bird Flu: The New Emerging Infectious Disease* (New York: Nova Science, 2008) at p. 2.

[7] J. H. Beigel et al. 'Avian Influenza A (H5N1) Infection in Humans' (2005) *New England Journal of Medicine* 353 (13) 1347–85.

[8] These are only the laboratory confirmed cases, see WHO Pandemic (H1N1) 2009—update 93, available at <http://www.who.int/csr/don/2010_03_26/en/index.html> (last accessed March 2014).

[9] Commission Decision 2009/547/EC of 10 July 2009, amending Decision 2000/57/EC on early warning and response system for the prevention and control of communicable diseases under Decision No. 2119/98/EC of the European Parliament and of the Council (OJ L 181/57, 11-07-2009); Decision No. 2119/98/EC of the European Parliament and of the Council of 24 September 1998 setting up a network for the epidemiological surveillance and control of communicable diseases in the Community (OJ L 268/1, 03-10-1998); M. Liverani and R. Coker 'Protecting Europe from Diseases: From the International Sanitary Conferences to the ECDC' (2012) *Journal of Health Politics, Policy and Law* 37 (6) 913–32.

[10] Article 168 TFEU.

[11] See L. O. Gostin and J. M. Mann 'Towards the Development of a Human Rights Impact Assessment for the Formulation and Evaluation of Public Health Policies' (1994) *Health and Human Rights: an International Quarterly Journal* 1 (1) 50–78.

[12] See European Commission (2005) supra note 1 35–7.

1.1 The role of EU institutional actors

There are numerous institutions and actors involved in an EU response to a health emergency. The main political actors in Europe are the Member States, the World Health Organization (WHO), and the European institutions. However, more particular, national public health authorities, European agencies (such as the European Center for Disease Control (ECDC), the European Medicines Agency (EMA), and the Health Security Committee (HSC)), expert committees, pharmaceutical companies, and the medical community all play important roles. Table 5.1 outlines some of the major institutional actors involved in an EU response to a health emergency.

Table 5.1. EU institutional actors involved in health emergency response.

Institutional actor	Role	Legal nature
World Health Organization	Global coordination and policy on public health (events)	International organization, EU has observer status in UN
Commission General Secretariat, Crisis management unit	Coordination between and among Commission services	EU institutional actor
European Commission, DG Health, Health threats Unit	Surveillance, early warning and response, manages information systems and exchange, including contact tracing	EU institutional actor
European Centre for Disease Control (ECDC)	Surveillance, early warning and response, scientific input/output, and information on public health threats. Limited operational capabilities through public health teams. Resorts under DG Health	EU Agency
European Medicines Agency (EMA)	Approval vaccines and antivirals, information dissemination, resides under DG Health	EU Agency
Early Warning and Response Committee (EWRS)	Information exchange and dissemination and coordination of surveillance and early warning and response on Communicable diseases, based on Decision 2119/1998 on early warning and response to Communicable diseases	Comitology Committee
Health Security Committee (HSC)	Member States' coordination of public health events, beyond communicable disease, including chemical, biological, and radio-nuclear threats, resides under DG Health	Informal cooperation
Friends of the Presidency	Horizontal council group	Informal and ad hoc

1.2 Commission services' role in early warning and response

Under the auspices of the Commission, the coordination of a European public health emergency falls under the responsibility of Directorate-General SANCO. However, there is also a crisis-management unit within the General Secretariat of the Commission, which uses a system for information exchange called 'ARGUS' that in times of a crisis is used to keep all the EU services up to date internally.[13] Through this unit, the President of the Commission and the college of Commissioners are kept informed of what is going on in terms of managing a public health crisis, and the unit coordinates the EU services involved in the crisis.[14] Within DG SANTE, Unit C3, the 'Health Threats Unit', is especially invested in health threats such as influenza. This unit was constituted in 2003 and is generally responsible for the surveillance and early warning of, and of the alerting to, communicable diseases and diseases of that are caused as a result of acts of bioterrorism. In this respect, the unit also conducts surveillance and early warning of biological and chemical threats in the EU. The unit is in charge of the operation of the Commission's Health Emergency Operations Facility in Luxembourg.[15] However, it also facilitates and manages the regulatory process for the network Committee for Early Warning and response to Communicable Diseases (EWRS).

1.3 The network committee for communicable diseases

After strengthening the legal basis for public health in the Treaty of Amsterdam in 1997, in 1998 a network for communicable disease was set up, initially as a bottom-up initiative on the basis of the advice of a charter group of the heads of public health institutions with responsibility for communicable disease in the Member States.[16] The network on communicable diseases had already been around since the start of the 1990s as an initiative of epidemiologists across the EU to tackle particular communicable diseases together, primarily for the sake of epidemiological data sharing and exchange.[17] The legislative basis given by the 1998 Decision formalized the already existing Network Committee and established it as a regulatory committee, composed of two representatives from each Member State, usually one epidemiologist and one

[13] 'It's purely internal and this system builds on top of a multitude of sector specific alert systems; Rapid Alert Systems, called RAS', Respondent 8 (Representative Secretariat General European Commission, 2010).

[14] Ibid.; Respondent 9 (Representative General Secretariat European Commission, 2010).

[15] The Health Emergency Operations Facility is located in Luxembourg and is used for the management of alerts and emergencies notified by Member States. During an emergency situation the responses of the Commission, Member States, and Agencies residing under the Commission including the liaison with international organizations such as the WHO are coordinated from this facility. European Commission, DG SANTE, The Commission Health Emergency Operations Facility: for a coordinated management of public health emergency at EU level, 2007, available at: <http://www.ec.europa.eu/health/archive/ph_threats/com/preparedness/docs/heof_en.pdf> (Last accessed March 2014).

[16] J. Weinberg et al. 'On Behalf of the Charter Group: Establishing Priorities for European Collaboration in Communicable Disease Surveillance' (1999) *European Journal of Public Health* 9 (3) 236–40.

[17] L. MacLehose et al. 'Responding to the Challenge of Communicable Disease in Europe' (2002) *Science* 295 2047–50; also see M. R. Roberts 'The European Centre for Disease Prevention and Control: Science and Political Integration in Europe' (2013) UCL STS Observatory blog at <https://blogs.ucl.ac.uk/sts-observatory/2013/08/02/the-european-centre-for-disease-prevention-and-control-science-and-political-integration-in-europe/> (last accessed November 2018).

representative of the Ministry of Health. A representative of DG SANTE's unit on health threats chairs the committee. Under the auspices of this Committee, a surveillance system and an early warning and response system (EWRS) were set up.[18] At the same time, the committee determines the case definitions for communicable diseases and data and methods for surveillance, and can also issue guidelines on the countermeasures to be taken in emergencies.[19]

With regard to the EWRS, similarly to the surveillance network, the exchange of information for the operation of this system is limited to information on new or unknown communicable diseases or to the list of diseases covered under the annex of Decision 2119/98/EC, including emergency situations.[20] The EWRS is a 'legally binding system'[21] in that the public health authorities of the Member States are obliged to report any information on existing and proposed mechanisms and procedures for the prevention and control of communicable diseases and the countermeasures that are being implemented.[22]

1.3.1 Other instruments for response: surveillance and Rapid Response Systems (RAS)

Besides the Early Warning and Response System, there are also a number of other ways through which information is shared in case of an emergency, particularly on information that goes beyond the communicable diseases framework. Some suggest there may even be too many information-exchange networks and systems at the moment: 'There are lots of different systems, all of which were very logical when they were created.'[23] Within the network on communicable disease, the surveillance systems and EWRS were first managed under the Health Surveillance System for Communicable Diseases within the European Public Health Information Network (EUPHIN-HSSCD).[24] The surveillance network

> is more the long-term surveillance, so they are not designed for an immediate outbreak. In other words, if somebody is spotted in the airport with cholera (this happened in Germany last week) this is an emergency situation and they have to use the EWRS and it is urgent. Now if you want to develop the statistics for cholera for the whole year then you use one of these surveillance networks.[25]

[18] See Article 1 Decision No. 2119/98/EC (1998) supra note 9; also see MacLehose et al. (2002) supra note 17 at p. 2048.

[19] At the time of the swine flu outbreak based on Articles 3 (c,d, and f) Decision No. 2119/1998/EC)

[20] Article 4 Decision No. 2119/98/EC.

[21] Respondent 15 (High level representative Commission Services SANCO, 2010).

[22] Article 4 (e and f) and Article 6 (3) Decision No. 2119/98/EC. See further relevant at the time of swine flu, Commission Decision 2000/57/EC of 22 December 1999 on the early warning and response system for the prevention and control of communicable diseases under Decision No. 2119/98/EC of the European Parliament and of the Council (OJ L 21 26-01-2000 at p. 32), amended by Commission Decision 2008/351/EC of 28 April 2008 amending Decision 2000/57/EC as regards events to be reported within the early warning and response system for the prevention and control of communicable diseases (OJ L 117, 01-05-2008).

[23] Respondent 15 (High level representative Commission Services SANCO, 2010).

[24] Commission Decision 2000/96/EC on the communicable diseases to be progressively covered by the Community network under Decision 2119/98/EC of the European Parliament and of the Council (OJ L28/50 03-02-2000).

[25] Respondent 8 (Representative Secretariat General European Commission, 2010).

In terms of Rapid Response Systems, the EWRS is reserved for 'events that have the potential to become public health threats'.[26] It operates on three levels: the first is basic information exchange, the second is that of a potential threat, and the last is in case of a definite threat.[27] At the same time, besides the EWRS there is also the MedIsys (Medical Intelligence system), which is operated by the health threats unit of DG SANTE. This system analyses and identifies potential threats to public health using information from the Internet. These threats include communicable disease, but also extend to chemical, biological, and radio-nuclear threats. The system analyses news outlets and articles online and categorizes this information. One version of this system is open to the public, but there is also a restricted version only accessible to public health authorities.[28] Dealing with cases of a public health threat that is the result of a deliberate release of chemical, biological, and radio-nuclear agents is the RAS-BISCHAT system, which in terms of chemical threats only covers those in relation to terrorist activities. This system is newer than the EWRS system, and although it works similarly to the EWRS, the Commission is the moderator of the system rather than a special regulatory committee. If a threat is posted through this system, an on-duty Commission officer acknowledges the message and authenticates the sender and the message before sending the information through to the other Member States.[29] There is also an RAS in development for chemical threats specifically,[30] including chemical agents relevant to terrorism and other events leading to the release of chemicals (RAS-CHEM).[31] However, rather than linking the public health authorities of the Member States, this RAS links national poison centres (the EU Poisons Centre (EUPC) forum). Last, as a response system, there is HEDIS, which is similar to ARGUS (internal crisis coordination system, operated by the Commission General Secretariat) in that it only becomes operational in a crisis.[32] The HEDIS system provides the Commission and the Member States with support and information during an outbreak on a *specific* health threat. This means that for each crisis a sub-portal is created where all the relevant information—such as advice from the international and national public health authorities, situation maps, and the actions that have been taken to respond to the threat—is brought together for the stakeholders. The members of the EWRS have access to this platform, as do the members of the HSC.[33] Altogether there are a wealth of information-surveillance and -exchange systems that may become operational at some point in an EU response to a public health emergency. Depending on the system and

[26] See Article 1 Decision 2000/57/EC Commission Decision 2000/57/EC (2000) supra note 22, which was applicable law during the swine flu outbreak.

[27] Article 2 (1,2,3) Decision 2000/57/EC. See further working of the EWRS in Annex 1 and 2 of Commission Decision 2008/351/EC (2008) supra note 22.

[28] Respondent 15 (High level representative Commission Services SANCO, 2010) and see <http://medisys.newsbrief.eu//medisys/homeedition/en/home.html>.

[29] European Commission, Programme of Cooperation on Preparedness and Response to Biological and Chemical Agent Attacks (Health Security) Luxembourg, 17 December 2001 (G/FS D(2001) GG).

[30] European Union Public Health Programme funded the European Commission, European Public Health Programme Project, Alerting System and Health Surveillance System project (ASHTI), Newsletter February 2011(2) available at: <http://webarchive.nationalarchives.gov.uk/20140714110153/http://www.hpa.org.uk/webc/HPAwebFile/HPAweb_C/1296683124874> (last accessed November 2018); RAS-CHEM is housed in the Health Emergency Operations Facility (HEOF), alongside other Rapid Alert Systems such as the Early Warning and Response System for communicable diseases (EWRS) and the Rapid Alerting System for CBRN health threats (RAS-BICHAT).

[31] This RAS follows the protocols and operating procedures of the EWRS.

[32] Respondent 15 (High level representative Commission Services SANCO, 2010).

[33] European Commission (2001) supra note 29.

on the type of information exchanged through it, there are different security clearance levels. However, for EU citizens that are being traced as a matter of contact tracing, for instance through the EWRS system, it is not clear how many civil servants and who exactly will have access to the data involving their person. In light of this fact, the role of the HSC, and the fact that its members have access to most of the RAS systems mentioned, is particularly interesting, especially given that its legal status, at least at the time of the 2009 swine flu outbreak, was basically informal.

1.4 The Health Security Committee

During the swine flu outbreak, the HSC provided a setting in which emergency decisions could be taken on a European level, beyond the committee structure of the EWRS. The Council installed the HSC in tandem with the Commission Health Emergency Operations Facility in 2001 after the 9/11 terrorist attacks.[34] In principle, the Member State representatives in the HSC were authorized by their health ministers to make coordinated decisions and commitments with respect to responding to major health threats:[35] 'It's another kind of ad hoc committee, but defined in advance, that was activated because circumstances asked for that.'[36] However, representatives of DG SANTE and other relevant Commission services and agencies, such as the ECDC and the EMA, also gave input for the HSC. Currently still, experts can be invited to the meetings and there are working groups that reside under the HSC.[37] In a sense this Committee assesses the political, social, and economic implications European health emergency decisions would have:[38] 'It's about assessing the situation and acting.'[39]

It is not a pure expert group, you also have experts group like: people meeting on cancer, [. . .] and then you have on the other side the formalised council working groups and in between you have such things as the Health Security Committee, where it is not only experts, it is about governmental questions, what is the government doing, but not in this EU legislative sense [. . .].[40]

This means that in terms of Union law the HSC at the time of the swine flu outbreak was an informal forum, and really created an intergovernmental way of working

[34] The Health Emergency Operations Facility is located in Luxembourg and is used to manage the alerts and emergencies notified by Member States. During an emergency situation the responses of the Commission, Member States, and Agencies residing under the Commission, including the liaison with international organizations such as the WHO, are coordinated from this facility.

[35] 'So for us it is mainly the deputy general director or the deputy for him, who participates in this security committee' Respondent 3 (MS Representative Working Party on Public Health in the Council, 2010); also see Respondent 4 (MS Representative Working Party on Public Health in the Council, 2010); see Communication from the Commission to the Council on transitional prolongation and extension of the mandate of the Health Security Committee in view of a future general revision of the structures dealing with health threats at the EU Level (COM (2006) 699 final); Council of the European Union, 2786th Council Meeting Employment, Social Policy, Health and Consumer Affairs, Brussels, 22 February 2007 (6226/07 Presse 23).

[36] Respondent 6 (Assistant to MEP, 2010).

[37] After the Swine Flu outbreak the HSC became formalized under Decision No.1082/2013/EU, 'Decision No 1082/2013/EU of the European Parliament and of the Council of 22 October 2013 on Serious Cross-Border Threats to Health and Repealing Decision No 2119/98/EC (O.J. L 293/1 5-11-2013)'.

[38] See ibid.; also see Respondent 3 (MS Representative Working Party on Public Health in the Council, 2010); Respondent 8 (Representative Secretariat General European Commission, 2010); Respondent 15 (High level representative Commission Services SANCO, 2010).

[39] Respondent 3 (MS Representative Working Party on Public Health in the Council, 2010).

[40] Respondent 2 (Deputy Permanent Representative for Health in the Council, 2010).

together with the input of EU institutionalized health actors, such as the different agencies and experts within the Commission services:

The idea is that Member States send high-level representatives. If you want the Health Security Committee to really be able to decide on something [. . .] you put someone there that has a direct line with your minister. Since there are very important, politically sensitive issues if it is a crisis. I mean, how many ministers had to resign because of this kind of crises? It is very sensitive and once that people are dying for example, your minister, politically, is being asked questions almost daily. It's fear. The national parliament is feared. The press is alert. Citizens or civil society groups put pressure on the minister. If you want the Health Security Committee to reach something, you need a representative who has the authority and the possibility to engage his minister. Otherwise it is useless, to have an agreement in the Health Security Committee when you have representatives who are not covered politically by the minister.[41]

In principle the idea is that the HSC can take relatively ad hoc executive decisions in short circuit with the national health departments (although this may depend on Member State), and this may explain why the decisions taken in this Committee are perceived by some as de facto binding:

It [the HSC] has to take into account the ECDC recommendations and it has to take into account what the WHO says; we are also members of the WHO, another isolated thing, but that is all connected in Member States. Altogether you could say it is de facto binding.[42]

Another representative called it 'morally binding, because it is not a legally binding created Committee; it is not created by a decision of the Council'. The fact that the legal status of this Committee has remained vague, however, seemed to have served the Member States in terms of the relative flexibility this brings: 'If the crisis assessment is different for our country, we want to have the flexibility to do it a little bit different.'[43] Moreover, Member States perceive its informality as a safeguard for their autonomy in managing and responding to a public health emergency:

Member States did not want to base the Security Committee so quickly on a real legislative act, where maybe much more binding questions would come up. [. . .] Member States are rather happy in some situations to have some flexibility.[44]

The Health Security Committee came together under Commission auspices, but in practice it is 'a rather special animal'[45] that is neither exactly under Commission, nor under Council auspices:[46]

The Member States asked for a venue: Hey, I want to meet with counterparts and I want to decide among the big boys and girls [. . .] and so the Commission agreed to facilitate [. . .]. If you ask me what the legal basis is, I can tell you we are debating this as we speak.[47]

[41] Respondent 4 (MS Representative Working Party on Public Health in the Council, 2010) and further: 'For us this is really the forum where Member States can talk and discuss and decide. So, for us it is very clearly a forum with an intergovernmental way of working. And it should be, because we are talking about Member States' competences once again.'

[42] Respondent 3 (MS Representative Working Party on Public Health in the Council, 2010).

[43] Respondent 2 (Deputy Permanent Representative for Health in the Council, 2010).

[44] Respondent 4 (MS Representative Working Party on Public Health in the Council, 2010); Respondent 8 (Representative Secretariat General European Commission, 2010); Respondent 15 (High level representative Commission Services SANCO, 2010).

[45] Respondent 15 (High level representative Commission Services SANCO, 2010).

[46] Ibid.

[47] Respondent 13 (High level representative Commission Services, DG SANTE, 2010).

After the swine flu outbreak the HSC became formalized under a new Decision, based on Article 168 TFEU.[48]

1.5 Ad hoc policy coordination in the Council: friends of the presidency

Another informal, intergovernmental, and executive forum for managing swine flu was a special ad hoc 'friends of the presidency' group activated by the Swedish presidency in order to respond to issues outside the public health policy sector, for example on multi-sectoral issues relating to business continuity and the transport sector: 'It is not just the public health department that needs to decide on things. If you are talking about closing schools, closing public transport, cancelling big manifestations for example, asking people to stay home, this is something that goes far beyond public health department.'[49]

The 'friends of the presidency' group is a horizontal Council group that can meet in different configurations. One of these configurations is on pandemics and influenza:

> The idea [behind] the 'friends of the presidency' is that we only activate them when necessary [...]. You have health security committee people; these are public health people. The idea of the friends of the presidency is that the people who are there can also liaise on for example the transport sector, education sector and public services—everything that has to do with business continuity.[50]

The representatives in this group are supposed to have a high-level mandate, and should be individuals who either come over from the capital or a (deputy) permanent representative:[51]

> The Friends of the Presidency is an informal structure and therefore very strong—because everything that is informal here in Brussels is far more powerful than formal structures, which is very strange in terms of opinion forming and paving the way for decisions.[52]

At the time of the swine flu pandemic, this friends of the presidency group worked together closely with the different agencies and the HSC. The work with the HSC was reported in order to facilitate the meetings of the group and as such 'the Commission had all of a sudden a very good platform to communicate its messages and so on. And that worked quite well, particularly in times of crises.'[53] However, the next incoming presidency decided that this active work in this particular configuration was no longer necessary, given the relatively mild symptoms of the flu.[54]

[48] Decision No.1082/2013/EU (n 37).

[49] Respondent 13 (High level representative Commission Services, DG SANTE, 2010.

[50] Respondent 4 (MS Representative Working Party on Public Health in the Council, 2010).

[51] Respondent 2 (Deputy Permanent Representative for Health in the Council, 2010); Respondent 4 (MS Representative Working Party on Public Health in the Council, 2010).

[52] Respondent 2 (Deputy Permanent Representative for Health in the Council, 2010).

[53] Respondent 13 (High level representative Commission Services, DG SANTE, 2010).

[54] See further Council conclusions on Lessons learned from the A/H1N1 pandemic—Health security in the European Union 3032nd General Affairs Council meeting Brussels, 13 September 2010; also see Respondent 4 (MS Representative Working Party on Public Health in the Council, 2010) and Respondent 2 (Deputy Permanent Representative for Health in the Council, 2010).

1.6 The agencies: the ECDC and the EMA

With the establishment of the ECDC in 2004, the coordination of the surveillance systems and related public health networks from the communicable diseases network committee was handed over to this new agency.[55] The ECDC also publishes surveillance reports on the specific diseases, and manages electronic systems, which allows Member States to upload health data in order for the ECDC to produce the statistics; it also carries out risk assessments.[56] The EWRS has been operated by the ECDC since 2007, and although the Commission remains responsible for the users' manager's authorization—that is, who has access to the information exchange[57]—the ECDC otherwise manages the system and the information updates. The Centre has no regulatory powers,[58] but it does coordinate and is in permanent contact with Member States, the ECDC, the WHO, and public health departments and centres throughout the world through the Global Health Initiative channel.[59]

The ECDC can also send teams for inspections, and although it has not been legally set up as such, in practice the Centre does have operational powers in health emergencies. For instance, 'they can dispatch people on the ground; this means crisis management teams, real assets'.[60] During the swine flu crisis the ECDC was important in terms of information updates, and science and information exchange and dissemination. In the EU context the Centre coordinated especially with the EMA, the HSC, and the network committee (EWRS) and its international counterparts. All in all, although there are some more entrenched institutional actors and mechanisms at EU level to respond to a health emergency, as has been shown here there were also some more informal and ad hoc mechanisms and actors at work in the EU in response to swine flu.

2. EU Countermeasures to Swine Flu

The main countermeasures taken at EU level in response to swine flu outbreak were the market authorization of vaccines and antivirals, contact tracing or information exchange on specific patients, passenger screening, defining priority groups for first

[55] See Regulation (EC) No 851/2004 of the European Parliament and of the Council of 21 April 2004 establishing a European Centre for Disease Prevention and Control (OJ L 142/1, 30-04-2004); Decision No. 2119/98/EC (1998) supra note 8; Commission Decision 2009/312/EC of 2 April 2009 amending Decision 2000/96/EC as regards dedicated surveillance networks for communable diseases (OJ L91/27 03-04-2009) at Resolution 7; Respondent 15 (High level representative Commission Services DG Health, 2010); the ECDC was also put in charge of the implementation of the IHRs.

[56] Respondent 15 (High level representative Commission Services DG Health, 2010).

[57] The national permanent representations formally assign the national contact points request the Commission and the EWR network committee for access.

[58] See Commission Decision 2009/312/EC (2009) supra note 55 at r. 6.

[59] The Global Health Security Initiative (GHSI) is an informal, international partnership between countries to strengthen health preparedness for pandemic influenza amongst other public health threats. This network was initiated in November 2001 by Canada, the European Union, France, Germany, Italy, Japan, Mexico, the United Kingdom, and the United States. The World Health Organization serves as an expert advisor to the GHSI. The network is made up of the Public Health Agency of Canada, the Health and Consumer Protection Directorate-General of the Commission, Ministère de la Santé et des Solidarités of France, the Federal Ministry of Health of Germany, the Ministry of Health of Italy, the Ministry of Health, Labour and Welfare of Japan, the Ministry of Health of Mexico, the Department of Health of the UK, the Department of Health and Human Services of the USA, and the WHO.

[60] Respondent 8 (Representative Secretariat General European Commission, 2010).

access to medicine, and creating guidelines on school closures and on communicating with the public.

2.1 Market authorization of vaccines and antivirals, and defining priority groups for vaccination

Although the procurement and use of vaccines and antivirals is the responsibility of Member State governments, the EU and Member States share responsibility for authorizing medicines and for pharmacovigilance.[61] The EU in this respect is a central actor for making vaccines and antivirals available to the community, which is a primary countermeasure against a pandemic viral infection.[62] At the European level a central authorization procedure is mandatory when launching influenza vaccines onto the European market. However, at the same time national authorities can approve vaccines. In that case, the mutual recognition regime applies for distributing the vaccine across the EU. Nevertheless, most pharmaceutical companies use the European central authorization procedure.[63]

In order to authorize the sale and distribution of a pandemic vaccine, the EMA's Committee for Medicinal Products for Human Use's (CHMP) Vaccine Working Group (VWG) scientifically assesses the medicines, and the Commission ultimately decides on authorization.[64] On 1 May, before the WHO declared the pandemic on 11 June, three so-called mock-up dossiers were developed by the pharmaceutical industry in tandem with the EMA. This meant that when the pandemic was declared, these mock-ups could be converted and granted authorization to introduce the pandemic vaccine strain by the end of September:[65]

> The difference between the assessment of this vaccine and regular products is that this had to go on a rolling basis. The reason for this is that you can only make a vaccine if there is a virus. But once there is a virus, everybody want[s] to have the vaccine.[66]

Two years before the outbreak of the pandemic, three vaccines had been licensed in advance on the basis of the relatively small proof of some principle studies. 'When the pandemic hit, all that needed to be done was to go through the authorisation assessment, just like the annual update that is usually done for the normal influenza season.'[67] This meant that although the pharmaceutical companies had licences for

[61] See Regulation (EC) No 726/2004 of the European Parliament and of the Council of 31 March 2004 laying down Community procedures for the authorisation and supervision of medicinal products for human and veterinary use and establishing a European Medicines Agency.

[62] Ibid.

[63] Respondent 20 (High level representative European Medicines Agency, 2010); Respondent 21 (Representative European Medicines Agency, 2010); Respondent 25 (High level representative ECDC, 2010).

[64] Regulation (EC) No 726/2004 (2004) supra note 61.

[65] 29 September Pandemrix and Focetria and 6 October Celvapan; See European Medicines Agency, Pandemic report and lessons learned Outcome of the European Medicines Agency's activities during the 2009 (H1N1) flu pandemic (29 April 2011), available at: <http://www.ema.europa.eu/docs/en_GB/document_library/Report/2011/04/WC500105820.pdf> (Last accessed March 2014) at p. 6.

[66] Respondent 22 (MS representative for the CHMP in the EMA, 2010).

[67] See European Commission Staff Document, Regulatory process for the authorisation of antiviral medicines and vaccines in the protection against Pandemic influenza H1N1 2009, accompanying document to the Communication to the Commission to the Council, the European Parliament and the European Economic and Social Committee and the Committee of Regions, Pandemic Influenza H1N12 2009 (COM(2009) 481-SEC(2009)119 final).

these vaccines, they could only be used during a pandemic. Since the Commission had already approved the 'generic' part of the medicine, the process of approving the specific vaccine for the pandemic could happen much faster. At the same time, two other vaccines were approved using the so-called emergency procedure in March and June 2010.[68] Once a pandemic is declared, the process of approving a vaccine can be sped up. A central conditional marketing authorization may then be granted on the basis of less comprehensive data in terms of safety and efficacy compared to the regular authorization procedure if this happens in order to fulfil unmet medical needs and there is sufficient proof of a positive risk–benefit balance.[69] Whereas usually the process may take up to 210 days, in this case the procedure only has to take seventy days.[70]

The EU also played a role in procurement, even though this falls outside EU competence.[71] In an informal Health Council meeting on 6–7 July, vaccination policies and the possibility of pursuing joint procurement of vaccines—especially for the Member States that did not have advance purchase agreements with pharmaceutical companies—were discussed. For those Member States, a mechanism was set up for the joint procurement of vaccines.[72]

With respect to antivirals, in May 2009, soon after the first data came in concerning the outbreak of a new virus from Mexico, the EMA (CHMP) recommended the extension of the shelf life of tamilflu (oseltamivir capsules) from five to seven years.[73] In the following months, the CHMP and the WHO issued guidance on the use of these antivirals in at-risk populations, which were children under one year of age and pregnant and breastfeeding women.[74] Recent research suggests however that tamilflu may lack effectiveness in preventing complications from flu.[75]

[68] See supra note 24; Respondent 19 (High level representative European Medicines Agency, 2010); Respondent 22 (MS representative for the CHMP in the EMA, 2010); Respondent 23 (MS representative for the CHMP in the EMA, 2010).

[69] Article 14(7) Regulation (EC) No 726/2004 (2004) supra note 61; Commisson Regulation (EC) No 507/2006 of 29 March 2006 on the conditional marketing authorisation for medicinal products for human use falling within the scope of Regulation (EC) No. 726/2004 of the European Parliament and of the Council (OJ L 92/6 30-03-2006). However, these authorizations only have a validity of one year, need to be backed up with extra scientific data, and may have to involve specific additional obligations concerning collecting data for pharmacovigilance.

[70] See ibid. In this regard the EMEA has developed specific technical guidelines: <https://www.ema.europa.eu/documents/scientific-guideline/guideline-influenza-vaccines-quality-module-revision-1_en.pdf>.

[71] Article 168(7) TFEU.

[72] See the reference in the Communication from the Commission to the Council, the European Parliament and the European Economic and Social Committee and the Committee of Regions, Pandemic (h1N1), Commission Staff Working Document on Joint Procurement of Vaccine against influenza A H1N1 2009 (COM (2009)481 – SEC (2009)1188).

[73] On 8 May the EMA issued guidance on the use of antivirals. However, as it turns out there are some doubts about the effectiveness of antivirals generally. In parallel, but not by use in the mutual recognition procedure, the shelf life of another antiviral that needs to be inhaled (Relenza) was also extended; see European Commission Staff Document, Regulatory process for the authorization of antiviral medicines and vaccines in the protection against Pandemic influenza H1N1 2009, accompanying document to the Communication to the Commission to the Council, the European Parliament and the European Economic and Social Committee and the Committee of Regions, Pandemic Influenza H1N12 2009 (COM(2009) 481-SEC(2009)119 final).

[74] WHO Guidelines for Pharmacological Management of Pandemic Influenza A(H1N1) 2009 and other Influenza Viruses, Part I Recommendations, revised February 2010, available at: <https://www.who.int/csr/resources/publications/swineflu/h1n1_guidelines_pharmaceutical_mngt.pdf> (last accessed November 2018).

[75] D. Cohen 'Complications: Tracking Down the Data on Oseltamivir' (2009) *British Medical Journal* 339 (b5387) 1342–7.

2.1.1 Defining priority groups for vaccination

Approving pandemic vaccines is one aspect of the role of medicines as a countermeasure in a public health emergency. The *use* of these vaccines is also an important aspect that can make a difference for their effectiveness as a countermeasure. However, generally each of the Member States in principle has autonomy on the use. In the words of a Member State CHMP representative,

> [w]hat is difficult is that although the vaccines are approved at EU level, how they are used in the end is up to the Member States and the state vaccination programme.[76]

This caused some conflict in coordination according to a high-level EMA representative:

> Health care authorities [...] did not work with us to regulate this [the use of vaccines]. Before they started to react with vaccination policies [...] we said 'hey why don't you come to us? Because, do we have a vaccine even to vaccinate pregnant women? Do we have data? What age group? One dose, two doses?'[77]

Nevertheless, on 25 August 2009 the Member States did coordinate in the EU context on a shared strategy on *priority groups* for vaccination,[78] that is, on the basis of three objectives as outlined on 7 July of that year by the WHO Strategic Advisory Group of Experts (SAGE) on immunization.[79] On 15 September the Commission came out with strategies and priority groups for vaccination. In order to maintain essential services, the Commission prioritized health-care workers and other workers in essential services. Furthermore, as the virus seemed to be potentially more dangerous for pregnant women, children, and people with underlying chronic conditions, the Commission prioritized very young children up to two years old and people with chronic conditions, then pregnant women and people aged 65 and over.[80] The Council conclusions on 12 October 2009 'take note' of this communication, but more formally refer back to the similar shared strategy for target and priority groups for vaccination (based on the recommendation of the WHO/SAGE).[81]

As to the amount of vaccines and actual strategies for vaccination, it was assumed that since this was a completely novel virus, people would not have any antibodies, which meant everybody would need two injections for immunization: 'So originally we [the EMA] said you need to have two vaccinations. Why? Because we expect everybody to have no immunity whatsoever [...].'[82] However, over the course of the summer,

[76] Respondent 22 (MS representative for the CHMP in the EMA, 2010).

[77] Respondent 19 (High level representative European Medicines Agency, 2010).

[78] EU Health Security Committee (HSC)/Early Warning and Response System (EWRS)HSC EWRS Statement on Influenza A(H1N1) 2009: target and priority groups for vaccination, 25 August 2009, avaliable at: <http://www.ec.europa.eu/health/archive/ph_threats/com/influenza/docs/hsc_ewrs_statement_en.pdf> (last accessed March 2014).

[79] This expert group is currently under investigation by the Parliamentary Assembly of the Council of Europe, since it is suspected that its advice might have been relied on too heavily by the WHO executives, especially in light of some conflicts of interest of its members within the pharmaceutical industry.

[80] Commission staff working document, Vaccination Strategies against pandemic (H1N1)2009 accompanying the Communication from the Commission to the European Parliament, the Council, the European Economic and Social Committee and the Committee of the Regions (Pandemic H1N1 2009) (COM(2009)481-SEC (2009)1189 final) p. 7.

[81] See Council Conclusions on Influenza A/H1N1 infection 30 April 2009, 2965th employment, social policy, health and consumer affairs Council meeting (Luxembourg, 12 October 2009).

[82] Respondent 23 (MS representative for the CHMP in the EMA, 2010).

the data that indicated that people to some extent were already protected and would most likely only need one jab came in relatively late, because it was in August when people were really pressing that they wanted to have a vaccine, and nobody wanted to reveal it [that one jab might be enough]. So this data we needed only came in during the autumn.[83]

With respect to the use of the vaccines then as an effective (and cost-effective) countermeasure, the European coordination system was perceived as flawed:

I had hoped that policymakers and regulators should have a little better dialogue. It improved during the process when it became clear that we were sitting on an important decision that had huge implications for the ministries, because they [the Member States] didn't think about all the complicated issues in order to get a safe and effective vaccine on the market, or recommendations on how it should be used [. . .], and when the data and the facts came out that we do not need two doses, only one, all the governments were sitting there with a lot of unused vaccines [. . .].[84]

2.2 Information exchange, contact tracing, and passenger screening

Beyond the approval of pandemic vaccines, one of the first steps in taking countermeasures at the EU level was to adopt a legally binding case definition for swine flu. This decision was taken on 30 April 2009, under Commission auspices and with the advice of the ECDC and the WHO.[85] The adoption of a case definition meant that, from that moment onwards, Member States were obliged to report incidences of the influenza in accordance with this definition through the ERWS.[86] A case definition then is important,

to make sure that everyone reports the same thing. You need to have a legally adopted case definition, which says what the disease is and so on. [. . .] [T]he case definition, however technical, is also a legal pillar as it defines what the Member States should be reporting to one another.[87]

The case definition is also a legal identification that for instance allows for the preparation of vaccines.[88] In that same time period, the WHO and the ECDC also added technical guidance to the case definition of what should be done regarding persons that had been infected or had been in contact with infected persons in terms of prophylaxis and treatment.

Another countermeasure was to trace the contacts of infected persons.[89] This means that at the national level the persons that might have been exposed to the virus are traced in order to make sure they are not sick and do not expose others to infection. An example of what takes place in a case of contact tracing is a case where Germany notified the European public health authorities of a Lassa fever patient who had travelled

[83] Respondent 22 (MS representative for the CHMP in the EMA, 2010).

[84] Respondent 19 (High level representative European Medicines Agency, 2010).

[85] See Commission Decision of 10 July 2009 amending Decision 2002/253/EC as regards case definitions for reporting Influenza A (H1N1) to the Community network (2009/540/EC) (O.J L 180/25 11-07-2009).

[86] See further on this system section 2 of this chapter; ibid.

[87] Respondent 15 (High level representative Commission Services SANCO, 2010); Commission Decision 2009/547/EC (2009) supra note 9.

[88] Ibid.

[89] See P. Dąbrowska-Kłosińska, 'Tracing Individuals under the EU Regime on Serious, Cross-Border Health Threats: An Appraisal of the System of Personal Data Protection' (2017) 8 *European Journal of Risk Regulation* 700.

from Freetown (Sierra Leone) through Brussels and Frankfurt. The patient was sick during the flight and was carrying a dysfunctional urinary tract catheter that leaked. Although the ECDC thought the risk to the other passengers was low, contact tracing procedures were agreed and coordination between the Commission, the ECDC, the German and Belgium health authorities, Sabena airlines, and the WHO was put in place. A list of ninety-two people, forty-three of whom were Europeans, was distributed and these passengers were sought out and traced. In the end no other case was found and thus no information was put out to the public.[90]

Contact tracing in the manner described had previously taken place in coordination with the Commission. However, in response to swine flu, on 10 July a decision was adopted which formally makes contact tracing part of the ERWS.[91] A high-level Commission representative explains:

> Last year we needed a legal text on contact tracing which defines the elements which can be circulated between the Member States respecting data privacy and data protection and so on, which allows the Member States to communicate, using this electronic system, details of individuals who have to be traced for the purposes of contacts tracing.[92]

Here the public health exception with regard to the protection of personal data in Article 8(3) of Directive 95/46/EC and Article 10(3) of Regulation EC 45/2001 is made explicitly applicable, insofar as the exchange of data takes place between recognized health professionals.[93] The patients should be informed that their contacts are being traced, unless 'this proves impossible or involves a disproportionate effort'.[94] The indicative list in Annex 3 to this Decision outlines that not only personal details such as name, identification numbers, and home address are exchanged and traced, but also the travel specifications and the people this person has been in contact with and *their* personal data.[95] A related measure is screening passengers on airlines and public transportation. Council Conclusions in April 2009 had already outlined that in order to curb the spread of the pandemic, Member States should take 'all appropriate measures' with regard to travel (bans) and liaise with one another, the ECDC, and the WHO on this.[96]

2.3 School closures, delaying strategies, and information to the public

Other measures discussed at the European level related to providing information to the public. The EU issued advice on information to the public on personal protective measures, travel advice for persons planning to travel to or returning from affected areas, guidelines for case management and treatment, and advice on medical countermeasures for health professionals. Moreover, on 6 June the ECDC published non-binding

[90] See Report form the Commission to the Council and the European Parliament, Operation of the EWRS of the Community Network for epidemiological surveillance and control of communicable diseases during 2006 and 2007 (Decision 2000/57/EC) (COM(2009) 229 final) at p. 4.

[91] See section 2 of this chapter for further information on this system. Decision No. 2119/98/EC (1998) supra note 8; Commission Decision 2009/547/EC (2009) supra note 9.

[92] Respondent 15 (High level representative Commission Services SANCO, 2010).

[93] Moreover, Article 23(1) of the World Health Organization (2008), International Health Regulations 2005 2nd edn also provides that the WHO may require state parties to exchange data on passengers travelling and contact tracing of infected patients.

[94] Commission Decision 2009/547/EC (2009) supra note 9.

[95] See ibid., Annex 3.

[96] See EPSCO Council Conclusions (2009).

mitigation and delaying strategies for the use of EU countries. Other statements on school closures were given on 13 August.[97]

2.4 The role of the EU in taking countermeasures to the swine flu outbreak

The above outline of EU countermeasures shows that the EU is also involved in the management and containment of public health emergencies beyond surveillance and early-warning and response coordination. However, in some areas (e.g. approving pandemic vaccines) the EU has more powers than in others (e.g. on the use or procurement of vaccines). In this respect EU countermeasures to a pandemic outbreak reveal a mix or overlap of hard regulation and soft coordination measures. Furthermore, the way in which the EU is involved is characteristically different from the involvement of the Member States at national level, where vaccination strategies directly affect particular groups of citizens. However, even in the cases where the formal authority is completely in the hands of the Member States (e.g. vaccination strategies or communication with the public), the EU is highly involved. In the next section we look at the way informal health policy in the swine flu case intertwined with more formal regulation, with this sometimes even being deliberately staged by the European Commission.

3. Expanding EU Health Policymaking: Linking Practices to Law

As this chapter has illustrated, the institutional actors involved in responding to the H1N1 pandemic were sometimes ad hoc or informal, but operating in the context of more formal mechanisms. Some of these actors may remain ad hoc, such as the friends of the presidency group. However, paradoxically this group was set up in response to the slow institutionalization of the Health Security Committee, which in its conception is also an intergovernmental actor initiated by the Council:

> So there was the Health Security Committee and that was good, but the Commission is now a driver behind this and we did not want the Commission, who has limited power in this area; that is why we established Friends of the Presidency.[98]

With regard to these two actors, the Member States seem to have been seeking informal actors/ways to coordinate their response to swine flu. However, during the swine flu pandemic actors at EU level with more formal roles also stepped outside their designated scope of tasks. The EMA, although its formal role is limited to the authorization and registration of pandemic medication, became more involved in the determination of what countermeasures it deemed appropriate. This particularly concerned the use of the pandemic flu shots and the determination of priority groups for vaccination, even though Member States are principally responsible for procurement

[97] European Commission, Statements of Health Security Committee and Early Warning and Response System (MEMO/09/362,13-08-2009); Influenza A (H1N1) 2009: EU Health Security Committee agrees statements on school closures and travel advice (IP/09/1234 03-08-2009); Outcome of the Health Security Committee meeting, 12 and 13 November 2009, Luxembourg, available at: <http://www.ec.europa.eu/health/archive/ph_threats/com/influenza/docs/hsc1311_en.pdf> (last accessed March 2014).

[98] Respondent 3 (MS Representative Working Party on Public Health in the Council, 2010).

and vaccination strategies nationally. There was even some disagreement between the ECDC and the EMA in this regard:

> The ECDC told for example that in their point of view for critical target groups we probably need to wait till December to vaccinate them, because there are no sufficient medical trials to rate the benefit risk of the users of the vaccine [. . .] and what the ECDC said was not in line with some ministries of health of the Member States. For instance, they said the first people to be vaccinated are to be pregnant women. But for the sake of humanity (!) they are one of the last groups you should use a vaccine on.[99]

As can be seen, one risk created by the involvement of the different agencies and EU actors is that these then come out with inconsistent scientific advice. In order to counter this scenario there are some working arrangements between the agencies. Besides, the fact that this is needed reflects that there is a growing awareness of the possible political backlash that particular scientific advice can have, in high-risk situations in particular.[100]

3.1 Linking the Health Security Committee with the EWRS Committee

Hence, although informality was sought to coordinate and respond more swiftly to the quick spread of the virus, at the same time more binding procedures and regulation were needed in order to adopt countermeasures. Going back to the HSC, as mentioned, although already somewhat institutionally entrenched it was still an informal actor at the time of the swine flu outbreak. Set up as an informal response to the 9/11 attacks in 2001, the mandate of the HSC was expanded and extended over time. In 2006 the mandate of the Health Security Committee was formally expanded from health threats from attacks in which biological and chemical agents might be used to the more generic preparedness for health emergencies and influenza preparedness and response.[101] Yet it never obtained formal status with specific procedures for decision-making. Regardless of its unclear formal status, however, declarations from the HSC still had authoritative strength, or, in the words of a representative quoted here, it was able to present Member States with a 'moral bindingness'. If the scientific basis of such a declaration is backed up by EU agencies and experts and also by public statements and possible legal obligations vis-à-vis the WHO, Member States may find themselves in a 'bind' to adopt particular policies or give similar advice to the public.

Besides the 'double hattedness' of similar people in different configurations, the Commission also organized some of the meetings in ways to ensure that informal co-operation would be linked with more binding regulatory decision-making: during the pandemic, the Commission set the agenda of the meetings. In order to deal with the legal ambiguities, or in order to have the formal mandate to make a decision in case

[99] Respondent 19 (High level representative European Medicines Agency, 2010).

[100] Respondent 20 (High level representative European Medicines Agency, 2010):

> We have working arrangements with the ECDC in order to cooperate whenever we have overlapping field of responsibilities, [. . .] and especially in the case of pandemic issues or contagious specific disease that may happen from time to time. We establish some sort of pool of people, some from our agency, some from ECDC, in order to cooperate with them on this [. . .] because the worst scenario would be if general opinion received inconsistent messages from two different EU agencies, because they would undermine the accountability of the system.

[101] See Commission Communication (2006).

this fell under Union competence, it often combined the regulatory EWRS Network Committee with the HSC:

> So if there was any legal action required and we would have to explain it all again to the other crowd, we would have them both in the same room. So when we had the audio conferences every day during the pandemic, you had both the members of the HSC and the EWRS together.[102]

This means that even with regard to the countermeasures for which the EU may *not* have a settled legislative competence to create policy, binding obligations could still have been created through interlinking issues and institutional actors that have stronger EU regulatory powers.

3.2 Ad hoc policymaking as bedrock for law

As has been described, the Commission exercised creativity in interlinking formal and informal policy practices for responding to the health emergency; but this was not the only problem that needed to be solved at the time of the crisis. In the evaluation of the role of the EU in the response to swine flu, a number of other problems came to the fore. The way swine flu was handled made policymakers aware of the problematic opaqueness of the legal framework at EU level on how to respond to a public health crisis. On one hand, the WHO International Health Regulations (IHR) is the main legal instrument for managing a transnational public health emergency. Hence, for the Member States, EU involvement is an extra layer to consider in terms of coordination during a crisis. On the other hand, the EU coordinates with the WHO as well.

Specifically with respect to the IHR, the first involvement in communicable disease monitoring of the European Union developed in the context of an exchange of letters with the WHO in 1972.[103] Over time, cooperation increased between the WHO and the Communities and also within the Community itself.[104] In this context, in 2005 the revised International Health Regulations were adopted with intense involvement of the European Commission.[105] This means, however, that currently the governance of health emergencies—specifically also of communicable diseases—is divided between the international, European, and Member State level.[106] The EU, though, is not a signatory to the IHR, which caused confusion over the legal framework and who has responsibility:

[102] Respondent 15 (High level representative Commission Services SANCO, 2010).

[103] Exchange of letters between the European Communities and the World Health Organisation laying down the procedure for cooperation between the two organizations -Memorandum defining the arrangements for cooperation between the World Health Organisation and the European Communities (72/725/ECSC, EEC, Euratom) (OJ L 300, 28-10-1982 at pp. 20-22).

[104] Exchange of letters between the World Health Organization and the Commission of the European Communities concerning the consolidation and intensification of cooperation (2001/C1/04) (OJ C1/7 2001).

[105] See World Health Assembly, Global Health Security: Epidemic Alert and Response (WHA 54.14) 21 May 2001 and World Health Assembly, Revision of the International Health Regulations (WHA 56.28) 28 May 2003.

[106] The IHRs now form the legal basis for Member States' responsibilities towards the WHO. This means that when there is a public health risk, defined as events 'posing a serious and direct threat to the health of human populations', the WHO can make binding recommendations with regard to international public health measures, such as travel restrictions and bans on trade, to be taken by Member States; however, there is no enforcement mechanism. Nevertheless, there is a dispute resolution procedure. As to cooperation with the EU, Article 57 of the IHR prescribes that 'states that are members of a regional economic integration organization shall apply in their mutual relations common rules in force in that regional economic integration organization'. This means that if the WHO made a recommendation, the EU would have to act collectively on the initiative of the Commission.

All the Member States signed this document, but not the European Commission. So you have a plan in the national states, but the European Union doesn't have to follow the plan. They did not prepare this plan, an official one, because public health is a national matter, not a European one. But in this case it's a trans-border risk. So there is a lift that begins to go up, go down, up, down, etc. So it was panic.[107]

The forest of alert systems that became active at the time of the crisis exacerbated this panic. At least three different alert systems were active during the swine flu pandemic. The first was the two-level alert system of the Commission itself, which is managed by the Secretariat General's crisis-coordination unit.[108] The emergency system also responds to the alert system of the WHO with respect to communicable diseases. If the level is raised to 6 (pandemic), the EU's emergency authorization of medicines becomes possible. The EU DG SANTE health threats unit also has an alert mechanism vis-à-vis the Member States.[109]

After the WHO declared alert level phase 6 on 11 June 2009, a cascade of emergency provisions became possible.[110] Particularly important in this respect is that the approval of a pandemic vaccine becomes legally possible after this kind of declaration. This means that in the case of a public health emergency, the EU central authorization procedure for medicines is dependent on another international organization's (the WHO) declaration of a pandemic. If there were a public health emergency that does not spread beyond the borders of the EU, it is questionable if at EU level it would be legally possible to declare a public health emergency on a grand scale, or a pandemic for that matter.[111]

Another problem that rose on the agenda during the swine flu outbreak was the *procurement* of pandemic vaccines and antivirals. For years, the Commission had been trying to create a stockpile of antivirals. However, this potentially directly impacts on Member States' ability to manage the welfare entitlement of access to medicines in the case of a public health emergency.

We discussed the EU stockpile of antivirals until we were all exhausted and then decided that there was no agreement. And when the pandemic happened they [Member States] suddenly found themselves in the situation that some countries had far too much and some countries had none. And there was no way to deal with this in the middle of the crisis so we need to [...] develop sufficiently good arguments in advance that convince people to adopt the measures in good time rather than afterwards. 'Cause it is very easy to adopt measures after Katrina for example or after the Tsunami or after something awful happens—everybody can be an expert then—but the real challenge I think is to look into the future and say what do we think we need to do on the basis of our past experience.[112]

This is also reflected upon by the Member States:

107 Respondent 6 (Assistant to MEP, 2010).

108 Ibid.; Respondent 8 (Representative Secretariat General European Commission, 2010); Respondent 15 (High level representative Commission Services SANCO, 2010).

109 See Commission (2007) in which the former EU 3 level emergency structure was still outlined.

110 Respondent 6 (Assistant to MEP, 2010); ibid.; Respondent 15 (High level representative Commission Services SANCO, 2010).

111 Respondent 15 (High level representative Commission Services SANCO, 2010). Arguably the Network Commission under the Communicable Disease Decision would be able to declare a pandemic at EU level. However, this is a relatively low-level body of EU bureaucrats. And although the pharmaceutical regulation provides for the possibility for the EU to declare an official pandemic, the Communicable Disease Decision did not create a (formal) procedure for the declaration of a pandemic.

112 Ibid.

We [the Member States] have been trying since 2005 to come to a mechanism for joint procurement. It took the pandemic to find an agreement [. . .]. So, in a sense it will always be crisis driven, like lot of policies are [. . .].[113]

These accounts illustrate that an important dynamic for policymaking in the area of public health, beyond the regulation public health in the area of, say, food and medicines, is crisis response. In this regard other examples are the BSE crisis, with the ensuing setting-up of DG SANTE and the risk assessment architecture, and also the 9/11 attacks, with the subsequent set-up of a health threats unit and HSC. This general effect of public health crises is well recognized by public policymakers: 'Crises which hit the consumer are excellent ways of speeding up policies.'[114] The swine flu pandemic in this respect created bedrock for legislative proposals and further policy with regard to 'health threats and security'. For instance, with regard to the 'forest' of alert mechanisms, the Commission outlines that:

we now are proposing an alert system of our own. Before, the Member States were rather reluctant, and you see they only move forward when really there is a crisis striking them in the face.[115]

In December 2011 the Commission proposed a new decision on all serious cross-border threats in order to address some of the problems identified here.[116] So, instead of dealing with the particulars of managing a communicable disease, the proposal extends the existing framework to all serious cross-border threats. This means that it includes responses to, for instance, the release of biological agents responsible for non-communicable diseases; threats of chemical release and antimicrobial resistance; environmental threats to public health, such as heat waves and cold spells; and threats of unknown origin, including those of malicious intent.[117] This proposal was adopted in 2013.[118] This newly adopted decision also creates a voluntary system for the joint procurement of medical countermeasures, which directly impacts the Member States' role to provide for (welfare) access to medicines and possibly also vaccine strategies. Moreover, the new decision also formalizes the HSC to some extent.[119]

The adoption of the new Health Security Decision, expanding and institutionalizing EU involvement in the area of public health protection, illustrates how a crisis allows for ad hoc policy as a matter of practice to interlink with law and thus create a basis for its further development: 'This is what the experience is: with each crisis the Commission becomes stronger, and usually during a crisis Member States are willing to let go.'[120] Policymakers at the European level are well aware of this mechanism; in the words of a Commission representative:

A very common known, studied effect is that after a crisis, the Union [. . .] is given more powers in an area, and that is why, part of the reasons why, the various mechanisms and sectors have developed over time.[121]

[113] Respondent 4 (MS Representative Working Party on Public Health in the Council, 2010).

[114] Respondent 2 (Deputy Permanent Representative for Health in the Council, 2010).

[115] Ibid.

[116] Commission proposal for a decission of the European Parliament and of the Council on serious cross-border threats to health Brussels (COM(2011)866 final).

[117] Article 2 Decision No. 1082/2013/EU of the European Parliament and of the Council of 22 October 2013 on serious cross-border threats to health and repealing Decision No. 2119/98/EC (OJ L 293, 15-11-2013).

[118] Ibid. [119] de Ruijter (n 2).

[120] Respondent 4 (MS Representative Working Party on Public Health in the Council, 2010); Respondent 15 (High level representative Commission Services SANCO, 2010).

[121] Respondent 8 (Representative Secretariat General European Commission, 2010).

4. The Impact of EU Public Health Policy on Fundamental Rights and Values

In the framework of EU fundamental rights in the context of EU health policy, particular focus with respect to individual rights is placed first on the right to informed consent and second on the right to privacy and data protection. These individual rights have particular meaning and weight in the health policy context. The right to informed consent is deeply connected with the right to human dignity and integrity of the person.[122] Human dignity in this regard can refer to the individual in terms of personal integrity, but also to protecting society in general.[123] The provisions on informed consent in Article 3 CFREU generally are also part of the ECtHR case law. However, the ECHR has no specific provision on informed consent.[124]

The second aspect focuses on is the right to privacy and confidentiality.[125] The right to private life in Article 7 CFREU relates to the information that is gathered and stored about an individual, such as the collection of medical data and medical records. Moreover, the right to privacy also entails the physician's duty to secrecy about the patient's medical and mental wellbeing as a matter of dignity and of preserving the patient's confidence in the medical profession and health services in general.[126] Article 8 CFREU asserts the right to protect personal data that is accessible or may be accessible to third parties. This is an important right when health-care providers or public health authorities exchange medical data about a patient across a border.[127] In this regard, the protection of personal data and the right to protection of a patient's health status are explicitly protected at EU level. Nevertheless, public health grounds may limit the right to have one's personal data protected.[128]

4.1 Individual rights

The countermeasures that were taken at EU level to curb the spread of swine flu can potentially impact individual rights of Europeans. A public health emergency generally can create an exception for the protection of informed consent and patients can be forced to undergo medical treatment, involuntary testing, or medical examination

[122] Articles 1 and 3 CFREU.

[123] Case C-377/98 *The Netherlands v. European Parliament and Council of the European Union*, [2001] ECR I-07079 (see paras 77 and 78 on the basis of human dignity for not allowing patentability of elements of the human body).

[124] Case C-404/92 *X v. Commission of the European Communities* [1994] ECR I-04737 (on informed consent); also see Case C-62/90 *Commission v. Germany* [1992] ECR 1-2575.

[125] Articles 7 and 8 CFREU.

[126] R. Reintjes et al. 'Benchmarking National Surveillance Systems: A New Tool for the Comparison of Communicable Disease Surveillance and Control in Europe' (2007) *European Journal of Public Health* 17 375–80; S. Gainotti et al. 'Ethical Models Underpinning Responses to Threats to Public Health: A Comparison of Approaches to Communicable Disease Control in Europe' (2008) *Bioethics* 22 466–76.

[127] Decision No 1082/2013/EU of the European Parliament and of the Council of 22 October 2013 on serious cross-border threats to health and repealing Decision No 2119/98/EC (OJ L 293/ 1 5-11-2013).

[128] Regulation (EU) 2016/679 of the European Parliament and of the Council of 27 April 2016 on the protection of natural persons with regard to the processing of personal data and on the free movement of such data, and repealing Directive 95/46/EC (General Data Protection Regulation) recital 52.

against their will if mandated by public authorities.[129] Furthermore, also concerning the secrecy of personal medical data, a public health emergency can create exceptional circumstances in which these rights of individuals are suspended.[130]

4.1.1 Market authorization of vaccines and defining priority groups for vaccination

In the authorization of pandemic vaccines, informed consent can be an individual right that may come into play with respect to the clinical trial. However, this is no different to the normal context for the approval of medicines at EU level. This means that even if a vaccine goes through an emergency procedure for its approval, in the clinical trial informed consent of the test subjects is always mandatory.[131] As to the determination of priority groups for vaccination, given the relatively mild symptoms of the swine flu, arguably the fundamental right to informed consent was not impacted, because Member States did not adopt measures for mandatory vaccinations. However, in its nature, and as we also saw with the Ebola outbreak, the determination of a priority group could potentially affect the right to informed consent. In order to curb the Ebola outbreak people arriving from West Africa were sometimes quarantined at airports and had to undergo mandatory medical examinations. To offer an example in the swine flu case, in the US response to swine flu, some members of the first priority group for immunization, the health-care workers, were told to immunize themselves against the influenza, or they could be fired from their job.[132]

At the same time, it is questionable if the determination of priority groups for immunization against swine flu was binding *at European level* and could formally have had a direct effect for European citizens. *Legally* the determination of an actual mandatory vaccination programme for certain priority groups would be a matter for the Member States, as Article 168(7) TFEU limits EU competence with respect to the delivery of medical care. However, Article 3(f) of the 1998 Decision on communicable diseases applicable at the time of the swine flu outbreak allowed for the adoption of implementing measures, but only concerning 'guidelines' on the protective measures to be taken by Member States in emergency situations.

Given the relatively broad interpretations of the Court with respect to bringing an EU measure into 'the scope of EU law', if a Member State effectuates a EU guideline it

[129] The ICCPR of the United Nations High Commission for Human Rights allows the public good to take precedence over individual rights in a number of situations, including when there are threats to public health. See C-28/05 *Doktor and Others* [2006] ECR I-5431 (on foot-and-mouth disease in animals and the general EU principle of the right of defence); Also see Joined Cases C-317/08, C-318/08, C-319/08, and C-320/08, *Alassini and others* [2010] ECR I-2213 at para. 63:

> [I]t is settled case-law that fundamental rights do not constitute unfettered prerogatives and may be restricted, provided that the restrictions in fact correspond to objectives to general interest pursued by the measure in question and that they do not involve, with regard to the objectives pursued, a disproportionate and intolerable interference which infringes upon the very substance on the rights guaranteed.

Also see S. Gruskin 'Is There a Government in the Cockpit: a Passenger's Perspective, or Global Public Health: the Role of Human Rights' (2004) *Temple Law Review* 77 313–34; and see Nuffield Council on Bioethics (2007) 'Public Health: Ethical Issues', available at: <http://nuffieldbioethics.org/wp-content/uploads/2014/07/Public-health-ethical-issues.pdf> (last accessed February 2014).

[130] See supra note 54. [131] See further Clinical Trial Directive.

[132] US Centers of Disease Control and Prevention, Prevention and Control of Influenza with Vaccines: Recommendations of the Advisory Committee on Immunization Practices (ACIP), Weekly August 26, 2011/60(33) at 1128-1132.

is possible that EU fundamental rights apply. Therefore, although in the case of swine flu no countermeasures were adopted that could seriously have infringed Europeans' right to informed consent, a measure such as the determination of priority groups for vaccination—particularly now that the legislative basis for the EU in the area of public health threats is expanded and EU decisions can more easily be formulated as an 'EU obligation'—could have such an impact in the future. Furthermore, the authority and number of *institutional actors* involved at EU level did entail authoritative allocation of value through the determination of priority groups in this respect. EU and Member States representative in this regard perceived the agreements made at EU level as 'de facto binding',[133] or 'morally binding'.[134] This means that although legally it may have been a stretch to argue a right to informed consent, the value of the right to informed consent was impacted in that some people, for instance medical workers, may have been pressured to undergo immunization against swine flu as a result of European agreements and coordination.

4.1.2 *Information exchange, contact tracing, and passenger screening*

As far as the rights to privacy and personal data are concerned, public health considerations have been considered a legitimate reason for interfering.[135] Although the general rule on medical data is that access by a third party is prohibited, in some cases this might nonetheless be allowed as long as it respects fundamental rights.[136] In this regard information about the patient's health status is duly recognized as a fundamental patient right in the EU context.[137] A public health threat could require a physician to notify the authorities when s/he suspects that a patient's condition might pose a threat to public health. In the EU this information would then be shared between the EU and Member States' public health authorities. Additionally, in an international context International Health Regulations also prescribe an obligation to report.[138] In some countries there are even financial incentives for physicians to report on possible threats.[139] This means that personal (medical) data may be made accessible to third parties, which was certainly the case with regard to the countermeasure of contact tracing for swine flu.

The countermeasures taken at the EU level regarding contact tracing and passenger screening and exchange of information between health authorities can impact on a

[133] Respondent 3 (MS Representative Working Party on Public Health in the Council, 2010).

[134] Respondent 15 (High level representative Commission Services SANCO, 2010).

[135] Articles 7 and 8 CFREU.

[136] Case C-369/98 (*Fisher) The Queen v. Minister of Agriculture, Fisheries and Food, ex parte Trevor Robert Fisher and Penny Fisher* [2000] ECR I-06751 paras 31 and 32:

> In order to answer the question whether certain information contained in the database may be disclosed, the competent authority must balance, on the one hand, the interest of the person who provided the information and, on the other, the interest of the person who has need of that information in order to meet a legitimate objective. However, the respective interests of the persons concerned in regard to data of a personal nature must be assessed in a manner which ensures protection of fundamental freedoms and rights.

[137] Case C-404/92 *P, X v. Commission* [1994] ECR I-4737.

[138] See R. Reintjes et al. 'Benchmarking National Surveillance Systems: A New Tool for the Comparison of Communicable Disease Surveillance and Control in Europe' (2007) *European Journal of Public Health* 17 375–80; World Health Organization *International Health Regulations 2005* 2nd edn (2008).

[139] S. Gainotti et al. 'Ethical Models Underpinning Responses to Threats to Public Health: A Comparison of Approaches to Communicable Disease Control in Europe' (2008) *Bioethics* 22 466–76.

patient's fundamental right to privacy and the protection of personal data.[140] The EU, at the time of the swine flu crisis, took implementing measures on the basis of the then applicable the Decision on communicable diseases. Although in principle Member States' authorities initially perform the contact tracing, specifics in the case of swine flu were outlined in a separate decision.[141] Moreover, given the fact that Member States are obliged to share this data under the Decision on communicable diseases, it would fall within the scope of Union law. Hence, contact tracing, information exchanges on 'public health events' regarding individual patients, and passenger screening at airports were all countermeasures that impact the right to privacy and data protection, although safeguarding the public (the right to health) may provide a legitimation for this infringement.

4.2 The right to health

The right to health in Article 35 CFREU encompasses the right to access health care. Although the Court has not ruled on this point, assuming that the right to health is a 'principle' in the Charter,[142] it can be used to assess the legality of EU health policy generally.[143] Article 263 TFEU creates a high threshold for individuals to take action against the EU, particularly when this concerns legislative measures. In that case individuals have to be able to show both direct and individual concern.[144] However, private parties can challenge regulatory acts (acts adopted other than through the Article 289 TFEU procedure) if they can show direct concern.[145]

With regard to the Member States, the assumption that the right to health is a principle in the Charter context affects the possibility for justiciability.[146] It is still a precarious matter, as discussed in Chapter 3, how the rights that are considered principles in the Charter can become operational. Individuals may be able to invoke a Charter provision together with a directive, if national law is *contra legem* and cannot be interpreted in line with a fundamental right expressed through a directive.[147] However, if the underlying right in the Charter, for the purpose of its justiciability, is considered a principle, individuals can still not invoke it against the Member States.[148] Furthermore, the right to *health care*, even for legality review in terms of Article 263 TFEU, would be difficult to invoke vis-à-vis EU institutions.

Article 35 CFREU, with regard to the right to access health care provides an extra safeguard, which is that 'national law and practices' establish its conditions. In simple

[140] Dąbrowska-Kłosińska (n 88).

[141] Decision 2009/547/EC of 10 July 2009 amending Decision 2000/57/EC on early warning and response system for the prevention and control of communicable diseases under Decision No 2119/98/EC of the European Parliament and of the Council (OJ L 181/57, 11-07-2009).

[142] See Chapter 3 at section 3 recalling that there is no certainty whether or not the right to health in the European (Charter) context is to be regarded as a 'principle' or a 'right'.

[143] Article 263 TFEU, Article 52(5), and Article 35 CFREU.

[144] See Chapter 2 at section 3.3.1 (n 87), reference to para. 31 of Case 25/62 *Plaumann & Co v. Commission* [1963] *ECR 95*, but see later case law, infra note 8.

[145] Case T-262/10 *Microban International and Microban (Europe) v. Commission*, [2011] ECR II-07697; Case T-18/10 *Inuit Tapiriit Kanatami and Others v. Commission*, nyr, [2011] (the *Microban* case involved an implementing act by the European Commission in order to protect public health).

[146] But see T. Hervey and J. McHale 'Article 35 Health Care' in S. Peers et al. (eds) *The EU Charter of Fundamental Rights* (Oxford: Hart, 2014) at p. 967 (who refer to this right as a 'right'—although one hedged with exceptions and caveats).

[147] Case C-555/07 *Seda Kücükdeveci v. Swedex GmbH & Co* KG [2010] ECR I-00365.

[148] Case C-176/12 *Association de médiation sociale v. Union locale des syndicats CGT (CGT)* nyr [2014] at para. 46.

terms, this implies that the EU can guarantee the recognition of this right *at EU level*, by not interfering in the national provisions realizing the right to access health care. Arguably, as long as a Member State has only the most limited provision establishing the right to access health care, the EU has no legal basis for review of national acts. Nevertheless, as put forward by Hervey, the right to health and access to health care in many instances can be coupled with an individual right (a 'social rights-plus' approach).[149] Herewith, the right to health could be justiciable for individuals when it *also* impacts on an individual right, such as the right to life, the right to dignity, or the right to non-discrimination (which may even have a horizontal effect).[150]

Outside the Charter, the right to health can be invoked as a general principle given that all Member States have signed up to Article 11 of the European Social Charter which covers the right to the protection of health,[151] and most Member States have also signed up to Article 13 ESC which outlines the right to medical assistance.[152] Beside the actual possibility of claiming a right to health in court, the right to health also creates a benchmark for analysing the legitimacy of EU health policy given that it is a principle that needs to be observed and promoted in the EU context.[153] The right to health in this respect is not only a purely legal provision, but it also expresses a 'value' common to the European Member States on which is the Union is founded,[154] particularly as it gives expression to a specific aspect of human dignity and promotes the wellbeing of citizens of the EU.[155]

Given the breadth of EU *public health* policy, in order to analyse the implications of EU public health policy on fundamental rights the current analysis looks at the EU handling of swine flu in relation to the institutional practices in this respect. The EU measures to counter the outbreak—the authorization of vaccines, contact tracing and information exchange on specific patients, passenger screening, defining priority groups for first access to medicine, the creation of guidelines on school closures, and communicating to the public—were generally aimed at the population at large. In adopting countermeasures, both aspects of the right to health—the responsibility of public authorities to protect health, and the facilitation of access to health care—can come into play. With respect to health emergencies, Article 168 TFEU outlines that the EU may take action to complement national policies:

> [S]uch action shall cover the fight against the major health scourges, by promoting research into their causes, their transmission and their prevention, as well as health information and education, and monitoring, early warning of and combating serious cross-border threats to health.

The procedure for doing so is outlined in Article 168(5) TFEU by use of the ordinary legislative procedure through adopting 'incentive measures' that may not in fact harmonize national laws.[156]

149 See Chapter 3 at section 3.1.1.

150 T. K. Hervey 'The Right to Health in European Union Law' in T. Hervey and J. Kenner (eds) *Economic and Social Rights Under the Charter of Fundamental Rights* (Oxford: Hart, 2003) at p. 196.

151 Article 6 TEU.

152 T. K. Hervey and J. V. McHale *Health Law and the European Union* (Cambridge: Cambridge University Press, 2014).

153 Article 51 CFREU and also expressed in the work of the Fundamental Rights Agency.

154 Council *Council Conclusions on Common values and principles in European Union Health Systems* (OJ C 146/1, 2006).

155 See the reference to European Social Charter in the Preamble of the Treaty on European Union and Articles 2 and 3 TEU.

156 The exact meaning of 'incentive measures' remains opaque.

For the countermeasures the EU took in response to swine flu the legal bases ranged from the primary health provision on 'complementing' Member States' policies in monitoring, early warning of and combating serious cross-border threats to health, to the use of internal market on the basis of Article 114 TFEU, where the EU has regulatory powers with respect to approving medicines and other forms of (informal) cooperation. In this respect, the basis for establishing whether EU health policy impacts the right to health directly and how this can be analysed depends on the countermeasures taken, by what institutional actor, and through what procedure.

4.2.1 Market authorization of vaccines and defining priority groups for vaccination

The first measure under consideration is the authorization of pandemic vaccines at EU level. The EU has an obligation to ensure a high level of health in all its policies.[157] This means that the EU only has the obligation to protect health as it comes up in the context in other policies; otherwise the right to health would be the basis for expanding the role of the EU beyond its legislative powers.[158] Generally, the availability of medical countermeasures is seen as an obligatory effort for public authorities to make.[159] However, even when Member States have conferred competences to the EU to approve pandemic medicines, if for some reason the EU decided not to do so, it is questionable whether there would be a right to health that in and of itself would impose an obligation on the EU to act. As it stands, there is no provision based on the right to health that permits the EU to oblige pharmaceutical companies to apply for central authorization to approve pandemic medicines (if these are available at all).

However, another question is how the right to health is impacted once pandemic medicines are actually available—what obligations with respect to the right to health can be imposed on the EU and the Member States? With regard to the Member States, as far as access to medicines is concerned, in the case of pandemic vaccines many had pre-purchase agreements with pharmaceutical companies. This resulted in a situation where, regardless of the severity of the pandemic, some Member States had too many and others had too few vaccines available for their population.[160] Particularly for the Member States that had a potential shortage of vaccines available, the European Commission created an ad hoc public procurement programme where Member States that had too many vaccines could offer to sell them. However, by this time it had already become clear that this strain of swine flu was a relatively mild virus. This situation brought a lack of solidarity among Member States to light, showing that once crisis strikes Member States tend to take care of their own population first.[161] That the European Commission attempted to mitigate the effect of a lack of coordination in terms of public procurement of vaccines, even though Member States only participated in its programme on a voluntary basis, promotes the right to access health care because

[157] Articles 6, 9, and 168 TFEU, and Article 35 CFREU.

[158] Article 51(2) TFEU.

[159] See H. P. Hestermeyer 'Access to Medication as a Human Right' (2004) *Max Planck UNYB* 8 101–80 at 178. See in this regard for instance the UN ICCPR Article 4 in relation to Article 6.

[160] And that some Member States paid much more for the same vaccine than other Member States. See Respondent 15 (High level representative Commission Services SANCO, 2010); Respondent 19 (High level representative European Medicines Agency, 2010); Respondent 25 (High level representative ECDC, 2010).

[161] Commission Communication from the Commission to the European Parliament, the Council, the European Economic and Social Committee and the Committee of the Regions on Action Against Cancer: Euroepan Partnership (COM(2009) 291/4).

the EU in this case was involved in coordinating more equitable access to medicines. At the same time, it is unlikely that this policy activity could result in directly enforceable rights for EU citizens vis-à-vis the EU or their Member State. The Member States were under no EU obligation to participate in the ad hoc public procurement/exchange of vaccines between Member States; therefore no justiciable fundamental rights claim can be made. Even when coupled with the right to equal treatment in Article 21 CFREU, given that there is no EU obligation to act with regard to the public procurement of vaccines,[162] the right to access health care would in this respect be unlikely to create an enforceable right.

A second countermeasure under consideration is the determination of priority groups for vaccination.[163] Here, the build-up of institutional capacity creates possibilities for de facto impacting the right to health, through institutional practices. The legal status of the guidelines for determining priority groups for vaccination is institutionally relatively complex. The guidelines were adopted by the HSC together with the regulatory EWRS committee while at the same time building on the advice of the ECDC, the Commission, and WHO experts.[164] However, the nature of the guidelines is not mandatory in and of itself. This means that if a Member State decided not to implement the guidelines, this would not result in a directly enforceable fundamental rights claim on the basis of the right to health or health care, even when taking a social rights-plus approach, for instance on the basis of the right to life or the right to equal treatment.[165]

At the same time, guidelines on priority groups for vaccination do have an impact on fundamental rights in terms of expressing particular values. For, although the guidelines may not have resulted in a legally binding EU obligation, given the number and authority of the institutional actors involved in drafting the guidelines, they did possess *authoritative value*. Hence the guidelines made a difference to the lives of for instance health workers and pregnant women, given that these were among the prioritized groups. Their access to health care was improved as a result of the guidelines, whereas for those Europeans excluded from the prioritized groups the right to access health care was cut off.

Another consideration that is relevant in the approval of pandemic medicines and the selection of priority groups for vaccination is the *safety of the vaccines* and antivirals that were approved in response to the swine flu outbreak. As described in case of swine flu, pandemic vaccines were authorized by using an emergency procedure, and obtained 'temporary approval' even before the full procedure of scientific and regulatory assessment was completed. This process of conditional authorization was adopted for most of the first vaccines that were distributed and given to millions of Europeans. One of these vaccines, Pandemrix, created and distributed by the pharmaceutical company GlaxoSmithKline, was also given to the prioritized high-risk groups, which included children, particularly those with asthma and heart disease. In the EU around 30 million people received this particular vaccine.[166] This vaccine has now been found

[162] Article 168(7) TFEU.

[163] Communication from the Commission to the Council, The European Parliament and the European Economic and Social Committee and the Committee of Regions, Pandemic (h1N1), Commission Staff Working Document on Joint Procurement of Vaccine against influenza A H1N1 2009 (COM (2009) 481- SEC (2009) 1188); HSC/EWRS Statement on Influeza A(H1N1) 2009: target and priority groups for vaccination available at: http://www.ec.europa.eu/health/archive/ph_threats/com/influenza/docs/hsc_ewrs_statement_en.pdf> (last accessed March 2014).

[164] See Chapter 5 section 2.

[165] Articles 2 and 21 CFREU.

[166] Y. Dauvilliers et al. 'Post-H1N1 Narcolepsy-Cataplexy' (2010) *Sleep* 33 1428–30; I. Sample 'Swine Flu Vaccine Can Trigger Narcolepsy, UK Government Concedes, Review of Fresh Evidence

to increase the risk of narcolepsy, a serious neurological disorder in children, by 30 per cent.[167]

Problematic in this respect is that most of the pre-purchase agreements, between governments and pharmaceutical companies that under EU regulations would otherwise have been liable for this type of injury, had indemnity clauses so that the Member State governments in the end had to pay the damages.[168] In this case the right to health coupled with the right to life was impacted if it was found that the public health authorities at the EU level and ultimately the Commission through its authorization procedures did not take sufficient care to safeguard the health of these children. The fact children were part of a *prioritised risk group* under European guidelines is an additional aspect to take into consideration, particularly because the vaccines were approved through European fast-track procedures where less clinical data are available, especially not on the side effects of a vaccine, given that clinical trials generally exclude children.[169] If the precautions by the EU were indeed insufficient and caused an increase in health risks for these groups, the latter is a serious impact on their right to health.

4.2.2 Information exchange, contact tracing, and passenger screening

With respect to the countermeasures of information exchange, contact tracing, and passenger screening, the right to health is impacted if the EU did not undertake these types of efforts to curb the spread of swine flu. From this perspective the public authorities have a duty to do what they can to curb the spread of disease. However, exactly what these efforts should contain is ultimately up to the public authorities. The countermeasures mentioned took place at EU level on the basis of Article 168 TFEU, which asks the EU to complement monitoring, early warning of, and combating serious cross-border threats. The fact that the EU only needs to 'complement' national policies makes it questionable that an individual claim against the EU or the Member States for not undertaking efforts to stop the spread of the virus on the basis of the right to health would be effective.

However, with respect to the possibility of a legality review, Member States are relatively dependent on information on the public health situation in another Member State, for instance if a patient carrying a virus has been localized. The EU early-warning system is obligatory in that these types of events need to be exchanged. Hypothetically, a failure to facilitate exchange, for instance not adopting an implementing measure on defining a case definition for exchange, could be challenged in light of the right to health.[170] Nevertheless, in the case of the swine flu crisis, through the exchange of

Finds Jab Given to 6 Million People in Britain Can Occasionally Cause Sleep Disorder' (2013) *The Guardian* Thursday 19 September.

[167] I. Persson et al. 'Risks of Neurological and immune-Related Diseases, Including Narcolepsy, After Vaccination with Pandemrix: A Population- and Registry-Based Cohort Study with Over 2 years of Follow-Up, January 2014' (2014) *Journal of Internal Medicine* 1; EMA Press Release, European Medicines Agency recommends restricting use of Pandemrix (27 July 2011, EMA/CHMP/568830/20110).

[168] See Sample (2013) supra note 166; Respondent 15 (High level representative Commission Services SANCO, 2010); Respondent 19 (High level representative European Medicines Agency, 2010); Respondent 25 (High level representative ECDC, 2010).

[169] Commission Communication to the European Parliament and the Council, Better Medicines for Children, From Concept to Reality, Progress Report on the Paediatric Regulation (EC) 1901/2006 (COM (2013) 443 final).

[170] See Article 3(a) of what is now No. 1082/2013/EU of the European Parliament and of the Council of 22 October 2013 on serious cross-border threats to health and repealing Decision No. 2119/98/EC (OJ L 293/1 5-11-2013): '[A] "case definition" means a set of commonly agreed

information and screening passengers, the EU was engaging in actions that effectuate the right to health for European citizens. In this regard countermeasures impact on the right to health; moreover these measures can seriously impact individual rights, as will be discussed here.

4.2.3 School closures, delaying strategies, and information to the public

It is unlikely that the right to health is directly impacted through the adoption of EU guidelines on school closures in response to the swine flu pandemic, particularly as these were not created on the basis of any EU legal provision. The same would apply to the determination of delaying strategies, which were generally basic hygiene rules (washing hands, cough into your elbow). However, with regard to providing information on public health risks, the EU right to health is relevant. This is particularly the case if the right to health is coupled with the right to life. The ECtHR *Oneryildiz v Turkey* case implies that in the case of serious health risks, there may be an obligation on the authorities to warn the public so that preventive measures can be taken to safeguard against loss of life.[171] In parallel, given the responsibility of the EU to coordinate Member States' policies in case of cross-border threats, the EU needs to ensure that the public has access to information that is clear and reliable and that the Member States are not coming out with different and confusing messages. Such an obligation to warn could follow and thus impact the EU right to health, particularly if for instance the EU had approved a flawed vaccine.[172]

5. The Impact of Intertwining Informal Coordination and Formal Law

The role of the EU in responding to the 2009 swine flu crisis illustrates how a build-up of previous ad hoc responses to various disease outbreaks and crises can culminate and expand the EU's power in the field of human health. Moreover, the case exemplifies that the regulatory aspects of public health protection in the EU, such as in the area of pharmaceuticals, can intertwine with different ways of Member States' health policy coordination, resulting in an increased role for the EU. In the case of the swine flu outbreak, the regulatory power for medicines intertwined with the coordination of communicable disease control and informal and ad hoc ways for Member States to work together at EU level.

As a result, however, both during (in terms of countermeasures) and after the outbreak, it became possible to adopt more binding measures at EU level than had previously been available, thus expanding the EU's power in the field of human health. On one hand, *during* the outbreak of the swine flu countermeasures were adopted through combining the EWRS Committee with the (informal) HSC. On the other, *after* the virus was no longer considered dangerous, a basis was created for institutionalizing and

diagnostic criteria that have to be fulfilled in order to accurately identify cases of a targeted serious cross-border threat to health in a given population, while excluding the detection of unrelated threats.'

[171] Grand Chamber Judgement, Case of *Oneryildiz v. Turkey* (Application no. 48939/99) Strasbourg, 30 November 2004.

[172] EMA Press Release, European Medicines Agency recommends restricting use of Pandemrix (27 July 2011, EMA/CHMP/568830/20110).

formalizing the ad hoc solutions that were created during the response to swine flu, and new legislation was adopted.

The response to a public health emergency has the consequence of triggering the executive to take action; the EU is no exception in this respect. However, the difference is that its emergency powers in the field of human health are narrowly circumscribed. The Member States' reliance on informality and even intergovernmental methods of cooperation at EU level shows that although there is a perceived need to work together at this level, there remains a reluctance to invest the EU with more powers. Even so, and perhaps paradoxically, the EU's authority to address public health does expand, through the intertwining of these informal processes with areas where there are regulatory powers.

Both with respect to the EU's role and the Member States coordinating at EU level, the question is whether EU public health policy in this respect is legitimate. What is the impact on fundamental rights of the countermeasures taken in response to swine flu? Is the exercising of power by the EU, in light of protecting the public from health risks while balancing this with individual rights, legitimate? Although the fact remains that the EU has limited legislative power in the field of public health, its role in responding to the swine flu outbreak also illustrates that the precarious balancing of public health with individual rights is no longer done by Member States alone. The swine flu case also raises questions with regard to the legitimacy of the countermeasures taken at EU level in terms of the impact on fundamental rights. The next chapter introduces a case where formal legislative procedure creates a policy discourse on *health care* that was previously unimaginable at EU level.

6

EU Health Care: Access to Medical Care

After health was included in the Treaty of Maastricht we could only speak about public health—not health care at all, that was blasphemy in Church [...]—and then it took 15 to 20 years and we are openly discussing a Directive on patients' rights and cross-border health care. That would have been unthinkable after Maastricht.[1]

The present chapter examines developments regarding EU legislation in the area of health care, rather than public health. The chapter focuses on the processes and the involvement of different EU institutional actors and policy mechanisms in the adoption of the Directive on patients' rights in cross-border health care ('the Directive').[2] The adoption of the Directive illustrates a case that, in the words of a Member State representative:

is very touchy. It really concerns the whole health-care system [...] [I]t is also tricky, because it touches an area which mainly is in Member States' competence.[3]

First, the chapter introduces the Directive itself and whether it expands access to health care across the EU. Second, it turns to the way the Directive was adopted, focusing particularly on the different roles of EU institutional actors and the discourse and controversies that developed in health care in the EU as a result of the legislative process. Last, the chapter addresses the expansion of EU health-care policy beyond the adoption of the new Directive that resulted from the increased discourse on health care and its impact for individual rights and access to health care.

1. Access to Cross-border Health Care before and after the Directive

In the area of health care, which relates more specifically to the delivery and access to medical care, the EU is excluded from harmonizing national laws. Article 168(7) TFEU reiterates the principle of subsidiarity in this regard:

The Union shall respect the responsibilities of the Member States for the definition of their health policy and for the organisation and delivery of health services and medical care. The responsibilities of the Member States shall include the management of health services and medical care and the allocation of the resources assigned to them.

[1] Respondent 2 (Deputy Permanent Representative for Health in the Council, 2010).

[2] Directive 2011/24/EU of the European Parliament and of the Council of 9 March 2011 on the application of patients' rights in cross-border healthcare (OJ L88/45, 04-04-2011).

[3] Respondent 3 (MS Representative Working Party on Public Health in the Council, 2010).

EU Health Law & Policy: The Expansion of EU Power in Public Health and Health Care. Anniek de Ruijter © Anniek de Ruijter 2019. Published in 2019 by Oxford University Press.

Paradoxically, in 2011 a Directive regarding the delivery of medical care across borders was adopted. This Directive applies to 'cross-border health care'. But what is cross-border health care, and what situation does this refer to? In practice, *cross-border* health care can refer to a number of arrangements. In the EU in recent years there has been an influx of bottom-up coordination schemes in order to facilitate national health-care systems. This means that national health-care providers and health insurance authorities regularly cooperate with health institutions across borders.[4] However, patients can also require access to health care across borders in an individual setting. This can be as a consequence of travel or cross-border settlement (*patients move*).[5] Health services can be delivered from the territory of one Member State into the territory of another, such as telemedicine or remote-diagnosis, prescription, and laboratory services (*services move*). Moreover, the health professionals themselves move cross border (*health provider moves*) on invitation of a hospital or a health insurance authority, for instance to take care of a waiting list for a particular medical treatment.[6] In fact, the majority of cross-border health care is made up of these types of cooperative arrangements. This is especially due to under-capacity and to create local competition in terms of health-care pricing.[7]

[4] For example, Belgium sends hundreds of patients to France each year for MRI scans, Austria sends groups of patients with highly infectious diseases to Munich, Malta sends about 300 patients per year to the UK for specialized treatment, and Ireland sends transplant patients to the UK. In order to reduce waiting time, Germany sends about 500 patients per year with chronic conditions to Austria, Hungary, Italy, the Czech Republic, and Slovakia for preventative treatments; see L. Bertinato et al. (eds) *Policy Brief: Cross-Border Health Care in Europe* (Geneva: World Health Organization on behalf of the European Observatory on Health Systems and Policies, 2005).

[5] See R. Busse et al. (eds) *Mapping Health Services Access: National and Cross-Border Issues (HealthACCESS) Final Report* (DG SANCO: 2006) at p. 22; European Parliament legislative resolution of 23 April 2009 on the proposal for a directive of the European Parliament and of the Council on the application of patients' rights in cross-border healthcare (COM(2008)0414-C6-0257/2008-2008/0142 (COD)). They might require health care on a temporary visit abroad, either on vacation or travelling abroad year-round. Another important group of cross-border patients are those that retire to another country. A growing number of northern Europeans retire to southern Member States, and as these patients are part of an older demographic of Europeans, they are perhaps more vulnerable than an average tourist, especially since they have left their family networks: they have relinquished their rights to access to health care in their home state, which means they might need to seek authorization from the health insurer of the Member State authority they retired in, in order to return to their home state and seek medical care. Then there are a growing group of patients for whom it is hard to maintain that the principle of single territory is still applicable at all. These are patients from the newer Member States that provide skilled labour in another Member State, or financial service workers that spend the week in London and the weekend in France; Flash Eurobarometer, 'Cross-border Health Services in the EU', Analytical Report (2007); L. Bertinato et al. (eds) (2005) supra note 4.

[6] For example, English hospitals hire surgical teams from Germany. They fly over to England and perform surgery on a high number of English patients that require non-urgent surgery in order to reduce waiting lists.

[7] See Busse et al. (eds) (2006) supra note 5; also see I. A. Glinos et al. (eds) *Contracting Cross-border Care in Belgian Hospitals: An Analysis of Belgian, Dutch and English Stakeholder Perspectives* (Brussels: European Social Observatory, 2005).. Other types of cross-border health arrangements are emergency arrangements, arrangements among providers (hospitals in border regions), arrangements between insurers/purchasers in one country and providers in another country, or administrative arrangements designed to facilitate access to care abroad but not actually involved in the purchase or provision of care. See e.g. P. Harant 'Hospital Cooperation Across French Borders' in M. Rosenmuller et al. (eds) *Patient Mobility in the European Union: Learning from Experience* (Brussels, European Observatory on Health Systems and Policies: 2006).

1.1 Access to health care before the adoption of the Directive

Access to health care for individual patients is regulated through European coordination of social security schemes. This coordination through the 'Social Security Regulation' has been around since 1958, and its last amendments became effective in 2010.[8] If a European becomes ill during a temporary stay in another Member State, she will be entitled to receive all medically necessary treatments that would be available to nationals, as long as she has her European Health Insurance Card, which is usually on the back of the national health insurance card.[9] In this case, the authorities of the host Member State insure cross-border health care without any additional requirements in the case of an emergency.[10] Article 20(2) of Regulation 883/2004 provides the right to cross-border health care for patients in a Member State even if there is no emergency, if the medical treatment is among the benefits that they are normally entitled to in the state that they are from and if they have obtained prior authorization from their competent institution.[11] This competent institution of the country of residence of the patient *has* to provide authorization if the treatment cannot be given in the time that is normally necessary for obtaining it at home, also taking into account the current state of health and the course the disease can take.[12] The home institution pays the full costs of the treatment received abroad directly to the host provider, without the need for the individual to pay in advance for medical treatment, unless the home authority would usually reimburse the patient under the rules of the national health-care system.

1.1.1 Planned care: prior authorization

If a European obtains prior authorization under Regulation 883/2004, all the costs of medical care abroad are either reimbursed or paid directly to the cross-border service provider. At the same time, there is a second 'scheme' for accessing cross-border health care developed by the Court of Justice of the EU on the basis of free-movement principles. The context of these cases is that patients only had limited rights regarding the access to health care cross border on the basis of the Social Security Regulation. Over the course of the nineties, patients started seeking health care across the border on the basis of their right to free movement, circumventing the 'prior authorization' patients need from the competent health institution in their home states, in order to travel abroad for health care and have their costs covered under their health insurance scheme on the basis of the Social Security Regulation.

[8] Regulation (EC) No 883/2004 of the European Parliament and of the Council on the Coordination of Social Security Systems (OJ L 166, 03-04-2004); Regulation No. 3 of the Council on Social Security for Migrant Workers (OJ 3025-09-1958 at p. 561).

[9] Communication from the Commission concerning the introduction of a European health insurance card (COM(2003)73 final); Regulation (EC) No 883/2004 of the European Parliament and of the Council on the Coordination of Social Security Systems (OJ L166, 03-04-2004) at p. 12.

[10] Article 19 Regulation 883/2004, ibid.

[11] Article 20(1) Regulation 883/2004, ibid.

[12] Article 20(2) Regulation 883/2004, ibid.

1.2 Access to cross-border health care on the basis of the free movement principles

Access to cross-border health care developed by the Court of Justice is primarily based on the freedom to provide and receive services freely across borders in the EU.[13] Although in the early nineties there had been some cases in which the free-movement principles were made applicable,[14] the 1998 *Kohll* case brought together all the elements developed in previous cases,[15] determining that the prior authorization procedure of the Social Security Regulation could be in direct breach of primary treaty law.[16] The case dealt with a Luxembourg national who sought the reimbursement of the costs of dental treatment received in Germany by his daughter without seeking prior authorization as per the Social Security Regulation. The Court explains: 'the special nature of certain services does not remove them from the ambit of the fundamental principle of the freedom of movement'.[17] This meant that the requirement of prior authorization was in breach of the freedom to provide services. In a judgment delivered on the same day, the ECJ determined the same with respect to goods, in the *Decker* case, which concerned a Luxembourg national who had purchased a pair of spectacles in Belgium.[18] The *Kohll* case is particularly important as it determined that, regardless of the fact that the prior authorization procedure might be in accordance with the Social Security Regulation, the Member States first and foremost have to act in accordance with the free-movement principles in the Treaty. In doing so, this case opened up an alternative route to access cross-border health care, outside the legal reach of the Member States (by use of prior authorization in the Social Security Regulation). This basically took access to cross-border care beyond the autonomy of Member States' health-care systems and into the European internal market.[19]

An important objection of Member States to the *Kohll* and *Decker* cases was that a prior authorization procedure was necessary in order to sustain the financial balance of a social security system.[20] The Court accepted this justification with regard to the planning of hospital services, which requires a level of foresight regarding the influx of patients.[21] However, since the medical services in these two cases did not involve

[13] Art. 57 TFEU, Case C-204/90 *Hanns-Martin Bachmann v. Belgium* [1992] ECR I-149; J. B. Cruz 'The Case Law of the European Court of Justice on the Mobility of Patients: An Assessment' in J. W. Van De Gronden et al. (eds) *Health Care and EU Law* (The Hague: Asser, 2011).

[14] T. K. Hervey 'Re-judging Social Rights in the EU' in G. de Búrca et al. (eds) *Critical Legal Perspectives on Global Governance* (Oxford: Hart, 2014).

[15] See ibid.; also see Joined cases C-283/82 and C-26/83 *Luisi and Carbone v. Ministero del Tesoro* [1984] ECR-377; Case C-159/90 *Society for the Protection of Unborn Children Ireland (Ltd) v. Stephen Grogan* [1991] ECR I-4685; See S. de la Rosa 'The Directive on Cross-border Healthcare or the Art of Codifying Complex Case Law' 2012 *Common Market Law Review* 49 15–46.

[16] Case C-158/96 *Raymond Kohll v. Union des caisses de maladie* [1998] ECR I-1931.

[17] Ibid. at para. 10.

[18] Case C-120/95 *Nicolas Decker v. Caisse de maladie de employes prives* [1998] ECR I-1831.

[19] See critically on what the Court could have decided otherwise: Hervey (2014) supra note 14.

[20] Respondent 2 (Deputy Permanent Representative for Health in the Council, 2010); Respondent 4 (MS Representative Working Party on Public Health in the Council, 2010). Interestingly, the Court had ruled before that this exception could only apply in cases where the barrier to the freedom of movement was in principle non-discriminatory, see R. Giesen 'Annotation Case C-120/95, *Nicolas Decker v. Caisse de maladie des employés privés*, Judgment of 28 April 1998, Case C-158/96, *Raymond Kohll v. Union des caisses de maladie*, Judgment of 28 April 1998' (1999) *Common Market Law Review* 36 (4); however, in the underlying cases, the measure was explicitly discriminatory.

[21] See Advocate General Tesauro's Joint Opinion C-158/96 *Kohll* and C-120/95 *Decker* [1998] ECR I-1831.

hospitalization, this exception was not deemed applicable.[22] In later cases the Court specified exactly that, with regard to *hospital care*, national health-care authorities could require that patients obtain prior authorization, regardless of whether they go abroad on the basis of Regulation 882/2004 in order to receive a full refund on the basis of the costs of care in the *host state*, or on the basis of the free-movement principles and receive refunds on the basis of the national rules.[23] The Court in this respect accepted that capacity planning, imbalance in the supply of hospital medical care, and logistical financial wastage could legitimate an exception to the freedom-of-movement principles.[24] Further, the Court in later cases determined that authorization on the basis of the freedom of services could be given even when this could not be based on the Social Security Regulation, or when, as in the *Vanbraekel* case, the refund under the national system is higher than in the host state. Moreover, it decided that the nature of the health-care system—whether care is usually provided through a benefit-in-kind scheme (where no refund is required and the price of treatment does not specifically have to be determined) or through a system of reimbursement—was not considered relevant (*Watts* case).[25] For patients to have the right to reimbursement of the costs of care, they need to have gone abroad and incurred costs.

To summarize, in general the Court only accepted limited justification for not applying the internal market provisions to health care. The maintenance of the balance of a social security system, however, may provide an overriding exception to the application of the freedom-of-movement principles.[26] Nevertheless, justification for this exception needs to be proportional and carried out in accordance with objective and non-discriminatory criteria, which means that as long as the respective hospital service was reimbursed in accordance with home state requirements, reasons for creating a barrier to free movement would not be easily accepted.[27]

[22] Moreover, with regard to protecting patients from poor quality of care abroad, the Court held that given the harmonization and coordination in the area of the mutual recognition of medical degrees this could not be used as a public interest exception; see ibid.

[23] The court established that for non-hospital care, prior authorization was no longer necessary. Patients could go abroad for treatment, pay the costs of medical care in advance, and ask for a refund from their home institution for the costs they would have been covered for if they had not gone abroad. However, if a patient sought prior authorization on the basis of what is now Article 20 Regulation 883/2004, then there should be a timely and transparent procedure subject to judicial or quasi-judicial control that should not result in receiving less than what they would have been reimbursed had the patient stayed in their home country. Case 368/98 *Abdon VanBraekel and Others v. Alliance nationale des mutualités chrétiennes (ANMC)* [2001] ECR I-5363. Prior authorization could also not be denied on the basis of national criteria with regard to the experimental nature of medical care. Moreover, the Court outlined that prior authorization cannot be denied if the necessary treatment cannot be offered in the Member State of affiliation within a reasonable time, especially taking into consideration the specific situation of each patient. Case C-385/99 Joint case *V.G. Muller-Faure and E.E.M. van Riet v. Onderlinge Waarborg Maatschappij ZAO Zorgverzekeringen* [2003] ECR I-4509; Case C-466/04 *Yvonne Watts v. Bedford Primary Care Trust, Secretary of State for Health* ECR [2005] I-4325.

[24] Case C-385/99 *Joint case V.G. Muller-Faure and E.E.M. van Riet v. Onderlinge Waarborg Maatschappij ZAO Zorgverzekeringen* [2003] ECR I-4509 at 77-81; also see Case C-158/96 *Raymond Kohll v. Union des caisses de maladie* [1998] ECR I-1931 at para. 104.

[25] Case C-466/04 *Yvonne Watts v. Bedford Primary Care Trust, Secretary of State for Health* [2005] ECR I-4325.

[26] See inter alia Case C-158/96 *Raymond Kohll v. Union des caisses de maladie* [1998] ECR I-1931 at para. 41; also see Case C-157/99 *B.S.M. Geraets-Smits v. Stichting Ziekenfonds VGZ and H.T.M. Peerbooms v. Stichting CZ Groep Zorgverzekeringen (Smits and Peerbooms)* [2001] ECR I-5473 at para. 73; also see *Case 368/98 Abdon VanBraekel and Others v. Alliance nationale des mutualités chrétiennes (ANMC)* [2001] ECR I-5363 at para. 47.

[27] Case C-368/98 *Abdon VanBraekel and Others v Alliance nationale des mutualités chrétiennes (ANMC)* [2001] ECR I-5363; Case C-158/96 *Raymond Kohll v Union des caisses de maladie* [1998] ECR I-19310; Commission Staff Working document, accompanying document to the Proposal for

This history of access to cross-border health care through the Court of Justice reveals the political upset concerning the EU's role in health care.[28] Whereas at first Member States could reassert and keep control through use of and amendments to the Social Security Regulation, after the *Kohll* case and subsequent cases it became clear that the internal market created a separate and alternative route to access health care, hence 'harnessing the needs and wishes of the individual to re-constitute the European space'.[29]

This realization also brought about a shift in the debate on the coordination of health-care systems and the legislative routes for doing so. In the early years of the new millennium, the Commission (DG MARKT) published a first report on the application of the internal market rules on health care.[30] Not long after, the first proposal for a Directive on Services included a provision on health care.[31] These events and the active role of the Court of Justice in the end formed the stepping-stones for the adoption of a separate Directive on patients' rights in cross-border health care. Before we look at the institutional setting in which this Directive was adopted, we will first examine the changes brought about by the Directive.

1.3 Access to health care after the adoption of the Directive

The Directive on patients' rights in cross-border health care was adopted in 2011.[32] The Directive had to be implemented before the end of October 2013; however, in some Member States implementation is still lagging.[33] The legal basis of the Directive is Article 114 TFEU on the enhancement of the functioning of the internal market and Article 168 TFEU on public health. This is in itself contradictory, since Article 168(7) TFEU clearly outlines the principle of subsidiarity regarding the definition of *health*

a Directive of the European Parliament and of the Council on the Application of Patients' Rights in Cross-Border Healthcare, Impact Assessment (COM(2008)414 final) (SEC (2008) 2164).

[28] D. Sindbjerg Martinsen, *An Ever More Powerful Court?: The Political Constraints of Legal Integration in the European Union* (Oxford: Oxford University Press 2015) 133 et seq.

[29] G. Davies 'Legislating for Patients' Rights' in J. W .van de Gronden et al. (eds) *Health Care and EU Law* (The Hague: Asser, 2011) at p. 207.

[30] Commission Staff Working Paper, Report on the Application of Internal Market Rules to Health Services, Implementation by the Member States of the Courts Jurisprudence, (SEC(2003) 900).

[31] European Commission, Proposal for a Directive of the European Parliament and of the Council on services in the internal market (COM(2004) 2 final).

[32] There is a wealth of literature on the legal ramifications of this Directive: A. P. van der Mei 'De nieuwe richtlijn betreffende de toepassing van de rechten van de patiënt bij grensoverschrijdende zorg' (2011) *Nederlands Juristenblad* 2717; D. Delnoij and W. Sauter 'Patient Information Under the EU Patients' Rights Directive' (2011) *European Journal of Public Health* 271; E. Szyszczak 'Patients' Rights: A Lost Cause or Missed Opportunity?' in J. W. van de Gronden et al. (eds) *EU Health Care and EU Law* (The Hague: Asser, 2011); F. Pennings 'The Draft Patient Mobility Directive and the Coordination Regulations of Social Security' in J. W. van de Gronden et al. (eds) *Health Care and EU Law* (The Hague: Asser, 2011); M. Peeters 'Free Movement of Patients: Directive 2011/24 on the Application Of Patients' Rights in Cross-Border Healthcare' (2012) *European Journal of Health Law* 19 (56); R. Baeten and W. Palm 'Preserving General Interest in Healthcare Through Secondary and Soft EU Law: The Case of the Patients' Rights Directive' in U. Neergaard et al. (eds) *Social Services of General Interest in the EU* (The Hague: Asser, 2013) at p. 391; de la Rosa (2012) supra note 15; K. Tomasevski 'Health Rights' in A. Eide et al. (eds) *Economic, Social and Cultural Rights* (Dordrecht: Martinus Nijhoff, 1995); W. Sauter 'Harmonisation in Healthcare: The EU Patients' Rights Directive' (2011) *Tilec Research Paper* 8.

[33] H. Nys 'After the Transposition of the Directive on Patients' Rights in Cross-Care Healthcare in National Law by the Member States: Still a Lot of Effort to Be Made and Questions to Be Answered' (2014) *European Journal of Health Law* 21 1–14; and see a number of contributions in that same issue of the *European Journal of Health Law*.

care policy, the organization of the delivery of health-care services, and the management of health services and medical care.[34] Article 168 TFEU cannot really be called a legal basis in this respect, but, in the words of a Member State representative, 'it was put in for mere optic reasons, but you know of course the whole history behind it was internal market'.[35] At the same time Article 168(1) TFEU clarifies that in the formulation and explication of all Union legislation a high level of health protection needs to be ensured, which echoes a similar provision in Article 114(3) TFEU. While this refers directly to *public health* matters rather than *health care*, with respect to the quality and safety of health-care services one could still argue that a specific basis for public health and safety provisions is needed in the context of the Directive.[36] The scope of the Directive is relatively broad. In Article 3(a) of the Directive, 'health care' is defined as health services provided by health professionals to patients to assess, maintain, or restore their state of health, including the prescription, dispensation, and provision of medicinal products and medical devices, regardless of how health care is organized, delivered, or financed.[37] The Directive aims to facilitate access to safe and high-quality health care provided or prescribed in a Member State other than the Member State of affiliation.[38] At the same time, however, it also has the objective of promoting cooperation on health care and clarifying the relationship of patients' rights (developed in the context of the internal market (Article 1)) with cross-border health care in the context of the Social Security Regulation.[39]

1.3.1 Two schemes for access to cross-border health care: what difference?

The Directive does not change the fact that there are still two schemes through which the patient can obtain access to cross-border care. The first scheme is as outlined above on the basis of the Social Security Regulation 883/2004.[40] The other scheme now is no longer just Article 56 TFEU on the freedom to provide services and the case law of the Court of Justice in that respect, but rather the Directive. However, the relation between the two regimes has now become regulated by Article 8(3) of the Directive. If a patient requests prior authorization for cross-border health care, first the public authority of the Member State of affiliation will ascertain whether the conditions for prior authorization in accordance with the Social Security Regulation have been met. In that case, prior authorization is granted pursuant to the Regulation, unless the patient requests otherwise. In paragraph 2 of Article 8 of the Directive, the kinds of health care that may be subject to prior authorization are listed.

Where the Court limited the possibility of denial of authorization to hospital care, the Directive expands the possibility of prior authorization to health care that is subject to planning requirements, especially to ensure equal access to health care in the

[34] Article 168 (7) TFEU:

> Union action shall respect the responsibilities of the Member States for the definition of their health policy and for the organisation and delivery of health services and medical care. The responsibilities of the Member States shall include the management of health services and medical care and the allocation of the resources assigned to them.

[35] Respondent 2 (Deputy Permanent Representative for Health in the Council, 2010).

[36] W. Palm and R. Baeten 'The Quality and Safety Paradox in the Patients' Rights Directive' (2011) *European Journal of Public Health* 21 (3) 272–4.

[37] Article 1(2) Directive. [38] Articles 1 and 2(e) Directive.

[39] Longterm care, the allocation of organs for the purpose of organ transplants and public vaccination programmes against infectious diseases are excluded from the Directive.

[40] Article 48 TFEU.

Member State, health care that involves at least a one-night stay in a hospital, and/or health care that requires a highly cost-intensive medical infrastructure. The reasons for a possible refusal of prior authorization are extensive, which implies that, compared to the exceptions that had been accepted by the Court, the list in the Directive is more specific. At the same time it leaves more grounds for Member States to deny prior authorization.[41] If there is reasonable certainty in accordance with clinical evaluation of a patient safety risk, this can also give a basis for denial of authorization to obtain cross-border health care. When there is a chance the general public will be exposed to a safety risk as a result of the cross-border health care, or if the health-care provider in the Member State of treatment raises serious and specific concerns regarding the upholding of safety and quality standards and guidelines, authorization can also be denied.

The case law is echoed regarding the possibility for denial of prior authorization when the health care can be provided in the state of affiliation, within a time limit that is medically justifiable, taking into account the current state of health and the probable course of the illness of the patient concerned.[42] The Member State of affiliation has to reimburse the costs of cross-border health care if the care in question is among the benefits to which the patient is entitled in the Member State of affiliation, without exceeding the actual costs of the health care received.[43] The calculation of the costs of care has to be done transparently, based on objective non-discriminatory criteria.[44]

This is a rather sensitive issue, as in many Member States the exact costs of treatment are difficult to determine, and in some Member States where health care is centrally and publicly funded, there are no schemes available to determine the costs of care.[45] In order for a patient to be reimbursed, no extra administrative burdens or conditions may be imposed as would have been usual under their health-care system, unless these administrative burdens can be objectively justified by planning requirements related to the provision of enduring, sufficient, and permanent access to a balanced range of high-quality treatments or by a wish to avoid costs and waste of financial, technical, or human resources.[46] For reasons of overriding general interest, the rules on reimbursement of cross-border health care can be limited,[47] restricted to what is necessary and proportionate in order to safeguard the general interest. Moreover, the Commission needs to be notified if this limitation is applied.[48]

1.3.2 Implementation and delegation: possibilities for expanding the EU's role in health care

One of the more controversial issues in the adoption of the Directive has been on settling the powers of the Commission with respect to further regulation on the basis of the rules of the Directive, or the creation of implementation measures.[49] The Directive sets up a committee for the purpose of implementing its particular aspects.[50] In regard to the creation of mutual guidelines on quality of care and safety, the Member States

[41] de la Rosa (2012) supra note 15.
[42] Article 8(6)(d) Directive.
[43] Article 8(6)(d) Directive.
[44] Article 6(7) Directive.
[45] See the UK for instance, where health care is provided 'in kind'; see J. Schreyögg et al. 'Defining the "Health Benefit Basket" in Nine European Countries' (2007) *European Journal of Health Economics* 6 (1) 2–10 and also see Case C-466/04 *Yvonne Watts v. Bedford Primary Care Trust, Secretary of State for Health* [2005] ECR I-4325.
[46] Article 7(7) Directive.
[47] Article 7(9) Directive.
[48] Articles 7(10) and 7(11) Directive.
[49] Articles 290 and 291 TFEU.
[50] Article 16 Directive.

have only accepted cooperation in the form of exchanging information through their national contact point.[51] However, on the recognition of prescriptions for medicinal products and with regard to medical devices, the Commission can adopt measures, and on the interoperability of e-prescriptions guidelines can be adopted in accordance with the regulatory procedure.[52] The regulatory procedure is also applicable with regard to facilitating the cooperation of Member States on an e-health network. The aim of this network is to create interoperable e-health systems and services for patients and health-care providers, and to create the rules on the use of the information in these e-health systems for public health and research.[53]

Moreover, a network is created for cooperation on health technology assessment.[54] The Directive also creates European reference networks between health-care providers and centres of expertise in the Member States, particularly in the area of rare diseases, in order to create cooperation in the EU in the area of highly specialized health care for patients. The Commission is given delegated authority to adopt measures in order to facilitate the creation of these networks on the basis of Article 17 of the Directive. The fact that the Commission has obtained, albeit specifically circumscribed, possibilities for expanding its involvement in health care through the use of these newly established committees and networks, in itself creates a platform for further increasing the EU's role in the field of human health.

1.4 Cross-border health care: a hot-button issue

The above outline of the different paths to access health care across the border in another EU Member State illustrates the tug of war that has played out over the last two decades between different institutional actors on health care in the EU. Particularly, the political response that was created in the slipstream of this string of case law has been minutely detailed in the policy discourse. The outline in this book does not do any justice to the intricacy of the matters involved, particularly the technical questions as regards creating access to cross-border health care and the different legal considerations that may be involved.[55] However, this political debate also indicates that health care—dealing with certain highly volatile health issues concerning access to medical care for individual patients and the community values involved[56]—can trigger a debate on values and fundamental rights.[57] In this respect, the adoption of cross-border health care formed the basis for a relatively explicit debate on the impact of EU policy on fundamental rights and values. The next section hones in on this aspect of European health-care policy, discussing the way the Directive was adopted in more detail.

[51] Article 10 Directive

[52] Article 16 Directive and Article 5 of Decision 1999/468/EC.

[53] Article 14 Directive.

[54] Article 15 Directive.

[55] See e.g. Martinsen (n 28). J. W. van de Gronden et al. (eds) *Health Care and EU Law* (The Hague: Asser, 2011), and numerous contributions to the *European Journal of Health Law*; and also see further references in supra note 32.

[56] C. Newdick 'Disrupting the Community—Saving Public Health Ethics from the EU Internal Market' in J. W. van de Gronden et al. (eds) *Health Care and EU Law* (The Hague: Asser, 2011); D. da Costa Leite Borges 'Making Sense of Human Rights in the Context of European Union Health-care Policy: Individualist and Communitarian Views' (2011) *International Journal of Law in Context* 7 (3) 335–56.

[57] E. Muir 'The Fundamental Rights Implications of EU Legislation: Some Constitutional Challenges' (2014) *Common Market Law Review* 51 219–46.

2. The Adoption of the Directive: Creating a Policy Discourse on Values and Rights

In the adoption of the Directive, three evolutionary stages can be identified, each with their own protagonist. At the onset DG MARKT was in the driving seat due to the application of internal market rules to health care by the Court, but over time parallel activities in DG SANTE gained momentum. When the controversy of the inclusion of health services in the Services Directive proposal of 2004 arose,[58] DG SANTE ended up taking over the lead from DG MARKT. In the end, however, once the negotiations in the Council were well underway, the Council decided 'the hell with the Commission's proposal, gently we are going to draft our own proposal as a Council'.[59]

2.1 The first evolutionary stage: DG MARKT

In the first evolutionary stage, DG MARKT was in control. After the first rulings of the Court in the eighties, Member States merely responded by adapting the Social Security Regulation. However, after the 1998 *Kohl* and *Decker* cases the Member States were unable to ignore that the Social Security Regulation no longer served as a buffer against the increasing effect of EU law on Member States' autonomy to regulate their own health-care systems. The Court cases caused a big stir:

> They [the Member States] were screaming in the House of Council that these Court decisions would destroy health systems, so there was this need to have reflection being carried out. [60]

The reflection that was felt needed was organized in the context of DG SANTE. DG SANTE, established only in 1999, was seeking to forge a central role for itself in EU health-care policy.[61] For instance, DG SANTE organized the European Health Policy Forum, in which health stakeholders were able to scrutinize proposals of DG MARKT, DG ECFIN, DG Enterprise (in the area of pharmaceuticals), or DG EMPL from a more singular health perspective.[62] However, in order to channel the discussion on the consequences of the Court rulings on health and the internal market, the newly instituted DG SANTE installed a High Level Committee, which created a working group on Internal Market and Health.[63] The High Level Committee, its members designated by the departments for health, advised Commission services on the development of the Health Strategy and exchanged information between the Commission services and Member States' health authorities.[64] In DG MARKT, this development was viewed with some hesitation:

[58] European Commission (2004) supra note 31.

[59] Respondent 2 (Deputy Permanent Representative for Health in the Council, 2010).

[60] Respondent 10 (Representative Commission Services DG MARKT, 2010).

[61] Respondent 5 (MEP (ENVI Committee), 2010); also see S. L. Greer *The Politics of European Union Health Policies* (Maidenhead/Philadelphia: Open University Press, 2009); T. K. Hervey and B. Vanhercke 'Health Care and the EU: The Law and Policy Patchwork' in E. Mossialos et al. (eds) *Health Systems Governance in Europe: The Role of European Union Law and Policy* (New York: Cambridge University Press, 2010).

[62] S. L. Greer et al. 'Mobilizing Bias in Europe: Lobbies, Democracy and EU Health Policy-Making' (2008) *European Union Politics* 9 (3) 403–33.

[63] See High Level Group on Health Services and Medical Care—information from the Commission (15190/04, Brussels) at p. 25.

[64] David Byrne, Commissioner for Health and Consumer Protection, 'Enabling Good Health For All, A reflection process for a new EU health strategy', European Communities (2004), available

I think it was a good idea; I think it was a good idea when there is such an emotion created by Court decisions to create a forum for discussion. But there was a danger. Court decisions are court decisions and they ought to be respected and these forums should not be used to reverse Court decisions; that was the risk of the exercise.[65]

The general objective that came out of the High Level Committee was that policy areas that were previously regulated in an internal market context should be brought into a health policy framework.[66] Additionally, the Committee concluded that although total harmonization of health systems seemed practically unfeasible, European health-care policy could be mainstreamed using the open method of coordination in the Lisbon Agenda.[67] At the same time, however, DG MARKT was already preparing a proposal for a Directive on services in the internal market, which was to include a provision on health care.[68] Moreover, there were still cases coming from the Court of Justice limiting and defining the rules for prior authorization.[69] At this time, the Council of health ministers called for a high-level process of reflection.[70] The actors involved in this process of reflection include a working group on ministerial level, but also civil society players such as the International Mutual Association; representatives of hospitals and doctors; and groups representing patients, health managers, and social insurance.[71] Although it was the Council that initiated the process this time, in order to find a common response to the Court cases the Member States also used the forum to express their adamant intention to retain responsibilities in health.[72] In the words of a DG MARKT representative:

This group in the end did not satisfy its purpose. The *natural outcome* would have been to accept the jurisprudence of the Court and to accept therefore that health services would be included in the services directive [...]. In fact, at the end of the day, the Member States did not move one centimetre and just refused jurisprudence.[73]

And indeed, in DG MARKT—simultaneously with the high-level reflection process—a parallel path was set out. In a working paper of July 2003, the Commission researches the extent to which the case law of the Court has been implemented by the Member States. This takes particular consideration of the 1998 *Kohll* and *Decker* cases, the

at: <http://www.ec.europa.eu/health/archive/ph_overview/documents/pub_good_health_en.pdf> (last accessed March 2014).

65 Respondent 10 (Representative Commission Services DG MARKT, 2010).

66 European Commission, The Internal Market and Health Services, Report of the High Level Commitee on Health, Brussels, 17 September 2001 (the basis of the document was research by the EHMA that 233 regulations, directives, decisions, recommendations, and rulings of the ECJ related to internal market, issued between 1958 and 1998, had the potential to affect Member States' health-care systems); see European Health Management Association, 'The European Union and Health Services: The Impact of the Single European Market on Member States', Summary of a Report to the European Commission Directorate General for Research (BIOMED2) Dublin (2001) at p. 19.

67 Report of the High Level Committee on Health, The Internal Market and Health Services (2001); also see K. Armstrong and C. Kilpatrick 'Law, Governance, or New Governance? The Changing Open Method of Coordination' (2007) *Columbia Journal of European Law* 13 649–79.

68 European Commission (2004) Commission Communication on patient mobility and health care developments in the EU (COM (2004) 301 final).

69 J. B. Cruz (2011) supra note 13.

70 2002 Council Meeting, Ministers for Health, Conclusions of the Council and the Representatives of the Member States Meeting in the Council of 19 July 2002 on Patient Mobility and Health Care Developments in the European Union (OJ C 183/01).

71 Minutes of the Meeting on the High level Reflection process on Patient Mobility and Health care Developments in the European Union, 3 February 2003 (HLPR/2003/2 REV1).

72 Respondent 2 (Deputy Permanent Representative for Health in the Council, 2010).

73 Respondent 10 (Representative Commission Services DG MARKT, 2010) (emphasis added).

2001 *Smits and Peerbooms* case, and the *Vanbraekel* judgment. The main conclusion of this report is that the Member States are not taking the consequences of the Court's case law on board sufficiently. The report found that prior authorization was still used almost across the board for both hospital and non-hospital care. Moreover, the decision on whether or not treatment was experimental was still usually based on national medical standards, rather than on international evidence-based standards as the case law had prescribed.[74] This communication on the whole sought to create a need for the inclusion of health care in the 2004 Services Directive in Article 23, reasoning that the added value of creating a market of services would probably outweigh initial resistance to a binding health-care framework.[75] Nevertheless, this provision and the general application of the country-of-origin principle across the board of the Services Directive caused substantial protest by the Council and the European Parliament, the latter threatening to get rid of the Services Directive altogether. Moreover, the proposal led to fierce protests by European labour unions.

In that context the European Council of March 2005 outlined that the proposed Services Directive could not be adopted if it included health care.[76] Moreover, in a 2005 report on patient mobility and health-care developments, the European Parliament voiced strong objections against the inclusion of health care in the Services Directive.[77] Therefore the provision on health care was removed (Article 2(f) Services Directive); according to the Commission, this was because of the technical complexity, the sensitivity of public opinion, and the fact that such major amounts of public funds are involved in health care, which meant that the singular provision in the Services Directive could not do justice to the special case of health care.[78]

2.2 The second evolutionary stage: DG SANTE—taking a 'health values and rights' approach

After the demise of the inclusion of health in the Services Directive, DG SANTE was still involved in the processes in the context of the High Level Committee. Moreover, in the context of DG EMPL an open method of coordination on health care and long-term care was launched.[79] In this respect then, even though there was no provision on health care in the Services Directive, the discussion and policy exchange about health care had not ceased. However, DG SANTE now became the protagonist. The ideas that had been developed parallel with the proposal for the inclusion of health services in the Services Directive were now expanded. The Communication in the follow-up

[74] Commission Staff Working document, Report on the application of internal market rules to health services. Implementation by the Member States of the court's jurisprudence (SEC(2003)900) Case C-368/98 *Abdon VanBraekel and Others v. Alliance nationale des mutualités chrétiennes (ANMC)* [2001] ECR I-5363.

[75] Respondent 10 (Representative Commission Services DG MARKT, 2010); Respondent 12 (Representative Commission Services DG SANCO, 2010).

[76] See European Council, 22 and 23 March 2005 (7619/1/05, REV 1).

[77] Report of the European Parliament, 29 April 2005, on patient mobility and health care developments in the European Union (2004/2148(INI)).

[78] European Commission, Amended proposal for a Directive of the European Parliament and of the Council on services in the internal market (COM/2006/0160 final) European Parliament, Resolution of 23 May 2007 on the impact and consequences of the exclusion of health services from the Directive on services in the internal market (P6 TA(2007) 0201).

[79] See A. de Rujiter and T. K. Hervey 'Healthcare and the Lisbon Agenda' in P. Copeland and D. Papadimitriou (eds) *The EU's Lisbon Strategy, Evaluating Succes, Understanding Failure* (New York: Palgrave MacMillan, 2012).

to the high-level reflection process of 2004 covered not only patient mobility but also general ideas on cooperation on health-care policy, which included ideas on health information technology, e-health, and health technology assessment.[80] Moreover, it introduced the setting-up of a permanent High-Level Group on health services and medical care, institutionalizing the former High-Level Committee. This High-Level Group has thus far created a number of strategies with regard to cross-border care, for instance with regard to health-care purchasing and common principles of care.[81]

In the 2006 Health Council meeting, the Member States decided that before they took up the issue of health care in the EU context once more, some constitutional boundaries needed to be outlined. Therefore the Health Council adopted a 'Statement of common values and principles in EU health systems' so as to create the legislative benchmark for how health care was to be organized and coordinated on the European level, especially with respect to patients' rights and universal access to health care.[82] A little later, in 2007, the European Parliament adopted a Resolution which called for binding legislation to ensure patients' rights.[83] In response DG SANTE launched a public consultation on health services, which aimed to bring together data on patient mobility but also proposed some broader ideas on creating a more binding legislative instrument on cross-border health care. It included ideas on a medical liability and compensation regime, European Centres of Reference (medical centres that specialize in rare diseases), the management of innovation, and sharing data that had been developed in the context of the High Level Group as a basis for creating European evidence-based health-care policy.[84] And while the Communication suggested that it would also be possible to reform the Social Security legislation,[85] the draft of a *Directive* on patients' rights in cross-border health care was already in the making and was ultimately published in July 2008.[86] The proposal for the Directive came as part of the renewed social agenda for twenty-first-century Europe.[87] This marked a shift in approach compared to the first proposal in the Services Directive. The European Social Agenda had the explicit aim of creating a counterweight to the developing economic growth agenda. And although at this point binding legislation on health care was back on the table, in DG MARKT they remained downbeat:

> [We] were very pessimistic about what would be the outcome of the Patients' Rights Directive; all most Member States wanted was a legal frame to refuse authorization to patients, and I find that shocking.[88]

[80] European Commission (2004).

[81] See e.g. European Commission HLG, Work of the high level group on health services and medical care during 2005 (HLG/2005/16); European Commission HLG, Work of the high level group in 2006 (HLG/2006/08, 2006); Centres of Reference for rare diseases in Europe: State-of-the-art in 2006 and recommendations of the Rare Diseases Task Force to the the High Level Group on Health Services and Medical Care (December 2006), available at: <http://www.ec.europa.eu/health/ph_threats/non_com/docs/contribution_policy.pdf> (last accessed February 2014).

[82] Council Conclusions on Common values and principles in European Union Health Systems (2006/C 146/01) (OJ 146/1).

[83] European Parliament resolution of 23 May 2007 on the impact and consequences of the exclusion of health services from the Directive on services in the internal market (2006/2275(INI)).

[84] Communication from the Commission, Consultation regarding Community action on health services (SEC(2006)1195/4); European Commission, Summary report of the responses to the consultation regarding 'Community action on health services' (SEC (2006) 1195/4).

[85] Commission Communication (2006) supra note 84.

[86] Commission Proposal for a Directive of the European Parliament and of the Council on the Application of Patients' Rights in Cross-Border Healthcare (COM(2008)414 final).

[87] Commission Staff Working Paper, Towards a Renewed Social Agenda for Europe-Citizens' Well-Being in the Information Society (SEC(2008)2183) (COM (2008) 414 final).

[88] Respondent 10 (Representative Commission Services DG MARKT, 2010).

2.3 The third evolutionary stage: the 'Council proposal'—bringing in the Member States

The proposal of the Directive drafted by DG SANTE was delayed in 2007 and again at the beginning of 2008. It was structured around three main areas: first, it outlined common principles in all EU health systems; second, it described a specific framework for cross-border health care that resembled the case law of the ECJ; and third the ground rules for European cooperation on health-care policy were drawn out.[89] The delay at the start of the negotiations was caused by fierce disagreement over the Directive's content between the Member States, the European Parliament, and the Commission. This debate became so heated that it was feared the proposal would stall the adoption of the Lisbon Treaty.[90] These difficulties also had to do with *conflicting discourses*:

> [A]t the beginning DG SANCO [DG SANTE] had one of the civil servants from MARKT dealing with the dossier, and at the first meetings with the Commission the discussion was really difficult because of this. They came with such arrogance to the meeting room: 'Here we are with our proposal and we have the legal basis—it's internal market—you are going to have to accept it whether you want to or not.' And that is why it took almost a year, if you ask me.[91]

Important in this respect was that the proposal, now coming from DG SANTE, was to be negotiated in the Public Health Working Party in the Council context, which meant that the Council representatives did not approach health care as a 'market product':

> The Commission came with someone coming from MARKT to the health working party. They thought they were untouchable, because they do this in MARKT all the time. And then they fell from one surprise to another because they knew so little about the way our health-care systems are organized.[92]

After the first year of negotiations, in the Council there was the widespread feeling that the Directive would never be adopted unless they became more proactive with respect to the drafting process itself:

> The first proposal was completely exaggerated, completely overshooting. There was absolutely not an effective discussion between the Council and the Commission. So we gently decided to draft our own proposal within the Council, and then it was our text and no longer the bloody Commission's text—a very important psychological element. The Commission was shooting a fly with a bazooka; that was really the feeling.[93]

Nevertheless, negotiations within the Council were also relatively ineffective. The first focus for the negotiations in the Council was the issue of subsidiarity relating to health care, which in the context of the Treaty on the Functioning of the EU in Article 168 had recently been reaffirmed as the Member States' exclusive responsibility. On this issue, however, neither in the Working Party on Public Health nor COREPER I, or for

[89] See Commission Proposal (2008) supra note 86.

[90] L. Kubosova 'Brussels Postpones Landmark Bill on EU Cross-border Health Care Until 2008' (2007) *European Observer* at <https://euobserver.com/economic/25361>; H. Mahoney 'EU Health Bill Pulled Amid National and MEP Criticism' (2008) *European Observer* at <https://euobserver.com/social/25426>.

[91] Respondent 3 (MS Representative Working Party on Public Health in the Council, 2010).

[92] Respondent 4 (MS Representative Working Party on Public Health in the Council, 2010).

[93] Respondent 2 (Deputy Permanent Representative for Health in the Council, 2010); and 'Half of the consequences we foresaw in the proposal, they had not foreseen themselves, so they came up with a market-based proposal that took no account of the way health-care systems are organized', Respondent 4 (MS Representative Working Party on Public Health in the Council, 2010).

that matter in the Council, could agreements be forged. And compromise proposals from the French, Czech, and Swedish Presidencies were all rejected.[94]

2.4 Opposing values: market versus health

In the European Parliament, amendments were adopted under the first reading of the co-decision procedure 124,[95] especially with regard to the chapter relating to Member States' responsibilities for allowing access to cross-border health care.[96] The debate polarized the Parliament, splitting it down the middle.[97] Within the Parliament controversy also arose about which Committee would lead on the health-care proposal, the IMCO or the ENVI Committee: 'All the way through there was pressure from the other committees to have equal rights on the proposal.'[98] At the same time the continued infighting in the Commission between DG MARKT and DG SANTE was also noticed in the European Parliament:

> So the problem here is also in the Parliament. There is a rivalry between the Commission services, internal market, health and environment.[99]

But negotiations were also difficult between the European Parliament and the Council:

> The European parliament had adopted a completely different mission: 'We are for Patients' rights', that was the new cosmetic element Directive [...]. so there were very many tensions there too, because they had to come down from the moon to the earth: Don't you have any sense of the operational aspects of what we are discussing at the moment? It was flabbergasting.[100]

At the same time, a complicating factor was created by the fact that DG MARKT had begun to launch infringement procedures on access to health care. DG MARKT had a number of complaints in the context of health care:

> [T]he infringements were kept by DG EMPL, but they didn't do anything about them; they kept that in a little corner, in a little cupboard [...] and then after all the Court decisions they decided to transfer them to DG MARKT.[101]

[94] See e.g. Czech Presidency proposals and amendments proposal for a Directive of the European Parliament and of the Council on the application of patients' rights in cross-border healthcare (2008/0142 (COD) 7379/090); Questions from the Presidency to the Council, in preparation for the Council meeting on 8 and 9 June 2009 on the Proposal for Directive of the European Parliament and of the Council on the Application of Patients' Rights in Cross-Border Health Care (2008/0142 (COD) 10027/09); Committee of Permanent Representatives to Council of the European Union, Proposal for a Directive on the Application of Patients' Rights in Cross-Border Health Care (2008/0142 (COD) 1600/09), in preparation for Council Meeting on Employment, Social Policy, Health and Consumers Affairs, 30 November and 1 December, 2009) Working Document on the Proposal for a Directive of the European Parliament and of the Council on the Application of Patients' Rights in Cross-Border Healthcare from the General secretariat of the Council to the Working Party on Public Health (11307/08 SAN 136 SOC389 MI 234 CODEC 904) ((2008/0142 (COD)15655/08) at p. 11.

[95] Draft Report by Parliamentary Committee on the Environment, Public Health and Food Safety, Rapporteur John Bowis, on the proposal for a directive of the European Parliament and of the Council on the application of patients' rights in cross-border healthcare (COM (2008) 0414-C6-0257/2008-2008/0142(COD)).

[96] European Parliament legislative resolution of 23 April 2009 on the proposal for a directive of the European Parliament and of the Council on the application of patients' rights in cross-border healthcare (COM(2008)0414-C6-0257/2008-2008/0142 (COD)).

[97] Most 'nays' came from the left, see H. Mahoney 'Cross border Health Proposal Splits Parliament' (2009) *European Observer*.

[98] Respondent 5 (MEP (ENVI Committee), 2010).

[99] Respondent 7 (MEP, 2010).

[100] Respondent 2 (Deputy Permanent Representative for Health in the Council, 2010).

[101] Respondent 10 (Representative Commission Services DG MARKT, 2010).

This meant that after health was removed from the Services Directive, DG MARKT had started launching infringement procedures on health-care issues in order to create case law on the subject. This caused friction between DG MARKT and DG Health. The continuing launch of infringements by DG MARKT while negotiations on the Directive were ongoing was not wholly appreciated in DG Health.

> We [DG Health] said let's especially not launch infringements in this area that encourages the Court to make announcements in this area, where we have to sit back and scratch our head and say, what does this mean to our proposal?[102]

Interestingly however, apparently DG SANTE did not have enough pull within the Commission to stop the launch of these infringements:

> [W]e do liaise with DG MARKT on this, but not with a lot of success sometimes, so we ask them 'What are you doing this for?' We told them not only not to launch, but also to discontinue because you are going to lose this, and we have lost in the Court of Justice [...]. [T]he last case against France was lost not only on the facts, but also on legal grounds unsubstantiated, a pretty big slap in the face of the Commission.[103]

2.5 The paradoxical expansion of power through limits and circumscriptions

Although many of the subjects in the Directive caused substantial discussion, especially issues such as e-health and the rules on prior authorization, in the negotiations about delegation and implementation some of the distrust felt by Member States towards the Commission's intentions for the health-care field becomes increasingly clear. However, another important complication was that negotiations were ongoing at the time of the adoption of the Lisbon Treaty, when there was no actual certainty as to what it would mean to hand over implementing powers or delegated powers to the Commission under Articles 290 and 291 TFEU: 'Of course we still don't know what the Commission will be able to do under delegated acts and implementing acts'.[104] This issue for instance played out with respect to how and by whom the quality of care would be regulated.

The Commission had proposed that in terms of quality, solidarity, and universal access international standards would apply in Article 5(a) of the initial proposal. However, the Council wanted to replace this language with a system whereby patients would need to have easy access to transparent information as to the quality standards and medical guidelines and protocols that apply cross border.[105] This meant that health care in the Member States remained to be provided on the basis of national standards:[106]

[102] Respondent 13 (High level representative Commission Services, DG SANCO, 2010).

[103] Ibid., and see Case C-64/09 *European Commission v. French Republic* [2010] ECR I-03283 (on the reimbursement of cross-border care involving major medical equipment outside a hospital setting).

[104] Respondent 3 (MS Representative Working Party on Public Health in the Council, 2010).

[105] Draft Progress Report from the Working Party on Public Health to the Permanent Representatives Committee in Preparation of the Council Meeting of 16 and 17 December on the Proposal for a Directive of the European Parliament and of the Council on the Application of Patients' Rights in Cross-Border Healthcare (2008/0142 (COD) 16781/08).

[106] Working Document Council Working Party on Public Health (2008).

On quality of care they wanted to have guideline competence; they did not speak about comitology. But guideline competence is much more than OMC for instance; it would be the Commission determining the standard of care [. . .] but it is up to us to decide how broad the catalogue of treatments is.[107]

They gave themselves a complete blank cheque on quality and safety in Article 5, original paragraph 3. They said the Commission was going to facilitate through guidelines, without any reference to comitology. We said: 'You have no legal ground to propose this.' The answer was: 'We do this all the time in MARKT.'[108]

[T]he Commission was trying to grab more power [. . .] the more they can gain control on how to do things in health care, the more they can show that Europe is achieving something.[109]

When the Directive was finally adopted in 2011, the initial proposal of the Commission was substantially cut back with regard to the ability to impose prior authorization for cross-border health care and delegated powers to the Commission and in many other areas. In the Commission in the end there was a deep sense of disappointment: 'yes, it is *a dream* being watered down'.[110] However, there was also pragmatism:

You can't force legislation on the Member States that they don't want, 'cause in the end you will get implementation problems; they will fight you through the back door by not applying the legislation.[111]

3. A Thousand Stones and You Have a Wall: Health Policy and Law beyond the Market

The case of the adoption of the Patient's Rights Directive illustrates that the creation of a policy discourse in a politically sensitive policy area can 'prepare the ground' for more binding legal rules—particularly as the controversy around the Directive, dealing with access to health care as a welfare entitlement, available at EU level, creates conflicting discourses at the EU level that play out in the institutional setting. To sum up the different positions in the institutions:

The Commission was driven to protect the system as part of the internal market, the Parliament was driven to protect and defend the patient and the Commission was close to the Parliament, and then they were both tapped on the nose by the Council, so there was a natural alliance against the Council.[112]

The Council represented the point of view of the management of health-care systems and their financial sustainability.

Of course with respect to the Member States Article 114 [TFEU] is harmonization and Article 168 [TFEU] excludes harmonization and this paradox is very important for the Member States. In the beginning to me it was clear that the Commission thought, 'We are going to use the judgments of the Court to liberalise the health care sector.' That's how it was perceived anyway.

107 Respondent 3 (MS Representative Working Party on Public Health in the Council, 2010).

108 Respondent 4 (MS Representative Working Party on Public Health in the Council, 2010); also see COREPER (2008); also see Case C-208/07 *Petra von Chamier-Glisczinski v. Deutsche Angestellten-Krankenkasse* [2009] ECR I-6095.

109 Respondent 3 (MS Representative Working Party on Public Health in the Council, 2010).

110 Respondent 13 (High level representative Commission Services, DG SANCO, 2010) (emphasis in original).

111 Ibid.

112 Respondent 2 (Deputy Permanent Representative for Health in the Council, 2010).

They wanted to get a grip on the health-care market, that is what they called it. But we said no, providing a good health care system is a basic task of our governments.[113]

There were some major clashes and infighting at the time of the adoption of the Directive, both within and among institutions, 'coming from their different tunnelled perspective'.[114] Indeed, a representative from DG SANCO remarked:

They [DG MARKT] have a different perspective from us: They advocate free services and we have the perspective of ensuring patients' rights and people's wellbeing.[115]

These conflicting discourses exemplify in a nutshell the intertwining of the EU's role in health through 'market-correcting' policy and welfare policy with the objective of creating health-care entitlements and rights at EU level. In this regard the EU policy discourse may have already started with the first court case that affected the provision of health care in a Member State, because running through it all is always the salient matter of the autonomy of the Member States with regard to their national budgets and the substantive discussion on market policies versus health policies.

3.1 Institutionalizing the policy discourse

However, as a result of the policy debate that is created through balancing policy objectives (health versus market versus fundamental rights) ad hoc or informal mechanisms for policymaking became institutionalized. The High-Level Group, already institutionalized during the negotiations on the Directive, became subsumed under a European Health Strategy, and part of a 'structured implementation' mechanism under Council auspices.[116] Moreover, a number of networks were institutionalized under the Directive, such as Centres of Reference and health technology. Parallel to this, the open method of coordination was set up, in an attempt to address macroeconomic policy issues with regard to health care.[117] The nature of the policy discourse on health care evolved from being an 'internal market discourse' to a 'health and rights discourse' which includes considerations on balancing values and rights in the context of health. This change in discourse is mirrored by institutional developments; in the words of a representative of the EMA with regard to medicines: '[N]ow we have created an internal market [on medicinal products], we can shift attention to be based mainly on the health implication.'[118]

3.2 From a policy debate on health values to law

At the same time, the case of the adoption of the Directive shows that the institutional evolution of the policy in this field is not a linear process, but rather a slow build-up of soft coordination and a process of negotiating legislative competence.

All these softer key intentions and Council conclusions .... After a while you see the Commission is a real master at quotations from these Council conclusions, building up a kind of pseudo or

[113] Respondent 4 (MS Representative Working Party on Public Health in the Council, 2010).
[114] Respondent 2 (Deputy Permanent Representative for Health in the Council, 2010).
[115] Respondent 13 (High level representative Commission Services, DG SANCO, 2010).
[116] See Council Conclusions on a cooperation mechanism between the Council and the Commission for the implementation of the EU Health Strategy 2876th EPSCO Council meeting (Luxembourg, 10 June 2008).
[117] de Ruijter and Hervey (2012) supra note 79.
[118] Respondent 20 (High level representative European Medicines Agency, 2010).

real urgency to come up with tougher measures. All this exchange of information, etc. etc..... If you pile up 1,000 of these stones you have a wall, and you have enough critical mass to come up with serious proposals such as legislation on cross-border health justified by the internal market [...]. The work done for the directive, a lot was done in relation to non-binding activities, such as on shared values, a High Level Group of reflection, all these non-legally binding platforms and interactive mechanisms, conferences, reflection groups, etc. It is a tool to invest once again and it prepares the minds a little bit for coming up with a finished product which is legally binding.[119]

Hence in the end, the power of the EU in the field has grown, if only because there is now a basis for discussion on further legislation and regulation, regardless of the limitations Member States have tried to obstruct the Directive with, for instance with regard to prior authorisation. One important reason for this is that the adoption of the Directive strengthened EU health-care policy through the reconfiguration of institutional actors involved in it, which are now more than ever health policy specialists rather than, say, agriculture or internal market specialists. The Directive creates a number of policy fora (committees and networks) through which the authoritative role of the EU may grow further.

4. Access to Medical Care in the EU: Impact on Values and Rights

This section focuses on the impact, in terms of fundamental rights and values, of the expansion of EU power in the field of health care—particularly in the context of the Directive on the quality and safety of health-care services and prior authorization. The reason for choosing these two elements for analysis is that both are central and contentious issues regulated by the Patients' Rights Directive. The provisions on prior authorization constitute the central aspect that the Directive aims to regulate, which is under what circumstances can Member States deny access to health care across their borders? The other provisions on quality and safety are highly contentious given that the quality and safety of medical care across the EU is varies greatly, and improvements in this respect can be costly for Member States.

The title of the 'Directive on patients' rights to cross-border health care' is suggestive, as the term 'patients' rights' implies a relation to the individual rights that are usually gauged under this term. However, as many commentators have mentioned, the Directive does not explicitly address patients' rights in the term's usual sense.[120] Although the Directive addresses aspects that fall within the realm of the right to access health care, the right to health generally can also be brought to bear in the health-care policy context, particularly if it pertains to preventing the loss of life, for instance concerning the safety and quality of health-care facilities. The main explicit purpose

[119] Respondent 2 (Deputy Permanent Representative for Health in the Council, 2010).

[120] See Chapter 3, section 3.2; H. Nys 'After the Transposition of the Directive on Patients' Rights in Cross-Care Healthcare in National Law by the Member States: Still a Lot of Effort to Be Made and Questions to Be Answered' (2014) *European Journal of Health Law* 21 1–14; M. Peeters 'Free Movement of Patients: Directive 2011/24 on the Application of Partients' Rights in Cross-border Healthcare' (2012) *European Journal of Health Law* 19 (56) 29–60; de la Rosa (2012) supra note 15; W. Sauter 'Harmonisation in Healthcare: The EU Patients' Rights Directive' (2011) *Tilec Research Paper* 8; also see R. Baeten and W. Palm 'Preserving General Interest in Healthcare through Secondary and Soft EU Law: The Case of the Patients' Rights Directive' in U. Neergaard et. al. (eds) *Social Services of General Interest in the EU* (The Hague: Asser, 2013), p. 391.

of the Directive is effectuating the access of patients to health care.[121] Article 4 of the Directive lists the responsibilities of the Member State of treatment and specifically provides that the principles of universality, access to good-quality care, equity, and solidarity need to be adhered to. The underlying idea is that the Member State of treatment has to guarantee that patients from another Member State are treated on the basis of their needs and that there is a set of common values and principles that are shared across the EU on how health systems respond to the needs of the population and the patients health systems serve.[122]

4.1 The right to health: the quality and safety of health care in the Directive

In terms of the right to health, quality and safety could become relevant when a patient loses his life or becomes injured as a consequence of lack of safety or quality of care in the context of cross-border care. Generally, EU regulatory policies impact the quality and safety of care.[123] However, there is no European regulation that determines the standard of care across the EU, and any harmonizing effort in this respect was excluded from the Directive.[124] At this point the information on the standard of care in the Member State of treatment has to be provided by National Contact Points.[125] This is due to the fact that Member States wanted to retain control over this issue. Instead of any harmonization in this respect there is a provision in Article 10 of the Directive that outlines a soft form of governance, where Member States have to give mutual assistance and cooperate with respect to quality and safety standards in health care.[126]

At the same time, Member States can refuse access cross-border care to a patient if they have specific and serious concerns that the standards of care are not guaranteed in the Member State where the patient seeks access.[127] Given the fact that the Directive facilitates access to cross-border health care for patients, this brings a particular medical treatment in a cross-border situation within the scope of EU law.[128] This means that if a problem arose with regard to the standard of care provided in a cross-border situation, fundamental rights would be applicable.

On the basis of the Directive, however, there are only limited information requirements regarding the quality and safety of health care that needs to be provided in a Member State of treatment—but the possibility remains of the Member State of affiliation refusing the patient access to cross-border treatment because of quality and safety concerns, or refusing prior authorization for patients that are attempting to escape the poor quality of care in their home state.[129] The Member State of affiliation may

[121] Implicit purposes have clearly been assumed among legislators and in the literature, as the different discourses that were brought to bear in the legislative process would indicate; also see references in supra note 32.

[122] Recital 21 of the Directive and see Council Conclusions on Common values and principles in European Union Health Systems (OJ C 146/1, 2006).

[123] H. D. C. Roscam Abbing 'Patients' Right to Quality of Healthcare: How Satisfactory Are the European Union's Regulatory Policies?' (2012) *European Journal of Health Law* 19 (5) 415–22.

[124] M. Peeters (2012) supra note 36 at p. 43.

[125] Articles 4(1) and 4(2)(a) and (b) Directive.

[126] Ibid. at p. 55 also see W. Palm and R. Baeten 'The Quality and Safety Paradox in the Patients' Rights Directive' (2011) *European Journal of Public Health* 21 (3) 272–4.

[127] Article 8(2)(c) and Article 5(a) Directive.

[128] Case C-617/10, *Åklagaren v. Hans Åkerberg Fransson* [2013] ECR 1-0000.

[129] Case C-268/13 *Elena Petru v. Casa Județeană de Asigurări de Sănătate Sibiu and Casa Națională de Asigurări de Sănătate* (ECLI:EU:C:2014:2271). See also M. Frischhut and R. Levaggi, 'Patient

do so in cases where there is a 'specific and serious concern'. However, it is doubtful whether health-care authorities will have enough information available with respect to what goes on in the health-care facilities cross border, or that this information will be provided to them, to aptly safeguard their patients. There are only limited information-provision requirements to address the protection of patients from unsafe situations in the context of the health care in the Member State of treatment. The information that is available to the 'visiting patient' through the National Contact Point of the Member State of treatment is limited in that this information does not have to be translated, and nor does it need to be ensured that the patient has understood the information, for instance by taking into account cultural differences, expectations, and the organization of the health-care system.[130]

Therefore, if a patient is injured or passes away as a consequence of poor quality of care that is systemic and due to negligence of public authorities, they (or their next of kin) could bring a claim against the national health institution (depending on the organization of the health-care system) based on the right to health, possibly combined with a right-to-life claim. However, the question can also be asked if the protection of the patients' life and health is actually guaranteed by the Directive itself, given the lack of protection and the basic assumptions regarding the patient's ability to obtain and understand the possible risks of cross-border care sufficiently. Hence, on one hand the Directive facilitates access to cross-border care, but does not guarantee the safety of that medical care, which impacts the right to health. On the other hand, opening up the ability to access cross-border care promotes access to health care that in terms of quality and safety may go beyond what is available at national level.[131] The outline of the above considerations indicates connection of the Directive with the right to health and also the right to access health care.

4.2 The right to health: prior authorization in the Directive

After the adoption of the Directive, the possibilities for patients to seek health care cross border of their own accord have been limited,[132] when taking into consideration the expansion of possibilities for Member States to exercise their right to prior authorization. Hence, regardless of the fact that the Directive creates the possibility for going cross border, by creating further bureaucratic barriers, the adoption of the Directive has limited the 'European route' and impacts the right to access health care at EU level.

However, the question is what the right to health *requires* with respect to accessing health care at European level. To begin with, Article 35 of the Charter, read together with the right to life, can provide the basis for an individual claim, for instance when access to health care is denied on the argument that resources are limited.[133] This could be in a case where a patient is denied prior authorization and therewith is denied life-extending treatment, which in some Member States might be discouraged for reasons of quality of life and even for rationing health care. Another claim can be made when Article 35 EUCFR is read in relation to Article 4 EUCFR on the infliction of inhuman or degrading treatment. In this situation, a patient in pain or disabled, who is made to

Mobility in the Context of Austerity and an Enlarged EU: The European Court of Justice's Ruling in the Petru Case' (2015) 119 *Health Policy* 1293.

[130] Article 4(2)(b) Directive. [131] Frischhut and Levaggi (n 129).

[132] S. de la Rosa (2012) supra note 15 at p. 39.

[133] As also suggested by Respondent 15 (High level representative Commission Services SANCO, 2010).

wait for health care in the home state while access to cross-border health care is denied, could potentially claim the infliction of inhuman or degrading treatment in combination with a right to health care.[134]

The need to ensure prior authorization for patients brings to light the difficulty the EU presents with respect to the right to health. The right to access health care, created at EU level by the Directive, can impede on the right to access health care at Member State level. Member States use a number of ways to ensure equitable access to health care, including different ways of rationing care. The fact that the Directive creates access to health care across borders can simultaneously ensure and impede the right to health care. Article 35 CFREU, however, puts emphasis on the right to access health care at Member State level, which can be seen as an indication that access in the home Member State trumps possibilities to access health care cross border. In the following section, the analysis turns to the consequences of EU health policy for individual rights.

4.3 The impact of EU health policy on individual rights

In the framework for analysis of EU fundamental rights particular focus with respect to individual rights is placed first on the right to informed consent and on the right to privacy and data protection. These individual rights have particular meaning and weight in the health policy context. The right to informed consent is deeply connected with the right to human dignity and integrity of the person.[135]

4.4 Individual rights: informed consent in the Directive

Generally, health-care policy can impact on individual rights in a number of ways. In this respect the right to equal treatment is particularly relevant for the right to access health care.[136] However, for the purpose of illustrating the impact of EU health policy on fundamental rights, the choice was made, because of their specific importance in the health context, to put the focus on the right to informed consent and the right to privacy and data protection.

Article 4(1) Directive outlines that cross-border health care is provided in line with the legislation of the Member State of treatment. This means that to establish an infringement of the fundamental right to informed consent, in principle the legal doctrine of the Member State of treatment applies. In this respect different standards of medical care apply in the Member States. Important differences here relate especially to the information the physician has to provide to the patients in order for them to be able to consent to medical treatment. The different models regarding the duty of care for informed consent can be arranged on a spectrum. On one end of the spectrum the doctor is legally entitled to determine on the patient's behalf what she needs to know. At the other end of the spectrum, the physician has to take into consideration the patient's specific and individual needs.[137] In the UK, for example, the legal doctrine

[134] For example Case C-466/04 *Yvonne Watts v. Bedford Primary Care Trust, Secretary of State for Health* ECR I-4325.

[135] Articles 1 and 3 CFREU.

[136] J. V. McHale 'Fundamental Rights and Health Care' in E. Mossialos et al. (eds) *Health Systems Governance in the EU: The Role of EU Law and Governance* (New York: Cambridge University Press, 2012); TK Hervey and JV McHale, *European Union Health Law* (Cambridge University Press 2015).

[137] See L. L. Emanuel 'Four Models of the Physician–Patient Relationship' (1992) *Journal of the American Medical Association* 267 (16) 2221–6; also see R. R. Faden and T. L. Beauchamp *A History and Theory of Informed Consent* (New York: Oxford University Press, 1986).

on information provision in a medical setting is determined by what a 'prudent doctor' would have told a reasonable patient in similar circumstances. In Germany, the standard for informed consent is determined by the answer to the question: what is important for this 'individual patient' in order to consent to treatment?[138]

With regard to the Directive, the standard for determining what information a patient needs in order to consent is not left completely to the physicians of the Member States of treatment. Article 4(2)(b) of the Directive determines that health-care providers are to provide the relevant information to help individual patients to make an informed choice, including on treatment options, and the quality and safety of the health care they provide. In Article 4(2)(a) of the Directive it is outlined that upon request the patient should receive information on the standards and guidelines of quality and safety applicable in the Member State of treatment from the national contact point.[139]

Concerning the provision of relevant information in order for the patient to reach informed consent, the Directive does not oblige physicians to provide more information to patients than they would to patients from within the health- care system of the Member State of treatment.[140] However, the information always needs to be provided, whether or not the patient requests it. Moreover, the Member State of treatment can assign other actors in the health-care system, such as the health insurer, to provide information to patients as well.[141] Additionally, Article 6(3) determines that the national contact point shall provide patients with information on health-care providers, including, on request, information relating to the providers' rights to provide services, or any restrictions on licences to practice; information about the applicable legislation in the Member State of treatment; and information on patients' rights, complaints procedures, and the legal and administrative options that are available to settle disputes in the event of harm arising from cross-border health care.[142]

The Directive poses a complication with respect to informed consent in that a physician does not need to provide more extensive information to patients from other Member States. Language in particular could be a barrier in this respect, as the physician is not obliged to provide information in the language of the patient's home state.[143] Another problem is the cultural and legal expectations a patient might have with respect to the information they will receive. As the examples of Germany and the UK showed, a patient from Germany would expect to receive all the information s/he deems important for their particular situation, whereas in the UK a physician has more autonomy to decide what a reasonable patient would need to know under the circumstances. In this respect the Directive offers no alternative indications as to what the standard of care for informed consent in cross-border health care entails. If it were up to the legislation and legal doctrines of the Member States alone, the patient's lack of actual understanding of the treatment options due to language or cultural mismatch could result in a violation of the right to informed consent on the basis of the CFREU.

[138] See generally A. de Ruijter 'Patient Autonomy in Europe' in J. Rutgers (ed.) *European Contract Law and the Welfare State* (Groningen: Europa Law, 2010).

[139] Article 6 of the Directive deals with the tasks and responsibilities of the national contact points.

[140] See generally H. Nys 'The Right to Informed Choice and the Patients' Rights Directive' (2012) *European Journal of Health Law* 19 (4) 327–31.

[141] Recital 20 Directive.

[142] Related is Article 10(4) Directive, which obligates the Member State of treatment to ensure that information on the right to practise of health professionals listed in national or local registers established on their territory is made available to the authorities of other Member States upon request for the purpose of cross-border health care, taking into consideration the rules on data protection.

[143] Article 5(5) Directive.

Hence, the indications of what a doctrine of informed consent in the context of the Directive would entail are meagre, as the Directive does not guarantee substantial aspects of all information necessary for informed consent specifically, such as the risks of the treatment and the possible complications. This means that the Directive itself does not safeguard the right to informed consent—for the Member States the Directive creates a low threshold for determining that patients are sufficiently informed to make a decision with respect to their health, which means that in individual cases the right to informed consent can also be impacted.

4.5 Individual rights: the right to privacy and data protection

The protection of the right to privacy is important as a general matter of human dignity and medical secrecy, as otherwise patients might be inclined to lie to their physician about certain aspects of their condition, which could lead to a wrong diagnosis, or patients might not seek health care at all. Article 7 CFREU outlines the right to privacy and Article 8 CFREU the right to data protection. The Directive also makes special provisions relating to the protection of privacy and personal data. Article 4(2)(e) of the Directive determines that the Member State where the treatment takes place needs to ensure that a private life and data protection are protected. This needs to be ensured in conformity with national legislation that aims to implement Union provisions on the protection of data.[144] Moreover, Article 4(2)(f) outlines that patients that have received cross-border health care are entitled to a written or electronic medical record of this treatment and access to at least a copy of the medical record in conformity with the national measures implementing the directives on data protection.

Recital 25 of the Directive acknowledges that cross-border health care has the potential to impact Article 8 CFREU by ensuring that, in the continuity of cross-border health care, the transfer of personal data concerning the patient's health should flow from one Member State to the other. Moreover, it states that the access to one's own medical dossier should be ensured,[145] for instance on the diagnosis, examination results, assessments by treating physicians, and treatment interventions that were provided. However, what is not clear is whether the personal notes taken by the physician should be part of the medical dossier, whereas presumably these do fall within the context of the right to privacy under Article 7 CFREU.[146] Therefore, the right to data protection and the right to privacy are both directly impacted by the Patients' Rights Directive.

5. The Impact of the Struggle over Policy Frames: The Market, Health, Values, and Rights

The power struggles, and the role of conflicting policy frames therein, mark the controversy surrounding the adoption of the Patients' Rights Directive. On one hand

[144] Directive 95/46/EC (1995); Directive 2002/58/EC of the European Parliament and of the Council of 12 July 2002 concerning the processing of personal data and the protection of privacy in the electronic communications sector (OJ L 201, 31-07-2002, pp. 37–47).

[145] Defined in Article 3(m) Directive.

[146] Case F-46/09 *V & EDPS v. European Parliament* (5-7-2011) (not yet published in Reports of Staff Cases 'Civil Service Tribunal' section) decided on the basis of Article 8 ECHR; ECtHR Case of *Z v. Finland* Application no. 22009/93 (25 February 1997).

power struggles were played out between institutional actors, and on the other between the EU and the Member States. There was a struggle between the different DGs in that DG MARKT wanted control over the health-care 'market', whereas DG SANCO claimed a role on the basis that health care is a special policy area with specific health considerations that need to be taken into account. However, the struggle between the Council and the Parliament concerned who was going to represent European citizens. In this respect the Directive is a real 'citizen directive' in a European sense,[147] as it affects inclusion or exclusion from welfare entitlements. The European Parliament was driven by the protection of the individual patient in this regard, whereas the Council and the Member States were driven to protect the communal or national solidarity-based health care systems. These struggles were largely the result of conflicting policy frames on fundamental values and the importance of health-care policy.

In the course of these struggles a number of institutional actors and fora were developed and institutionalized in which health care policy could become part of a European conversation. For instance, the high-level processes initiated by DG SANCO were initially seen as a way to cool the tempers on the EU debate on the role of the EU in health care generally, but eventually this 'cooling down' created a safety zone where Member States could discuss a number of other health-care issues that went far beyond the codifications of the CJEU's case law. A number of these fora for discussion have now been institutionalized within the Directive. E-health, Centres of Reference, and the transferability of prescriptions were all issues that were not strictly necessary in order to codify the Court's case law. These actors are not merely coordinating but in some case the EU has actual delegated or implementing powers to regulate particular aspects regarding medical care that can impact on fundamental rights. Moreover, even where the EU is merely facilitating a debate on particular policy issues or on coordinating Member States' health-care systems, the authority and the possibility to 'pile on more stones to wall' as the above-quoted civil servant called it, can eventually lead to actual legal rules. However, perhaps surprisingly, fundamental rights were never discussed explicitly, even when the title of the Directive refers to patients' rights. At the same time, fundamental rights are seen by the Commission as the opportunity to build and strengthen the reach of the EU in health care through litigation:

> I think what is important is to see is how the equal status of the Charter of fundamental Rights [to the primary Treaties] will play out. Because, how will citizens use this as a tool, or how will health stakeholders try and mobilize support for European health policy and use litigation?[148]

The following chapter will expand on this point the Commission representative raises and on the further implications of the impact of European health policy on fundamental rights.

[147] Davies (2011) supra note 29 at p. 207.
[148] Respondent 13 (High level representative Commission Services, DG SANCO, 2010).

7

The EU Constitutional Constraints on the Intrinsic Relationship of Values, Rights, and Human Health

> EU health policy […] is like if you are walking on the mountain. The mountain is very high and you are walking right on the top. It is steep on the one side and steep on the other side and we have to balance through these interests that are both justified.[1]

In the introduction to this book the EU's involvement was characterized by a civil servant as a 'silent revolution'. This characterization highlights the two leading threads in the book: The first is the ongoing 'silent' expansion of EU public authority with regard to health policy and law, regardless of the limitations in the legal possibilities for EU policy and law. The other thread is the 'revolution' of the impact of this policy with regard of the guiding fundamental rights and values that Member States share, in the protection, provision, and promotion of public health and health care. In this concluding chapter these threads are brought together. The main thrust of this chapter is that, while the EU's power in public health and health care is expanding, the current constitutional doctrines for constraining EU power in the field of human health are not designed specifically with human health in mind and therefore are not capable of safeguarding the values and rights that are intrinsically related to human health law and policy. This begs the question of whether there is legal room and common ground between the shared values and rights of the Member States to alleviate the current tensions.

1. The Juxtaposition: Health Law and the EU Internal Market

In health law, values and human rights make up the central aspects that form the fabric of most of its legal instruments, in the Western world and beyond. By contrast, according to most accounts, including that in this book, *EU* health law developed as a side issue of internal market law. Furthermore, EU health law came about as national health laws and regulations became *exceptions* in light of the overarching objective of creating the EU internal market (deregulation). A relevant famous and foundational CJEU decision is the *Cassis de Dijon* case, in which the CJEU ruled on the extent of

[1] Respondent 3 (MS Representative, Working Party on Public Health in the Council, 2010). Some parts of this chapter have been pulblished in T. K. Hervey, C. A. Young, and L. E. Bishop (eds) *Research Handbook on EU Health Law and Policy* (Cheltenham: Edward Elgar, 2017).

EU Health Law & Policy: The Expansion of EU Power in Public Health and Health Care. Anniek de Ruijter © Anniek de Ruijter 2019. Published in 2019 by Oxford University Press.

national power to adopt health-related alcohol laws.[2] EU health law and policy have also been a means to re-regulate the EU market in areas where national regulatory barriers to trade were removed to create the internal single EU market. In the *Tobacco Advertising* case it was established that the European legislator cannot create legislation with health as a central and single objective. There must be an internal market connection as a legal basis for most EU health law (Art. 114 TFEU, but see certain paragraphs in Art. 168 TFEU).[3] There are numerous examples here in the area of food safety, medicines, and access to medical benefits in another Member State, where the market connection is the (legal) basis for EU health regulation. In contrast, over the last half-century in the Member States, health law has developed on rather different foundational bases.

Generally, in the Member States health law regulates relationships of solidarity, ethics, professional trust, and the protection of human physical dignity, in the face of shared risks and opportunities related to life, disease, and mortality.[4] Health laws in the Member States on the whole express the values of solidarity, universal access, equality, and human dignity, which are also reflected in health-related fundamental rights. These values are translated in national public health programmes and health-care systems in various ways.[5] The values of equality and solidarity are expressed in the general rule across EU Member States that all citizens have 'universal access' to medical treatment.[6] Human dignity is expressed in rules regarding the protection of informed consent in medical research and medical treatment or in national laws that guarantee a 'right to know and not to know' and the right to the inviolability of physical integrity. In public health human dignity is expressed in rules about eugenics and other research-related regulations. Besides the general national laws and policies that express the values and principles of health law, these values are expressed in constitutional law and in the application of (EU or Council of Europe ECHR) human rights.[7]

Hence, Member States' national health laws largely protect a number of specifically health- and human dignity-related rights,[8] such as informed consent, the protection of medical and health data, secrecy and professional medical standards, medical liability,

[2] In Case 120/78 *Rewe-Zentral AG v. Bundesmonopolverwaltung für Branntwein (Cassis de Dijon)* ECLI:EU:C:1979:42, [1979] ECR 649, the public health exception for goods in the Treaty (currently Article 36 TFEU) was broadened through the establishment of a Rule of Reason doctrine that applies only to national measures that treat products from another Member State equally.

[3] Case C-376/98 *Germany v. European Parliament and Council (Tobacco Advertising I)* ECLI:EU:C:2000:544 [2000] ECR I-8419.

[4] T. K. Hervey and J. V. McHale *European Union Health Law: Themes and Implications* (Cambridge: Cambridge University Press, 2015).

[5] E. D. Kinney and B. A. Clark 'Provisions for Health and Health Care in the Constitutions of the Countries of the World' (2004) *Cornell International Law Journal* 37 285–355. B. Toebes 'Introduction: Health and Human Rights in Europe', *Health and Human Rights in Europe* (Cambridge: Intersentia, 2012).

[6] Nobody can be denied access to medical care.

[7] Kinney and Clark (2004) supra note 5; H. J. Leenen 'Health Law in the Twenty-First Century' (1998) *European Journal of Health Law* 5 341; H. J. Leenen, J. K. M. Gevers, and G. Pinet *The Rights of Patients in Europe* (Deventer: Kluwer, 1993); J. Legemaate 'Integrating Health Law and Policy: A European Perspective' (2002) *Health Policy* 60 101; T. Hervey 'We Don't See a Connection: The "Right to Health" in the EU Charter and European Social Charter', *Social Rights in Europe* (Oxford: Oxford University Press, 2005); J. V. McHale, 'Fundamental Rights and Health Care', *Health Systems Governance in the EU: The Role of EU Law and Governance* (Cambridge: Cambridge University Press 2012).

[8] M. Frischhut '"EU": Short for "Ethical" Union? The Role of Ethics in European Union Law' (2015) *Heidelberg Journal of International Law* 75 531.

and the right to equal 'universal' access to medical care.[9] The shared foundations of rights and objectives that can be found in national health laws are the 'values' of health law. The current setup of the EU's constitutional order—that is, the manner in which the EU can exercise power in the field of human health and the setting in which the growing role of the EU in human health regulation is taking place—begs the key question of how EU law can safeguard the central values and rights inherently related when regulating human health issues. This question is especially relevant in light of the findings in this book, in the specific case studies, that EU health law and policy in the fields of health care and public health has (implicit) fundamental rights and values impact.

2. Silent Revolution: Implicit Fundamental Rights and Value Implications

This book principally looks at EU public policy and law through a 'health law' lens, which implies consideration of its intrinsic bioethical values and fundamental rights. This is not to put forward a view that health care and public health law and policy are different from other sensitive EU policy areas. However, the case of human health clearly puts into view some of the constitutional conundrums for the EU. The starting point for the analysis is the fact that Article 168 of the Treaty on the Functioning of the European Union (TFEU) does not reflect the EU's actual involvement in and impact on human health. Instead, in order to capture the power of the EU in human health, EU health policy and law are conceptualized essentially as an authoritative allocation of value through the EU political system aimed at protecting and promoting human health. This conceptualization aims to describe the exercise of EU power through the ability to frame and impact policy objectives regarding human health through, for example, formal legislation on various legal bases (internal market, health, agriculture, etc.) and through different regulatory and policy modes. Conceptualizing EU health policy as an 'authoritative allocation of value' recognizes the fact that EU involvement cannot always be captured legally—or may not even be binding on Member States or individuals. However, it can still have authoritative value, which eventually may have an impact on fundamental rights and values.

This book illustrates ways in which the EU expands its power in the field of human health and the case studies show that—because of the intrinsic relationship of human health policy and law with certain rights and values—in expanding its power, the EU explicitly *and implicitly* takes on obligations and impacts fundamental values and rights. In some of the described instances this impact gives rise to possibilities for litigation or legislative review in light of fundamental rights and values, also in areas when health policy is merely created as a by-product of EU internal market law. However, even when it is not necessarily intended that legal effects are brought about by health policy, fundamental rights and values can come into play when addressing human health.

[9] A. de Ruijter 'EU Integration in the Field of Human Health, Review Article' (2016) *Journal of European Integration* 38 (7) 837–43.

2.1 Vertical implications: between the EU and the Member States

2.1.1 Health care

The analysis of the Patients' Rights Directive in light of the right to health shows that the EU *right to access care* depends on this right existing at Member State level. At Member State level, providing universal health coverage is generally a constitutionally mandated responsibility of the Member States and a shared value.[10] Moreover, the health-care systems that have evolved over the years are extremely intricate and demand intensive planning and governance.[11] Hence, simply effectuating a right to access health at EU level could infringe on the obligations of Member States to guarantee universal coverage, or equal access to health care, and paradoxically, impinge on the right to health *at EU level.*

This impact can be illustrated by the example of the Spanish health-care system. The manner of balancing the redistributive right to access health care through rationing in Spain is to demand that patients go to a physician or hospital within their respective network. The fact that the right to access health care at the European level is, by definition, out of network (i.e. in another Member State) directly impacts the regulation of the national health-care system in Spain.[12] It not only affects the possibility for the Spanish authorities to redistribute health entitlements; it affects the logic and mechanism of the system itself, which is developed and accepted by the Spanish citizens as a moral way of rationing and redistributing access to health care. The introduction of going out of network may harm the system as a whole and hence the right to health at *EU level* may be impacted, given that this could hypothetically affect all Europeans seeking access to health care in Spain.

2.1.2 Public health

The matter of the right to health in *public health* demands that public authorities strike a 'fair balance [...] between the competing interests of the individual and the community as a whole'.[13] The EU implicitly strikes this balance between the individual and the community through its involvement in human health. An example from the public health case study is that when the contacts of individuals that are suspected of carrying a communicable disease are traced, personal information of patients is exchanged across Member States for the common good of protecting the community against a particular disease.[14] Moreover, in balancing the rights of the individual and the community, the EU also adds another constitutional layer to the Member States, which in their turn are also balancing legitimate rights claims of citizens and their community. Adding the EU layer to this implicit balancing of rights immediately puts

[10] Kinney and Clark (2004) supra note 5. Council Conclusions, 'Council Conclusions on Common Values and Principles in European Union Health Systems (O.J C 146/1, 2006)'.

[11] F. W. Scharpf 'The European Social Model: Coping with the Challenges of Diversity' (2002) *Journal of Common Market Studies* (40) 645–70.

[12] T. Requejo 'Cross-border Healthcare in Spain and the Implementation of the Directive 2011/24/EU on the Application of Patient's Rights in Cross-border Healthcare' (2014) *European Journal of Health Law* (21) 79–96.

[13] ECtHR *Nikky Sentges v. the Netherlands* (Admissability) [2003] Application no. 27677/02 (8 July 2003).

[14] P. Dąbrowska-Kłosińska 'Tracing Individuals under the EU Regime on Serious, Cross-Border Health Threats: An Appraisal of the System of Personal Data Protection' (2017) *European Journal of Risk Regulation* 8 700.

into question the legitimacy of the scope of this 'community' and who is to have a say regarding these sensitive balancing acts between the public and the individual in the field of human health.[15]

2.2 Horizontal implications: between (institutionally defined) policy domains

2.2.1 Health care

In several places in the Treaties human health is mentioned, most importantly in outlining that the EU has no general legislative power in the field of human health (Art. 168(5) public health and (7) health care), which, in light of the general principles on attribution of power in Article 5 TEU (Treaty on European Union) might seem like an overload of prohibitions on the EU legislator to adopt human health law and policy. At the same time, the protection and promotion of human health as a mainstreaming provision is mentioned in several places across EU primary law: Article 35 CFREU; Articles 4 and 6 TFEU on shared and supportive competence; Articles 9, 114(3), and 168(1) TFEU, etc.

The horizontal struggle for authority and a rightful policy space that is visible in the current EU primary law is reflected in the debate on the legal basis for the Directive in the case study in this book on the adoption of the Patients' Rights Directive. This debate went to the heart of the EU's limited formal role for affecting access to health care.[16] The particularly heated discussion around the legal basis of the Directive revolved around the fact that the Directive would be based on Article 114 TFEU (functioning of the internal market), because Article 168(7) TFEU explicitly prohibits the regulation of health-care services. This struggle also took place between institutions, DG MARKT, DG Health, and even DG Employment, over where to situate the dossier of access to health care.

The horizontal struggles are fed by the role of the Member States, who have wanted to include some recognition of the fact that the EU regulation and coordination of health-care systems was more than an internal market issue; that the proposed legislation involved values that are inherent in Member States' health systems. This view has led to the adoption of Council Conclusions, brought to defend against what were seen as the inroads of EU internal market law into the politically sensitive area of access to medical care at Member State level.[17]

The legal basis of Article 114 TFEU for a directive that bore 'Patients' Rights' in the title was also seen as problematic. One civil servant commented that although the Directive had to be based on Article 114 TFEU, Article 168 TFEU was added as a legal basis 'for aesthetic reasons'.[18] These 'aesthetic reasons' point to the problematic legitimation of the Directive in that the reference to Article 168 TFEU indicates that

[15] G. Davies 'Democracy and Legitimacy in the Shadow of Purposive Competence' (2013) *European Law Journal* 21 2; G. Davies, 'The Process and Side-Effects of Harmonisation of European Welfare States' *Jean Monnet Working Paper No 2/06* (2006).

[16] D. Sindbjerg Martinsen, *An Ever More Powerful Court?: The Political Constraints of Legal Integration in the European Union* (Oxford: Oxford University Press, 2015) chapter 5; D. Sindbjerg Martinsen and H. Vollaard 'The Rise of a European Healthcare Union' (2015) *Special Issue Comparative European Politics* 15(3) 337–52.

[17] Council Conclusions, supra note 10.

[18] Respondent 2 (Deputy Permanent Representative for Health in the Council, 2010).

the Directive is not merely internal market law, but also balances public authority obligations along the lines of the right to access health care.

These—at times—paradoxical legislative bases that were deemed necessary in adopting the Patients' Rights Directive exemplify the ever-present intrinsic connection between health policy and fundamental rights and also the related political distributary welfare concerns at stake in this field of regulation. The fact that the Directive in itself also has an important impact on access to health care may be an indication that more of this debate will follow in the future.[19]

2.2.2 Public health

Whereas in Member States' health law the fields of public health and health care are reasonably defined, in the EU the different functions of public power within its involvement in human health are not as clear cut. As outlined above, the references to human health and public health run across the Treaties. In addition to the legislative references outlined, human health in Article 36 TFEU is a ground for exception, and Articles 45 and 52 TFEU are also notably important for *public health* as an exception to the free movement of workers and the right of establishment, which are also provisions that feature relatively centrally in the context of Union free-movement law.

In this vast field of EU public policy, the focus is on the more 'technical'—arguably less value-charged—area of *EU public health*. However, the analysis in the book renders visible EU health policy's implications for fundamental rights and values. As illustrated, the large number of public health regulations in the field of the internal market and agriculture that the EU adopts each year may *horizontally* intertwine with classical public health functions that the EU has taken on over the years. For instance, the case study on the swine flu outbreak showed that the EU has no formal powers to create vaccination strategies. In fact, the Patients' Rights Directive explicitly excludes national vaccination policies.[20] Yet given that the EU regulates the approval of pandemic vaccines, in case of an emergency—as the swine flu case study indicated—the EU also becomes involved in national vaccination strategies (which are an important aspect of safeguarding the right to health), engaging a number of formal and informal EU institutional actors.

The public health case study further shows how the EU's obligation to protect the right to health may go beyond its policies that aim to create a free market. Consequentially EU 'market-correcting policy', such as safe medicines, intertwines with the classic welfare policy of making medicines available to everyone, even—as the case of swine flu shows—in highly morally challenging issues such as vaccine strategies, where questions are asked of who gets a vaccine first in an emergency.

Furthermore, with regard to individual rights, the impact of EU health law and policy brings into view the constitutional difficulties faced in dealing with a sensitive policy area such as human health in the EU context. For example, the regulation of vaccines during a pandemic, as the public health case study showed, is approved on less clinical evidence than the usual centralized authorization procedure calls for. As outlined in the previous chapter, one vaccine, approved as an EU-wide pandemic

[19] Request for a preliminary ruling from the Fővárosi Közigazgatási és Munkaügyi Bíróság (Hungary) lodged on 28 March 2018—*VIPA Kereskedelmi és Szolgáltató Kft v. Országos Gyógyszerészeti és Élelmezés-egészségügyi Intézet* (Case C-222/18).

[20] Directive 2011/24/EU of the European Parliament and of the Council of 9 March 2011 on the application of partients' rights in cross-border healthcare (OJ L 88/45, 4-4-2011).

vaccine against swine flu, was found to cause the neurological disorder narcolepsy. In this case a right-to-life claim could possibly be made in considering the legitimacy of the EU authorization procedures regarding pandemic medicines in terms of fundamental rights. At the same time, the social right to access medicines in case of a pandemic may limit a right-to-life claim, or, paradoxically, a right to life together with the right to health could be claimed with regard to the obligation of the EU to ensure access to medicines. However, in general, this tension between rights is not new to health lawyers:

> Health law has contributed much to the growing awareness that health and human rights are closely interlinked, especially in those areas where tension may rise between the interests of the individual and the needs of society at large.[21]

The implications of, on one hand, the EU's role to protect and promote human health and, on the other, the limits of this role in terms of individual rights are particularly precarious in areas of EU health policy where the legal nature of this policy is unsure and where there is a build-up of different institutional actors that are involved in an issue.

For instance, as the public health study showed, when in responding to the swine flu outbreak the Health Security Committee determined that contact-tracing was necessary for curbing the spread of the virus, while it had no legal basis to decide on contact-tracing. Hence the Commission had to involve the EWRS Committee's legal powers to adopt a decision in order to track and trace the contacts of patients across the EU. Although formally there may not be a problem with this, the substantive decision regarding the infringements of the right to secrecy of personal medical information was taken informally.[22] And even though these exchanges of information may be well within the public health exception of the Data Protection Directive, they still impact the individual rights of patients' privacy and data protection. The body that makes this decision should also be able to be held responsible.

Generally, the implications of EU health policy are that the EU *de facto* and often *implicitly* balances the positive responsibilities to protect and promote health with the limits of this responsibility in terms of both the right to health and individual rights. Yet this balancing often occurs as an unintended consequence of EU health policy-making. At the same time, given the particular nature of the European legal system as a 'layer' on top of Member States' legal systems, the balancing of EU obligations takes place not only in relation to the autonomy of individual Europeans, but also in relation to the legal autonomy of Member States.

[21] J. Legemaate 'Integrating Health Law and Policy: A European Perspective' (2002) *Health Policy* 60 101–10 at p. 102

[22] Immediately after the swine flu outbreak the position of the Health Security Committee became more formalized. Communication from the Commission to the Council on Transitional Prolongation and Extension of the Mandate of the Health Security Committee in View of a Future General Revision of the Structures Dealing with Health Threats at the EU Level (COM (2006) 699 Final); Commission Proposal for a Decision of the European Parliament and of the Council on Serious Cross-Border Threats to Health Brussels (COM(2011)866 Final); Decision No.1082/2013/EU, Decision No 1082/2013/EU of the European Parliament and of the Council of 22 October 2013 on Serious Cross-Border Threats to Health and Repealing Decision No 2119/98/EC (OJ L 293/1 5-11-2013).

3. Depoliticization as a Constitutional Constraint on Human Health Regulation

The general constitutional conundrum that places constraints on the ability of the EU to take into consideration the full spectrum of health rights and values involved in human health law and policy is not a new phenomenon. Indeed, as outlined by others, the combination of 'purposive powers'—where generally the internal market objective provides the overriding legitimation for legislation—and the principle of subsidiarity—which holds that the EU should only have the power to act in cases where Member States themselves cannot achieve a particular objective effectively[23]—may not constitute an apt tool to balance other values and fundamental rights and at what level of governance these are best protected.[24]

3.1 Limiting values, rights, and welfare perspectives

At Member State level these constitutional constraints also have an effect on the ability to take into consideration other legitimate objectives, such as the protection of human health and its related values and fundamental rights on their own account. Scharpf proposes for example that the EU's limited legislative competence in areas outside the internal market objectives create a constitutional asymmetry.[25] The institutional and legal constraints for the EU to adopt 'market-correcting policies' favour economic liberal interests and policies, which in turn constrain Member States at national level to pursue other welfare and value goals. Furthermore, as outlined in the introduction to this book, if EU health policy impacts on fundamental rights as a result of informal ad hoc practices, neither the conferral nor the use of EU legislative competences can determine the legitimacy of the EU's role, as EU involvement takes place as a matter of fact, rather than as a matter of law. One strategy for protecting the values inherent in health law and regulation at Member State level of solidarity, equality, universal access, and human dignity generally could be through the above-indicated legal expression in fundamental rights. However, the application of fundamental rights guarantees under the CFREU and the Principles of EU law is also limited to the scope of EU law. This might mean that in cases where Member States are under no obligation to follow the EU's policy coordination in public health, they still may do so, without there being EU protection of individual rights.

Dieter Grimm has proposed that constitutional constraints in the EU derive from an 'over-constitutionalisation'. In most political systems, constitutions function to legitimize and limit political power. Constitutional rules form, in his words: 'the framework for politics, not the blueprint for all political decisions'.[26] This 'over-constitutionalisation' of the EU refers to the notion that the four freedoms and the objective of the creation of an internal market override all other legitimate policy

[23] Article 5(3) TFEU.

[24] Davies (2006) supra note 15 (subsidiarity as a tool for EU integration is a matter of assessing the effectiveness of law in view of a particular (legislative) objective, rather than balancing values).

[25] A. de Ruijter and T. K. Hervey 'Healthcare and the Lisbon Agenda' in P. Copeland and D. Papadimitriou (eds) *The EU's Lisbon Strategy: Evaluating Success, Understanding Failure* (Basingstoke: Palgrave, 2012); see F. Scharpf 'The Asymmetry of European Integration or why the EU cannot be a "Social Market Economy"' (2010) *Socio-Economic Review* 8 (2) 211.

[26] D. Grimm 'The Democratic Costs of Constitutionalisation: The European Case: Democratic Costs of Constitutionalisation' (2015) *European Law Journal* 21 460.

objectives, due to the lack of hierarchy in the Treaties and their constitutional status and function in the Treaties as constitutional review standard for the CJEU.

The field of health in the EU exemplifies Grimm's thesis, given that the CJEU has had a central role in reaffirming the recasting of national public health considerations as 'exceptions', even beyond those exceptions that are mentioned in the Treaties.[27] Importantly, however, in the field of human health, Member States' health law is directly impacted by European Union inroads into this field.[28] Liberalization and privatization, together with the effects of globalization and the constitutional context of the EU, make it difficult for the Member States to uphold their standards of social welfare in order to retain their economic competitiveness.[29]

This impact is exacerbated by the fact that the EU only has a very limited budget that can be used to alleviate these effects in light of values such as equality, solidarity, and universal access and the related fundamental rights. The European public health programme only has a small budget, which pales in comparison to the national budgets for public health and health-care services and programmes. But it is also true that the EU public health programmes are an example of positive integration at EU level that actually *redistributes* funds in the area of social welfare. And although the public health programmes over the years have had to make do on very low budgets,[30] they have links with the much larger budget of the EU research programme that allocates over 6 billion euros for health. The priorities defined in the Programme Committee for public health filter through in the funding priorities that are chosen under the heading of DG Research.[31] Moreover, much of the public health budget is distributed through co-funding, which means any activity or action usually needs at least 40 per cent funding from other sources. Another aspect that plays into this is that the EU public health programmes play a role in the distribution of EU structural funds, in that objectives of the public health programmes are mirrored with respect to the budget for health priorities in the structural funds.[32]

These budgetary constraints also explain much of the struggles over the EU's competence across EU primary law. Furthermore, the impact of the EU on health laws' fundamental values and rights is not limited to the cases and examples in this book. EU macroeconomic policy has a deep and increasingly important impact on the protection of health values in the Member States. In a recent study, Sokol and Mijatović show the impact on human health policy of the EU's European Stability Mechanism, which is the governance structure established by (or for) the eurozone countries.[33] For the countries that received financial aid during the euro crisis, the ESM established Memorandums of Understanding (MoU), monitored by the European Commission.

[27] See *Cassis de Dijon* and 'The Rule of Reason', supra note 2.

[28] T. K. Hervey and J. V. McHale *Health Law and the European Union* (Cambridge: Cambridge University Press, 2004). In this first edition, this dynamic is meticulously mapped.

[29] Grimm (2015) supra note 26. [30] Averaging 300 to 500 million euros.

[31] This link with research and health at EU level goes back to the 1950s, since the ECSC funded research programmes in the area of occupational diseases. Over the course of the 1970s and especially in the 1980s, research into communicable diseases was also funded by the Community; this was mainly in the context of the common market and agriculture. However, in the field of research and technology, biomedical research became funded at the European level in the area of biotechnology. Commission, 'Biology and Health Protection Programme: Research Programme 1976–1980' (Proposal) COM (75) 351 final..

[32] J. Watson 'Health and Structural Funds 2007–2013 (2013): Country and Regional Assessment' (Report for DG SANCO, 2009), and see ibid.

[33] T. Sokol and N. Mijatović 'EU Health Law and Policy and the Eurozone Crisis', in Hervey, Young, and Bishop (2017) supra note 1.

Non-compliance with these MoUs can result in sanctions. As a result, the health-care systems of these Member States, and particularly the ability of Member States to determine their own budgets for health-care spending, were immediately affected. Given that the European Stability Mechanism is outside the EU legal realm, the first question is whether EU law on fundamental rights even applies. Furthermore, Member States are subject to the European Semester, which is an EU governance mechanism for national macroeconomic and fiscal policies based on the Stability and Growth Pact. In this regard the Member States have also been pushed towards cutting public spending in the field of health.[34]

3.2 The legitimating function of human health considerations, without constitutional protection

The constitutional place of human health in the Treaties and the difficulty Member States encounter in seeking common constitutional grounds at EU level has everything to of the health-care market and the sensitive balancing act that is involved in protecting public health. In the meantime, the EU has been muddling through: the promotion and protection of human health as a constitutional problem for the EU can be traced back in most of the Union's important constitutional moments in its integration through law. One only has to consider the CAP's tuberculosis-contaminated milk in the sixties, the impact of the BSE crisis, the Tobacco advertising directive saga, *Cassis de Dijon*, and so on. Without offering one theoretical explanation, human health considerations have been pivotal in the constitutional history of the EU, and its increasing powers generally, and—paradoxically, always with opposition from the Member States—in the field of human health.

The Member States' opposition to a formal role for the EU also potentially lowers the protection of values and rights that are intrinsically involved when regulating the field of human health in the Union. In this regard, aside from deregulation and (EU) macroeconomic policies, re-regulation of human health law and policy at EU level is a third factor to consider in terms of its effect on the upholding of health values. Particularly in the field of public health, a massive regulatory effort has been undertaken in the EU to create markets by ensuring health and safety. However, and as the Tobacco Advertising saga foretold, the EU has only limited legislative basis for recreating health protection regulation at EU level. As Marjolein van Asselt, Ellen Vos, and Michelle Eversen have argued persuasively, the manner in which the EU re-regulates in the field of public health is also depoliticized through what Sheila Jasanoff calls the 'constitutional role of' science.[35]

Their central thesis is that, through science, the EU obfuscates political disagreement about balancing health risks with economic aims.[36] Moreover, the EU constitutional order—and here the observations are similar to those of Dieter Grimm—puts

[34] R. Baeten and B. Vanhercke 'Inside the Black Box: The EU's Economic Surveillance of National Healthcare Systems' [2016] *Comparative European Politics* <http://link.springer.com/article/10.1057/cep.2016.10> (accessed 7 July 2016).

[35] See S. Jasanoff 'Constituting Public Health Surveillance in 21st Century Europe', in M. Weimer and A. de Ruijter (eds) *The Co-Production of EU Expert and Executive Power in the Field of Public Health and the Environment* (Oxford: Hart, 2017).

[36] Hervey and McHale (2015) supra note 4. M. van Asselt, M. Everson, and E. Vos, *Trade, Health and the Environment: The European Union Put to the Test* (Abingdon: Routledge, 2013); M. van Asselt and E. Vos, 'The Precautionary Principle and the Uncertainty Paradox' (2006) *Journal of Risk Research* 9 313. See also Chapter 6 in this book.

executive actors in charge, particularly on politically sensitive policy issues.[37] These analyses highlight the EU regulators' use of health regulation and policy as a tool to enhance the EU's legitimacy. Science, in this analysis, takes on a role that is needed to align economies in order to limit market forces for the establishment of health regulation. Yet this excludes the rights and value (also ethical) considerations that are actually at play. Values and ethics, specifically bioethics, are formally still largely determined at Member State level.[38] In some specific areas of EU secondary regulation, ethics committees are involved. However, their contribution is fragmented and in a recent overview of the EU's approach to ethics it was outlined that many gaps remain at EU level, also in areas affected by EU internal market regulation.[39]

The constitutional constraints as outlined have an impact in the field of human health, particularly with regard to the underpinnings of both public health and health-care policy and law that in in current EU developments might not easily be solved. More powers at EU level would also involve more redistributionary capacity to ensure a comparable and feasible level of protection of rights and values in the Member States. On the other side, the current constitutional system for ensuring the protection of Member States' 'other concerns' outside market concerns is difficult as the principle of subsidiarity is always related to the objective as stated in the legal basis provisions,[40] which in the field of health is usually not human health itself, but rather other concerns, where human health concerns come in as a mere corollary.

4. Common Values and Rights in EU Human Health Policy and Law?

The central conclusion, that the EU's growing role in human health is problematic, given constitutional constraints on the EU's ability to take into consideration other legitimate objectives—such as the protection of human health and its related values and fundamental rights—automatically raises the question of whether there could, at least legally, be an EU common ground for values and fundamental rights as a basis for its human health law and policy. Values in bioethical research and analysis have a separate meaning from fundamental rights or human rights. As outlined in Chapter 2, 'fundamental rights' in the jurisprudence of the CJEU refers to the legal *praxis* that is used in balancing the legitimacy of the EU's policies, legal rights claims against the Member States, against institutions of the EU, or in some cases even in horizontal, private relationships.[41] Human rights usually have a broader (international) or more abstract connotation.[42] In this more abstract connotation, human rights can also refer to what are understood here as 'values'.

[37] See Grimm (2015) supra note 26. Also see D. Curtin, *Executive Power of the European Union: Law, Practices and the Living Constitution* (Oxford: Oxford University Press, 2009).

[38] Frischhut (2015) supra note 8. [39] Ibid. [40] Davies (2015) supra note 15.

[41] Commission, '2013 Report on the application of the EU Charter of Fundamental Rights' COM (2014) 224 final; C. Mak, *Fundamental Rights in European Contract Law: A Comparison of the Impact of Fundamental Rights in Contractual Relationships in Germany, the Netherlands, Italy and England* (Deventer: Wolters Kluwer, 2008) 6. See further Chapter 3 in this book.

[42] R. Alexy 'Discourse Theory and Fundamental Rights' in A. J. Menendez and E. O. Eriksen (eds) *Arguing Fundamental Rights* (New York: Springer, 2006) 17.

4.1 The relationship between values and fundamental rights in health

Bioethics and the human rights discourse in many ways grew up together after the Second World War, where the Nuremberg trials in particular had an important and contested role to play.[43] In the literature there are different approaches to the relationship between bioethical values (both in an individual health context, and with regard to population health) and rights. On one hand, it has been argued that to speak here of values or human rights in legal terms provides a universal language for 'the development of international legal standards for biomedicine'.[44] Values in this respect provide a normative basis for specific fundamental health-related rights. George Annas even refers to bioethics and law as 'estranged twins' in this respect.[45] On the other hand, there is also criticism of the immediate relationship between values and fundamental or human rights. Bioethicists have argued that rights have their own legitimacy problems which limit the moral concepts that are used and relevant when referring to broader values that have a self-standing importance. Moreover, a rights-based approach is only one of the many perspectives in this regard.[46]

The innate plurality of the EU legal order, the growing importance of fundamental rights, and the underlying 'ethical' (naturalistic) implications of rights make the impact of rights controversial in the European context. Rights are increasingly used to legitimate important decisions that affect the autonomy of the Member States.[47] In a political conception rights in the EU are also controversial, given the absence of a formal EU constitution.[48] Furthermore, rights, in the deeper sense of common humanistic values, are particularly controversial in the health context.[49] The different underlying reasons for the regulation of abortions across Member States is a striking example.

It is therefore important to reconcile the 'legal', 'political', and 'ethical' conceptions of values and human rights, for instance through democratic notions or by choosing an explicit political theory.[50] This is particularly the case for the EU, where an actual 'fundamental rights policy',[51] including Article 2 TEU itself, presupposes a specific

[43] E. Fenton 'Bioethics and Human Rights' in J. D. Arras, E. Fenton, and R. Kukla (eds) *The Routledge Companion to Bioethics* (Abingdon: Routledge, 2014).

[44] R. Andorno 'Human Dignity and Human Rights as a Common Ground for a Global Bioethics' (2009) *Journal of Medicine and Philosophy* 34 223–4. Also see L. P. Knowles 'The Lingua Franca of Human Rights and the Rise of a Global Bioethic' (2001) *Cambridge Quarterly of Healthcare Ethics* 10 253.

[45] G. J. Annas 'Human Rights and American Bioethics: Resistance Is Futile' (2010) *Cambridge Quarterly of Healthcare Ethics* 19 133.

[46] Fenton (2014) supra note 43. Other approaches could be the classical utilitarian or deontological approaches, or a capabilities perspective, etc. M. Freeman *Law and Bioethics* (Oxford: Oxford University Press, 2008).

[47] E. Muir, 'The Fundamental Rights implications of EU Legislation: Some Constitutional Challenges' (2014) *Common Market Law Review* 51 219.

[48] A. J. Menendez 'Some Elements of a Theory of European Fundamental Rights' in Menendez and Eriksen (eds) (2006) supra note 42, 156.

[49] Menendez and Eriksen (eds) (2006) supra note 42.

[50] S. Bagatur 'Toward a Democratic Conception of Human Rights' (2014) *Theoria and Praxis* 2; P. Gilabert 'Humanist and Political Perspectives on Human Rights' (2011) *Political Theory* 39 (4) 439; S. M. Liao and A. Etinson 'Political and Naturalistic Conceptions of Human Rights: A False Polemic?' (2012) *The Journal of Moral Philosophy* 9 (3) 327, and see Alexy (2006) supra note 42.

[51] P. Alston and J. H. H. Weiler 'An "Ever Closer Union" in Need of a Human Rights Policy: The European Union and Human Rights' (1998) *European Journal of International Law* 9 658; A. von Bogdandy, 'The European Union as a Human Rights Organisation? Human Rights and the Core of the European Union' (2000) *Common Market Law Review* 37 1307.

idea of shared values; an idea of which direction to take the EU in this respect,[52] rather than merely taking the status quo of fundamental rights protection as a matter of social practice, dependent on place and time, as is implied by a political conception of human rights.[53] Concluding, in order to look for guidance in determining the proper location of power for the formulation of EU health law and policy, fundamental rights are not unproblematic. Yet EU fundamental rights do give expression to values, and there are different aspects of EU health law that operationalize these values.

4.2 EU health values

In the context of health law, each Member State has formulated itself the values and principles that underlie its national health-care system(s).[54] When the Council adopted its Conclusions on Common Values and Principles in EU Health Systems,[55] it referred to 'common' values and principles among the Member States. The legal status of those common values and principles, and their relationship to fundamental rights in the sense of EU law, depends on whether the Council was referring to these values and principles in the sense of Articles 2 and 6 TEU.

The language of the Council's 2006 statement of Common Values (referring to 'values', rather than principles of EU law) suggests that it is not intended to constitute a statement of general principles of EU law that are on equal footing with fundamental rights. However, in combination with particular EU fundamental rights it could be argued that the Common Values may help shape the *interpretation* of fundamental rights in the context of EU health law. At the very least, the 2006 Common Values represent an indication of the baseline principles that are common to the Member States, and in that regard they can also at least be taken into consideration in the European Union legislative process, though this is not legally required.

The 2006 Common Values were also written so as to stress their importance in the context of the organization of national health-care systems, a matter over which the Treaty explicitly requires *national* competence. However, in the field of public health, where the EU enjoys greater competence, there is no explicit document that refers to for instance values of solidarity or equality. In the central legal provisions, Articles 9, 168, and 114(3) TFEU, the central objective is formulated as 'a high level (a protection) of human health'. What a 'high' level would prescribe, however, is difficult to determine.

At the same time, the values of solidarity, equality, universal access, and human dignity *are* addressed in EU fundamental rights.[56] Furthermore, the EU's adherence to the protection and promotion of fundamental rights, on the basis of EU primary law, is expressed as a constitutional value. Article 2 of the TEU lays the foundation of the EU's agreed 'common values' as the basis of the EU's constitutional structure.

[52] This also shows in some of the CJEU's case law on the Charter where the interpretation is usually based on a preconceived idea of rights 'that were already protected' in the EU legal order; see on this point and a discussion of these cases, P. Eeckhout, 'The EU Charter of Fundamental Rights and the Federal Question' (2002) *Common Market Law Review* 39 945.

[53] R. Forst 'The Justification of Human Rights and the Basic Right to Justification: A Reflexive Approach' (2010) *Ethics* 120 711, 727, emphasizing the 'internal' role (inside a political system) of human rights for assessing legitimacy, and see further Bagatur (2014) supra note 50, 9.

[54] Council Conclusions, Council Conclusions on Common Values and Principles in European Union Health Systems (OJ C 146/1, 2006).

[55] Ibid.

[56] Charter of Fundamental Rights, 'Charter of Fundamental Rights of the European Union (OJ C 364/01, 2000)' <0808210432text_en.pdf>.

Importantly, the *respect for rights* in itself is taken to be a foundational value of the European Union, and is assumed to be a value that is *common* to the Member States. Furthermore, Article 2 TEU refers to 'human rights' and not 'fundamental rights', which are protected under Article 6 TEU by reference to, for example, the CFREU and the common principles of EU law. As mentioned, 'human rights' as a term is usually used to connote a meaning that employs underlying, deeper values when speaking in terms of 'rights'. These deeper values are sometimes also referred to as 'rights', but rather in a particular ethical sense. The fundamental rights in the EU that express the EU health law values of solidarity, equality, universal access, and human dignity are outlined in Chapter 2.

Yet, the fact that these shared and common values can be distinguished at EU level in the field of health does not solve the ultimately political question of at what level these values and rights can best be protected. It remains that internal market freedoms form the very reason for EU health policy and law's existence.[57] The four freedoms as constitutional principles are currently stronger than the EU constitutional principle of subsidiarity in the field of health, which explains the recurrent conundrum that the internal market as legal basis forms the legislative ground for many aspects of EU health law, where Member States at the same time have limited EU powers to create a substantive health law at EU level. Hence the true protection of the rights and values intrinsically connected to health law and policy might lie in a more conservative approach to attributing the EU with the legal power to create legislation or policy in the field, with reference to the mainstreaming of fundamental rights and values and human health protection. This could possibly occur as part of a 'value-laden' effectiveness analysis under Article 5 TEU limiting the silent revolution of the EU's expanding powers in the field of human health.

5. EU Powers in Public Health and Health Care into the Future

The constitutional setting of the EU affects the place and protection of values and rights in EU health law that are central to the health law of the Member States; values and rights such as human dignity, equality, and solidarity. At Member State level, EU law affects health law, as it is approached as a barrier to trade, whereas at EU level, health law is re-created, but its inherent values are often depoliticized through science or lose significance in light of 'higher' internal market objectives. This is not to say that internal market objectives are necessarily always opposed to health rights and values. For example, as Hervey and McHale outline, EU competition law has likely contributed to consumer benefits and a lowering of prices in the health-care sector, important in ensuring universal access and upholding the values of solidarity and equality.[58]

This book has illustrated a number of ways the EU is expanding its power in the field of health care and public health, through the lens of health law, where rights and values are intrinsically related. EU power in human health—broadly defined by the EU's ability to authoritatively allocate value through the European political system

[57] For an alternative position, see Hervey and McHale (2015) supra note 4; T. K. Hervey 'Telling Stories about European Union Health Law: The Emergence of a New Field of Law' (2016) *Comparative European Politics* DOI 10.1057/cep.2016.4 <http://www.palgrave-journals.com/cep/journal/vaop/ncurrent/full/cep20164a.html> (accessed 1 June 2016).

[58] Hervey and McHale (2015) supra note 4, 229.

in light of a health-related framework of rights and values—may be stronger than was ever intended, because of the intrinsic relationship between health policy and fundamental rights. Even when the EU adopts 'soft' coordination measures or mere 'technical' public health and safety standards, health and fundamental rights are such a close-knitted pair that the EU's ability to determine authoritatively what rights are protected in human health is also expanded in areas where its competences are explicitly limited. Health policy and law-making in this respect are not 'value' neutral but have fundamental rights implications. In other words, the EU *de facto* balances fundamental rights through health policymaking, either affecting fundamental rights protection at national level or creating obligations for fundamental rights and values at EU level.

The underlying question here is ultimately about the legitimacy of EU power in the field of human health in terms of fundamental rights and values. Fundamental rights and values in the context of health policy are regarded as a particularly important instrument for analysing its legitimacy—that is, health law in the Member States generally functions to ensure the protection of fundamental rights in the context of health policy. In other words, health policy and fundamental rights are reciprocal in that the protection and promotion of fundamental rights safeguards human health, while the safeguarding of human health is a fundamental right. Fundamental rights provide health law with 'conceptual unity', especially the 'right to health' and respect for individual rights, which are central in the regulation of health. The importance of safeguarding and promoting fundamental rights in this regard is seen as a consequence of the growing power of the nation state in the field of health and in the growing powers of private actors in medical care. If the EU is also expanding its powers in this field, and there are constitutional constraints to offer protections to individuals and populations, the legitimacy of EU power in health can be questioned.

The EU, in exercising power in human health, often implicitly balances the rights of the community with individual rights. Through this balancing of rights, another balancing takes place between the EU and the Member States' powers to define their own health policies; all the while the legislative competence in the Treaty explicitly remains limited. As the quotation at the start of this chapter indicated, EU health policy is a balancing act.

Therefore, the expansion of EU power in the field of human health goes to the heart of questions on the legitimacy of the EU political system as a whole. This is particularly the case because the expansion of EU power in health is largely taking place 'by stealth' creating a 'silent revolution' in that it is largely the result of policymaking rather than part of explicit legislative objectives to create health law. Hence, the obligations for balancing the interests of the community with those of the individual that lay with the *Member States* are not sufficient in order to address the legitimacy of EU health policy. In this regard fundamental rights and values in the EU, beyond their legal power, provide a normative language that explicates the legitimacy of the EU's efforts to promote and protect human health.

EU health law and policy also raises questions on a deeper constitutional level of who will take care of us when it comes to human health, the EU or the Member States; are there bonds of solidarity that tie us to the EU? The fact that the bounds of the right to access care, although effectuated by Member States, are determined at the EU level is a significant implication if keeping in mind that in the founding Treaty the EU is completely excluded from having a role in the provision of medical care. In his seminal book *In Care of the State* sociologist Abram de Swaan shows the important role of health policy in legitimating and contributing to the success of the rise of the nation state in the nineteenth century. The question is, what is health policy and law doing for the legitimacy of the existence of the EU political system and our relationship to it? Considering the reciprocal implications of health policy for fundamental rights and values, EU health policy has an important role to play in the legitimacy of the EU political system itself.

Bibliography

Alexy, R. 'Discourse Theory and Fundamental Rights' in A. J. Menendez and E. O. Erkisen (eds) *Arguing Fundamental Rights* (Dordrecht: Springer, 2006) 15–30

Alfredsson, A. and K. Tomasevski (eds) *A Thematic Guide to Documents on Health and Human Rights* (The Hague: Martinus Nijhoff, 1998)

Alston, P. and J. H. H. Weiler 'An 'Ever Closer Union' in Need of a Human Rights Policy: The European Union and Human Rights' (1998) *European Journal of International Law* 9 658–723

Anand, S. et al. (eds) *Public Health, Ethics, and Equity* (Oxford: Oxford University Press, 2004)

Annas, G. J. 'Human Rights and Health: The Universal Declaration of Human Rights at 50' (1998) *The New England Journal of Medicine* 339 (24) 1778–81

Armstrong, K. and C. Kilpatrick 'Law, Governance, or New Governance? The Changing Open Method of Coordination' (2007) *The Columbia Journal of European Law* 13 649–79

Armstrong, K. A. and S. J. Bulmer *The Governance of the Single European Market* (Manchester: Manchester University Press, 1998)

Baeten, R. and W. Palm 'Preserving General Interest in Healthcare through Secondary and Soft EU Law: The Case of the Patients' Rights Directive' in U. Neergaard et al. (eds) *Social Services of General Interest in the EU* (The Hague: Asser Press, 2013) 391

Baeten, R. et al. (eds) *The Europeanisation of National Health Care Systems: Creative Adaptation in the Shadow of Patient Mobility Case Law* (European Social Observatory: European Social Observatory paper series, 2010)

Bagatur, S. 'Toward a Democratic Conception of Human Rights' (2014) *Theoria and Praxis* 2

Bauer, M. W. and G. Gaskell *Biotechnology: The Making of a Global Controversy* (Cambridge: Cambridge University Press, 2002)

Beauchamp, T. L. 'Universal Principles and Universal Rights' in A. den Exter (ed.) *Human Rights and Biomedicine* (Antwerp: Maklu, 2010)

Beigel, J. H. et al. 'Avian Influenza A (H5N1) Infection in Humans' (2005) *New England Journal of Medicine* 353 (13) 1347–85

Beitz, C. *The Idea of Human Rights* (Oxford: Oxford University Press, 2009)

Bergdolt, K. *Wellbeing: A Cultural History of Healthy Living* (Cambridge: Polity Press, 2008)

Bertinato, L. et al. (eds) *Policy Brief: Cross-Border Health Care in Europe* (Geneva: World Health Organization on behalf of the European Observatory on Health Systems and Policies, 2005)

Bircher, J. 'Towards a Dynamic Definition of Health and Disease' (2005) *Medicine, Health Care and Philosophy* 8 335–41

Birkland, T. A. *An Introduction to the Policy Process: Theories, Concepts and Models of Public Policy Making* 2nd edn (New York: M. E. Sharpe, 2005)

Boessen, S. and H. Maarse 'The Impact of the Treaty Basis on Health Policy Legislation in the European Union: A Case Study on the Tobacco Advertising Directive' (2008) *BMC Health Services Research* 8 (77) 1–13

Bogdandy, A. von et al. 'Reverse Solange: Protecting the Essence of Fundamental Rights against EU Member States' (2012) *Common Market Law Review* 49 489–520

Bogdandy, A. von 'The European Union as a Human Rights Organisation? Human Rights and the Core of the European Union' (2000) *Common Market Law Review* 37 1307–38

Bradsher, K. 'The Naming of Swine Flu, a Curious Matter' (2009, 28 April) *New York Times*

Brandsma, G .J. *Controlling Comitology: Accountability in a Multi-Level System* (Basingstoke: Palgrave Macmillan, 2013)

Briggs, L. 'The Race of Hysteria: "Overcivilization" and the "Savage" Woman in Late Nineteenth-Century Obstetrics and Gynecology' (2000) *American Quarterly* 52 (2) 246–73

Brouwer, O. 'Free Movement of Foodstuffs and Quality Requirements: Has the Commission Got It Wrong?' (1998) *Common Market Law Review* 25 237–62

Búrca, G. de 'Towards European Welfare' in G. De Búrca (ed.) *EU Law and the Welfare State: In Search of Solidarity* (New York: Oxford University Press, 2005)

Búrca, G. de 'After the EU Charter of Fundamental Rights: The Court of Justice as a Human Rights Adjudicator?' (2013) *Maastricht Journal of European and Comparative Law* 20 (2) 168–84

Búrca, G. de et al. (eds) *Critical Legal Perspectives on Global Governance* (Oxford: Hart, 2013)

Burley, A.-M. and W. Mattli 'Europe before the Court: A Political Theory of Legal Integration' (1993) *International Integration* 47 (1) 41–76

Busse, R. et al. (eds) Mapping Health Services Access: National and Cross-Border Issues (HealthACCESS) Final Report (DG SANCO) (2006)

Busuioc, M. E. *European Agencies: Law and Practices of Accountability* (Oxford: Oxford University Press, 2013)

Busuioc, M. E. *The Accountability of European Agencies, Legal Provisions and Ongoing Practices* (Utrecht: Eburon, 2010)

Callahan, D. 'The WHO Definition of "Health"' (1973) *The Hastings Center Studies* 1 (3) 77–87

Carlson, R. V. et al. 'The Revision of the Declaration of Helsinki: Past, Present and Future' (2004) *British Journal of Clinical Pharmacology* 57 (6) 695–713

Carrick, K. M. 'A Case Study Approach to Legal Research: The Kent State Case' (1980) *Law Library Journal* 73 (99) 66–78

Chambers, G. R. 'The BSE Crisis and the European Parliament' in C. Joerges and E. Vos (eds) *EU Committees: Social Regulation, Law and Politics* (Oxford: Hart, 1999)

Childress, J. F. *Who Should Decide? Paternalism in Health Care* (New York: Oxford University Press, 1982)

Cohen, D. 'Complications: Tracking Down the Data on Oseltamivir' (2009) *British Medical Journal* 339 (b5387) 1342–7

Cohen, I. G. (ed.) *The Globalization of Health Care: Legal and Ethical Issues* (New York: Oxford University Press, 2013)

Costa Leite Borges, D. da 'Making Sense of Human Rights in the Context of European Union Health-Care Policy: Individualist and Communitarian Views' (2011) *International Journal of Law in Context* 7 (3) 3335–56

Craig, P. *EU Administrative Law* (Oxford: Oxford University Press, 2012)

Craig, P. 'EU Accession to the ECHR: Competence, Procedure and Substance' (2013) *Fordham International Law Journal* (36) 1114–50

Craig, P. and G. De Búrca *EU Law: Text, Cases and Materials* (Oxford: Oxford University Press, 2008)

Crinson, I. *Health Policy: A Critical Perspective* (London: SAGE, 2009)

Cruz, J. B. 'The Case Law of the European Court of Justice on the Mobility of Patients: An Assessment' in J. W. van de Gronden et al. (eds) *Health Care and EU Law* (The Hague: Asser, 2011) 79–102

Cryer, R. et al. *Research Methodologies in EU and International Law* (Oxford: Hart, 2011)

Curtin, D. M. and R. van Ooik 'The Sting is Always in the Tail. The Personal Scope of Application of the EU Charter of Fundamental Rights' (2001) *Maastricht Journal of European and Comparative Law* 8 102–13

Curtin, D. M. 'Delegation to EU Non-Majoritan Agencies and Emerging Practices of Public Accountability' in D. Gerardin et al. (eds) *Regulation through Agencies in the EU: A New Paradigm of European Governance* (Cheltenham: Edward Elgar, 2005) 88–109

Curtin, D. M. *Executive Power of the European Union. Law, Practices and the Living Constitution* (Oxford: Oxford University Press, 2009)

Curtin, D. M. 'Holding (Quasi-) Autonomous EU Administrative Actors to Public Account' (2007) *European Law Journal* 13 (4) 523–41

Curtin, D. M. 'The Constitutional Structure of the Union: A Europe of Bits and Pieces' (1993) *Common Market Law Review* 30 (1) 17–69

Curtin, D. M. 'The Sedimentary European Constitution: The Future of 'Constitutionalisation' without a Constitution' in I. Pernice and E. Tanchev (eds) *Ceci n'est pas une Constitution—Constitutionalisation without a Constitution?* (Baden-Baden: Nomos, 2009) 76–85

Daniels, N. *Just Health: Meeting Health Needs Fairly* (Cambridge: Cambridge University Press, 2008)

d'Aspremont, J. *Formalism and the Sources of International Law: A Theory of the Ascertainment of Legal Rules* (Oxford: Oxford Monographs in International Law, 2013)

Dauvilliers Y. et al. 'Post-H1N1 Narcolepsy-Cataplexy' (2010) *Sleep* 33 1428–30

Davies, G. 'Legislating for Patients' Rights' in J. W. van de Gronden et al. (eds) *Health Care and EU Law* (The Hague: Asser, 2011) 191–210

Davies, G. 'Subsidiarity: The Wrong Idea, in the Wrong Place, at the Wrong Time' (2006) *Common Market Law Review* 43 63–84

Davies, G. 'The Effect of Mrs Watts' Trip to France on the National Health Care Service' (2007) *King's Law Journal* 18 158–67

Davies, G. 'The Price of Letting Courts Value Solidarity: The Judicial Role in Liberalizing Welfare' in M. Ross and Y. Borgmann-Prebil (eds) *Promoting Solidarity in the European Union* (Oxford: Oxford University Press, 2010) 106–22

Davies, G. 'Democracy and Legitimacy in the Shadow of Purposive Competence' (2013) *European Law Journal* 21 2

Delnoij, D. and W. Sauter 'Patient Information under the EU Patients' Rights Directive' (2011) *European Journal of Public Health* 21 (3) 271–2

Den Exter, A. P. *Health Care Law-making in Central and Eastern Europe* (Antwerp: Intersentia, 2002)

Dougan, M. 'The Treaty of Lisbon 2007' (2008) *Common Market Law Review* 45 (3) 617–703

Douglas-Scott, S. 'The European Union and Human Rights after the Treaty of Lisbon' (2011) *Human Rights Law Review* 11 (4) 645–82

Douglas-Scott, S. 'The Problem of Justice in the European Union' in J. Dickson and P. Eleftheriadis (eds) *Philosophical Foundations of European Union Law* (Oxford: Oxford University Press, 2012) 384–412

Dutheil de la Rochère, J. 'The Protection of Fundamental Rights in the EU: Community of values with Opt-Out?' in I. Pernice and E. Tanchev (eds) *Ceci n'est pas une Constitution—Constitutionalisation without a Constitution?* (Baden-Baden: Nomos, 2009) 119–30

Easton, D. 'An Approach to the Analysis of Political Systems' (1957) *World Politics* 9 (3) 383–400

Eckes, C. 'EU Accession to the ECHR: Between Autonomy and Adaptation' (2013) *The Modern Law Review* 76 (2) 254–85

Eeckhout, P. 'The EU Charter of Fundamental Rights and the Federal Question' (2002) 39 *Common Market Law Review* 945–94

Emanuel, L. L. 'Four Models of the Physician–Patient Relationship' (1992) *Journal of the American Medical Association* 267 (16) 2221–6

Faden, R. R. and T. L. Beauchamp *A History and Theory of Informed Consent* (New York: Oxford University Press, 1986)

Farrell, A-M 'Is the Gift Still Good? Examining the Politics and Regulation of Blood Safety in the European Union' (2006) *Medical Law Review* 14 155–79

Farrell, A.-M. 'The Emergence of EU Governance in Public Health: The case of Blood Policy and Regulation' in M. Steffen (ed.) *Health Governance in Europe: Issues, Challenges and Theories* (New York: Routledge, 2005) 134–54

Fluss, S. S. 'A Select Bibliography of Health Aspects of Human Rights 1984–1999' (1999) *Health and Human Rights: An International Quarterly Journal* 4 265–76

Flyvberg, B. 'Five Misunderstandings about Case-Study Research' (2006) *Qualitative Inquiry* 12 (2) 219–45

Forst, R. 'The Justification of Human Rights and the Basic Right to Justification: A Reflexive Approach' (2010) *Ethics* 120 711–40

Frank, S. *A New Model for European Medical Device Regulation: A Comparative Legal Analysis in the EU and the USA* (Groningen: Europa Law, 2003)

Gagliardi, D. et al. 'Occupational Safety and Health in Europe: Lessons from the Past, Challenges and Opportunities for the Future' (2012) *Industrial Health* 50 7–11

Gainotti, S. et al. 'Ethical Models Underpinning Responses to Threats to Public Health: A Comparison of Approaches to Communicable Disease Control in Europe' (2008) *Bioethics* 22 466–76

Garcia-Perez, M.A. et al. 'Physicians Migration in Europe: An Overview of the Current Situation' (2007) *BioMEd Central Health Services Research* 7 1–8

Gerring, J. *Case Study Research: Principles and Practices* (Cambridge: Cambridge University Press, 2007)

Gerring, J. 'What is a Case Study and What is it Good for?' (2004) *American Political Science Review* 98 (2) 341–54

Gevers, J. K. M. 'Medical Research and the Law: A European Perspective' (1995) *European Journal of Health Law* 2 (2) 97–9

Giesecke, J. and J. Weinberg 'A European Centre for Infectious Disease?' (1998) *The Lancet* 352 (9136) 1237–322

Giesen, D. *International Medical Malpractice Law: A Comparative Study of Civil Responsibility Arising from Medical Care* (Tubingen: Mohr, 1988)

Giesen, R. 'Annotation Case C-120/95, Nicolas Decker v. Caisse de maladie des employés privés, Judgment of 28 April 1998, Case C-158/96, Raymond Kohll v. Union des caisses de maladie, Judgment of 28 April 1998' (1999) *Common Market Law Review* 36 (4) 841–50

Gilabert, P. 'Humanist and Political Perspectives on Human Rights' (2011) *Political Theory* 39 439–67

Glinos, I. A. et al. (eds) *Contracting Cross-border Care in Belgian Hospitals: An Analysis of Belgian, Dutch and English Stakeholder Perspectives* (Brussels: European Social Observatory, 2005)

Gostin, L. O. 'A Theory and Definition of Public Health Law' (2007) *Journal of Health Care Law and Policy* 10 1–12

Gostin, L. O. and J. M. Mann 'Towards the Development of a Human Rights Impact Assessment for the Formulation and Evaluation of Public Health Policies' (1994) *Health and Human Rights: An International Quarterly Journal* 1 (1) 50–78

Gostin, L. O. Public *Health Law: Power, Duty, Restraint* (Berkeley, CA: University of California Press, 2000)

Gostin, L. O. 'Public Health, Ethics, and Human Rights: A Tribute to the Late Jonathan Mann' (2007) *The Journal of Law, Medicine and Ethics* 29 (2) 121–30

Gray, N. 'Tobacco Industry and EC Advertising Ban' (2002) *The Lancet* 359 (9314) 1264–5

Greely, H. T. 'Some Thoughts on Academic Health Law' (2006) *Wake Forest Law Review* 41 391–409

Greer, S. L. and P. Kurzer (eds) *European Union Public Health Policy: Regional and Global Trends* (New York: Routledge, 2013)

Greer, S. L. 'Choosing Paths in European Union Health Services Policy: A Political Analysis of a Critical Juncture' (2008) *Journal of European Social Policy* 18 (3) 219–31

Greer, S. L. et al. 'Mobilizing Bias in Europe: Lobbies, Democracy and EU Health Policy-Making' (2008) *European Union Politics* 9 (3) 403–33

Greer, S. L. 'EU Healthcare Services Policy' in J. Richardson (ed.) *Constructing a Policy-Making State? Policy Dynamics in the EU* (New York: Oxford University Press, 2012)

Greer, S. L. 'Standing Up for Health? Health Departments in EU Health Policy Formulation' (2010) *Social Policy & Administration* 44 (2) 208–24

Greer, S. L. 'The Changing World of European Health Lobbies' in D. Coen and J. Richardson (eds) *Lobbying the European Union: Institutions, Actors, and Issues* (Oxford: Oxford University Press, 2009)

Greer, S. L. 'The European Centre for Disease Prevention and Control' (2012) *Journal of Health Politics, Policy and Law* 37 1001–30

Greer, S. L. The *Politics of European Union Health Policies* (Maidenhead/Philadelphia: Open University Press, 2009)

Greer, S. L. 'Uninvited Europeanization: Neo-functionalism and the EU in Health Policy' (2006) *Journal of European Public Policy* 13 (1) 134–52

Griffin, J. P. et al. (eds) *The Text of Pharmaceutical Medicine*, 7th edn (London: Wiley Blackwell, 2013)

Gronden, J. W. van de et al. (eds) *Health Care and EU Law* (The Hague: Asser, 2011)

Gruskin, S. and D. Tarantola 'Health and Human Rights' in S. Gruskin et al. (eds) *Perspectives on Health and Human Rights* (New York: Routledge, 2005) 3–59

Gruskin, S. et al. 'Health and Human Rights: History, Principles and Practice of Health and Human Rights' (2007) *The Lancet* 370 449–55

Gruskin, S. *et al.* 'Rights-based Approaches to Health Policies and Programs: Articulations, Ambiguities, and Assessment' (2010) *Journal of Public Health Policy* 31 (2) 129–45

Gruskin, S. 'Is There a Government in the Cockpit: A Passenger's Perspective, or Global Public Health: The Role of Human Rights' (2004) *Temple Law Review* 77 313–34

Guerrieri, S. 'The Evolution of the European Parliament's Role before Direct Elections' in D. Preda and D. Pasquinucci (eds) *The Evolution of the EEC/EU Institutions and Policies* (Brussels: Peter Lang, 2010) 183–203

Haas, E. B. *The Uniting of Europe: Political, Social, and Economic Forces, 1950–1957* (Stanford, CA: Stanford University Press, 1958)

Hagen, P. *Blood Transfusion in Europe: A White Paper* (Strasbourg: Council of Europe Press, 1993)

Hagen, P. *Blood: Gift or Merchandise? Towards an International Blood Policy* (New York: A. R. Liss, 1982)

Hamalainen, R. *The Europeanisation of Occupational Health Services: A Study of the Impact of EU Policies* (Tampere: Juvenes, 2008)

Hancher, L. 'The EU Pharmaceuticals Market: Parameters and Pathways' in E. Mossailos et al. (eds) *Health Systems Governance in Europe: The Role of European Law and Policy* (New York: Cambridge University Press, 2010) 589–635

Harant, P. 'Hospital Cooperation across French Borders' in M. Rosenmuller et al. (eds) *Patient Mobility in the European Union: Learning from Experience* (Copenhagen: European Observatory on Health Systems and Policies, 2006) 157–77

Hart, H. L. A. 'Are There Any Natural Rights?' (1955) *The Philosophical Review* 64 175–91

Hart, H. L. A. *The Concept of Law* 2nd edn (1994) (Oxford: Oxford University Press, 1961)

Hatzopoulos, V. 'Health Law and Policy: The Impact of the EU' in G. de Búrca (ed.) *EU Law and the Welfare State: In Search of Solidarity* (Oxford: Oxford University Press, 2005) 89–111

Hatzopoulos, V. 'Public Procurement and State Aid in National Health Care Systems' in E. Mossailos et al. (eds) *Health Systems Governance in Europe: The Role of European Union Law and Policy* (Cambridge: Cambridge University Press, 2010) 379–418

Hatzopoulos, V. 'The ECJ Case Law on Cross-Border Aspects of Health Services' (2007) IIP/A/IMCO/FWC/2006-167/C3/SC1) Briefing to the European Parliaments' Committee on Internal Market and Consumer Protection

Hayes-Renshaw, F. and H. Wallace *The Council of Ministers* 2nd edn (Basingstoke: Palgrave Macmillan, 2006)

Hendriks, A. 'The Council of Europe and Health and Human Rights' in B. Toebes et al. (eds) *Health and Human Rights in Europe* (Cambridge: Intersentia, 2012) 21–51

Hendriks, A. 'The Right to Health in National and International Jurisprudence' (1998) *European Journal of Health Law* 5 389–408

Hermans, H. E. G. M. and M. A. J. M. Buijsen *Recht en Gezondheidszorg* 2nd edn (Amsterdam: Elsevier, 2010)

Herrmann, R. et al. 'The European Union and Health and Human Rights' (2011) *European Human Rights Law Review* 4 419–36

Hervey, T. K. and A. de Ruijter 'Healthcare and the Lisbon Agenda' in P. Copeland and D. Papadimitriou (eds) *The EU's Lisbon Strategy: Evaluating Success, Understanding Failure* (New York: Palgrave Macmillan, 2012) 130–48

Hervey, T. K. 'Community and National Competence in Health after Tobacco Advertising' (2001) *Common Market Law Review* 38 (6) 1421–46

Hervey, T. K. 'Mapping the Contours of European Union Health Law and Policy' (2002) *European Public Law* 8 (1) 69–105

Hervey, T. K. 'The Right to Health in European Union Law' in T. Hervey and J. Kenner (eds), *Economic and Social Rights under the Charter of Fundamental Rights* (Oxford: Hart, 2003) 161–93

Hervey, T. K. 'We Don't See a Connection: The "Right to Health" in the EU Charter and European Social Charter' in G. De Búrca and B. De Witte (eds) *Social Rights in Europe* (Oxford: Oxford University Press, 2005) 279–305

Hervey, T. K. and B. Vanhercke 'Health Care and the EU: The Law and Policy Patchwork' in E. Mossialos et al. (eds) *Health Systems Governance in Europe: The Role of European Union Law and Policy* (New York: Cambridge University Press, 2010) 84–133.

Hervey, T. K. and J. McHale 'Article 35 Health Care' in S. Peers et al. (eds) *The EU Charter of Fundamental Rights* (Oxford: Hart, 2014) 991–1011

Hervey, T. K. and J. V. McHale *Health Law and the European Union* (Cambridge: Cambridge University Press, 2004)

Hervey, T. K. and L. Trubek 'Freedom to Provide Health Care Services within the EU: An Opportunity for a Transformative Directive' (2007) *Columbia Journal of European Law* 13 (3) 623–49

Hervey, T. K. 'Re-judging Social Rights in the EU' in G. de Búrca et al. (eds) *Critical Legal Perspectives on Global Governance* (Oxford: Hart, 2014)

Hervey, T. K. 'The European Union and the Governance of Health Care' in G. De Búrca and C. Scott (eds) *New Governance and Constitutionalism in the EU and the US* (Oxford: Hart, 2006) 153–79

Hervey, T. K. 'The European Union's Governance and the Welfare Modernisation Agenda' (2008) *Regulation and Governance* 2 103–20

Hesselink, M. 'A European Legal Method? On European Private Law and Scientific Method' (2009) *European Law Journal* 15 (1) 20–45

Hestermeyer, H. P. 'Access to Medication as a Human Right' (2004) *Max Planck UNYB* 8 101–80

Hix, S. and B. Hoyland 'Empowerment of the European Parliament' (2013) *Annual Review of Political Science* 16 171–89

Hix, S. 'The EU as New Political System' in D. Caramani (ed.) *Comparative Politics* (Oxford: Oxford University Press, 2008)

Hix, S. *The Political System of the European Union* (London: Palgrave Macmillan, 2005)

Hix, S. *What's Wrong with the European Union and How to Fix It* (London: Polity, 2008)

Holland, W. W. and E. Mossailos (eds) *Public Health Policies in the European Union* (Aldershot: Ashgate, 1999)

Huber, M. et al. 'How Should We Define Health?' (2011) *British Medical Journal* 343 (4163) 163

Hunt, S. M. and J. McEwen 'The Development of a Subjective Health Indicator' (1980) *Sociology of Health & Illness* 2 (3) 231–46

Irwin, J. 'Migration Patterns of Nurses in the EU' (2001) *Euro Health* 7 (13)

Jacobs, J. G. 'The European Convention on Human Rights, The EU Charter of Fundamental Rights and the European Court of Justice: The Impact of European Union Accession to the European Convention on Human Rights' in I. Pernice et al. (eds) *The Future of the European Judicial System in a Comparative Perspective* (Baden-Baden: Nomos, 2006) 291–96

Jacobsen, H. 'European Semester's Increased Target on Healthcare Reform' (2014) Euractiv (available at: <https://www.euractiv.com/section/health-consumers/news/european-semester-s-increased-target-on-healthcare-reform/ >, last accessed November 2018)

Jadad, A. R. and L. O'Grady 'How Should Health Be Defined?' (2008) *British Medical Journal* 337 2900

Jaspers, K. *General Psychopathology* (Baltimore, MD: John Hopkins University Press, 1997)

Joerges, C. 'Law, Science and the Management of Risks to Health at the National, European and International Level—Stories on Baby Dummies, Mad Cows and Hormones in Beef' (2001) *Columbia Journal of European Law* 7 1–19

Johnston, M. J. 'European Council and the Council of the European Union' in P. Van der Hoek (ed.) *Handbook of Public Administration and Policy in the European Union* (Boca Raton, FL: Taylor & Francis, 2005) 113–49

Jost, L. J. and R. A. Shiner (eds) *Eudaimonia and Well-Being: Ancient and Modern Conceptions* (Kelowna, BC: Academic Printing and Publishing, 2003)

Kahlmeier, S. et al. 'Health in All Policies in Practice: Guidance and Tools to Quantifying the Health Effects of Cycling and Walking' (2010) *Journal of Physical Activity and Health* 7 (1) 120–5

Kammerhofer, J. 'Uncertainty in the Formal Sources of International Law: Customary International Law and Some of Its Problems' (2004) *European Journal of International Law* 15 (3) 523–53

Kapteyn, P. J. G. et al. *Inleiding tot het recht van de Europese Gemeenschappen. Na Maastricht* (Deventer: Kluwer, 1995)

Kennedy, I. and A. Grubb *Medical Law* (London: Butterworths, 2000)

Kentikelenis, A. et al. 'Greece's Health Crisis: From Austerity to Denialism' (2014) *The Lancet* 13 (9918) 748–53

Kinney, E. D. and B. A. Clark 'Provisions for Health and Health Care in the Constitutions of the Countries of the World' (2004) *Cornell International Law Journal* 37 285–355

Koch, I. E. *Human Rights as Indivisible Rights* (Leiden: Martinus Nijhoff, 2009)

Krapohl, S. 'Credible Commitment in Non-Independent Regulatory Agencies: A Comparative Analysis of European Agencies for Pharmaceuticals and Foodstuffs' (2004) *European Law Journal* 10 (5) 518–38

Krapohl, S. 'Risk Regulation in the EU Between Interests and Expertise: The Case of BSE' (2003) *Journal of European Public Policy* 10 (2) 189–207

Kubosova, L. 'Brussels Postpones Landmark Bill on EU Cross-Border Health Care until 2008' (2007) *European Observer* (available at: <https://euobserver.com/economic/25361 >, last accessed November 2018)

Lacey, M. and D. G. McNeil 'Fighting Deadly Flu, Mexico Shuts School' (2009, 24 April) *New York Times*

Lambert, J. and C. Hoskyns 'How Democratic is the European Parliament?' in C. Hoskyns and M. Newman (eds) *Democratizing the European Union: Issues for the Twenty-first Century* (New Brunswick, NJ: Transaction, 2007)

Langford, M. (ed.) *Social Rights Jurisprudence: Emerging Trends in International and Comparative Law* (Cambridge: Cambridge University Press, 2008)

Larson, J. S. 'The Conceptualization of Health' (1999) *Medical Care Research and Review* 56 123–36

Lee, K. et al. (eds) *Health Policy in a Globalising World* (Cambridge: Cambridge University Press, 2002)

Lee, R. L. and D. Morgan *Human Fertilisation and Embryology: Regulating the Reproductive Revolution* (London: Blackstone, 2001)

Leenen, H. J. J. et al. *Handboek Gezondheidsrecht, deel 1 rechten van mensen in de gezondheidszorg* 5th edn (The Hague: Boom Juridische, 2011)

Leenen, H. J. J. et al. *The Rights of Patients in Europe* (Geneva: World Health Organization, Kluwer, 1993)

Leenen, H. J. J. 'Health Law in the Twenty-first Century' (1998) *European Journal of Health Law* 5 341–8

Legemaate, J. 'Integrating Health Law and Policy: A European Perspective' (2002) *Health Policy* 60 101–10

Leikola, J. 'Achieving Self Sufficiency in Blood across Europe' (1998) *British Medical Journal* 316 489–90

Lenaerts, K. and J. A. Gutierrez-Fons 'The Constitutional Allocation of Powers and General Principles of Law' (2010) *Common Market Law Review* 47 1629–69

Lenaerts, K. and P. Foubert 'Social Rights in the Case-Law of the European Court of Justice: The Impact of the Charter of Fundamental Rights of the European Union on Standing Case-Law' (2001) *Legal Issues of Economic Integration* 28 (3) 267–96

Lenaerts, K. 'Exploring the Limits of the EU Charter of Fundamental Rights' (2012) European Constitutional Law Review 8 375–403

Liao, S. M. and A. Etinson 'Political and Naturalistic Conceptions of Human Rights: A False Polemic?' (2012) *Journal of Moral Philosophy* 9 327–52

Liverani, M. and R. Coker 'Protecting Europe from Diseases: From the International Sanitary Conferences to the ECDC' (2012) *Journal of Health Politics, Policy and Law* 37 (6) 913–32

Llewellyn, K. N. and the Committee on the Curriculum of the American Association of American Law Schools 'The Place of Skills in Legal Education' (1945) *Columbia Law Review* 45 345–91

London, L. 'What is a Human rights Based Approach to Health and does it Matter?' (2008) *Health and Human Rights: An International Quarterly Journal* 10 (1) 1–15

Lupton, D. *Medicine as Culture: Illness, Disease and the Body* 3rd edn (London: SAGE, 2012)

McConville, M. and W. H. Chui (eds) *Research Methods for Law* (Edinburgh: Edinburgh University Press, 2007)

McHale, J. V. 'Fundamental Rights and Health Care' in E. Mossialos et al. (eds) *Health Systems Governance in the EU: The Role of EU Law and Governance* (New York: Cambridge University Press, 2012) 283–315

McKee, M. et al. (eds) *Health Policy and European Enlargement* (New York: World Health Organization, European Observatory on Health Systems and Policies, 2004)

McKee, M. et al. 'Public Health Policies' in E. Mossialos et al. (eds) *Health Systems Governance in Europe: The Role of European Union Law and Policy* (New York: Cambridge University Press, 2010)

McKee, M. et al. 'The Influence of European Law on National Health Policy' (1996) *Journal of European Social Policy* 6 (4) 263–86

McKee, M. et al. (eds) (2002) *The Impact of EU Law on Health Care Systems* (Brussels: Peter Lang)

MacLehose, L. et al. 'Responding to the Challenge of Communicable Disease in Europe' (2002) *Science* 295 2047–50

Mahoney, H. 'Cross Border Health Proposal Splits Parliament' (2009) *European Observer* (available at: <https://euobserver.com/economic/25361>, last accessed November 2018)

Mahoney, H. 'EU Health Bill Pulled Amid National and MEP Criticism' (2008) *European Observer* (available at: <https://euobserver.com/social/25426>, last accessed November 2018)

Mair, P. 'Popular Democracy and the European Union Polity' (2005) *European Governance Papers* C-05-03

Majone, G. 'The European Community Between Social Policy and Social Regulation' (1993) *Journal of Common Market Studies* 31 153–70

Majone, G. 'The Regulatory State and Its Legitimacy Problems' (1999) *West European Politics* 22 (1) 1–24

Majone, G. 'The Rise of Statutory Regulation in Europe' in G. Majone (ed.) *Regulating Europe* (London: Routledge, 1996)

Mak, C. 'Europe-Building through Private Law: Lessons from Constitutional Theory' (2012) 2 *European Review of Contract Law* 326–41

Mak, C. *Fundamental Rights in European Contract Law: A Comparison of the Impact of Fundamental Rights in Contractual Relationships in Germany, the Netherlands, Italy and England* (The Hague: Wolters Kluwer, 2008)

Mann, J. M. and D. Tarantola 'Responding to HIV/AIDS: A Historical Perspective' (1998) *Health and Human Rights: An International Quarterly Journal* 2 (4) 5–8

Mann, J. M. et al. 'Health and Human Rights' (1994) *Health and Human Rights: An International Quarterly Journal* 1 (1) 6–23

Mann, T. 'Human Rights and the New Public Health' (1995) *Health and Human Rights: An International Quarterly Journal* 1 (3) 229–33

Marchand, S. et al. 'Class, Health, and Justice' (1998) *The Milbank Quarterly* 76 (3) 449–67

Marrus, M. R. 'The Nuremberg Doctors' Trial in Historical Context' (1999) *Bulletin of the History of Medicine* 73 (1) 106–23

Martinsen, D. S. 'The Europeanization of HealthCare: Processes and Factors' in T. Exadaktylos and C. M. Radaelli (eds) *Research Design in European Studies, Establishing Causality in Europeanization* (Basingstoke: Palgrave Macmillan, 2012) 141–60.

Martinsen, D. S. 'The Europeanization of Welfare: The Domestic Impact of Intra-European Social Security' (2005) *JCMS* 43 (5) 1027–54

Mason, J. K. and G. T. Laurie *Law and Medical Ethics* (New York: Oxford University Press, 2006)

Mei A. P. van der 'De nieuwe richtlijn betreffende de toepassing van de rechten van de patiënt bij grensoverschrijdende zorg' (2011) *Nederlands Juristenblad* 2712–3

Mei, A. P. van der *Free Movement of Persons within the European Community: Cross-Border Access to Public Benefits* (Oxford: Hart, 2003)

Menendez, A. J. and E. O. Eriksen (eds) *Arguing Fundamental Rights* (Dordrecht: Springer, 2006)

Menendez, A. J. 'Some Elements of a Theory of European Fundamental Rights' in A .J. Menendez and E. O. Eriksen (eds) *Arguing Fundamental Rights* (Dordrecht: Springer, 2006) 155–86

Meron, T. 'On a Hierarchy of International Human Rights' (1986) *American Journal of International Law* 80 1–23

Michalowski, S. 'Health Care Law' in S. Peers and A. Ward (eds) *The EU Charter of Fundamental Rights: Politics, Law and Policy* (Oregon: Hart, 2004) 287–309

Miles, S. H. 'Hippocrates and Informed Consent' (2009) *The Lancet* 374 (9698) 1322–3

Minogiannis, P. *European Integration and Health Policy: The Artful Dance of Economics and History* (New Brunswick, NJ: Transaction, 2003)

Montgomery, J. *Health Care Law* 2nd edn (Oxford: Oxford University Press, 2002)

Mossialos, E. et al. (eds) *Health Systems Governance in Europe: The Role of European Union Law and Policy* (New York: Cambridge University Press, 2010)

Mounier-Jack, S. and R. J. Coker 'How Prepared is Europe for Pandemic Influenza? Analysis of National Plans' (2006) *The Lancet* 367 (9520) 1405–11

Moynihan, R. 'The Making of a Disease: Female Sexual Dysfunction' (2003) *British Medical Journal* 326 (7379) 45–7

Muir, E. 'Fundamental Rights: An Unsettling EU Competence' (2014) *Human Rights Review* (15) 25–37

Muir, E. 'The Fundamental Rights Implications of EU Legislation: Some Constitutional Challenges' (2014) *Common Market Law Review* 51 219–46

Muller, A. 'Limitations to and Derogations from Economic, Social and Cultural Rights' (2009) *Human Rights Law Review* 9 (4) 557–601

Neuman, M. et al. 'Tobacco Industry Strategies for Influencing European Community Tobacco Advertising Legislation' (2002) *The Lancet* 359 (9314) 1323–30

Neureither, K. 'Transformation of a Political Role: Reconsidering the Case of the Commission of the European Communities' (1972) *Journal of Common Market Studies* 10 (3) 233–48

Newdick, C. 'Disrupting the Community—Saving Public Health Ethics from the EU Internal Market' in J. W. van de Gronden et al. (eds) *Health Care and EU Law* (The Hague: Asser, 2011) 211–41

Nicholas, S. 'The Challenges of the Free Movement of Health Professionals' in M. McKee et al. (eds) *Health Policy and European Union Enlargement* (New York: Open University Press/McGraw-Hill, 2004) 82–109

Nugent, N. *The Government and Politics of the European Union* 7th edn (Basingstoke: Palgrave Macmillan, 2010)

Nys, H. 'The Right to Informed Choice and the Patients' Rights Directive' (2012) *European Journal of Health Law* 19 (4) 327–31

Nys, H. 'After The Transposition of the Directive on Patients' Rights in Cross-Care Healthcare in National Law by the Member States: Still a Lot of Effort to Be Made and Questions to Be Answered' (2014) *European Journal of Health Law* 21 1–14

Nys, H. and T. Goffin 'Mapping National Practices and Strategies Relating to Patients' Rights' in M. Wismar et al. (eds) *Cross-Border Health Care in the European Union Mapping and Analysing Practices and Policies* (London: World Health Organization, European Observatory on Health Systems and Policies, 2011) 159–217

Obermaier, A. J. *The End of Territoriality? The Impact of ECJ Rulings on British, German and French Social Policy* (Farnham: Ashgate, 2009)

Orme, J. et al. (eds) *Public Health for the 21st Century: New Perspectives on Policy, Participation and Practice* 2nd edn (Berkshire: Open University Press, 2007)

Palayret, J. et al. (eds) *Visions, Votes and Vetoes: The Empty Chair Crisis and the Luxembourg Compromise Forty Years On* (Brussels: Peter Lang, 2006)

Palm, W. and R. Baeten 'The Quality and Safety Paradox in the Patients' Rights Directive' (2011) *European Journal of Public Health* 21 (3) 272–4

Peers, S. and M. Costa 'Court of Justice of the European Union (General Chamber) Judicial review of EU Acts after the Treaty of Lisbon; Order of 6 September 2011, Case T-18/10 Inuit Tapiriit Kanatami and Others v. Commission & Judgment of 25 October 2011, Case T-262/10 Microban v. Commission' (2012) *European Constitutional Law Review* 8 82–104

Peeters, M. et al. 'EU Law and Health Professionals' in E. Mossailos et al. (eds) *Health Systems Governance in Europe: The Role of European Union Law and Policy* (Cambridge: Cambridge University Press, 2010) 589–635.

Peeters, M. 'Free Movement of Patients: Directive 2011/24 on the Application of Patients' Rights in Cross-Border Healthcare' (2012) *European Journal of Health Law* 19 (56) 29–60

Pennings, F. 'The Draft Patient Mobility Directive and the Coordination Regulations Of Social Security' in J. W. van de Gronden et al. (eds) *Health Care and EU Law* (The Hague: Asser, 2011) 133–61.

Permanand, G. and E. Vos 'EU Regulatory Agencies and Health Protection' in E. Mossialos et al. (eds) *Health Systems Governance in Europe: The Role of EU Law and Governance* (New York: Cambridge University Press, 2010) 134–86

Permanand, G. *EU Pharmaceutical Regulation: The Politics of Policy-Making* (Manchester: Manchester University Press, 2006)

Persson, I. et al. 'Risks of Neurological and Immune-Related Diseases, Including Narcolepsy, after Vaccination with Pandemrix: A Population- and Registry-Based Cohort Study with over 2 Years of Follow-Up, January 2014' (2014) *Journal of Internal Medicine* 1 172–90

Plato Laws, XI (360 BC) (available at: http://classics.mit.edu/Plato/laws.11.xi.html, last accessed November 2018)

Poland, G. A. 'The 2009–2010 Influenza Pandemic: Effects on Pandemic and Seasonal Vaccine Uptake and Lessons Learned for Seasonal Vaccination Campaigns' (2010) *Vaccine* 28 (4) D3–D13

Pollack, M. A. 'Creeping Competence: The Expanding Agenda of the European Community' (1994) *Journal of Public Policy* 14 (2) 95–145

Pollack, M. A. 'Theorizing EU Policy-Making' in H. Wallace et al. (eds) *Policy-Making in the European Union* (Oxford: Oxford University Press, 2005) 15–45

Porta, D. della and M. Keating 'How Many Approaches in the Social Sciences? An Epistemological Introduction' in D. della Porta and M. Keating (eds) *Approaches and Methodologies in Social Sciences: A Pluralist Perspective* (Cambridge: Cambridge University Press, 2008) 19–39

Porta, M. A. *Dictionary of Epidemiology* 5th edn (New York: Oxford University Press, 2008)

Powers, M. and R. Faden So*cial Justice: The Moral Foundations of Public Health and Health Policy* (Oxford: Oxford University Press, 2008)

Preda, D. and D. Pasquinucci (eds) *The Evolution of the EEC/EU Institutions and Policies* (Brussels: Peter Lang, 2010)

Randal, E. *The European Union and Health Policy* (New York: St Martin's Press, 2000)

Rawls, J. *Political Liberalism* (New York: Columbia University Press, 1993)

Rawls, J. *The Law of Peoples* (Cambridge: Harvard University Press, 2002)

Raz, J. 'Human Rights Without Foundations' in S. Besson and J Tasioulas (eds) *The Philosophy of International Law* (Oxford: Oxford University Press, 2010)

Reinicke, W. H. *Global Public Policy: Governing Without Government?* (Washington: Brookings Institution Press, 1998)

Reintjes, R. et al. 'Benchmarking National Surveillance Systems: A New Tool for the Comparison of Communicable Disease Surveillance and Control in Europe' (2007) *European Journal of Public Health* 17 375–80

Requejo, T. 'Cross-border Healthcare in Spain and the Implementation of the Directive 2011/24/EU on the Application of Patient's Rights in Cross-border Healthcare' (2014) *European Journal of Health Law* 21 79–96

Richardson, J. (ed.) *Constructing a Policy-Making State? Policy Dynamics in the EU* (New York: Oxford University Press, 2012)

Richardson, J. 'The Onward March of Europeanization: Tectonic Movement and Seismic Events' in J. Richardson (ed.) *Constructing a Policy-Making State? Policy Dynamics in the EU* (Oxford: Oxford University Press, 2012) 334–60

Rieger, E. 'Agricultural Policy: Constrained Reforms' in H Wallace et al. (eds) *Policy-Making in the European Union* 5th edn (Oxford: Oxford University Press, 2005) 181–207

Rittberger, B. and F. Schimmelfennig 'The Constitutionalization of the European Union: Explaining the Parliamentarization and Institutionalization of Human Rights' in S. Meunier and K. R. McNamara (eds) *The State of the European Union* (Oxford: Oxford University Press, 2007)

Roberts, M. R. 'The European Centre for Disease Prevention and Control: Science and Political Integration in Europe' (2013) UCL STS Observatory blog at: <https://blogs.ucl.ac.uk/sts-observatory/2013/08/02/the-european-centre-for-disease-prevention-and-control-science-and-political-integration-in-europe> (last accessed March 2014)

Rosa, S. de la 'The Directive on Cross-Border Healthcare or the Art of Codifying Complex Case Law' (2012) *Common Market Law Review* 49 15–46

Roscam Abbing, H. D. C. 'Patients' Right to Quality of Healthcare: How Satisfactory Are the European Union's Regulatory Policies?' (2012) *European Journal of Health Law* 19 (5) 415–22

Rosen, G. *A History of Public Health* (Baltimore, MD: John Hopkins University Press, 1958)

Ruijter, A. de and T. K. Hervey 'Healthcare and the Lisbon Agenda' in P. Copeland and D. Papadimitriou (eds) *The EU's Lisbon Strategy: Evaluating Success, Understanding Failure* (New York: Palgrave Macmillan, 2012) 130–48

Ruijter, A. de 'Patient Autonomy in Europe' in J. Rutgers (ed.) *European Contract Law and the Welfare State* (Groningen: Europa Law, 2010) 43–65

Sabel, C. and J. Zeitlin 'Learning from Difference: The New Architecture of Experimentalist Governance in the EU' (2008) *European Law Journal* 14 (3) 271–327

Sample, I. 'Swine flu vaccine can trigger narcolepsy, UK government concedes, Review of fresh evidence finds jab given to 6 million people in Britain can occasionally cause sleep disorder' (2013, 19 September) *The Guardian*

San Giorgi, M. *The Human Right to Access to Health Care* (Antwerp: Intersentia, 2012)

Sandholtz, W. and J. Zysman '1992: Recasting the European Bargain' (1989) *World Politics* 42 (1) 95–128

Sarmiento, D. 'Who's Afraid of the Charter? The Court of Justice, National Courts and the New Framework of Fundamental Rights Protection in Europe' (2013) *Common Market Law Review* 50 1267–304

Sauter, W. 'Harmonisation in Healthcare: The EU Patients' Rights Directive' (2011) *Tilec Research Paper* 8

Scharpf F. 'Perpetual Momentum: Directed and Unrestrained?' (2011) *Journal of European Public Policy* 19 127–39

Scharpf, F. 'The Asymmetry of European Integration or why the EU cannot be a "Social Market Economy"' (2009) KFG Working Paper Series 6

Scharpf, F. 'The European Social Model: Coping with Challenges of Diversity' (2002) *Journal of Common Market Studies* 40 (4) 645–70

Scharpf, F. W. 'Negative and Positive Integration in the Political Economy of European Welfare States' in G. Marks (ed.) *Governance in the European Union* (London: SAGE, 1996) 15–40

Scharpf, F. 'Perpetual Momentum: Directed and Unconstrained?' (2012) *Journal of European Public Policy* 19 127–39

Schneider, A. L. and H. M. Ingram *Policy Design for Democracy* (Kansas: Kansas University Press, 1997)

Schreyögg, J. et al. 'Defining the "Health Benefit Basket" in Nine European Countries' (2007) *The European Journal of Health Economics* 6 (1) 2–10

Schutter, O. de 'Article 52' in S. Peers et al. (eds) *Commentary of the Charter of Fundamental Rights of the European Union* (Brussels: European Union, 2006) 397–409

Scott-Samuel, A. and E. O'Keefe 'Health Impact Assessment, Human Rights and Global Public Policy: A Critical Appraisal' (2007) *Bulletin of the World Health Organization* 85 212–17

Sen, A. 'Why Health Equity?' in S. Anand et al. (eds) *Public Health, Ethics, and Equity* (Oxford: Oxford University Press, 2004)

Shaw, J. 'Importing Gender: The Challenge of Feminism and the Analysis of the EU Legal Order' (2000) *Journal of European Public Policy* 7 406–31

Sheldon, S. and M. Thomson (eds) *Feminist Perspectives on Health Care Law* (London: Cavendish, 1998)

Shore, C. *Building Europe: the Cultural Politics of European Integration* (New York: Routledge, 2000)

Simpson, J. and E. Weiner (eds) *The Oxford English Dictionary* Oxford: (Clarendon Press, 1989)

Snape, L. and L. Spencer 'The Foundations of Qualitative Research' in J. Ritchie and J. Lewis (eds) *Qualitative Research Practice* (London: SAGE, 2003)

Stahl, T. et al. (eds) *Health in all Policies: Prospects and Potentials* (Brussels: European Observatory on Health Systems and Policies, Finnish Ministry of Social Affairs and Health, 2006)

Steffen, M. (ed.) *Health Governance in Europe: Issues, Challenges, and Theories* (New York: Routledge, 2005)

Stone Sweet, A. and K. Stranz 'Rights Adjudication and Constitutional Pluralism in Germany and Europe' (2014) *Journal of European Public Policy* 19 92–108

Sunstein, R. C. 'Against Positive Rights' in A. Sajo (ed.) *Western Rights? Post-Communist Application* (The Hague: Kluwer, 1995) 225–33

Sunstein, R. C. *Designing Democracy: What Constitutions Do* (New York: Oxford University Press, 2001)

Swaan, A. de *In Care of the State: Health Care, Education and Welfare in Europe and the USA in the Modern Era* (New York: Oxford University Press, 1998)

Szyszczak, E. 'Experimental Governance: The Open Method of Coordination' (2006) *European Law Journal* 12 (4) 486–502

Szyszczak, E. 'Patients' Rights: A Lost Cause or Missed Opportunity?' in J. W. van de Gronden et al. (eds) *EU Health Care and EU Law* (The Hague: Asser, 2011) 103–33

Tiefer, L. 'Female Sexual Dysfunction: A Case Study of Disease Mongering and Activist Resistance' (2006) *PLoS Medicine* 3 (4) 178

Titmuss, R. *The Gift Relationship: From Human Blood to Social Policy* (1970) (London: Reprinted by the New Press, 1997)

Toebes, B. 'Introduction: Health and Human Rights in Europe' in B. Toebes et al. (eds) *Health and Human Rights in Europe* (Cambridge: Intersentia, 2012) 1–21

Toebes, B. 'The Right to Health and Other Health-Related Rights' in B. Toebes et al. (eds) *Health and Human Rights in Europe* (Cambridge: Intersentia, 2012) 81–111

Toebes, B. *The Right to Health as a Human Right in International Law* (Amsterdam: Hart/Intersentia, 1999)

Tomasevski, K. 'Health Rights' in A. Eide et al. (eds) *Economic, Social and Cultural Rights* (Dordrecht: Martinus Nijhoff, 1995) 169–91

Trubek, L. et al. 'The Construction of a Healthier Europe: Lessons from the Fight Against Cancer' (2008) *Wisconsin International Law Journal* 26 (3) 1–39

Veitch, K. *The Jurisdiction on Medical Law* (Aldershot: Ashgate, 2007)

Vos, E. 'EU Committees: The Evolution of Unforeseen Institutional Actors in European Product Regulation' in C. Joerges and E. Vos (eds) *EU Committees: Social Regulation, Law and Politics* (Oxford: Hart, 1999) 19–46

Vos, E. 'EU Food Safety Regulation in the Aftermath of the BSE Crisis' (2000) *Journal of Consumer Policy* 23 227–55

Vos, E. *Institutional Frameworks of Community Health and Safety Regulation: Committees, Agencies and Private Bodies* (Oxford: Hart, 1999)

Vos, E. 'The Rise of the Committees' (1997) *European Law Journal* 3 (3) 210–29

Vos, E. 'The Role of Comitology in European Governance' in D. M. Curtin and R. A. Wessel (eds) *Good Governance and the European Union: Reflections on Concepts, Institutions and Substance* (Antwerp: Intersentia, 2005) 107–21

Wallace, H. and F. Hayes-Renshaw *The Council of Ministers* 2nd ed. (Basingstoke: Palgrave Macmillan, 2006)

Walt, G. *Health Policy: An Introduction to Process and Power* 5th edn (London: Zed Books, 2001)

Ward, A. 'Article 51 Field of Application' in S. Peers et al. (eds) *The EU Charter of Fundamental Rights* (Oxford: Hart, 2014)

Watson, J. *Health and Structural Funds 2007–2013 (2013) Country and Regional Assessment (Hungary)* (2009) EUROEGIO III Project for DG SANCO

Watson, R. 'Focus: Brussels Which "Europe" Should Deal with Ethical Issues?' (1994) *British Medical Journal* (308) 362

Weatherill, S. 'Competence Creep and Competence Control' (2004) *Year of European Law* 23 (1) 1–55

Weiler, J. H. H. 'The Community System: The Dual Character of Supranationalism' (1982) *Year of European Law* (1) 267–306

Weiler, J. H. H. 'The Transformation of Europe' (1991) *Yale Law Journal* 100 (8) 2403–83

Weimer, M. 'Risk Regulation, GMOs, and the Challenges to Deliberation in EU Governance: Politicization and Scientification as Co-Producing Trends' in C. Joerges and C. Glinski (eds) *The European Crisis and the Transformation of Transnational Governance* (New York: Hart, 2014) 293–315

Weinberg, J. et al. 'On Behalf of the Charter Group: Establishing Priorities for European Collaboration in Communicable Disease Surveillance' (1999) *European Journal of Public Health* 9 (3) 236–40

Westlake, M. and D. Galloway (eds) *The Council of the European Union* 3rd edn (London: John Harper, 2004)

Wicks, E. *Human Rights and Health Care* (Oregon: Hart, 2007)

Williams, A. *European Union Human Rights Policies: A Study in Irony* (Oxford: Oxford University Press, 2004)

Wismar, M. et al. 'Is HIA Effective? A Synthesis of Concepts, Methodologies and Results' in M. Wismar et al. (eds) *The Effectiveness of Health Impact Assessment: Scope and Limitations Supporting Decision-Making in Europe* (Copenhagen: European Observatory on Health Systems and Policies, World Health Organization, 2007) 15–37

Wiwanitkit, V. *Bird Flu: The New Emerging Infectious Disease* (New York: Nova Science Publishers, 2008)

Yin, R. K. *Case Study Research: Design and Methods* (Thousand Oaks: SAGE, 2003)

Zweigert, K. and H. Kotz *Introduction to Comparative Law* (Oxford: Oxford University Press, 1998)

Index

Tables are indicated by an italic t following the page number

The manufacturer's authorised representative in the EU for product safety is Oxford University Press España S.A. of el Parque Empresarial San Fernando de Henares, Avenida de Castilla, 2 – 28830 Madrid (www.oup.es/en or product.safety@oup.com). OUP España S.A. also acts as importer into Spain of products made by the manufacturer.

www.ingramcontent.com/pod-product-compliance
Lightning Source LLC
LaVergne TN
LVHW011756200926
848484LV00003B/722

* 9 7 8 0 1 9 8 7 8 8 0 9 6 *